Walkabout Year

Walkabout Year

Twelve Months in Australia

Samuel F. Pickering, Jr.

University of Missouri Press   Columbia and London

Library of Congress Cataloging-in-Publication Data

Pickering, Samuel F., 1941–
    Walkabout year : twelve months in Australia / Samuel F. Pickering, Jr.
        p. cm.
    ISBN 0-8262-1043-0 (acid-free paper)
    1. Pickering, Samuel F., 1941– —Journeys—Australia. 2. English teachers—
Australia—Biography. 3. Australia—Social life and customs. 4. Americans—
Australia—Biography. I. Title.
PE64.P53A3   1995
820.9—dc20
    [B]   95-35344
                                                                                                                               CIP

∞ This paper meets the requirements of the
American National Standard for Permanence of Paper
for Printed Library Materials, Z39.48, 1984.

Designer: Kristie Lee
Typesetter: BOOKCOMP
Printer and binder: Thomson-Shore, Inc.
Typefaces: Giovanni, Runic Condensed, Mistral

For the members of the English department
at the University of Western Australia.
"I have owed to them, / In hours of
weariness, sensations sweet."

Also by Sam Pickering

Essays

A Continuing Education

The Right Distance

May Days

Still Life

Let It Ride

Trespassing

Scholarly Studies

The Moral Tradition in English Fiction, 1785–1850

John Locke and Children's Books in Eighteenth-Century England

Moral Instruction and Fiction for Children, 1749–1820

Contents

Preface

In December my friend George Seddon sent a postcard from Fremantle, Western Australia. "When I swim in the Indian Ocean on Christmas," George wrote, "I will think of you." A cold rain fell outside our house. Water washed down the driveway, curving like fish scales before sloshing into the pachysandra, pushing hickory nuts under the green leaves. On the front of the card stood a gray kangaroo, its fur loose, dangling warmly over its bones like a coat on a rack. "Gosh," Vicki said, picking up the card, "I haven't thought about Australia in weeks. Did we really go there?"

Vicki and the children and I spent twelve months in Australia. We lived in Perth, the capital of Western Australia. Perth is a big city, inhabited by 1.4 of the 1.7 million people who live in Western Australia. Despite its size Perth seemed small and familial. The Indian Ocean was ten minutes from the house we rented. The bush lay twenty minutes away, and within fifteen minutes I could drive downtown, park the car, and start shopping.

Western Australia is three and a half times as big as Texas, and the land seemed to open like a hand beckoning us to explore. "Hurry up, Daddy," Edward said; "I am going to be late for soccer, and we probably won't practice long in this rain." I lay the postcard on the kitchen table. I wanted to be nostalgic about the year, but the little doings of life distracted me. After leaving Edward at Lions Field, I picked Eliza up at her piano teacher's house and took her to Southeast School for her soccer practice. Francis was at the Middle School studying for a math contest, and next I fetched him.

Later that night I looked at the postcard. I missed George. He was an extraordinary man and during his life had held university chairs in history, philosophy of science, geology, and environmental science. Last year in Perth he worked at the Centre for Studies in Australian

Literature at the University of Western Australia. His most recent book, *Searching for the Snowy,* an environmental history of the Snowy River in Victoria, lay on my desk. Beside George's book slumped a pile of yellow papers, the manuscript of this book.

Often I had morning tea with George in the English department at the university. Almost every day I drank tea with members of the department: Hilary Fraser, Brenda Walker, Delys Bird, Veronica Brady, Sue Lewis, Caroline Horobin, Bob White, Dennis Haskell, Ron Shepherd, Bob Nussbaum, Ian Saunders, Gareth Griffiths, Colin O'Brien, Andrew Lynch, Kiernan Dolin, and Chris Wortham, among others. I enjoyed the mornings. The English department welcomed me, and when I left Perth, I felt despondent. Yet I have not described members of the department and other friends at the university in this book. Knowing what not to write is more important than knowing what to write, at least for me. Despite the row of books I have written, I don't think myself an author but just a person: father, husband, and neighbor, a man trying to get through his years with decorum, laboring to do "the right thing" by other people. Friends in Perth treated me kindly, and to have written things that might have embarrassed them would have been shoddy return.

Twenty-five years ago I decided that I would not write about English departments in which I taught. Many times I have been tempted to scribble things down about colleagues. When I taught in New Hampshire, an older member of the department came into my office one afternoon. He shut the door behind himself then said, "Sam, if I should die suddenly, I want you to clean out my desk immediately. Make sure my family does not see the contents." The man was studiously conventional. I could not imagine him with vine leaves in his hair or misbehavior on his mind. That night I speculated about what lay in his desk, and for years I wanted to write about his visit to my office. I resisted the temptation, at least until now. The man has been dead for a decade. When he died, the contents of his desk, like his very life, startled no one. The most outlandish thing I heard said about him later was that he occasionally voted Democratic.

The man who travels with his family rarely escapes home. Wherever I travel, I carry a suitcase bulging with home. Although most of the doings described in this book occurred in Australia and the appointments of the rooms in which I lived for a year were Australian, I remained American. Being in a different country did not change me. Surrounded by children who wanted to go to birthday parties and play baseball much as they did in Storrs, I behaved as I did in Connecticut. Although I learned to recognize different birds and trees, I worried about the children's suffering an attack of asthma, something I do in Connecticut. I always let worries go to my head, as my friend Josh puts it. When Edward came down with a case of viral conjunctivitis and had to miss his class trip because his eyes resembled oranges, I stayed up night after night. No matter where I lived in the world I would have worried excessively and sat through nights reading and sipping tea, my concerns first exhausting then irritating Vicki.

In this book I do not describe the Australian character or dissect the country. While age has made me bawdy, it has also made me modest. Like all peoples the Australians were wonderfully various. To describe the inhabitants of any country as a people takes more naïveté or presumption than I possess. About all I can say about the Australians I met is that they were quiet and gentle, decent folks addicted to graciousness and honesty.

According to an old saying the typical man devotes his youth to the devil and his old age to God. I am not on first-name terms with the deity, yet. But I know his cousin Temperance well. Temperance and I did not beat the bush for odd characters in Australia, and I spent evenings at home with my family. Instead of roaming the night and bars, I wandered gardens, sipping the milk and honey of blossoms, not Emu Bitter from cans. Consequently I describe more flowers than people in this book. "That is nothing new," Josh said; "in your writings plants are always thicker than mouse turds in a meal barrel."

I was happy in Australia. Only occasionally did my parents preach to me when I was a child. They did, however, urge me to look for the bright side of life. "Resist mood," Mother said; "only selfish people inflict their moods upon others. We do not spend much time in this world, and we ought to make other people smile." I wanted the children to enjoy the year in Australia. No matter how tired I felt, I forced myself to be enthusiastic, and during the course of the year I swallowed a case of the tonic I peddled.

I wrote the essays in this book month by month as the year unraveled. Little things cluttered and colored my days, and I wrote about them. No matter where I am I notice small matters. Just last week, for example, I rummaged through an old dresser. At the bottom of a drawer I found a battered cookbook, *Tried and True Recipes* compiled by Elizabeth Bashinsky, "Chairman" of the Education Committee of the Alabama Division of the United Daughters of the Confederacy. The book was published in Troy, Alabama, in 1937, and the Daughters of the Confederacy sold it to raise money for college scholarships. When I removed *Recipes* from the drawer, a bookmark slipped to the floor. The bookmark was a page torn from a newspaper. Printed on the page were advertisements for businesses in Carthage, Tennessee: W. F. Cothern's groceries, the Walton Hotel, and then my grandfather's insurance business. Sam Pickering, the advertisement stated, "writes FIRE, LIGTNING AND TORNADO INSURANCE for the Farm Department of The Home Insurance Company of New York."

Finding the advertisement with the word *lightning* misspelled brightened the moment. In Australia little things similarly perked up the hours, and I described them. "Some men," Josh said to me recently, "are peach orchard crazy. When a fiddle starts to play, they feel the devil's fingers in their trousers. You wouldn't even hear the music. But throw a scrap of moldy paper on the ground, and 'it is all over with you,' as the waffle said when the pancake was turned over." Josh knows a lot of moldy, corny sayings, and that is one of the reasons I enjoy his company.

Three generations of my family, including Mother and Father, are buried in Carthage. Six books ago Carthage popped into my writing, at first only one or two fictional characters who grew tobacco. Now a whole section of town accompanies me no matter what I write or where I travel. Carthage traveled to Australia in that suitcase bulging with home, and its inhabitants appear in the book. The characters are not very bright, but I like them. Not long ago when Coker Knox visited Carthage from Nashville, he met Jodrell Tayler outside the Walton Hotel. To make polite conversation Coker inquired about the weather, asking, "What kind of weather do you have in Smith County?" "Mixed," Jodrell answered; "long spells are frequent, and sunshine comes principally during the day."

Time changes opinions. Going to Perth was not, I now think, quite so spontaneous as I made it seem in the first essay in this book. When I was a boy, I studied maps and dreamed of traveling. I was especially fond of the map of Australia, and I imagined living in Perth and Darwin, not because I knew anything about either city but just because they were far from my home in Tennessee. The English poet Wordsworth wrote that the child was father of the man. If Wordsworth was right, then childhood reading might have influenced my going to Perth. I have also changed my opinion about school education in Perth. Rarely did the children have homework in Perth, something that worried me during the year. Because the children had few time-consuming assignments, they educated themselves, reading libraries of books, writing sheaves of poems and stories, and designing houses and computer circuits. In Storrs homework so fills the children's hours that they read and create less. Forever busy with school projects, they rarely teach themselves. Maybe the children were better off educationally in Perth.

George Seddon's postcard now stands on my desk, leaning against the shell of a wood turtle. Hanging on the wall behind my desk is a calendar sent to me by Brenda and Brian Bannon, newsagents in Broadway Fair, the small shopping center near the house we rented. Printed above the months are pictures taken in or around Perth. At the bottom of each page below the grids for days are sketches of houses, the drawings resembling a border on a skirt. Over March the Fremantle town hall rises like a white pencil, the sky in the background blue and thick as construction paper. The lower half of the picture is bushy with Canary Island date palms, their fronds heavy green smudges. Drawn beneath March are four houses on Birdwood Parade, a street just around the corner from our house. I even know the number of one of the houses, twenty-seven. I remember the number because the children said the house was their favorite house on the street.

Looking at the calendar makes me momentarily melancholy, in fact homesick for Perth. I suspect that if I had been ten years younger and Vicki's parents had been stronger, we would not have returned to the United States. Since coming home we have been happy. Storrs is a nice community. Still, the horrible violence in this country frightens me. In Australia, I sometimes think, my children would have a better, gentler future. Would that Vicki, the children, and I could have swum with George on Christmas morning. I would have loaded a hamper of champagne into the car. From the snack bar above Cottesloe Beach I would have bought hot dogs and ice cream, and we would have had a fizzy, family day.

Walkabout Year

First Days

I never thought about going to Australia on my sabbatical. Instead I dreamed of going to Greece. Before Vicki and I had children, we explored the Dodecanese. We wore floppy hats, sandals, and shorts. We drank retsina in cafés with red and yellow flowers on tables and walked along dusty roads bordered by olive trees. Last spring I taught a course on "nature writing." The first book assigned was Gerald Durrell's *My Family and Other Creatures,* an autobiography describing five years Durrell lived on Corfu with his family. Durrell was a boy, but instead of spending days in a classroom, he roamed hill and shore. He caught zoos of the crawling and flying creations. In the process he educated himself and trapped shelves of anecdotes. As I taught the course, I imagined roaming an island with my children, leading them through a library of natural history. Together we followed deep paths across limestone hills. In shadows beneath gray boulders red and black poppies bloomed. Along a ravine lemon trees were yellow with fruit. I imagined us sitting on rocks and eating oranges, the juice clinging to our chins like honey, words rustling sweet about us. In my class students read poems written by William Wordsworth, the nineteenth-century English poet. Late at night verses of Wordsworth's poetry turned through my mind. Instead of thoughts sublime, however, I had feelings fleshly and dreamed of strolling beaches with Vicki, recapturing moments of "splendor in the sand," or so I imagined at my desk.

I decided to go to Kos. Four hours northwest of Rhodes by steamer, Kos had a population of twenty thousand people. Forty miles long and one mile wide, the island resembled a bottle opener, one sticky with fruit: grapes, melons, and pomegranates. In ancient times Kos was famous for its Asklepieion dedicated to medicine and named after Asklepios, the god of healing. Fifteen years ago I explored the ruins of the Asklepieion. Cicadas chattered in pines at the top of the hill. I looked across the sea at Turkey. Houses in Bodrun floated through the edge of sight like white motes. Suddenly a tortoise crawled out of brush at my feet. The animal's right eye was swollen shut, resembling a golf ball that had been rolled through mud then scraped on a rock. Jutting out of the corner of the tortoise's eye was a thorn. I grasped the tortoise's neck and stretched it, wrapping my left hand around it like a collar so that the animal's head stuck out between my thumb and index finger. Then using the thumb and index finger on my right hand as tweezers, I gripped the thorn. At first the thorn would not come out, but then it slid loose, glistening and followed by a spurt of brown pus. I saved the tortoise's eye, and maybe its life. A year on Kos, I told Vicki, would remove all the splinters that bothered us and made us rub irritatingly against each other.

"That's well put," Vicki said opening the oven and taking out a chicken casserole, "but turtles are not children. Children want to go to school and have friends." "I will teach the children," I said, "and I'll be their friend." "Do you know how cold the winter will be on Kos?" Vicki said, pausing before she answered her own question; "damn cold, I can tell you. And if you think," she continued, taking the lid off the casserole, steam rising in a cloud to the ceiling, "that I am going to walk naked with you on the beach you are mistaken. We are too old for that sort of thing." Compromise, nay, giving way completely is not simply the blood of marriage, it is also the muscular stuff of narrative. Deciding not to go to Kos was the first step I took toward Australia.

At the time of my last sabbatical, Edward was three, Francis, five, and Eliza, a baby. Doings for the children so filled hours that I stayed in Storrs and didn't dream of elsewheres. Although I was taking the year off at half salary in hopes of traveling abroad, remaining at home was also appealing. At home I would not stagger beneath suitcases bulging with worries about schools, houses, and doctors. At home days would fold seamlessly into each other. "Where are you going on your sabbatical?" Jack asked me two weeks later at a reception for faculty of the College of Arts and Sciences. After I explained that I wanted to go to the Dodecanese but had decided against it because of the children, he said, "Go to Australia." "Where?" I asked. "Perth or Adelaide," he answered; "Perth is a children's paradise."

"Vicki," I said that night in bed, "let's go to Australia; people speak English, and the children could go to school and make lots of friends." "That sounds fine to me," she said, turning off the light, "but I'm tired now and want to go to sleep. You make the arrangements and tell me about them." The next morning I called the Australian Embassy in Washington and talked to a member of the cultural affairs staff. "Perth is wonderful," he said, adding that he had a friend at the University of Western Australia. "I will call him," the man said, "and see what he can do for you." And that was simply that. Before Vicki and I considered the trip, we were on our way. Moreover, I decided to write essays about the year. Seven or eight years ago, a former governor of Tennessee spent six months in Australia with his family. Afterward he wrote a book about the experience. The man was decent and bright, but the book was poor. "That's what happens," an Australian told me, "when you live in a Lear jet. If you stay on the ground you will do better."

Our deciding to go to Australia resembled an engagement, made in the passion of a moment but over time shaping its own identity, no matter the wishes of anyone involved. Vicki spent the night before our wedding crying in her bathroom at home. The engagement to which she agreed almost carelessly had hardened into stone. Invitations having been sent and friends having assumed expectations as weighty, in her mind at least, as iron bars, all she could do was weep then march to the altar the next morning. Similarly, once I mentioned that I was thinking about going to Australia, people transformed consideration into fact. "How exciting," a woman said, telephoning Vicki, "what a trip! I wish Carl would plan something like that." Alas, I planned little, and preparations were mostly time-consuming, not exciting. I canceled my automobile insurance for the year and paid home and life insurance in advance. I bought short pants, loose cotton shorts made in the Philippines, from the legs of which my knees and calves hung down and swayed like thin, rusty bell clappers. I wrote automobile and airline companies trying to enlist sponsors for my essays. I was not successful. "I have to love a project before I give an advance," an editor wrote, "and your idea just doesn't thrill me." We spent a morning in Willimantic having passport pictures taken. We spent another morning at the post office filling out forms for passports. For visas I gathered a folio of papers and mailed them to the Australian Consulate in New

York. After receiving them, an official asked me to send a copy of Vicki's and my marriage certificate. I refused. "The request," I answered, "is common." Six days before the children went to summer camp in Maine I learned they needed physicals. Dr. Dardick squeezed them into an afternoon, charging eleven dollars apiece for the examinations.

Once the children were at camp, Vicki cleaned and packed the house. I mailed checks to Brian Gamache and to Grasshopper Lawns so that they would clean the gutters and rake the leaves in the fall. Mr. Fish regrouted the bathrooms, and I hurried through essays and reviews that I had agreed to write. Because of George the dog I did not rent the house. Instead I arranged for two graduate students to be house sitters. Rents on our street ranged from a thousand to fifteen hundred dollars a month. My charging nothing for the house made George the most expensive four-legged mongrel in Storrs, if not in Connecticut. Two days before leaving, Vicki wrote instructions for the house sitters. I typed them on the computer. The instructions were eighteen pages long. Four pages pertained to George. My old sweaters became George's bedding. "George's sweaters," Vicki wrote, "may be washed with detergent except for wool ones. Two are particularly nice; one is cashmere! Always cover the cushions with a sweater. Use one or two or three sweaters for blankets. George will need lots of covers in winter. Tuck him in like a baby. Use sweaters on the TV room dog pillow also. Try not to let the wicker touch the radiator. George will hibernate in its heat in winter. We turn the heat down or off at night. George always sleeps downstairs in one of his beds."

At ten-thirty in the morning on August 25, we left for the airport. I hired a limousine to take us, a white Cadillac with a claret interior and lines of orange lights flickering around the ceiling. Loaded with six suitcases, three duffel bags, ten backpacks, and five people, the limousine was the only vehicle that could have carried us, aside from a paneled van or a dump trunk. The limousine cost $90.75, by this time an almost meaningless expense as the airplane tickets for the five of us cost $8,337 round-trip, Francis at twelve being classified as an adult. The suitcases and duffel bags were new, bought on sale for $452.59 at Sears and Kabels in the Buckland Hills Mall. The ride in the limousine was a success. None of us had ridden in a limousine before, and after Edward forgot George and stopped crying, all three children put on sunglasses with reflecting lenses and pretended to be celebrities. Eliza's glasses had scarlet rims. When she draped herself against the seat and lifted a champagne glass, she looked to the limousine born. For earrings Vicki wore a pair of stainless steel kangaroos. Whenever she moved, the kangaroos hopped, "anticipating going home," Francis said. For my part I wore loose khaki trousers, cowboy boots, and a red T-shirt. Across the front of the shirt, an orange bird of paradise bloomed. Two blue tree frogs hunkered on a green leaf, one pulling itself over the back of the other and bringing thoughts inappropriate for airplane travel to mind. "When people see us arrive at the airport," Eliza said, waving languidly at a man driving a Ford, "they will think we are movie stars." "Not," I thought, "when they see us unload. Then they will think we work for a circus. Only clowns could stuff so much junk into a car."

The ride to the airport was the easiest part of the trip to Australia. Forty and a half hours and five flights loomed ahead of us. From Hartford to Chicago we sat in the last seats in the plane, only jet motors visible out the windows. From Chicago to Los Angeles we flew in a DC-10. We sat in the first seats facing the bulwark that divided tourist from business class, the movie unwatchable but shaking like rain before our eyes. Stewards thrust platters of food at us. I ate little because I do not like to use bathrooms on planes. More relaxed, the children devoured everything put before them. From Los Angeles we flew to Hawaii. Unfortunately the electricity on the 747 scheduled to take us to Sydney went haywire, and we spent five hours in the airport at Honolulu, watching the sun rise over the tarmac. During the day I drank so many cans of orange juice that I became citric and, bloated with criticism, paced about and muttered. In contrast the Australians waiting for our flight sat quietly, my first indication that citizens of the continent did not resemble characters from their films, extravagant individuals long on personality and knives. I looked out the window. Eight men stood under the airplane, each with a flashlight and a set of plans in his hands, all the men looking in different directions. Minutes turned slowly, and as Australians chatted or dozed, I longed for a seasoning of brash New Yorkers. To pass time I shaved once and brushed my teeth twice. Eventually airline personnel served Hawaiian souvenir pastries, or so Vicki dubbed them. The pastries resembled ancient volcanoes, the sharp edges of which had been eroded by time. In the mouth of each volcano squatted the lava, a red plop of hard, waxy jam. Instead of serving the pastry, Qantas representatives instructed the three hundred and fifty passengers to form a single line. Without protest people followed the instructions, and after standing for twenty minutes, we each received a souvenir pastry and a tepid cup of tea.

Once the flight took off, I read Thomas Carlyle's extended essay *Sartor Resartus,* a book I last read as a student thirty years ago. Supposedly a biography compiled from paper bags containing the autobiographical leavings of the learned German professor Diogenes Teufelsdröckh, *Sartor Resartus* was a device enabling Carlyle to write his own philosophy. On a plane, or really anywhere, I am not up to philosophy, and so I read Carlyle for snippets, underlining crochets stitched out of irritation, statements such as "Custom doth make dotards of us all" and Teufelsdröckh's remark, "Of the insignificant portion of my Education, which depended on Schools, there need almost no notice be taken." When I read that language was "the Garment of Thought," I wondered about my red T-shirt and cowboy boots, simple sentences and metaphors stretched ragged. I finished *Sartor Resartus* over the South Pacific halfway between Honolulu and Sydney. My reading then became mundane. For the Department of Immigration, Local Government, and Ethnic Affairs, I filled out five Incoming Passenger Cards, forging the names of the rest of the family. The instructions for a section entitled "Main Reason for Coming to Australia" read "Please Mark ONLY ONE Box." The card provided nine choices: In Transit, Convention, Business, Accompanying Business Visitor, Visiting Relations, Holiday, Employment, Education, and Other. I wondered if business travelers and their spouses had to provide marriage certificates. "No," a man told me later, "if a chap comes from Japan with a bag full of yen he can bring a geisha house with him." On my card I marked Other. On the four remaining cards I drew a caret before the O of Other and wrote in the word *Accompanying.*

The flight on which we were supposed to fly to Perth had long departed when we landed in Sydney. After we retrieved our bags, Qantas bustled us through Customs and onto a plane. Four hours later we landed in Perth. Australian airlines are more relaxed than those in the United States. After leaving Sydney the pilot opened his door, and keeping it open until just before landing, he invited children and interested adults to visit the cockpit. One by one people traipsed forward, including a group of retarded adults returning home from a trip to Disneyland. On flights in the United States I become nervous whenever I see a person walk toward the front of a plane to use a bathroom. There are so many nutcases in America that I want the cockpit door bolted. "Jesus," I thought as I watched a very large retarded man wedge himself through the door, "if one of these people stumbles, much less gets frightened and has a seizure, that's the end of us."

No one met us in Perth. The telex that Qantas officials in Hawaii assured me would be sent to the University of Western Australia giving our new schedule had not been sent. Two weeks earlier I talked on the telephone to Bob White, professor of English at the university. Bob booked an apartment for us and said he would meet us at the airport. If I had known the address of the apartment, I would have hired two cabs to take us and our luggage there. I tried to call Bob, but the Perth telephone book listed eighty-seven Whites with Christian names beginning with R. We arrived late in the afternoon, and the university was shut. For a moment I did not know what to do. Then I remembered Charles Edelman. An American born on Staten Island, Charles taught in the English department at Edith Cowan University. On Bob's advice I had telephoned Charles from Connecticut. Charles described schools in Perth and suggested neighborhoods in which to live. Only one C. Edelman appeared in the telephone book. Charles and Leslie, his wife, were eating dinner when I called. They put dinner in the icebox and twenty minutes later arrived at the airport in separate cars. When we reached the apartment, Bob was waiting for us, presents in his hands: for me, a book, *The Living West of Australia;* for the children, cookies and soft drinks; and for Vicki, two bottles of Australian champagne.

We drank the champagne, and after Bob, Charles, and Leslie left, I walked down Fairway and found a fish and chips store where I bought dinner, the first fish and chips the children ever ate. At a corner grocery run by a Chinese family Vicki bought milk and cereal for breakfast. Bob had arranged for us to stay in the apartment for a month, the English department paying the first week's rent as a welcoming present.

Although I eventually liked the apartment, it did not appeal to me that first night. Upstairs were a bathroom and three small bedrooms, one with bunk beds, another with a single twin bed, and a third with a double bed. Downstairs were a kitchen, a combination living room and dining room, and a small washroom with a toilet at one end. Furnishing the living and dining room were a gas heater, a ceiling lamp, a sofa, two armchairs, a standing lamp, and a coffee table. Behind the sofa stood a laminated table with six wooden chairs around it. The night was cold, but I was too tired to figure out how to operate the gas heater, so we went to bed right after dinner. The mattress on which Vicki and I slept resembled a V. A deep trench ran down the middle, and throughout the night we rolled down from the raised edges and thumped against each other. Because it tumbled mates against one another, such a mattress might be a wise investment for the man, or woman, experiencing a domestic chill. For the couple exhausted by traveling halfway around the world, I do not recommend the mattress. At three o'clock Edward went to the bathroom. Flushing the toilet started water coursing through the bowl. I got up and took the top off the tank to examine the innards. The ball and levers differed from those in Connecticut, and for a moment I couldn't dam the stream cascading through the bowl. "Oh, God," I exclaimed, and putting down the plastic seat, I sat on the toilet and cried. "What have we done," I said to Vicki when I returned to bed, "why did we leave our nice house and little dog in Connecticut?" "You are asking that question long after the plane has bolted the hanger," Vicki said, trying to claw a way up her side of the mattress and out of the gulch.

The next morning was sunny. I looked out a window. Immediately I felt better. Trumpet vine twisted over a fence. A singing honeyeater dropped onto a pink grevillea and thrusting its bill into a blossom dusted the crown of his head with yellow pollen. On the roof of a nearby house two laughing pigeons bubbled at each other. In the distance a magpie called, its song bouncing, resembling a coil in a music box. By the front door bottlebrush bloomed. Eight inches long and round as the mouth of a jar, the flowers dangled in scarlet spikes, smelling cool and clear. Suddenly I heard a shrill, rapid piping, reminding me of the sound made by smoke detectors. In a coral tree four parrots shredded blossoms. The flowers swept upward in red gusts like flame, the pink stamens glowing then becoming ash and falling out and downward. The parrots were ring-necks, feathery tapestries of red, green, blue, black, purple, and gray, the colors bound together by a yellow band cinched around the birds' necks. Never had I seen a parrot outside a zoo, and I didn't expect to see them in Perth. "Vicki," I shouted, "come look. You won't believe your eyes."

When I first saw the birds and plants, I could not identify them. So long as the language in a new place is the same as the language spoken at home, adjusting to difference is easy. Custom and quirk are quickly learned. Thought runs shallow, no matter the terrain, and bending words to fit local expectation is simple. Birds and trees are harder matters. Plant life in Western Australia was stunningly lush. The luminous reds and purples of Perth dismayed me, and I felt like a stranger. "I have never managed to lose my old conviction that travel narrows the mind," G. K. Chesterton wrote at the beginning of *What I Saw in America*. Chesterton was right, I thought, as I stood on the sidewalk watching the parrots. I knew the birds and flowers, trees, snakes, and insects of New England. When I studied a meadow in Connecticut, I knew how to look and what to look for. As a result I could probe beneath the topsoil of things. In Australia I did not know how to focus. By the time I learn to see, I thought, I will be back in Connecticut. "Don't worry," Vicki said later that morning, "at worst you will write a superficial book. Actually that might increase sales. As things are now your sales couldn't be much smaller. Anyway," she continued, "you can buy handbooks and learn the names of things. What I want to know is what are you going to do about the children's schools?"

Chesterton said that only a "double effort" of "imaginative energy" could prevent travel from narrowing the mind. For the next three weeks the practical, not the imaginative, sapped my energy. For Edward and Eliza, Charles recommended Nedlands Primary School. The school was three blocks from the apartment, and on the afternoon of our second day in Perth we walked to it. On the school grounds a pair of kookaburras foraged through holes in the trunk of a date palm. Above them the crown of the tree sprayed upward, ferns growing like weeds amid the fronds, and orange dates hanging down in strings. Along a walk black pods of kurrajong lay open, exposing rows of yellow seeds.

Above our heads a red-capped parrot twisted noisily through a marri, digging into the fruits.

The school buildings were red brick. Over them tin roofs rolled in the sunlight like waves. The school resembled a small complex of stables and carriage houses attached to a Georgian estate: the library, the saddlery, the administrative offices, the blacksmith's shop. In the largest courtyard grew great clumps of lavender. Scattered about the buildings were bits of playgrounds: playscapes painted blue and yellow, sets of parallel bars, tractor tires, heavy stumps of eucalyptus, then sticking out from a peppermint tree, a walkway resembling the bow of a ship, the tree itself forming both sides of the boat, the figurehead a limb white with blossoms.

Behind the school were a small green playing field, an asphalt basketball court, and a swimming pool. The school looked quiet and old-fashioned, and early on Monday we enrolled Edward and Eliza. In Connecticut, Edward was supposed to start fifth grade in September and Eliza third. The school year in Perth being two-thirds over and the children good students, we registered Eliza for the remainder of third grade and Edward for fifth. After Christmas, Edward would start the sixth grade and Eliza the fourth. The children found the work easy. "I added and subtracted thousands in the second grade," Eliza said, "and here we don't do hundreds." Reading assignments consisted of small books in big type. To supplement her schoolwork Eliza read through a bookcase in the Nedlands Public Library, during the first two weeks of school completing L. M. Montgomery's novels describing the life of Anne of Green Gables. Classes in Storrs rarely consisted of more than eighteen or nineteen students. In Nedlands, Eliza joined a class of twenty-seven while Edward entered one with twenty-four. In contrast to public schools at home, Nedlands Primary did not furnish children with books and supplies. Instead parents purchased them from a local merchant. Children wore uniforms: boys, gray shorts and a light blue cotton shirt with a soft collar; girls, a blue skirt and blue blouse or a black and gray dress, loose and flowing, a good outfit in which to play tag. Both boys and girls wore blue sweaters. Printed in white letters on the left side of the front of the sweater was NEDLANDS. Above the letters lumbered a pelican, his near wing clawing sharp above his body, pulling him upward.

In Storrs schools stressed creativity and individuality, often to the detriment of community. At Northwest School children bustled along halls, and classrooms rang with discussion and laughter. In Perth order was more important than creativity. When their teacher entered the classroom, students stood and in unison said, "Good morning, Miss Taylor." Before being dismissed at the end of the school day, they said, "Good afternoon." Lessons emphasized rote learning, and curiosity, although not repressed, was not encouraged in many classes. "Students here," Eliza said after two weeks in the third grade, "are a little bit behind, and the teachers yell a little more." "In games," Edward said, "children are rougher and say the F-word all the time, but it doesn't mean anything. At recess if you score in soccer, the goalie will call you a bastard, but he doesn't really mean it." Although talk on the playing field was abrasive, that in classrooms was smooth. "When a student misunderstands a teacher," Eliza said, "she has to say *pardon*. If she says *what*, the teacher corrects her."

The school did not have a cafeteria or a gymnasium, and children spent much time outdoors, having a twenty-minute break at ten-thirty, a fifty-minute recess at noon, then a ten-minute break at two o'clock. During the breaks children ate and played games: Eliza, tag, sleepwalk, and piggy in the middle; Edward, soccer, basketball, or Australian rules football. Teachers didn't supervise the recesses closely, and the games themselves were old-fashioned, particularly those played by girls. In the future, recess in Australia will lose its innocence as it has done in the United States. Fences will be built around school yards, and teachers will hover like guards. Edward and Eliza took lunches to school, but a child could order a meal from Hunka's, a local shop. Steak and kidney pies cost $1.40; a hot dog, $1.50; lasagna, $2.00, and a large fruit salad, $2.50. For drink a child ordered juices ranging in price from $0.65 for those containing sugar and water to $1.30 for "100% fruit juice." Large milks cost $1.00 and came in four flavors: chocolate, coffee, strawberry, and spearmint. Dessert cost $1.10, and a child could buy apple or apricot crumble, a custard tart, or carrot cake.

Classes at the school reflected the mix of people in Perth. Most students were descended from European ancestors, but a goodly number were Chinese, the sons and daughters of comparatively recent emigrants to Australia. Unlike Storrs, in which retarded and severely disabled children attended many regular classes, no retarded children attended Nedlands Primary, or at least I did not see any. "I am going to miss walking to school when we return to Connecticut," Edward said at breakfast soon after he began school. "Me, too," Eliza said; "I don't want to ride the school bus any more." Nedlands Primary was a neighborhood school, and although some parents drove children to school, many children walked or rode bicycles. Classes started at eight forty-five. From the house we eventually rented, walking took fourteen minutes, and Vicki and I accompanied Edward and Eliza, stopping often to look at flowers growing in yards along Kingsway: hibiscus; daisies; nasturtiums; diosma, green shrubs covered with small papery blossoms resembling forget-me-nots; bouvardia, the blossoms orange cornets jutting out brassily; freesia; stock; red holly flame pea; and golden guinea, yellow petals surrounding a bushy crown smelling like sweet, curdled cream. Fences served as trellises for vines: morning glory; bougainvillea; Rangoon creeper, red and white and sugary as icing; jasmine, fresh as fruit juice; then on a damp side of a garage golden chalice vine, the blossoms ornate yellow horns streaked with red and so large they seemed swollen, exploded by bursts of notes.

Geraldton wax hung over walls in bushy canes. In the blossoms five round petals surrounded beveled sunken cups thick with red wax and resembling muffins that refused to rise. When crushed, the blossoms smelled like milk and sliced bananas. Each morning I rolled two or three blooms through my hands, spreading the wax over my palms. After the first weeks in Perth, I stopped worrying about the lack of academic matter in Eliza's and Edward's classes. What a child gains from an experience, or for that matter what an adult retains from spending a year away from home, cannot be predicted. Yesterday as we walked to school, Edward scanned the sidewalk. "Daddy," he said, "Australia is wonderful. Pill bugs are everywhere. I don't ever want to go back to Storrs." At dinner Vicki said that Perth so appealed to her senses that life seemed almost decadent. "In New England," she said, "hills and ridges rise hard around a person limiting not only movement but also vision and dream." In Perth colors awakened the senses. Unlike oaks and maples, the leaves of which bunched in thick masses and forming tall hedges blocked sight, eucalyptus trees, she said, were open. Often leaves clumped together only at the ends of limbs, cloud and distant sky filling spaces between branch and trunk, drawing the eye toward the horizon, beyond the immediate and the parochial.

Unlike Edward and Eliza, Francis does not play sports. Instead of a sweeper or shortstop, he has always been a full-time student. Good grades flesh out his identity. In Storrs, Francis would have started the seventh grade in September. Although Nedlands Primary included a seventh grade, Francis did not think classes would challenge him. "I don't want to fall behind my friends at home, and I want to work more with computers," he said. Charles suggested that he attend John XXIII College, a private Catholic school. Across the Stirling Highway some four miles from our house, John XXIII consisted of twelve grades and thirteen hundred and fifty students. The campus was new. Walkways covered with red tile twisted between stone buildings, and the school appeared medieval and academic. An opening existed in the eighth grade. In sixth grade in Connecticut, Francis and a small group of science students studied some quantum physics. After Francis discussed physics and showed him the algebra book that he would have used in Connecticut, the headmaster enrolled Francis in the eighth grade. School proved easy for Francis. His classmates, though, asked many questions about the United States. "Have you ever seen anyone murdered?" a boy asked. "Do you live in Hollywood?" a girl asked. "The kids are nicer to each other here than at home," Francis said at dinner, "but the teachers aren't as good, and the kids don't pay any attention to them, but that's all right because the teachers ignore them, too."

Like the children at Nedlands Primary students at John XXIII wore uniforms. For Francis I bought a closet of second-hand clothes, among other items, gray trousers, a black belt, blue long-sleeved shirts, two pairs of blue shorts, a blue cap, a school tie, and several pairs of tall yellow socks with blue stripes. The clothes cost $304. When this amount was added to the price of books at $164 and of tuition at $2,164 for the year, I spent seventeen times more on Francis's schooling than for Edward's and Eliza's schooling combined. I taught Francis how to tie his necktie. When he wore his gray trousers and sweater the first time, he looked like a young man, not a boy, something that both pleased and saddened me. Children in Perth were less sheltered than in Storrs. In Connecticut the school bus stopped at the mouth of our driveway. The day after registering for John XXIII, Francis caught a city bus at seven-fifty in the morning. He rode to Claremont, a nearby suburb. There he got off and waited twenty minutes before taking a second bus to John XXIII. When school ended, he took another city bus home, getting off at a stop around the corner from our house.

Once Edward and Eliza enrolled in Nedlands Primary, I had to rent a house nearby. Travel does not free parents from the fetters of ordinary living. Instead of making a person more flexible by developing the capacity to cope with and enjoy the new, travel often makes one rigid. Worn out by the trip, I did not have energy enough to wander Perth searching for a house. A block from our university apartment was Broadway Fair, a quadrangle of shops surrounding an open courtyard. The shops were small, and the people managing them friendly. Amid the disruptive aftermath of the trip, the stores seemed homey, if not home. After spending hours amid the new, reading maps or, for example, brochures explaining the mechanics of banking, I looked forward to going to the market. Shopping was the single thing that Vicki and I did together outside the apartment that was reassuringly the same each day. Soon butcher and greengrocer, newsagent and wine merchant knew our names. In the market we forgot about schools. We relaxed and wandering familiar aisles were comfortable. "I don't care where we live in Perth," Vicki said, "just so long as we live in Nedlands and are close to Broadway Fair."

Nedlands was a popular area. Not only did it border the Swan River and the campus of the University of Western Australia, but its streets were quiet and familial. Highways did not slice through it, cracking edges into used car lots and service stations. Finding a furnished house was difficult. Because I like things done yesterday and because I don't like to inconvenience people by asking for help, I wore myself into a sore throat and out of ten pounds. The apartment did not have a telephone. To call real estate agents I walked to my office in the English department. Whenever I saw an advertisement for a house in Nedlands, I hurried to the office, sometimes making five trips a day. Because I did not yet have a key to the office, I had to telephone house agents when the English department was open, fetching a passkey for my office from the department secretary. After eleven days of walking streets and worrying through newspapers, I found a house on Melvista Avenue. The house was one and a half blocks from Nedlands Primary. From the door of my office in the English department to the front stoop of the house was 2,193 steps. The house had three bedrooms, a dining room, a living room with a television, and a kitchen, in this last red cabinets and a floor made from dark jarrah wood. Built in the 1920s, the ceilings of the house were high and molded into geometric patterns: triangles, sunbursts, and sheaves of grain. Panes in the windows were made from leaded glass. Across the front windows stretched a design of columns, vines turning around them and their tops supporting a silver valance. Bottlebrushes grew by the front door, and beds of yellow daisies hung over the curb. In the backyard stood a lemon tree. From the top of a fence dangled bales of morning glory and trumpet vine. By the stoop polygala was purple with flowers, the blossoms resembling small butterflies wrinkling into flight.

Travel is more exhausting than exciting. Before I left Connecticut, a friend said she envied my "skipping out of the groove of ordinary life." No traveler, particularly the family traveler, escapes his accustomed life. Before I went to Australia, I said I would not buy a car. I was naive. Instead of leaving behind the middle-class existence I led in Connecticut, I replicated it in Australia. Despite intention I bought a car. Public transportation in Perth was good. Buses were clean, and the drivers saints, willing to answer all questions and even radio the bus terminal when asked a question they couldn't answer. Still, I needed a car. Edward wanted to play baseball. To enroll Francis in John XXIII and buy uniforms I took taxis, money seeming to wash through the meters like water. When Eliza began to suffer from asthma, I knew that I had to purchase a car. The day after paying the first month's rent for the house, I started searching for a car. New cars cost one and a half times as much in Australia as they do in the United States. At first I had no idea what to buy. I read advertisements in newspapers and studied lists of prices. Francis and I spent an afternoon uptown in Perth looking at the Lada Niva, a small Russian four-wheel drive vehicle. I imagined myself bouncing through the outback, a bush hat on my head and gritty, new words on my tongue. Four-wheel drive days are not, alas, family days. The Lada did not have an automatic transmission. Vicki had never driven a gear shift, and the last time I drove one was in 1975. "Do you really think," she said, "that you can shift gears and drive on the wrong side of the street at the same time? If you get that car, I will never drive."

Vicki was right. Only in dream could I wheel over sand dunes slamming gears back and forth. Instead of pitching through the bush I knew I would spend my days on city streets, with grocery bags, baseball gloves, and nebulizers piled on the backseat. Francis and I also investigated rental cars. The cheapest four-door with an automatic transmission rented for $680 a month, the most expensive for $1,530. "Buy a Toyota, Nissan, or Mazda," Charles advised; "you won't have trouble selling it when you go back home." On the Stirling Highway within walking distance of our house were Mazda and Toyota dealers. At both places I looked at Toyotas. The salesman at the Toyota dealership offered to take me to his farm and show me tiger snakes. I wanted to see the snakes, but unfortunately the best used car for sale at the dealership was a sedan. At the Mazda dealership I bought a 1987 Toyota Camry station wagon. The car had been driven 56,000 miles. I paid fourteen thousand dollars for it. I probably paid too much, but then the year itself was going to cost "too much," the price of the new kitchen and family room Vicki dreamed of adding to our house.

In order to escape daily concerns about money and so that I would not pinch pleasure in Australia, I gelded our savings. In August I cabled eighty thousand American dollars to Perth. At the time the Australian dollar was worth seventy-one cents American. Two days after we arrived in Perth, the Australian dollar sank in value to sixty-four American cents. My eighty thousand dollars suddenly shrank to seventy-two thousand dollars, a loss of eight thousand dollars before I even visited the bank. Instead of escaping mundane monetary concerns I spent more time on such matters than ever before in my life. Never had I worried so much about money. At night I often awakened, wondering why I gutted the savings. Our first days in Perth were more complicated than the same days would have been had we stayed in Connecticut. Little things disrupted peace of mind. Bank machines worked differently. When a teller explained the workings of a checking account, I didn't understand his explanation. Consequently I paid cash for everything I bought, including the car. Little nuisances cluttered hours. Each night I stapled receipts into a notebook in order to have a record of expenditures for the Internal Revenue Service in the United States. For the tax agency in Australia I spent a day getting a "Tax File Number." The next day I learned that Vicki also needed a number.

Included in the price I paid for the Toyota were the transfer fee, stamp duty, license fee, a year's warranty, and insurance. If my insurance company in the United States sent a fax saying that no claims had been paid against my policy during the past five years, then the cost of insurance in Australia would be halved. Getting the fax was a small matter, but one that absorbed a morning. Fortunately my driver's license was good for a year in Australia. Even better, I had no difficulty driving on the wrong side of the street. When Rod Evans asked me if I wanted to take the Toyota for a test drive before I bought it, I refused, explaining that I would be so nervous that I wouldn't notice anything about the car. After buying the car I wheeled out into the traffic on Stirling Highway. So far I have done well. Vicki has screamed at me just once. Only twice have drivers stuck their middle fingers up at me. The drivers were young, however, and I matched them finger for finger.

My inability to shed the trappings of middle-class life was reassuring. My character is formed. Although circumstance may knock me about, it will not shape me or even, I think, the children. Today Eliza went to a birthday party. She wore a flowery dress, just like she does in Connecticut, not rough play clothes. Francis has borrowed a laptop computer from John XXIII and is now in his room composing a newspaper. The Monday after we arrived I checked *Oliver Twist* out of the university library and started reading it to the children. On the first visit to the Nedlands Library the children checked out thirty-one books, only eight below their average in Storrs. When Eliza used the bathroom in the university library, she read graffiti scribbled on the wall just as she does at home. "Daddy," she said, describing what she saw, "why do lawyers carry shit in their pockets?" When I replied that I did not know, she said, "for identification." In Storrs my house stands on the edge of the campus of the University of Connecticut. In Perth I now live around the corner from the University of Western Australia. I enjoy exploring universities, and I like English departments. In Connecticut I often roamed the campus, studying trees and collecting seeds and flowers. Before me on the desk now are two seedpods from an illawarra flame tree. The pods are attached to a long wishbone-shaped twig. When I hold the wishbone up, the pods dangle down, reminding Vicki, at least, of "the knackers on a well-hung bull."

After we moved into the house on Melvista, life slipped into a familiar pattern. Every morning after walking Edward and Eliza to school, I went to the English department. I wrote, drank tea, and visited with folks, making myself not only a bore but also a bit ridiculous, much as I do in Connecticut. Late in the afternoon after the children came home from school, they walked to the campus. I bought them treats, usually Magnums, sticks of vanilla ice cream dipped in chocolate. After eating the ice cream, they haunted the university bookstore. In Connecticut they fed bread to the ducks on Mirror Lake, a pond in the middle of the campus. In Perth they tossed crumbs to peacocks living in the courtyard of the Arts Building.

"I hope your trip was not too exhausting," a friend wrote from Massachusetts shortly after we arrived; "the year sounds like a wonderful experience for you and your family. Have a great time." Wonder opens the door to a great time. In traveling, Chesterton wrote, a person shakes off the bonds that tie him to home and leaving "the inside" draws "dangerously near the outside." From the outside one sees little. Bound not by root or friendship, he judges quickly and usually too harshly. From Connecticut I brought not only habits of seeing and writing but also the paraphernalia I carried on walks about Storrs: binoculars, hand lenses, rulers, and an orange work vest stuffed with pads and pencils. As the university farm lay a short walk from my house in Storrs, so Kings Park, four hundred hectares of bush and garden, was only a fifteen-minute stroll from the house on Melvista. One morning eight days after we arrived, I donned my orange vest and wandered through Kings Park.

Prickly Moses curved yellow over the escarpment. Honeyeaters fed on the cream flowers of parrot bush: brown and singing honeyeaters; a flock of white-cheeked honeyeaters, white patches on their cheeks, yellow streaks along wings and tails; and a western spinebill, his bill curved, appearing almost filed, a white mask over his eyes then tied behind the neck, and falling down his chest a chestnut bib, stitched on its lower edges a border of white and black. Vanilla lilies burst into showers of blue and yellow stars. Wild sarsaparilla twisted purple through shrubs, and buttercups grew bushy along paths. Resembling remnants of sugar candy trickling down the centers of tongues, red lines streaked the lower petals of pink gladiola. Yellow feather flowers popped up through beds in clumps. The flowerheads were three-eighths of an inch in diameter. The petals resembled the feathery ends of arrows, butts of them being shot into each flower. Zamia sprayed up in rigid leaves resembling the fronds of palms. In the centers of female plants cones as tall as a forearm and as round as a child's thigh tilted sideways, resembling pineapples, scaled and prickly. Honeymyrtle glowed pink and yellow, and the tips of smokebush turned white, as if small hidden coals were burning down the stems searing the shrubs to ash. A kookaburra perched on the handle of a spade. I walked within a foot of him. "When I dig under bushes," a gardener said, "he hovers near me, and when I turn up an insect he pounces." While the stems of kangaroo paws were scarlet, the flowers were green. At the tip of the flower the petals rolled back like the fingers of a glove turned inside out. From the glove six yellow stamens unraveled. I ran my hand across the stamens, and the pollen left yellow tracks on my fingers.

On the way back to the apartment from the park, I stopped at Reid Library. I thumbed the card catalog to see how many of my books the university owned. I found one, more than most libraries. No matter where a person travels the past accompanies him. Before coming to Australia I dreamed of escaping *The Dead Poets Society* and my identification with John Keating, the teacher in the movie. "We'll slip quietly into a house," I told Vicki, "and the movie will vanish from our lives." I was mistaken. Instead of ebbing out of mind, the film whirled and gathering strength tumbled me through an undertow of interviews, articles, and telephone calls. Mornings and afternoons I repeated things I said in Connecticut. I wanted to hoist myself beyond the sound of my own words. The publicity office at the University of Western Australia scheduled interviews. Because people at the university had been gracious, I agreed to the interviews. "The movie," Vicki said, "would be waiting for you in the Sahara. Besides the publicity, even if undeserved, hasn't been bad. Because of the film you have traveled and met nice people. You probably wouldn't be here if not for the movie. With only one of your books in Reid Library, you are not exactly an academic name."

Vicki was right. The past determined the present. The year in Australia was bound to be a new limb on an old trunk, not a new tree. Lately trees have been on my mind as well as in wooden metaphors. "I smell cough drops," Edward said as we walked along Fairview. Across the street a man mowed a lawn, in the process shredding eucalyptus leaves into perfume. In *Sartor Resartus* appreciation of nature enabled Professor Teufelsdröckh to escape despondency and tormenting self-concern, ultimately leading him to love of God. Heaven lies beyond my thoughts and prose. On walks I have not carved trees into Jacob's Ladder. Trees, though, have helped me shed nagging worries about money and automobiles and made me feel more like an insider than an outsider. I first noticed barks: the trunks of coral trees smooth and streaked with orange; paperbarks resembling stacks of newsprint swollen by rain; and peppermints, the trunks twisting, rumpling the bark into strips, the leaves dangling down from above, the trees resembling soiled, shaggy mops. Almost every day I wandered the grounds of the university and looked at trees. Beside the Tropical Grove a New Zealand kauri towered bone straight, so imposing that even when out of sight it lowered ominous at the edge of consciousness. Near the Arts Building a Moreton Bay fig splayed above the sidewalk, its trunk resembling a deep gray stream breaking upward over rocks, its limbs thick currents running to green rivulets. Tree ferns draped over paths, the fronds spilling out like curtains, brown fruitdots running in rows under the leaves like stitching. From mouse ears flowers jutted out like red gills. While banksia bloomed in spikes, the sun turning the blossoms into turrets of light, the fruit on hakea resembled primitive, reptilian toes, gray hooks at the ends tearing claws.

More startling than other shrubs and trees were the eucalyptus, there being some two hundred and fifty species in Western Australia. The number unsettled me. If a person lives in a place long enough to recognize plants, he can fool himself into believing that he knows the world, or if not the world itself, at least its ways. Certainty is parochial. No matter how I worked, I realized that by the end of the year in Western Australia I would recognize only a grove of eucalyptus. I would return to Connecticut chastised, aware that I knew less about the world and about mankind than I thought I did. During the first month in Perth I whittled at my ignorance. I learned to recognize marri, its bark rough, flaking away to expose patches of moldy orange. While the bark of jarrah flowed in dry splintery gray strips reminding me of ash, that of tuart looked damp and rough, almost as if it had been scoured by a dirty pad of steel wool. In contrast karri was smooth, blue and white until it shed bark and orange seeped to the surface in pools like colored groundwater. On gungurru old orange bark rolled inward exposing sharp strips of red. While the flowers of gungurru hung down resembling scarlet brushes dipped into yellow, those on bell-fruited mallee were light green and tipped with white.

We have started to settle. We explored the arcades in Perth and wandered through Fremantle, exhausting the children then reviving them with chocolate croissants in the Mill Bakehouse, Vicki and I resuscitating ourselves with cappuccino and slabs of Jamaican coffee cream cake. At the Perth zoo we watched crocodiles being fed and were the only family taking pictures of kangaroos. For lunch we ate meat pies and Australian hot dogs, these last long, scarlet sausages. A white ibis landed on top of a table and raked his bill through the remains of a meal, scattering french fried potatoes over the ground. The children enjoyed the zoo, marveling at the diverse life. When younger I liked zoos more than I do now. The sight of caged animals depresses me. Now, when I look at them I think of friends whom age and disease have locked behind bars, not of hard iron but of weak flesh. At Cohanu Nature Park we saw koalas and fed Rice Krispies to wallabies. Pink and white galahs edged sideways up our arms and perched on our shoulders. The Sunday after buying the car, I drove to Whiteman Park, and we rode a steam train through the bush. Smoke made the children cough, and cinders spotted our clothes. After the ride I walked into the bush. In February a fire swept through the park, but grass trees thrived, their woody trunks solid, their crowns thick, leaves flowing out of them like green fountains. I wanted to explore the park, but near a wetland the trail disappeared. "You'll see tiger snakes in the wet part of the park," a volunteer told me. I wore low-topped sneakers, and so instead of stumbling nervously about in the wetland, I visited the pottery shop and the blacksmith's shed.

Although we have fast become comfortable, we are not Australian. People in Perth are quieter, less demonstrative, less openly individu-alistic than people in Connecticut. In the grocery Australians whisper.

We chatter and cluck, even shriek, resembling the bold wattlebirds who feed noisily in the bottlebrush by the front door. And despite the wonderful tapestry of emu and bustard, pink honeymyrtle, white sugar gum, and magpies singing in dinner jackets, I occasionally miss the brambles of home. Just yesterday I thought about Hoben Donkin and Googoo Hooberry. They caught a string of bass in Dunphy's Pond and afterward were walking along the highway when a man from Nashville stopped his car. He had fished all day at Crossville and had caught only a couple of minnows. "Good Lord," he exclaimed, rolling down his car window, "those are big fish." "Oh, this ain't nothing," Googoo said; "you should have seen the one what got away." "Bigger than those?" the man said, then, thinking to be witty, added, "was it a whale?" "No," Hoben answered, "nothing that small. We was baiting with whales."

On the Road

I had been in Perth for twelve days when Bill Bach telephoned from the American Embassy. The budget year of the United States Information Service ended on September 30. USIS had a small surplus, and Bill arranged a speaking tour for me beginning on the twenty-ninth of September. Slipping me through the maw of the budget in the new year required a loaf of paperwork. "Budgets are strange creatures," he said; "no matter the condiments I sprinkled you with you might rise to the gorge." Accepting invitations comes easily. Declining is harder. I like to accommodate people, and to stop *yes* from slipping pleasingly across my lips, I have to gird up throat and mind, something that takes mental effort. When Bill called, I lacked the strength to say *no*. I had spent the past twelve days finding schools for the children and roaming Nedlands looking for a house and a car. Almost every night I woke up at two or three o'clock and, making a pot of tea, sat in the living room and worried about matters easily resolved in the daylight.

As the twenty-ninth approached I dreaded the tour. Television and radio appearances do not attract me. The short form of an interview prevents a person from being thoughtful. I knew I would be asked what I thought about education in Australia. For me to discuss Australian education after having spent a month in the country was presumptuous. Moreover I was a guest in the country, and for a guest to be critical of his host smacked of poor taste. I dreaded fending off questions that begged for aphoristic answers and reduced me to a pundit, a personality whose lips waggled like ivy in a breeze while his mind remained as immobile as brick, plastered into platitude by the trowel of camera and microphone. Bill scheduled speeches for me in Melbourne, Sydney, and Canberra, places I wanted to visit. Nevertheless, if Bill had not gone to the trouble of arranging the tour, I would have backed out. Not only would I be away from my family on my birthday, but I would miss the wildflower festival at Kings Park.

The children settled happily into school, and each night story and event spiced dinner. One afternoon Edward brought home a jar stuffed with bran and mealy worms, forty-seven worms, he said, "more than in any other jar in class." "Today in religious education we saw a film," Francis said one evening before I left on the tour. "What sort of film?" I asked, wondering if he were being doused with dogma. "A film of *Bridge to Terabithia*," Francis said; "at the end of the film an advertisement for Jiffy condoms appeared on the screen, and we watched that, too." "What!" I said. "Jiffy condoms," Francis repeated, "it was neat." "Here's a present for you," Vicki said one afternoon; "you said you were having trouble getting Australians into your essays." Vicki handed me a stack of posters, each poster eleven inches wide and sixteen inches tall. Green with black letters stamped on them, the posters announced "Open Days" for "Science," Thursday, July 1, and Tuesday, August 3. "See the latest research in molecular biology," the posters urged; "bring your rock specimens to be identified" and "visit research laboratories in population genetics and marine biology." Eliza removed the posters from the wall of the women's bathroom near the coffee shop in the Hackett Building. Instead of scribbling on the walls of the bathroom, students wrote on the backs of old posters. Although the language of the students was more informal and slightly less enthusiastic than that stamped on the posters, it still dealt with matters biological and genetic, and if not with rock specimens, at least with a hard case or two.

"I broke up with my boyfriend five months ago," a girl said, using a blue pen and writing a round, lumpy script. "A week ago we went out and ended up making love. I knew it wouldn't mean we'd get back together but I thought it at least meant he feels something for me. I was really hurt when I found out he was hiding his b'day party from me. When I asked him he said he was trying to get away with not telling me. I had arranged to take him out to lunch anyway, just as a friend, but of course he didn't turn up. I can't believe he would do this to me. I really feel hurt and rejected. The worse part is I still really love him. I've spent five months trying to forget him, but he still dominates my life. Why is he being such a bastard to me and why won't I stop hurting?"

Written in capital letters by a pen with a fine point, the first response resembled a carved rectangle, not a single loop or line jutting beyond the sides of the rectangle. "Like lots of men," the answer explained, "he has a problem reconciling his sexual and emotional life. He is probably confused about what he feels for you and is running away because he doesn't want to find out. His immaturity is not your problem. Distance yourself. Give yourself time to get over him (You *will*). Maybe in ten years he will have grown up." "Why do you let him be a bastard to you? It is called codependency," another respondent wrote, attaching her remark to the girl's story with a long, curved tail. Scrawled sideways in big cursive letters, the last comment filled half the poster. "You are responsible for your own happiness," the writer advised; "don't set yourself up to be a victim. Tell him to fuck-off and get on with your life."

Using red ink and, alas, poor grammar, another girl wrote that she was thinking about taking a break from studying "to go overseas dancing. No, it is nothing sleazy," she explained. "I get paid $200 US; all food, accommodation, air fare is paid for. I know my parents will not want me to go, as they will want me to finish my studies as they will be scared I will like it. It is just that I am in 2nd year and though I like my course I am *bored* of studying. What do you think I should do? Should I finish my studies (2 more years) then go?" "No, go now," someone wrote, underlining her words; "take opportunities when they come along. If you are bored you won't do that well anyway." "Go for it," a second person advised; "you can come back and study if things don't turn out. One year is not a very long time in the grand scheme of things. You'll regret it after, if you don't go." "Good lord," I thought, "what does anyone know about the scheme of things." I picked up my pen and in crabbed black letters wrote, "Listen to your parents and stay home. Life is fragile. One day can destroy your happiness." "Vicki," I said that evening, handing her the poster, "would you mind taping this back on the bathroom wall? The child who wrote this note is not very smart. God knows what she is about to waltz into."

At five-thirty on the morning of the twenty-ninth a black-and-white taxi picked me up. By seven o'clock I was flying to Melbourne. My pay was not quite so good as that offered the dancer, $100 (U.S.) a day plus $119 for living expenses, including cabs, hotels, and food. Unlike the notes they scribble in bathrooms, young women, and for that matter young men, bore me. No longer do I talk to strangers on airplanes. When I look around, passengers appear the same: students, grandmothers, businesspeople, these last acting busier than they really are, adding columns of figures, filling in reports, and turning pages in spiral notebooks. Across the aisle from me a heavyset man opened a Toshiba laptop computer and began playing solitaire. A woman in a blue suit thumbed *Australia Way*, the airline magazine. She read the first paragraph of an article entitled "The Soul of Indonesia: A Journey through Time." After reading the paragraph, she crammed the magazine into the pocket attached to the back of the seat in front of her and putting her left hand under her chin leaned sideways and looked out the window at the gray clouds curving beneath the wings of the plane. For my part I folded a pillow in half and stuffed it behind my neck. Then I opened my backpack and removed a fat book containing three of Gregory McDonald's novels describing the doings of Fletch, an entrepreneurial journalist turned detective and adventurer. Lastly I put on headphones and turned the seat radio to the classical music station. For four hours I listened to rounds of Vivaldi, Ravel, Paganini, Tchaikovsky, Mendelssohn, Offenbach, and Rimsky-Korsakov.

In Melbourne I took a taxi to my hotel, the Sheraton on Spring Street. The hotel's better days were over. Along hallways rugs tattered and peeled away from doorways, rolling up into minute scrolls of fiber. Color had leached out of the walls of my room, the pastels not simply tired but exhausted, the breath of too many weary travelers rubbing across the wallpaper like erasures. The cabby who took me to the hotel was Greek. From Corfu, he said. Most cabbies who drove me were Greek, one emigrating from Naxos, another from Cyprus. The Lebanese who picked me up at the airport in Sydney was from Beirut. Both his parents, he said, had been killed in the civil war. Only one of the cabbies who drove me during the trip had been born in Australia. Dour and unshaven, he had been driving for thirteen hours when I got into the car. For a long time we sat silent in a traffic jam, but once the traffic broke up, he began to chatter. Talk and driving did not mix, neither in the driver's character nor in the pit of my stomach, for the cabby sped as fast as he talked, reaching speeds of 139 kilometers or 87 miles an hour on the highway leading to the Melbourne airport.

I didn't spend much time in my hotel room. After putting my suitcase down by the closet, I pocketed the ballpoint pen on the desk then looked into the bathroom. On the sink sat two small bars of soap wrapped in white paper. On the side of the bathtub was a plastic packet of shampoo, resembling a sea purse. Whenever I leave a hotel, I harvest the fruits of the bathroom. I am especially fond of bottles that resemble small jars of exotic spices. The Sheraton was barren ground. In the next two hotels, however, reapings were bountiful: shoe shine "mitts," shower caps, perfumed soaps in boxes decorated with bottle brushes and fringe lilies, shampoos, sewing kits, then two items I never use, "hand and body lotion" and "bath and body gel."

On a table in the lobby of the Sheraton sat a stack of small maps, supplied by Avis, the "rent-a-car" company. Map in hand, I set out along Flinders, crossed the Yarra River, and thirty minutes later entered the Royal Botanic Gardens, eighty-seven acres of hill, lagoon, lawn, and wood. In Canberra and Sydney I also wandered botanical gardens, in Sydney spending over seven hours in the garden. Often when I am in a critical mood, disposed to judge people and place harshly, I roam the outdoors. Among plants mood softens. Because I recognize few trees and flowers, gardens awaken curiosity. After a ramble I don't have sublime thoughts, but I feel better. Appreciation of plants leads me not only to appreciate people more but to sympathize with them as well. Instead of bolting doors and examining days through peepholes, I turn outward, eager for sun and rain, birdsong, laughter and tears, even the dry sounds of pens scratching and pages turning on a flight from Perth to Melbourne.

The first plants I noticed in the Royal Gardens were trees: bunya bunya pine, its bark thorny and rippled, in the trunk where branches had fallen out, holes puckered like brows and cheeks, bone surrounding empty eye sockets; gully peppermint, its bark appearing charred; water gum, white and gray, the bark pinched and shredded, making the trunk seem pleated; and cypress pine, the limbs not round but tall and thin, taller than they were wide, the lower portions resembling the atrophied triceps of a man gray and arthritic with old age. From the flowers of colchis bladdernut, fragrance melted like soft icing. On paulownia, blooms erupted in sprays of purple and white horns. "Take some seeds home," a woman said to me, seeing me admiring the tree. "That's against the law," I said; "if Customs caught me, they would throw me under the jailhouse." "Hide them in your washbag. That's what I always do," she said.

Wild elder smelled like country, or at least the way country smells in imagination, sourness and salt gone from the earth. On the grass by the ornamental lake black swans hovered over two cygnets. The bills of the adults resembled shoes that an eighteenth-century dandy would have fancied. While most of the bill appeared polished and red, the tip was pink. Behind the tip a white line crossed the top, separating toe from instep and heel. When I looked at the bills I recalled one of my favorite nursery rhymes, *Bobby Shafto*. "Bobby Shafto's gone to sea, / Silver buckles at his knee; / He'll come back and marry me, / Bonny Bobby Shafto!" "Yes," I thought, "and he will prance into the assembly at Bath, buckles winking, red shoes sparkling in the candlelight."

I roamed the park for three hours. That evening I attended a reception at the American Consulate honoring a photographer who won a fellowship to study in the United States. Afterward I ate dinner at a Vietnamese restaurant with the consul and her houseguest, an actress who just completed playing a role in an American television series. Because union fees made working in California expensive, the cast had flown to Australia, and the episode had been filmed in Queensland. The woman was strikingly pretty and so fit that I couldn't tell whether she was thirty-four or forty-four years old. At sixteen she left home and moved to California determined to become an actress. She succeeded and had appeared in several films and television shows.

She had also been a centerfold in a men's magazine, *Playboy*, three people at the reception told me. Although I have never purchased an issue of *Playboy*, eating dinner with a centerfold titillated me. Conversation left over from the meal would provide a tasty canapé or two that I could slap on a postcard and serve to friends in the English department in Connecticut. "That Sam is quite a lad," I could imagine Dick saying, his words not deciduous but evergreen in their envy. The actress was a vegetarian. I don't eat spicy foods, and accordingly conversation was mild and palatable. We discussed our mail, the consul describing the letters she received, many demanding vast amounts of money from the

American government. The actress did not answer her mail. In the past when she answered letters, fans wrote back, asking to borrow money or meet her. When she did not answer second letters, often fans became abusive and threatening. The actress kept her address secret, and her mail went to a post office box. A secretary sorted through it, panning out bills and professional matters before tossing the dross away.

I felt sorry for the actress. People saw her as the roles she played and wrote not to her but to fictional characters. Ever since my identification as one of the sources of John Keating the teacher in *Dead Poets Society* not only have people confused me with Keating but often they have insisted upon my being him. Occasionally when I emphasized that movies are fictions and that Keating was not me but a fictional creation, people became resentful. Happily, though, Keating was popular, and most of the people who insisted upon seeing me as him were not critical but admiring. Voluptuaries and femme fatales were among the roles the actress played, and letters written by people confusing her with such parts were provoked less by admiration than by lust or resentment. Even I wanted to imagine myself in the glossy company of a centerfold, not a real person. Before traveling to Queensland the actress played a lesbian in a movie filmed in Germany. "An interesting role," she said, "but I'm not a lesbian, far from it." "I'm not one either," I said. Appearing in a movie as a lesbian would, I suddenly thought, stop people from confusing me with John Keating. "But," I added, "I would not mind playing one. I'd be darn good at it."

On the postcard I sent to the English department I said that the actress replied, "Oh, no, you would be the world's worst lesbian." Actually she ignored my remark and asked, "what sort of mail do you get?" For an essayist dross glitters, and when I pan through my correspondence, I toss aside the gold. Today's mail brought three letters. From Florida a man sent an article, the headline of which read, "Running Acts as a Fairly Potent Laxative." From the *Seattle Times* a woman clipped an article describing the career of General William Pickering, governor of the Washington Territory during the Civil War. She underlined Pickering's nickname "William the Headstrong." She drew a line from the nickname to the margin where she wrote, "Is he kin to you?" From Victoria a man sent a tape on which he recorded his school hymn, all five verses. "Lord, Thy Holy Word revealeth, / As our coming years will show," the hymn began; "We shall surely reap the harvest / Of the good or ill we sow. / And as in the hour of testing, / Only what is good survives, / Give us grace to reverence virtue, / And by them shape our lives."

The consul brought two bottles of wine to dinner, good wine, or so I thought, until she said, "Can you believe this only cost five dollars a bottle?" If she had said "twenty dollars a bottle," not only would I have drunk with more panache but I would have thought better of myself. In Perth, Vicki and I drink wine that costs $3.95 a bottle. On the road I want to think that people see me as a twenty-dollar-a-bottle man. No matter the cost, however, we finished both bottles. Wine makes me hoarse, and three times during the night I got out of bed and drank four glasses of water. Getting up was easy. No matter the room, I sleep fitfully in hotels, and by the end of the speaking tour I was exhausted.

For a continental breakfast the hotel charged ten dollars. My fancies about wine aside, I am not a ten-dollar-breakfast man, and so I left the hotel and roamed streets until I found a sandwich nook on Collins Street that served bacon, eggs, toast, and coffee for $5.50. After breakfast I explored downtown Melbourne, strolling through arcades and poking into bookstores. The interviews I had on tour, the radio and television shows on which I appeared, would not increase sales of my books. None were available in Australia. In truth not many were for sale in the United States. Just before leaving Perth for Melbourne I received a royalty check for my latest collection of essays. The check was for $229.64. "I thought you would get at least a thousand dollars," Vicki said; "the book has been out just a year."

Later that morning I appeared on a radio show, after which a writer for a magazine interviewed me. The river of water I poured down my throat during the night soothed my voice, and wine bubbled through my brain only once, making me mispronounce *swath* on the radio. After returning from breakfast I checked out of the hotel, storing my suitcase in the luggage room. My flight to Canberra left at four-fifteen. The radio appearance ended at noon. "You have a lot of time to kill before your flight," the embassy official who escorted me to the interview said; "I'll drop you off across the river from your hotel. You can explore Southgate for a couple of hours. Then you can catch a taxi, pick up your bag, and go to the airport." Southgate was an esplanade of trendy boutiques and "eateries" stretching along the south bank of the Yarra River, not far from Princess Bridge. After eating a sandwich, I bought a ginger ice cream cone and sitting on a green bench looked across the Yarra at the Melbourne skyline.

I squinted, and my eyes bleared as grit gusted through the air. Trams knocked and thumped heavily on Princess Bridge. Gas fumes tumbled off the road, seeming to fall onto the esplanade in choking bundles, heavy with lead. The sky was overcast, and Melbourne resembled a collection of thick slabs, blocks tossed in a blanket by an impatient child. Big letters marked the upper stories of several buildings. In idleness I read them: SEC, MLC, ANZ, QBE, and WESPAC. Just under the roof of a building loomed a rectangular sign. The top half of the sign was yellow. Stamped across it in black letters was the word *Auction*. The bottom half of the sign was black. Printed on the left side in white was *Hooker;* on the right was *Richard Ellis.* Telephone numbers appeared in red under the names, 6701111 for Hooker and 6543333 for Ellis. The Flinders Street Railway Station stretched along the embankment, the low red bricks rusty, the taller clock tower and domes hunks of liverish yellow, tarnished silver trains sliding along tracks beneath them. Spires of St. Paul's Anglican Cathedral stuck up sharply, jabbing futilely through the smothering weight of steel and concrete around them. Moored to the far shore of the Yarra were three sight-seeing boats owned by Melbourne River Tours. With glass tops and faded blue hulls, the boats rode low in the water, resembling whirligig beetles. Rows of classroom chairs with vinyl seats filled the boats, turning them into floating auditoriums. Above the boats two office buildings owned by the Gas and Fuel Corporation of Victoria hung like stage curtains, blocking vision and stifling imagination.

"Jesus," I said aloud, suddenly realizing that the day was September 30, "what a way to celebrate a birthday!" The thought awakened curiosity, and forgetting the buildings I looked around to see who was at my party, or if not at my party, at least close enough to enjoy the festivities. On the railing in front of my bench a seagull perched on a single red leg. Under the railing an English sparrow pecked at vanilla-colored specks in the concrete. To my left eleven retarded people sat in a circle eating lunch. Six of the people were in wheelchairs, and two wore black helmets. To my right two buskers sang songs made popular by the Beatles. One of the buskers played drums, the other a guitar and a harmonica, this last locked into place near his mouth by a metal harness that fitted around his neck and shoulders, resembling a brace. Both buskers wore frayed jeans, but while the drummer wore a long-sleeve red-checked shirt unbuttoned down the middle of his chest, the guitar player wore a blue sweatshirt with the letters CCCP printed on the front in white. Nearby a girl stood astride a bicycle and listened. She wore a green helmet, a pink sweatshirt, and gray sweatpants and leaned slightly to the left, so she could tilt the bicycle and plant her feet on the sidewalk.

In Canberra, Bill Bach met me at the airport. Huong, his wife, prepared a Vietnamese dinner, and I ate with the Bachs and their two children. The children were eight and ten, the ages of Eliza and Edward, making me long for family and Perth. Knowing that creeping things interested me, Bill showed me a trapdoor spider he kept in a jar of preservative. The spider was hairy. When I held the jar against a light, the spider resembled a dark knot of letters. In Canberra I spent three nights at The Pavilion, rated "outstanding" in one survey. Although continental breakfast cost $13.50 at The Pavilion, I ate it, there being no cafés within convenient walking distance of the hotel. Businessmen stayed in The Pavilion, and every afternoon as I sat in the sauna, conversation ran to finance, the words *Hong Kong, Superfund,* and *Singapore* dripping about me. The weather was warm, and because I spoke more than once a day, my clothes became soiled. I washed underpants and socks in the bathroom sink, but I sent other things out to be cleaned, the first time I ever used a hotel laundry. I stuffed a sport coat, three white dress shirts, and a green T-shirt with a collar into a plastic laundry bag and set it outside my door at eight-thirty in the morning. That evening the clothes were back. The bill was $30.50: $8.70 for the jacket, $5.70 for each of the white shirts, and $4.70 for the T-shirt.

At eight-fifteen the morning of my first full day in town Bill took me to the Canberra Grammar School to film an interview for television. With cloisters and academic Gothic buildings surrounding a green, the oldest quadrangle of the school resembled the main court of a college at Cambridge. The cameraman was a perfectionist. Three times he filmed me walking up the front steps of the school. The interview took place in the dining hall. Afterward the cameraman filmed me and the interviewer walking through the cloisters. He filmed us twice from the front and once from the back. Then he asked us to walk slowly so he could film our feet. The day was full. From the school I went to a radio station. Later a reporter for a local newspaper interviewed me. I gave two talks, one at the National Library and another after dinner at the American Embassy. In the *Canberra Times* a reporter wrote that I had "the timing and the moves of a stand-up comedian and the undulating cadences of a secular evangelist who has seen not hell-fire and damnation in the life to come, but the almighty and often hilarious wonder of things in the life at hand."

The reporter understood that a good speaker is a performer, an actor delivering soliloquies, a conjurer creating props with words, his voice pulling a cast of supporting characters from the wings of recollection. For me, however, dissatisfaction always accompanies the fall of the curtain, whether my performance be on the stage or in the classroom. Although I shape essays and try to create reactions, rarely do I see the effects of my writings. The essays are published months after I write them. When a person mentions an essay to me, chances are that the essay has slipped so far out of mind that it seems written by a stranger. Because of the gap between writing and publication, reactions to an essay are unexpected, seeming spontaneous and individual, not a communal response to plotted manipulation. Onstage words bring immediate reactions. I know how to make audiences laugh and cry, how to silence people, how to make them turn and smile at their neighbors. My expertise lies behind my dissatisfaction with speaking. I think the speaking me a manipulator, not an educator, not the writer, the ordinary guy fumbling through thought laboring to explain or describe. Onstage words lose meaning and become tools, devices used to build shanties that resemble mansions, shacks that concerns of the next hour will tumble out of mind.

In hopes of forgetting my dissatisfaction with speaking I asked Bill to take me to the National Gallery. I spent two hours at the gallery. I hurried through a room in which exhibitors held cameras up to private parts. Hotels paper bathroom walls with mirrors, and no matter how the traveler tries he cannot avoid studying himself. In The Pavilion I had seen enough of my sagging middle-aged bottom not to want to see anyone else's, be it perky, puckered, or otherwise. In the National Gallery I selected pieces that I wanted to own, not great art but things to stand in the hall or sit on a mantelpiece in Connecticut. On the far end of the living room wall I nailed a picture by Eugene von Guerard, a view of Mount Kosciusko painted in 1863. Dark ledges of rock pushed out of the mountain like thick stubble. Dishcloths of snow trailed down valleys, crumpled and soiled. Soapy white clouds hung over the left distance; to the right the sky crinkled and splintered into oily colors: purple, pink, and yellow. Atop the piano in the living room I set a saucer and teacup, designed by Lulu Shorter in Sydney in 1908. The rim of the saucer was gold. Inside the rim was a band of soft black, almost brown. Bunched together in the center of the saucer was a bundle of green leaves. From them grew a waratah, the blossom itself resembling a cup. My "steal" was a bookcase made from cedar in Tasmania in 1840. The bookcase was tall, and to wedge it into the study I widened the front door of the house. The bookcase was worth the expense, however. Through the wood flowed the hot, grainy reds of sunset, that time just before stars and the first cooling purples of night.

The next morning Bill drove me and John Lake, director of the Australian-American Educational Foundation, to Namadgi National Forest. We hiked from Glendale Crossing to Nursery Swamp, where we sat on a hillock, drank wine, ate apples and ham sandwiches, watched gray kangaroos, and talked as three comfortable middle-aged men will do: with humor and taking pleasure in each other and in being able to walk through the bush. We did not climb a mound of big round boulders that we saw. We didn't say studiously bright things. Instead we ambled the lowlands, letting Nature make the path memorable. I chewed broad-leaved peppermint and picked up wombat droppings. A crimson rosella squawked from a gum tree, the sound red and blue like the bird's feathers. A white-eared honeyeater flew ahead of us. Austral indigo bloomed purple along the forest trail. Mountain grevillea was red and yellow, and silver banksia shone orange in the shade. While bracken curved upward in soft fronds, early wattle was spiky and sharp. Strips of red bark unraveled from candlebark gum, leaving the trees blue and white. Across the bumpy trunks of scribbly gum the larvae of moths carved shallow channels resembling spirals scratched on paper by a person turning a ballpoint pen about in order to start ink flowing. At the edge of Nursery Swamp black sallee shed bark. On the slopes above grew snow gum, clusters of white trunks snaggy and twisting, resembling icy rivulets spewing up from the ground then freezing hard and cloudy. That night I ate dinner at John's house, learning that thirty years ago John's father had been head of Nedlands Primary School.

The next day was Sunday, and I flew to Sydney. I was supposed to spend three nights in Sydney, not because I had much to do but because on Tuesday I was to be a guest on *Late Night Live,* a popular radio program broadcast throughout Australia. After lunch on Tuesday I spoke at the University of Sydney. University holidays had begun, and the man whom the consular official contacted to arrange my talk beat through the halls to flush out an audience: a secretary here, a graduate student there, and professors so dozy that they came to their offices not realizing that vacation had begun. In Sydney I stayed in the new Marriott, on the nineteenth floor, the "executive" floor for which I used a special key in the elevator. The Marriott was the poshest hotel in which I stayed, the bathroom seeming all mirror and tub. Fitted into a corner the tub resembled a marble home plate removed from a giant baseball field. I didn't know how to stretch out in it, whether to lie facing the pitcher or looking toward third or first base. Consequently I sat in the middle and splashed water over myself.

Beside my bed was a black digital clock. Life in a big city is digital. In the country days are slower and not so mechanical. Long and short hands appear to wander around the faces of clocks, and time itself seems to turn through a circle. For the person who owns old clocks, a missed opportunity matters little. As time revolves endlessly through the same circle, so opportunity or its twin must come round again. In contrast numbers on a digital clock snap the changing minutes, conveying finality. Unlike the long hand that stretches and languidly points a finger in a general direction, the numbers on a digital clock are related to those on cash registers and computers, attuned to the bustle of buying and selling, showing not simply what stock is up or down but who is up or down, who has kept or lost track of time.

On the executive floor continental breakfast was free, and from five-thirty to seven-thirty in the evening drinks were complimentary and

served with canapés. I did not drink, but every evening I munched trays
of canapés: smoked salmon and chives on toast; on black bread, brie
topped by strawberries; anchovies and hard-boiled eggs on toast; then
boat-shaped patties, swamped with avocados whipped into a frothy
paste. Two nights in Sydney I ate by myself. When being driven into
the city from the airport, I noticed restaurants on Oxford Street, just
around the corner from the Marriott. I explored Oxford Street before
eating. Men in shorts and tank tops, urban cowboys in boots and
leather, strolled arm in arm. After peering in the windows of two score
restaurants, I ate in the Tandoori Palace. I chose it because most of the
tables were occupied, and feeling lonely I wanted to be in a crowd. I
chose well. The food was so good I returned a second night. Each time I
had a plate of onion bahajees then a mild curry, one night chicken, the
next lamb. Drawn on the walls of the Tandoori Palace were colorful,
primitive sketches: the Taj Mahal white against a red sky; a mud fort
surrounded by an orange wall, elephants standing and pushing against
each other from opposite sides of the wall, their tusks buckled together
across the top of the wall; a blue pool, yellow spotted fish swimming
in it, white water lilies and brown mushroom-shaped plants sticking
above the surface, and finally elephants diving and sporting in the
water, a gray bottom topped by a ropy tail sticking up beside a flower
and next to a rock a trunk curling out of the pool like a sea serpent
and blowing a geyser of purple suds into the air.

When I checked into the Marriott, I received a map of Sydney. After
dropping my suitcase in my room and hiding money in the arm of
a white shirt, I hurried to the quay and for fifteen dollars bought a
ticket for the Captain Cook Harbor Highlights Cruise. The trip lasted
seventy-five minutes. Although the day was chilly, I stayed on deck.
The famous opera house resembled a fistful of gigantic scallop shells.
In the cold the shells appeared dry and brittle. Once the cruise ended
I hurried to the opera house and discovered tickets were available
for *Tosca* on Tuesday night. Ten minutes after the opera ended I was
supposed to be at the radio station, so I didn't buy a ticket. Alas, I
could have attended the performance, for events in Moscow bumped
me off the air, the host of the show preferring to interview an expert on
Russian affairs. From the water Sydney appeared big but not so lovely
as I expected. Along the bays apartment buildings rose sharply from

the water's edge. Stacked behind each other, they lost dimension and resembled playing cards pitched out of a shuffle and stuck into the ground, their windows marking suit and number.

I roamed downtown Sydney. The city vibrated to the digital rhythm of buying and selling. Everything was for sale: boys on Oxford Street, women at Kings Cross, opals on George Street, and clothes in the Pitt Mall. Even I imagined "a deal." I walked through The Rocks, the section of Sydney where the first fleet anchored two hundred years ago. Recently restored, many of the older buildings in The Rocks were restaurants, craft shops, patisseries, and hotels. In August we planned to return to the United States from Sydney. Hotels in The Rocks were expensive. If I promised to praise a hotel in my essays, perhaps, I thought, one might offer us complimentary accommodations. Then we could stay three or four days in Sydney, and maybe Vicki and I could attend an opera. To this end I climbed through The Rocks, munching a hunk of sacher torte and collecting brochures from hotels: the Old Sydney Parkroyal, the Russell, and the Harbour Rocks Hotel. My appetite for bargaining lasted only as long as the torte. After wiping the chocolate off my face with a napkin, I tossed both it and the hunger for wheeling and dealing into a garbage can and set out for the Royal Botanic Gardens. In Canberra, Guy Farmer, an official at the embassy, took me to the National Botanic Gardens. To enjoy a garden, a person should be alone. Alone one meanders and lets imagination roam. He putters or simply sits. He escapes being the self that others think him. He does not have to speak, much less groove word and observation to fit another's mood. Guy was good company, so good that I did not see the garden at Canberra.

In the gardens in Melbourne, noise tugged at awareness. Commerce splintered quiet as trains clattered and chains of traffic jerked through the city. The garden in Sydney was silent, rumpling above Farm Cove like an eiderdown. Because my throat was sore from talking, I chewed eucalyptus leaves. After testing several leaves, I decided the most effective came from maiden's blue gum. Beside paths in the Palm Grove cliveas bloomed in puffs of orange, and acanthus hung dark and waxy. Cape daisies bloomed in borders at the edge of green lawns. Black cormorants perched on trees in the islands in the Main Pool, and four sulfur-crested cockatoos scavenged through the grass, their bright yellow topknots appearing brushed and kept in place by hair jell. I looked at trees, the raised welts on the bark of Hill's weeping fig making the tree appear light and airy. The trunk of a white fig was so indented that the tree seemed to be sucking itself inward, out of substance. The leaves of weeping lilly pilly dangled, their margins scalloped and dripping through the clear light in rivulets. Branches of a Chinese elm swept out of the ground, making the trunk drape like a long, clinging gown. In the rose garden olympiads resembled dark red bowls, veins running brown and hammered through their petals. Iceberg was white; buccaneer, yellow; and the old Bourbon rose Zephirine Drouhin, lavender.

At the shop in the garden I bought a T-shirt for Vicki. Printed on the front of the shirt was a wheelbarrow overflowing with wildflowers: dryandra, banksia, wattle, honeymyrtle, and Sturt's desert pea. Much as I enjoyed the formal gardens, I wanted to see wildflowers and wilder parts of New South Wales. For eighty-nine dollars I took a day tour of the Blue Mountains. On Monday at eight-thirty a guide picked me up in a four-wheel drive. I got back to the hotel at seven that evening, 320 kilometers later. Four people beside me were on the tour, a couple from Western Australia on vacation and from Italy two honeymooners, the wife a teacher and the husband an engineer with a cellular phone company. Above Hawkesbury River apple gums bloomed white. A wedge-tail eagle floated above the Colo River. Beyond Mountain Lagoon mountain ash towered over the woods. Wattle blossomed along dry fire trails, and black currawongs watched us eat near Mount Wilson, their bright eyes gold coins. On high slopes snow gum twisted in snarls, their struggle to hold on to the earth making them seem undignified, even petty. I enjoyed being a tourist. At Katoomba I rode both the rail- and skyways. On this last the man in charge stopped halfway across the gorge and rocked the cable car, all the while grinning and pointing through a gap in the slats of the seats to the forest below. The man's expression was goofy, but I suppose taking a cable car across the gorge twenty or thirty times a day might make a person peculiar. Of course travel itself can make a person odd. When I travel, big matters slip through the slats of concern, and I notice small things, for example, a sign on a school bus near Blackheath declaring, "WE DON'T WANT TO LOSE YOUR MIND."

By the end of the trip my mind was truant. I had been asked so many questions that my responses became mechanical, requiring not thought but only energy enough to rewind then play the appropriate answer. In part my responses were recorded because I did not wish to offend. Whenever I was asked a question that I thought ill-considered, I pressed fast forward and changed the subject of conversation. On the flight back to Perth I replayed interviews, pondering questions, not providing answers but wondering why the questions had been asked. The outlandish and the acidic make good copy. Several times interviewers asked leading questions. "Is it good that Australia is so British?" one person asked. "Why do you suppose," another reporter asked, "that all Australians are racist?" "I haven't seen racism in Perth," I said. "Perth?" the reporter continued, "why in the world did you go there?" Several people asked why I chose to go to Perth, implying that the place I thought another Eden was a wasteland. "How was the trip?" Vicki said when I walked through the door. "Tiring," I said. "Well," she said, "the children and I have bought kangaroo, just the thing to perk you up. I am cooking it tonight for a belated birthday dinner." "Oh, boy," I said. "Yes," she said, "the meat will set you on your feet. We hop on the road the day after tomorrow."

Vicki bought the kangaroo at the Royal Agricultural Show. Kangaroo bones shatter easily. The man who butchered the animal had not wielded a subtle knife, and the meat was gravelly. "Grit for the craw," I thought. Enough grit, I hoped, to help me grind through the rocky week ahead. Western Australia, as a tourist pamphlet put it, "is renown for its spectacular wealth of wildflowers. No other place in the world produces a more prolific abundance of wildflowers than Western Australia during the months August, September, and October." Shortly after arriving in Perth, Vicki plucked a garden of brochures, all blooming with tours through "wildflower country." At first we considered a tour. One that lasted eight days and covered the southwestern part of the state cost forty-five hundred dollars for the five of us. By car a comparable tour cost thirteen hundred dollars, excluding, of course, the price of the car. During the first two and a half weeks of October the children were home on school holidays. Accordingly on the morning of the eighth, a day and a half after I flew home from Sydney, we set out. Despite my having urged her to organize the trip while I was away, Vicki did not make plans. "You are the traveling man," she said, "sashaying about with wombats and *Playboy* bunnies and god-knows-what-else while I vacuumed, cleaned clothes, and carted the children around. You organize the trip. This is my holiday." During the one full day in Perth, I bought maps and a pile of guidebooks. Still, when we turned on the Stirling Highway toward Fremantle, I knew only that we were heading south. Not knowing where we would spend nights bothered me, especially since acquaintances warned that we would have a "devilish time" finding places to stay during the holiday.

At the start of the trip my mind resembled the rear of the station wagon, crammed with backpacks; a new blue-and-white twenty-six-liter Esky cooler, "The Original Aussie Cooler," costing $45.48 and bought at Coles in Claremont the previous day; duffel bags; yellow raincoats; Edward's stuffed monkey, the elephant I bought Francis in London eleven years ago, then all twelve of Eliza's "babies," Kitty, Fuzzy, Corduroy, the whole gang; and finally an attic of boxes filled with, among other things, binoculars, pads and pencils, shelves of kitchen equipment including knives and forks, a cutting board, napkins, dish towels, straws, even a wine opener. In the front seat worries about our destination piled high, and at the start of the trip I did not notice the landscape. While I was in Melbourne, a crack began to inch across the windshield. When, I wondered, would the glass shatter? "Only fools," Mother once said, "buy used cars. Old cars are death traps." Not only did I worry that the car would break down, but I wondered where the breakdown would occur. I hadn't changed a tire in twenty years. With my bad back changing a tire would, I concluded, cripple me. In the pocket of the door beside me sat a plastic bottle of sunscreen. The ozone over Western Australia was thin, and skin cancer rates were boiling. From the Cancer Society I bought a white hat with a big brim and the first pair of sunglasses I ever owned.

Getting the children to swim in shirts and butter themselves with sunscreen was often difficult. Then, of course, beaches themselves were aquatic minefields, sowed with stone and scorpion fish, the blue-ringed octopus, and jellyfish appropriately dubbed sea wasps. Instead of being ornaments for a child's desk, seashells seemed the invention of terrorists. With red and brown twirling through it like sugar, the cone shell geographus had killed a dozen people in Australia. Inside the shell lurked a creature armed with a long hollow tooth, sharpened at the end. Thrusting the tooth out, the animal first harpooned then injected poison into its victim. Off the coast of southwestern Australia, sea snakes did not occur in large numbers, or so books said. If snakes were scarce in the sea, however, they were bountiful on land. Common across the southwest were, among other serpents, the death adder, its venom one and a half times as toxic as that of the Indian cobra; the dugite, its venom only 90 percent as poisonous as that of the cobra; the king brown, only 25 percent as toxic but a big snake whose venom sacks resembled barrels; then the tiger snake, whose poison was four times as toxic as that of the cobra. "At this time of the year," the owner of a farm told me, "snakes are coming out of hibernation and their poison is really strong. Later after they have killed a few things they won't have so much of the stuff." "And scorpions and spiders," I said aloud. "And kangaroos," Eliza said, overhearing, "don't forget kangaroos. I want to see kangaroos, too." On this trip kangaroos were easy to forget. Despite driving several hundred miles, we did not see a live kangaroo. By the side of the road, I counted six swollen dead kangaroos. These kangaroos, Vicki decided, were stuffed and placed on the shoulders of roads for tourists. "The only live kangaroos in Western Australia," she said, "are in zoos. The rest have been shot or poisoned. Each spring the tourist commission dumps several paddocks of stuffed kangaroos beside highways. If we examined one of the kangaroos," Vicki said, "we'd find a label sewed on it, reading 'Made in Japan.' "

With the exception of a small part of the Vasse Highway, I drove the entire trip. Driving was hard. Although once or twice I glanced into a field to see emus or a flock of Carnaby's cockatoos, I kept my eyes focused on the asphalt. Roads were narrow and two-laned. Surfaces were rough. Spring rains washed out hunks of pavement, and often shoulders fell sharply off into sand. Occasionally ash from forest fires drifted across the highway, hiding the asphalt under a gray blanket. Vicki drove from Nannup to the Donnelly River, or rather to the Donnelly River Winery. Unfortunately that portion of the trip was difficult. The shoulders of the highway were eroded, and the line down the center of the road had vanished. The land rolled, and the road bumped around hills and dipped pitching through small valleys. When Vicki stopped at the winery, she was dizzy. She stumbled out of the car and sat on the ground. The owner of the winery brought us a cold towel, and I wrapped it around Vicki's head. Because the owner was thoughtful I bought a bottle of wine, one costing sixteen dollars, more than I would have paid if Vicki had not stumbled. During the trip we stopped at several wineries, not for samples of drink but to break the drive. Rarely did I taste more than one wine. Not only did wine blow through my brain in a purple fog, but sampling made me convivial, binding me in glib, momentary friendship to owners, making me feel obliged to buy bottles.

I drove slowly the first day, traveling through Rockingham and Mandurah over to Pinjarra then to Waroona Dam. The names of the towns through which we drove during the vacation sounded romantic, and I imagined a poem of names, sounds creating moods, not thought: Cowaramup and Margaret River, Nannup, Pemberton, and Walpole, Denmark, Albany, and Kojonup, Busselton, Williams, and Mount Barker. Near the dam rangers burned bush, so I drove to Harvey. We ate beside a small stream. Above us open pastures were yellow in the sunlight. Jarrah and marri rose like shadows in the seams of crinkled slopes. Beyond them the sky was thick and blue, clouds passing in bundles. Throughout the trip I stopped at bakeries and small groceries, and Vicki kept the cooler full of bread, cheese, chocolate milk, bottles of Coca-Cola, cookies, and fruit, these last usually apples and mandarin oranges.

After lunch we followed a stream up a slope. Resembling thick dangling fingers, sawfly larvae hung on the stem of a seedling, white hair sticking out from their bodies like electrified spikes. A bobtail skink hissed at us. The reptile resembled a hunk of pipe wrapped in thick hide, the tail rounded at the end almost as if it had been sliced off and the wound bandaged with scales. The head of the animal was dirty yellow and worn to a dull flattened arrowhead. When we didn't move, the bobtail opened its mouth and thrust a blue tongue out at us, the tongue not flicking but lapping down over the lower jaw in threatening display, one that the children immediately tried to match, only Eliza succeeding. The bobtail impressed Eliza. Yesterday at school she sculpted a bobtail's head. "I tried to make the head of a tiger," she explained, "but the nose was too long, so I pressed the head into a triangle, opened the mouth, and lined it with blue clay. Miss Beck was pleased that I made an Australian animal. Everybody else made elephants or monkeys, creatures from zoos."

Grass trees grew in the scrub. Semaphore sedge stood knee-high, and ribbons of coral vine wound red through bushes. Bristly cottontails clumped together in bundles of yellow. Blue flowers sprayed up from the ground almost as if a stream flowing through a deep cave spurted up, the stems of the plants fresh green fountains, the blossoms damp goblets winy with color: royal robe; purple flag, yellow simmering in the centers like dollops of cream; tinsel lily; and demure bluebell creeper. During the trip we took many walks, some no longer than a football field, others stretching through morning into afternoon. Deep forests seemed cathedrals, the great trees columns and the flowers stained glass flickering in the sun. Beneath gray tuarts beyond Busselton wattle shimmered like pieces of yellow tissue paper tossed from car windows and blowing loosely through the woods. Resembling small open gloves cowslip lilies bloomed, the two lower petals, or the thumb and little finger, yellow, the upper three petals, the other fingers, streaked with red.

Behind a log four pink fairy lilies shone like stars. Bulldog ants patrolled the grass by the log. When I scraped a twig across the ground in front of an ant, it rushed forward and seized the twig between two long pincers resembling red clamps. In damp spots arum lilies bloomed, the white flowers so large they reminded me of shovels. Scooping up sunlight, the curved edges of the petals swept heat into the centers of the blossoms. Arum bloomed throughout the damp. In a dell formed when the roof of a limestone cave collapsed, the flowers drifted like snow across the forest floor. Hovea bloomed along the sides of the dell. A green ruffle of ferns wrapped the top of the dell, fishbone and the smooth velvety collar of maidenhair. Beyond the dell Billy buttons filled a bare spot, the yellow circle a corsage focusing the eye and ordering vision into a garden, paths twisting outward through white clematis, heart-leaved flame pea, and bull banksia, the leaves of this last scratchy and smacking of the desert but the blossoms great popsicles of humid, lemony summer.

Traveling alone is easy. A poor meal affects the digestion of only one person. Alone one drifts past meals and indulges in mood, creating a wardrobe of identities. On the trip south I was never alone. I had many identities, all thrust upon me: daddy, driver, banker, the tour guide who pointed out sights and chose hotels and restaurants, the alarm clock that roused the family in the morning, and the cheerleader who invigorated the weary and jollied the splenetic into smiles. I planned to keep track of the miles driven each day, but I did not. Familial concerns pushed the intention out of mind.

Similarly I did not have the leisure to study wildflowers. Once I returned to Perth only small patches of the southwest bloomed in recollection: beside tingle trees white crowea and tassel flower, a whorl of sharp leaves cutting upward, through them blossoms spilling down loosely scattering pink; a clump of vanilla orchids near a dirt road; sticky tailflower white and pastry sweet under a headland below Denmark; atop a rocky bluff overlooking the Southern Ocean, pigface plugging a gray seam with pink and yellow; pink rice flower beside a boulder atop Morgan's View in the Porongurup Mountains; and a red mountain pea in the Stirlings, the blossom almost a cartoon, a vamp from the late show, the furry calyx resembling a silver fox coat from the neck of which pursed lips protruded fleshly and scarlet.

I spent more time eating and searching for places in which to eat than I did examining wildflowers. While Edward and Eliza ate little other than hamburgers and french fried potatoes, Francis devoured everything, practically always ordering the most expensive item on a menu. In Bunbury we ate at the Friendship Chinese restaurant. Afterward I bought ice cream cones for the family in hopes of getting something down Edward and Eliza. In Augusta I cooked T-bone steaks at Jimmy's Grill. The day had been long, so I bought a bottle of red wine. After cutting Eliza's steak into small pieces, I poured the wine down my throat so fast that it backed up into my head and plugged my ears and I did not hear anything the children said. In Pemberton we ate at Chloe's Kitchen, all of us satisfied for a change, Eliza and Edward eating hamburgers, the rest of us donner kebabs. The next night in Denmark was a culinary disaster. No restaurant served anything Edward or Eliza would eat, so we ate a hamburger pizza at Kittles Deli.

Just beyond the booth in which we sat was a room containing video games. While we waited for pizza, a man entered carrying a bottle of Jack Daniels and a sack of coins. After drinking from the mouth of the bottle, he put the whiskey on the table and, scooping a handful of coins out of the sack, started playing the games. Neither the meats on the pizza nor the chili, onions, cheese, and tomatoes that accompanied it appealed to me, so I walked around the corner and at a grocery bought three pounds of mandarin oranges. I gave Vicki and the children an orange apiece. Then I ate the rest myself. The next night in Albany I repeated the dinner. Occasionally I managed to supplement meals, gulping down a squid salad in Busselton or sneaking into the Spot Coffee Shop in Denmark and bolting a cappuccino and a chocolate tart while the rest of the family mailed cards in the post office.

I slept better than I ate. I drove to Bunbury the first night. For a moment I was tempted to stay in the old hotel, the Rose. Bathrooms were at the end of the hall, though, not something to bother the lone traveler but the stuff of discontent for wives and children. Consequently we stayed in a motel facing the ocean. Early the next morning I walked two miles on the beach. Returning to the motel I met Edward and Eliza, their pockets bulging with shells. We spent the second night in Augusta, arriving at dusk. The Georgiana Motel did not have a room large enough for us, so the owner rented a house to us. Consisting of a living room, dining room, kitchen, washroom, bathroom, a long hall, two bedrooms, and a sunroom with beds along the walls, the house slept nine. On top of our bedspread Vicki found a gold ring. On it was engraved a jumble of mysterious signs and the words *CARPE DIEM*. "You will never escape the movie," Vicki said. The ring belonged to a man from Sydney. "It has sentimental value for him," the owner of the motel said, "and he will be pleased that it has been found." The next night we slept outside Pemberton at Forest Lodge. Only a small room was available. With the help of two trundle beds we fit inside. In an alcove outside the room stood a washing machine; before going to sleep, Vicki washed the children's clothes.

Wisteria hung over the porch of Forest Lodge, and the next morning birds hunted through the grounds. Outside our door splendid fairy wrens scratched in the dirt, the bodies of the males blue flames, yokes of black feathers around their necks and patches of silver gleaming behind their eyes like fish scales. A New Holland honeyeater scrabbled through parrot bush. Beside a pond tree martins plucked grass for nests. A western rosella sat on a bird feeder, the feathers on its head and breast red, a yellow patch on its check, and its wings tipped with blue. A small flock of red-eared firetails scratched about under a bird feeder, their breasts mottled black and white, their backs brown, but their bills, rumps, and the diamonds behind their eyes melting red.

On the trip I saw many birds I'd never seen before: nankeen kestrels hovering over pastures; in a clearing under tingles, gray fantails chasing insects, snapping and twisting through the air; a scarlet robin fluttering through understory in a karri forest; yellow-rumped thornbills on the ground under a lemon tree, the tops of their heads tattoos of speckles; and a black-shouldered kite perched on the tip of a bare limb, still as a flag becalmed atop a pole.

We spent the fourth night at a bed-and-breakfast farm, thirteen miles west of Denmark. In the tourist information booth in Walpole I found a flyer for "The Peppermints," and having seen no cars on the long road from Pemberton to Walpole, I decided to try The Peppermints, even though the farm had only a single tourist cottage. The farm was two kilometers up a dirt road, the Happy Valley Road. On the top of a hill the farmhouse faced south. Below the hilltop the land fell green through pasture and swamp. From the northwest, forests slipped down like shadows in the gathering dark. In the distance the Southern Ocean curved silver into William Bay. Mr. Parkes, owner of The Peppermints, was a retired engineer my age. He wanted to grow herbs and had found the farm only after a long search for land free from insecticides and fertilizer. "Herbs are astonishingly sensitive," he explained.

What began simply had fast grown complex. To keep the grass mowed he bought two hundred pregnant ewes and then sixteen Frisian steers. In a shed I saw a blue tractor and stalls of machines. In another shed were a stack of metal fence posts and coils of wire. I got up early the next morning and watched Mrs. Parkes feed three abandoned lambs. "We lost a lot of lambs the first year," she said, "because we didn't know what to do. We know more now, but," she added, "there is so much to learn." I walked down the drive lined by peppermint trees white with blossoms. I turned north along the Happy Valley Road then crossed into a pasture and walked along a fence. I carried a stick. "Tiger snakes are beginning to crawl about," Mrs. Parkes said; "one lives in rocks not far from the house, but most live around the swamp." Mrs. Parkes prepared breakfast for us, a good one of bacon, eggs, toast, and tomatoes.

I did not want to leave. The hero and heroine of Samuel Johnson's philosophic novel *Rasselas* lived in the Happy Valley. Although their wishes were always granted, they were unhappy and fled the valley. For years they wandered the world seeking contentment. Finally unable to discover lasting happiness they returned to the valley. Although teaching has enriched my life, I am tired of classrooms. Despite knowing that no job or place can provide lasting satisfaction, I, like the hero of *Rasselas,* forever dream of moving somewhere new and wondrously interesting.

Across the southwest farms were for sale. For $285,000, an advertisement in the *Great Southern Weekender* stated, one could buy 581 acres of "excellent grazing country with a full complement of buildings," including a four-bedroom homestead. Near Many Peaks in a "28 inch rainfall area" a 1,064-acre farm was for sale for $425,000. The land was "excellent sheep, prime lamb or cattle country," the advertisement stated, "also suitable for blue gum production." On the property were shearing sheds suitable for shearing six sheep at a time, sheep and cattle yards, a lean-to for machinery, two silos, and two houses. This second farm was too expensive for me. "But," I thought suddenly, "Geoff and I could buy it together." Geoff is Vicki's brother and a successful lawyer in New York, so successful that he could afford to give up law. He and I would never make a cent, but if we were careful our savings might last us to the grave. What a life the money would bring us, I mused. Geoff's wife, Barbara, designed clothes in New York, and she and Vicki could open a decorating shop in Denmark.

Away from gasoline fumes the children would grow hale and callused. I could throw away the asthma medicine we carried whenever we traveled. Instead of learning how to exploit the earth maybe the children would learn to conserve it. We might escape our digital existences and for a year or two wake up in a more humane time, one with a face and hands, one noisy not with the sound of money being shuffled but with the bawling of lambs, the thunk of postholes being dug, one electric with the tang of gum and the dust of hay being tossed.

Dreams are toys of the leisured and the affluent. Farmers are too weary to dream. The land would quickly break me and my pocketbook.

Moreover the very buying and selling from which I imagined escaping paid my salary and made my wanderings in Australia possible. In truth spending money was fun. Occasionally I thought the sounds I heard most often on the trip were not the songs of birds or the pulling hum of the car motor but the jangle of coin and crinkle of bill. We stopped at scores of shops along the road, buying bags of potato chips, brownies, Lamingtons, and great slabs of apricot cake. In Augusta, Vicki bought a jar of "Indian Wedding Chutney." In Walpole she bought a jar of "Sweet Cauliflower Pickles." At a church sale in Mt. Barker she bought "Tamarillo and Apple Jelly." The children bought T-shirts at Busselton and Cape Leeuwin. At craft shops in Nannup and Pemberton, Vicki bought Christmas presents for her family: boxes carved from grass trees, jarrah apples and pears, and salt and pepper shakers cut from the fruits of bull banksia. After settling the children into Gryphon's Restaurant, buying them each a doughnut and a milk shake, strawberry for Francis, vanilla for Edward, and chocolate for Eliza, I explored the Fine Woodcraft Gallery. Although our house in Storrs is more warehouse than home with both attic and basement bins for storing possessions, I wanted to buy pieces of jarrah to take home. I selected a baker's table, and if I have money enough left at the end of the year, I may buy it. "Where will you put it?" Vicki asked; "we don't have room. We will have to build a new house." "All right," I answered; "I'll sell the farm that Geoff and I were going to buy and build a new house."

Froth bubbling on top of waves and milk shakes attracted the children more than alluvial red seeping through jarrah. None of our walks, though, lacked fizz. With the children I climbed the stairs in the lighthouse at Cape Leeuwin and hunted rock crabs over the headland. I hiked to the end of the jetty at Busselton, the longest jetty in the southern hemisphere, the round-trip being two and a half miles. Not only did I go up and out, I went under, through Mammoth Cave in the Boranup Forest. I swam in Flinders Bay and at Green's Pool at William Bay. In the Land of the Giants I posed for and took a dozen photographs, standing in the burnt-out hearts of trees, the live outer bark rising in tepees above me. At Torndirrup National Park I got dizzy leaning over the Gap watching waves explode in fissures of spray. On the shore of Frenchman's Bay I ate a picnic lunch and afterward searched through the shallows at Vancouver Point for shells.

The lone traveler can explore new worlds. The family traveler carries old worlds with him. Except for brief chats in groceries and farmhouses, I did not talk to anyone other than Vicki and the children. Even if I had met someone "fascinating," my time belonged to family. Moreover, pushing us through the hours sapped strength, so much so that the thought of meeting a colorful character was unappealing. Such a person might have upset the flow of the trip, a disruption that promised only to make days more difficult.

Our hours were sound tracks of words, tapes the sounds of which differed little from what they would have been in Connecticut. I warned Francis and Edward not to tease Eliza. I told Eliza not to scream when she was teased. Each morning when we packed into the car, the children argued over whose turn it was to sit in the middle of the backseat. Concerned about asthma, I grilled Eliza and Edward on health. Vicki urged the children to put on sunscreen. Edward asked about money, worried that the trip would land us in the poorhouse. Francis counted the cars we met on lonely roads, announcing each number loudly. Eliza talked to "the babies." Vicki discussed food. I ordered Edward to eat more. Two score times a day I told Vicki that I thought the car was running poorly and was sure to break down. When we got within a hundred miles of Perth on the way home, Vicki told the children to be quiet. "Traffic makes Daddy nervous," she said; "if he doesn't concentrate, he will have a wreck and kill us all." We talked about animal droppings, those of both four- and two-legged creatures, never failing to comment when someone broke wind. Repeatedly we speculated about what friends were doing in Connecticut. Afterward we always said we were happy to be in Australia.

Much as our car was an enclosed but satisfactory world, so I enjoyed traveling through small towns. Simplicity, not complexity, attracts me, towns with a fleshly handful of streets, not a tooled grid of roads. The largest town in the southwest was Albany, with a population of just over fifteen thousand, not a big city but too big for my hankerings. I feel comfortable on main streets bordered by one- and two-story buildings. The dimensions of such buildings suit me. Instead of being plastered with signs proclaiming function and creating personality, skyscrapers exist almost as one-dimensional artifacts, the stuff not of real use but of abstract conversations about aesthetics and philosophy.

I like looking down streets and seeing buildings run out to field and hill. On such streets one imagines stories in which people change. On a street at the end of which a city stretches to the horizon, change does not come quickly to mind. Instead of moving from a beginning through a definite middle to an end, story stagnates, and although characters rush from corner to corner, they go nowhere.

One afternoon we ate lunch on a picnic table in Walpole. I drank soda and chewed hunks of bread and feta cheese, this last bought at a small store in Augusta and made from sheep's milk and seasoned with chives and garlic. Eleven seagulls strolled around the table. "Guests of the family," as Francis labeled them, they dined on french fries, bought across the highway at the Super Deli and served to them by Eliza and Edward. Vicki did not eat with us. She was across the road at Glassblower Gallery, buying two green glass candlesticks, each seven and a half inches tall.

While waiting for Vicki, I looked at the stores along the road. At the Shell station gas cost 76.5 cents a liter; the R & I bank was open only on Wednesdays from ten to three. If a person ran short of money some other time during the week, he could get two hundred dollars at the Four Square Grocery, provided he owned an R & I or a Commonwealth Bank card. Two other craft shops competed with the Gallery: Wildflowers and Walpole Crafts. For the artisan who needed new tools Walpole Hardware Supplies was open. Beside the Shell station stood three pay telephones, the booths bright orange, topped by bubbly, translucent plastic roofs. Walpole might be a place to buy a farm, I thought, for three real estate agents had offices on the highway: Harmon Ricketts, Burton Realty, and Denmark Real Estate. Geoff and I could probably get a good price, I decided, for business appeared slow. The windows of the metal building that housed Denmark Real Estate had been smashed, and a padlock hung on the front door.

Driving from Manjinup to Walpole tired me. Rangers burned bush, and smoke billowed over the road in choking white clouds. In places the asphalt was rough, and I passed a man changing a tire on his four-wheel drive, a car with big, thick tires. From side roads logging trucks entered the highway throbbing like trains. "It's getting late," Vicki said when she returned from the Gallery, "we'll have to hustle if we want to find a place to stay before dark." Dozy and comfortable, I was not eager to drive, and I longed to stay somewhere for a day or two, to stretch and absorb the tang of place, to sniff the petals of a Wildflowers and racket about in a Four Square Grocery.

Three days later I found a place in the Porongurup Mountains. Forty kilometers north of Albany and the ocean, the Porongurups rose in the middle of a plain, chins and elbows of granite, knees of stone, lumpy with cicatrices and worn rough, yet also soothed by weathering, the torn seams cooled and settled into smoothness and not inflamed by slide or toppled boulder. A karri forest surrounded the mountains. Thriving on wet loamy soil, the forest wrinkled up slopes like a sheet tossed in haste over a table set with dish and candelabra. The Porongurups looked old. Karri stood ponderous, their trunks resembling muscles aged into immobility, brown pushing up hazy through the blue bark like deep bruises, pouches of fungus and canker black and meaty against the flesh, ugly growths but not things that a man decades beyond dream and vanity would consider having removed.

The day before leaving Perth, I picked up a travel brochure published by the Western Australian Tourist Centre. The brochure listed four places to stay near the Porongurups. Close to the center of the range was a farm, the Bolganup Homestead. "We'll stay there," I said to Vicki; "it will be as good as The Peppermints." The Homestead was at the end of a dirt drive off the Mt. Barker Road. White arrows directed travelers to the house. Alas, suspended beneath an arrow was a sign saying "No Vacancy." Across the drive from the sign was the Porongurup Shop and Tea Room. Earlier during the trip I would have shrugged and driven on. After six days, however, I was tired enough to be persistent. I went into the tea room and asked where I could find the owner of the Homestead. Mrs. Bird lived a hundred yards up the highway. I walked to her house. When she came to the door, I asked her if no vacancy really meant "no vacancy." "To tell the truth," she said, "I might have a vacancy." A family who had booked a cottage had not arrived. "They were supposed to be here three days ago," she said; "let me call Perth to see if they are coming. If they are not, you can have the place."

At the farm were three cottages: Fernbrook, Burnley, and Hollyhock. We stayed in Burnley, part of the old farmhouse. Pale yellow plaster covered the outside of the house. Slats of dark brown wood ran through the plaster, dividing the outside walls into rectangles. The roof was tin. By the back door stood a lemon tree. Periwinkle bloomed by the stoop. Jasmine climbed a trellis, and a purple lilac blossomed next to a window. Our cottage was shaped like an L with the lower leg pointing to the left rather than to the right. The floors were jarrah, the dark boards as wide as the distance from elbow to wrist.

The back door opened into a big sitting room. Three large windows on the right faced the mountains. To the left was a bedroom with twin beds; the boys chose it while Eliza put her gang on the upper bunk of a double-decker bed in the sitting room, declaring that since she had never slept on an upper bunk the bed belonged to her and the babies. Scattered about the room were nine chairs, most with bottoms sagging like clotheslines. By the windows sat a round table, covered with red oilcloth. A square metal stove stood at the far end of the room near a doorway leading into the rest of the cottage. Before the stove stood a metal fire screen. Hammered into the surface of the screen was a sentimental scene depicting life on an English farm. A setter led three puppies through a creek. She seemed happy and almost smiling. Behind the dogs towered an oak. Thick with leaves the oak appeared all-wise, resembling a kindly patriarch or a benevolent rural deity. Beside the stove slumped a basket, bulging with firewood. Next to the basket was a cardboard box filled with newspapers.

A wall sliced through the farmhouse, dividing it into two cottages and in the process splitting rooms in half. What once was part of a parlor became an odd nonfunctional nook, a sugar chest in one corner, dried flowers in a vase on a table, and by a door an Edwardian hat rack. Hanging on the rack were two bowl-shaped caps smacking of flappers and the 1920s, one hat brown and the other white, but both moth-eaten and made in England. Beyond the sitting room was a hall. To the side was the bathroom. Beyond the hall lay the kitchen, then Vicki's and my bedroom. Beyond the bedroom was a front porch, a wrought-iron table and two iron chairs on it.

The porch faced a broad green pasture. To the left grazed a brown horse, and far from gulls and fried potatoes, the children fed it carrots. To the right a creek curved down from the mountains and seeming as old and as lethargic as the Porongurups themselves wound slowly through the grass. Sheep inched through the field, sometimes grazing, other times standing motionless. At night they gathered close to the farmhouse, in the moonlight glowing pale and ghostly. A dead tree stood in a depression. Orange lichens grew from the tips of the limbs back to the trunk of the tree, turning the branches into matches, flaring with color in the sunlight. Before breakfast I sat on the porch and drinking tea watched a kookaburra hunt lizards from the shelter of a mulberry tree.

The homestead had been settled in 1860, the same decade as our house in Nova Scotia was built. Under the Porongurups I felt comfortable, almost as if I were in Beaver River above the Gulf of Maine. After traveling halfway around the world I had arrived somewhere familiar. Decorating the plates in the kitchen at Bolganup was the willow pattern, the same pattern that appeared on dishes in our kitchen in Nova Scotia. In the morning in Nova Scotia I made a fire in the kitchen stove. At Bolganup I made a fire at night. After using all the wood in the basket by the stove, I fetched wood, not from the barn as I did in Nova Scotia, but from a pile stacked inside a cistern turned on its side.

In Bolganup I wandered the cottage exploring closets and crannies as I did in Nova Scotia. On top of a worn linen doily lay a guest book. I read the comments. "The Golden Dream" and "Arcadia," people wrote. "Just what the doctor ordered for a tired teacher," a man wrote in a red ink. "Magic!" a woman exclaimed; "I never realized this is where my sanity was hiding. Back to the kids, hubby, and work. I don't want to go." "Real cool trampoline," an adolescent wrote.

For the children Bolganup was the high point of the trip, not because of anything Vicki and I did but because of trampoline and pool table. The trampoline was suspended across a pit dug at the edge of a pasture. While I drank tea and looked at birds, Eliza jumped. For their part Edward and Francis busied themselves inside a building that had been a clubhouse. Along the north wall stood a stone chimney. In a corner a bar collapsed rotten with wet and decay. From rafters bundles of dried flowers hung down, their heads resembling dust rags. In the middle of the room was a pool table. In places the green surface was bald, and the netting under one of the pockets was missing. The table was good enough for the boys, though. "Daddy," Edward said; "this is really fun. We ought to buy a pool table in Connecticut." "Where would we put it?" I said; "we don't have room. We'd have to build a new house just for the table."

The Faulkner family had owned the farm since the turn of the twentieth century. On walls were reproductions of family photographs: a picture of a cowshed taken during the 1930s, another of a swimming hole at Karribank in the 1920s, and then from 1902 a picture that looked original, a portrait of the five Faulkner girls. All the girls had sharp eyes and long noses, each with a lump near the end resembling a bubble. Unless anger honed the eyes into needles, the bubbles, I imagined, could have been cute, floating lightly upward and sparkling with laughter. On our bedside table was a mound of moldy books, the bindings loose and the covers stained. For "Attendance and Good Conduct" at the Albany Wesleyan Sunday School *Wrongs Righted* by Annie S. Swan was presented to Nellie Faulkner on January 24, 1898. Swan was the pen name of Mrs. Burnett Smith, author of *Gates of Eden* and *Briar and Palm* among other books. Which of the girls was Nellie? I wondered as I held the book. Did some nice boy see her home when Sunday school ended?

The Albany Mechanics' Institute once owned *A Dream of the World's Tragedy*, volume 2,399 in the Institute Library. Fourteen days were "allowed" for reading the book, and the library was open on Mondays and Wednesdays from 7:00 to 8:30 P.M. and on Saturday from 4:00 to 5:00 P.M. "The fine for keeping this work beyond the allowed time," the librarian warned, was "three pence per week or any portion of a week. Fines may be enforced in the local court." In pages following the conclusion of *A Dream* Methuen and Company announced its list for April 1894. The first book advertised was *Cricket Songs* by Norman Gale. "Mr. Gale's rural poems," Methuen declared, "have made him wildly popular, and this volume of spirited verse will win him a new reputation among lovers of our national game."

The homestead was an operating farm, and in a raised concrete shed with corrugated tin for the roof and sides, an eight-man crew was shearing a flock of two thousand merino sheep. After unloading the car, we walked into the shed and watched. Four men sheared. Another swept and gathered loose bits of wool. Two tossed fleeces on a table and cut away frayed edges while another used a hydraulic press to pack the fleeces into bales. Clamped to a strut above each shearer was a motor. From it dangled a mechanical arm hinged with two elbows and a flexible spring. Beside the motor a metal T-bar hung upside down. Attached to the ends of the bar and resembling a child's swing, sagging down like the underside of a yoke attached to oxen, was a broad rubber band. When the shearer leaned through the band, it supported him, resting his back.

A fine shearer could shear one hundred and eighty to two hundred sheep a day, the boss told me, taking three minutes to shear an animal and receiving $1.47 a head. Behind each shearer was a pen of sheep. Outside in a corral sheep milled about. After pulling an animal from the pen, the shearer sat the sheep on its bottom and began to cut, starting with the wool on the belly, which he removed and tossed aside. Another man picked up the wool and threw it into a stall-like bin filled with similar wool. Shearing a sheep resembled peeling an orange. The shearer did not seem to cut the wool so much as turn the clippers through the fleece, sliding them down the legs then rolling them over the back and head.

After the fleece was off the animal, a man threw it on an iron rack resembling the frame of a big, tall bed. The man lifted and tossed the fleece almost as if he were casting a fishnet, floating it above the rack on the wind so it would spread wide and settle loosely. Immediately another man trimmed and graded the fleece, the loose wool being pitched into a bin. Then the fleece itself was thrown into another bin. Afterward the packer grabbed it and using the hydraulic press forced the wool into a tight bale. A full bale weighed almost four hundred pounds. Once the bale was wrapped, the packer marked it, spraying paint over cutout numbers and letters. Lastly he rolled the bale out of the way, near a landing against which a truck could back.

The shed was noisy, the humming of the clippers seeming to wash back and forth along the tin sides of the building, creating an undertow of sound. The workday was long, the men laboring in two-hour shifts. The work itself was exhausting, and the crew was always moving: sweeping, cutting, throwing, and baling. The work took skill, coordination, and youth. The crew moved gracefully, as if they were dancing. In the shed ballet suddenly seemed an imitation of work, an abstraction distilled from the reality of thick lanolin, the shuffle of foot and hoof, and the patter of hot oil dripping from a press. On a stage in the imagination a fleece could swim golden through the air. In the shed cakes of dirt clung to the wool. Still, when the fleeces were thrown, they flew, not lightly and deceptively like ballerinas transporting observers to fairyland, but heavily, making one see muscle and ache, the sweat necessary to accomplishing a task well.

Because we did not want to intrude and because we had not eaten lunch, we stayed in the shed for only ten minutes. Not far from the farm was the Tree-in-the-Rock picnic ground, named for a tree growing through a boulder. After eating in the picnic ground, we hiked into the mountains, walking for three hours, past Hayward Peak, scrambling over Nancy Peak, then returning through Morgan's View. Footing was soft, and the woods were damp and cool. Only when we crawled over a bald hunk of granite at the top of a mountain was I nervous. Like a raised shoulder joint linking collarbone and upper arm, the granite rolled roundly forward but tumbled away sharply on each side. I made the children shuffle across the shoulder on their hands and knees.

At the end of the hike we felt good, and on the way back to the farm I stopped at Jingalla winery and bought a shiraz. "A rich spicy elegant cool climate full-bodied dry red," the label said, "balanced with superb French oak and a soft tannin finish." Because the owner wanted to treat his employees to a meal in Albany, the tea room was not open for dinner. Before closing the shop, the owner prepared a meal for us, baking and buttering garlic bread and tossing a salad of lettuce and fresh vegetables from his garden. For the children he prepared spaghetti to heat in the oven. For Vicki and me he made meat pies rich with beef and mushrooms. That night after the long walk and the shearing, and amid mushrooms and garlic, the wine almost lived up to its label.

The next morning we ate breakfast at the tea room: eggs, bacon, toast, tomatoes, and mushrooms, topped off by a Devonshire tea, scones submerged beneath whipped cream and apricot jam. After breakfast we looked at the owner's garden behind the restaurant. A black dog lay under a bush, his jaw grizzled and his right front paw twisted. Staying in the hostel just opened by the owner of the restaurant was a herpetologist from Flinders University. He studied ticks on bobtails. "You haven't seen a snake," he said incredulously; "I see tiger snakes every day." He wanted to visit the United States, and I gave him the name of George Middendorf. George wrote a dissertation describing lizards in Arizona. George majored in English at Dartmouth. One semester he asked to take a reading course with me. "What on?" I asked. "Children's books," he said. "I don't know anything about children's books," I said. "Don't worry," he said; "I'll draw up the reading list, and you will know a lot by the end of the year." George's list was serpentine, coiling through centuries, and the books themselves were ophidian, front-fanged and injecting me with an interest that got into both blood and brain and became incurable.

I did not look forward to packing the car. I had traveled enough. Each morning when I set out, I did not know where I would sleep. To spend our last night away from Perth at the farm would be too easy, I thought. Not only would staying another night be indulgent, but it would be a sign that I had broken down. Instead of thrusting forward into the new, I would doze before the fire in a swaybacked chair, rocking through dreams as soft as muffins. "Death," I said to myself, "remaining here would be a kind of death." "Daddy," Eliza said, interrupting my reverie, "can we stay here another night? I want to jump on the trampoline, and the brothers want to play pool." "I don't know, Eliza," I said; "I was thinking about heading north and trying to see Wave Rock at Hyden." "Please, Daddy, let's stay here," Eliza said. "All right," I said; "we'll stay here and explore the area." At eleven o'clock Vicki stuffed the cooler into the car, and we drove to the Stirling Mountains, forty kilometers to the north.

Resembling a stage, a flat plain stretched between the Porongurups and the Stirlings. Across the plain the Stirlings rose dramatically, blue and angular, shadows dropping down from them through the pale spring light like curtains. If mountains can be thought theaters and travelers troupes of wandering actors, then the Porongurups appeared home to comedy, the karri forests screens behind which the middle-aged bumbled through misunderstandings. Having reached that span of life in which everyone's point of view seems partially true and certainly no opinion worth fighting over, the actors posed and postured. Through the fourth act they heaved extravagant words about. In the last act, however, differences dissolved. Afterward the actors pulled out long loaves of bread and rounds of yellow cheese, and tapping flasks of wine sat alone in the theater. Legs dangling over the edge of the stage, candles flickering behind them, wax dripping on the floor, they raised the curtain of recollection and let anecdote bowl dark time and his scythe from consciousness.

The Stirlings were dryer than the Porongurups. Instead of damp forests, blankets of heath covered them. While the highest point in the Porongurups was 670 meters, fourteen peaks in the Stirlings were over 900 meters tall, with Bluff Knoll the highest at 1,073 meters. The height of the mountains and the sun's beating hot upon the traveler's brow did not lend themselves to whimsy. The mountains were stages for physical exertion. On a hike through them perspiration not wit flowed freely. The Stirlings were for the young and earnest, ideologues and actors whose visions of the world were narrow, dramatists who did not shrug at betrayal and who lashed failure, people who, once the play ended, counted receipts, packed, and strode off to the next challenge.

The Stirling Range Drive crossed the mountain range. The drive was scenic, but the road unpaved. "I have come this far without a flat tire," I said; "and I am not about to get one the day before we return to Perth. We are not driving through the Stirlings. We are climbing Bluff Knoll." We ate lunch in the parking lot below Bluff Knoll. I wasn't hungry, and I fed most of my lunch to gray currawongs. The hike lasted three and a half hours. Because we started comparatively late in the day, we met people coming down. On meeting me, older climbers smiled and shrugged. Then they looked puzzled, and their sight turned inward as if they were thinking about something. Ultimately their expressions hardened into pique and exasperation, the series of expressions seeming to say, "I climbed the mountain, and for some reason I am proud of doing so. But the climb was one of those accomplishments that means nothing and was an absurd, damn-fool thing to have done."

Skinks darted across the trail. I caught several. So that I would not hurt them, I held them loosely. A big one twisted out of my hands, and as I tightened my grip, he snapped his tail off, fell to the ground, and disappeared through a crack in a rock. The tail thrashed for a long time. "At least fifteen minutes," Edward said, putting the tail into his pocket; "I'm going to take this home as a souvenir." Beside the path black gin grew. Many had been toppled, and the inner wood splintered. Red and tipped with black, the wood appeared shellacked and peeled away in curves, the splinters bowing out almost as if they had been poured hot over convex molds then stripped off once they cooled. "Is the snake still by that big rock?" a woman asked me as I hiked around a bend in the trail. "If it is still there," she said, pointing back down the trail, "I'm not going down." Bluff Knoll was home to dugites and tiger snakes. I had not seen any, however. "The snake is gone," I said; "dens vanish when I appear."

Francis, Eliza, and I completed the climb, Eliza in an inexpensive pair of green canvas slippers with flat soles. Edward climbed three-fifths of the way to the summit. Then the trail bulged to the right around the mountain, the shoulder of the path dropping off sharply. For a few steps Edward crept along the inside of the trail hugging rocks, but the mountain bowed out and the closer he pushed his chest to stone, the more his feet slid toward the drop. He fell to his hands and knees and tried to continue the climb, but his heart was not in the attempt and soon neither his arms nor his legs moved. Fear made him cry. I raised him off the ground and holding his hands led him back to a sheltered turn in the trail and told him to wait for Vicki. Vicki is a slow but determined hiker, and although behind us on the trail, she would have reached the top of the mountain. When she came upon Edward, though, she stopped and, not willing to let him wait alone, sat beside him until Francis, Eliza, and I returned from the summit.

That night we ate chicken kiev in the tea room. Vicki opened the wine bought at Donnelly River. After breakfast the next morning we left for Perth. We arrived home at five-thirty that afternoon. "That does the traveling for me," I said to Vicki; "from now on I'm not leaving Perth." Words are creatures of moments, hatched in mood, fluttering swiftly into sound then dying without echoes, much less effects. Two weeks have passed since our return. Combs of orange blossoms have appeared on the silky oak behind the garage. Indian lilacs have lost their fragrance, and pink and white sprays of bauhinia have turned brown and soft. Fat, lumpy fruits resembling moles have rained down from the climbing fig in the Great Court at the university. Every day this week rainbow lorikeets have foraged through the marri at the edge of the yard. After lunch yesterday we swam in the Indian Ocean. Last night we went to Parry Field and watched a baseball game.

Days are full. Still, travel appeals to me. On my desk is a fax outlining a tour of New Zealand. The tour will last a week, and I will speak in Auckland and Wellington, and maybe Christchurch. Under the fax is a letter from Alice Springs, describing a camel "safari." Spread open on the dining room table is my *South West Map and Guide*. I am thinking about taking a trip in January during the next school vacation. This time we will head east before going south, driving to York then down to Pingelly, Narrogin, and Wagin. From Wagin we will drive due east, all the way to Lake King. Then we will turn north and go to Hyden and see Wave Rock.

Incidentals

"Incidentally," Nigel said, "have you heard about the queer wine maker in the Swan Valley who'd get a couple of fellows stumbling drunk then knock them off?" I had not heard the story. But after I changed a few incidentals, the story was right for Carthage, Tennessee, if not for Main Street at least for Long Dog Cove, under the tail of which Dapper Tuttlebee kept a moonshine still. When his father, Tyrell, got struck by lightning while putting a new roof on his barn, Dapper inherited the still. Dapper took more pride in leading the choir at the Baptist Church on Spring Street than he did in brewing. Nevertheless he kept the still percolating, more, though, for social than for business reasons. Whenever a choir from Crossville or Lebanon visited Carthage for a revival, Dapper invited two of the tenors to the cove for drinks. For such occasions he ran off some high octane, one certain to knock his guests off the scales and lead to, as Turlow Gutheridge put it, "some friendly tail-wagging." The next morning Dapper's guests rarely remembered the evening's festivities. "What did you think about that fellow's whiskey?" a Pentecostal from Zarephath said to his companion after they awoke from a night of carousing. "Well," the friend said, "the whiskey was grand, but don't your ass hurt after you drink it? Jesus H. Christ, my ass is sore this morning."

Incidentals furnish essays and houses, and I collect them, reckoning that some day I will arrange them on a mantelpiece or scribble them over a page. Scraps of paper clutter my desk. Three mornings a week I swim. The Department of Human Movement and Recreation Studies manages the pool or, as the department's "Public Timetable" dubs it, the "Aquatics Laboratory." "I want to illustrate books," Eliza told me one morning. I wrote a selection of the books that she wanted to illustrate on the "Bus Timetable," the E/F1 timetable, listing the stops

61

and sketching the routes of buses 200, 201, 202, 208, 209, and 556. "My best bet is a fairy tale book," Eliza said, "not some story with a title like *Sally Won't Clean Up Her Room.*" Scratched on the back of the business card of Rod Evans, "Sales Consultant" at Brooking Mazda, is "Try not to beat up the avocados," an order shouted from the living room when Vicki heard me rummaging in the kitchen.

On a white sheet of paper torn from a school tablet is a description of ways in which plants in Western Australia have evolved in order to lessen the loss of water during hot, dry summers. Not only is the canopy sparse but leaves on some plants hang vertically to reduce their exposure to sunlight. To reflect light, leaves are often gray or silver. While some leaves have a waxy surface, other leaves are minute, so small they are difficult to see. Threadlike hairs cover the surfaces of other leaves, and the openings through which plants breath are sometimes on the shaded underside of leaves or surrounded by thick cuticles. Essayists gather incidentals in hopes that convergences will occur, not simply on desks but in the mind. In contrast, say, to politicians, essayists delight in the unexpected, thinking it mirrors the unpredictable doings of life itself. Because politicians try to anticipate the unexpected, indeed labor to control it, much that they do or say seems dull and contrived.

Incidentals are the fiber of life, not just story. My weeks are fabrics of small threads: getting a haircut, buying stamps, and talking to Brian the newsagent. This morning at eight-thirty I drove the Toyota to Brooking Mazda in order to purchase a new windscreen. While the screen was being put on, Rod and I chatted, first about the new Mazda 121, then about his house, finally about my writing. Because I am far from the crocheted routine of life in Connecticut, my hours hang loosely. Instead of being knotted to schedule, days slip and fray. As a result what I do often seems incidental, even the money I spend. Instead of purchasing things that last or give the illusion of permanence, I pay rent for a house I will not see again after August. The car will be sold before I leave Perth. Appointments of kitchen and desk will be left in drawers or thrown into the garbage. Because the places I visit in Western Australia will be foreign to friends in Connecticut, the trips will not be matter for conversation. Unframed by familiar words they will slip quickly through memory.

In great part the activities of the children stitch my days together. I am an older father. "The children will keep you young," acquaintances say. When weary I speculate about the best age to be a parent. Instead of young the children have kept me occupied, particularly in Australia. Mansfield, Connecticut, is home territory, a place the children can wander without a guide. Australia is bush, and despite having met many other children, they are not settled enough to telephone acquaintances and invite them to the house. "This isn't home, Daddy," Edward said; "my things are not here. There is not much for us to play with in this house." "Yes," Francis added, "we don't have a computer." In Connecticut the names of other children mark calendars, scribbled beside ballet, science club, baseball, and soccer. In Perth I write myself across weekends. In Connecticut weeks pass seamlessly from Monday to Monday. On Saturday and Sunday in Australia I snag the loose strands of weekdays and tie them off into event. Instead of occurring randomly, events are planned, designed to jerk the family out of the house.

One Saturday I drove to Underwater World, an aquarium where visitors, an advertisement declared, "can experience Western Australia's unique and spectacular marine life." A moving walkway carried us around the bottom of the aquarium. Thick glass curved overhead forming a tunnel. While moray eels rose out of holes and waved in the current to the left, stingrays and sea turtles glided above, and schools of fish flowed and pitched to the right. After my third trip through the tunnel, I drifted far from the Indian Ocean. Despite the current of Australian experiences I washed ashore on the red banks of the Cumberland River just below Carthage. Turlow Gutheridge had just returned from a vacation in Florida. Not many Carthaginians ever left Tennessee, and several people asked Turlow about his trip. One day during lunch at Ankerrow's Café, Turlow recounted, a storm swept jellyfish on to the beach south of Jacksonville. Mulling over a story he heard about Dapper Tuttlebee, Loppie Groat wasn't paying close attention to Turlow's account. Loppie had a sweet tooth, though, and when he heard the word *jellyfish*, he addressed Turlow. "Jelly fish," he exclaimed, "what kind were they: strawberry, peach, or fox grape?" "Do they fetch up in jars?" he continued before Turlow could reply; "can you spread them right away or do you have to scrape off sand and fish scales first?"

The next day I drove the family to Fremantle, and we visited Crocodile Park. Crocodiles are not fussy eaters. Just so long as the dish is meaty they will gulp it down, being considerably less fastidious, I thought, than Buster, Hink Ruunt's yellow hound. Hink always had an eye cocked for a bargain. When he heard Abner Turentine say he was going to throw away an ancient ham, Hink bought the ham for thirty-six cents, "just to spare Abner the trouble of disposing of it," he said. Tasting proved the ham inedible. Although Abner warned Hink that the ham was moldy and that the meat was certain to be crawling with skippers, Hink acted irritated when he next saw Abner. "That ham was so rotten," he said, "that I couldn't eat none of it, and neither could Buster. I tossed him a slice, but he spit it out almost before he bit into it. That meat was so nasty," Hink continued, "that Buster had to lick his bottom twice just to get the bad taste out of his mouth."

The following weekend my observations, if not thoughts, were in better taste. Saturday morning Vicki, the children, and I went to a kite festival on the Nedlands foreshore. The children watched kites and ate Wedges, hunks of vanilla ice cream impaled on sticks and covered with frozen chocolate. Overhead small kites spun like gnats, struts bending as the kites dipped in the breeze, their plastic bodies rippling and humming, color splashing behind them. Above the gnats smaller kites swirled like confetti. A man sat in a low brown cart mounted on tricycle wheels. With his left hand he turned a steering wheel. In his right he held a rope leading up to a big green kite shaped like a pastry cutter. The kite pulled the cart across the field in swift rushes, the man trying to wend a collisionless course between dogs and children, shouting and punching a throaty horn clamped to the steering wheel. Resembling jet planes performing in an air show, three triangular kites swept overhead. The three kites were linked; behind the last kite two long tails snapped and flared like vapor trails. Above the shoreline crawled a centipede, his twenty-four legs rising and falling in humps almost as if he were clambering over sandy dunes. An orange squid squirted upward. A large red octopus with yellow eyes shook its arms, seeming to grab at smaller kites that darted past in bright shoals. Nine black-and-white boxes composed a box kite. Against the sky the kite lost dimension and resembled a checkerboard.

I sat on the ground. Over my head a silver line swayed up to a kite. I tried to follow the line from hand to strut. A green and yellow platypus bustled by and so distracted me that I lost sight of the line. Even if the platypus had not left his burrow, I could not have traced the line to the kite. Never have I had elevated vision or a sublime thought. My attention runs to the ground and low incidentals, not low enough, alas, on this particular morning. Watching kites spiral overhead, I did not look where I trod. Buster and a pack of his canine compatriots had long wandered the foreshore. When I sat on the ground, not only did I sit on grass but also on a mound of droppings. Old, the droppings resembled Abner's ham. Unfortunately they had not lost all savor. After going home and changing trousers, I drove the family to Scitech in Perth, an exhibition of "science and technology" at which visitors could participate in "learning experiments."

The exhibition was held on the third floor of a square building. For three hours I enjoyed myself, walking through a large foam-rubber lung stained black to show the effects of smoking cigarettes, jumping back and forth in front of concave and convex mirrors, and strolling over wooden floorboards and seeing "special effects" turn the boards into a rickety bridge suspended above a canyon through which a red ribbon of lava flowed. I put my hands on a round silver ball charged with electricity, and my hair stood on end. I sat in a booth and switched lights on and off, turning my face different colors, "ghastly" and "ghostly" as the directions stated. After three hours I sagged. Windows in the building were closed, and the air was electric with experiment and fume. Sounds buzzed and rang, thudded, jangled, and sloshed. Although I wanted to reel in the children and go home, I stayed two more hours. The children raced about like kites, and we left only when the exhibit closed. "Daddy," Francis said, seeing me sitting on a bench, "are you tired?" "No," I answered paraphrasing a remark Hink made about Buster. "I'm a pretty young dog considering my age." "What?" Francis said. "Never mind," I answered; "go have fun."

I spent the next Sunday outdoors, watching the Perth Heat win a baseball game. We sat in the bleachers above first base. We ate chicken and french fried potatoes. All of us drank sodas, except for Francis, who had chocolate milk. Five young men sat in front of us. One, the driver I assume, drank Coca-Cola; the others drank beer, twenty-six cans, Edward announced after they left. Despite the tub of beer, the men remained quiet. Only during the eighth inning did they stir. By then the Heat had won the game. The stirrings were slow, however; the men tore their programs into sheets and made paper airplanes that they launched over the back of the bleachers. The field itself was a mixture of artificial turf and grass. On top of the outfield fence were signs advertising Kentucky Fried Chicken; Choc Chills, the kind of milk Francis drank; Midwaste Disposal and Recycling Company; Nissan; Hungry Jacks, a chain of fast-food restaurants specializing in hamburgers; the *West Australian,* the local daily paper; Houghton Wines; and Emu beer, "matured," the sign stated, "at less than zero degrees Celsius to keep its fresh draft brewed taste." Before the game began the Heat Wave ran on the field and jumped about to the tunes of old rock songs: "Tutti Frutti" and "Whole Lot of Shakin' Going On." The Wave consisted of twelve girls wearing white baseball caps with red bills, dark high-top athletic shoes, and shorts and halters. The midriff of the shorts was red, and the legs black. At the bottom of each leg, just above the knee, yellow flames flickered discretely.

I have never seen a Major League baseball game and have no desire to attend one. I like the small-town atmosphere of the minor leagues. Although not a farm team, the Heat was associated with the Baltimore Orioles. All the teams in the "Pepsi Australian Baseball League" were aligned, the program explained, with Major League teams. Four "imports" could play on each Australian team, imports being players whose salaries were paid by Major League teams in the United States and who had not played above "Single A" in the minor leagues. For a player who played previously in Australia, this last rule was waived. Indeed the offensive star of the Heat was Greg Jelks, a minor leaguer from Centre, Alabama, who came out of retirement to play for the Heat.

Kentucky Fried Chicken replaced balls fouled into the stands. Whenever a batter knocked a ball into the crowd, the announcer said, "That's another gift from KFC." When a ball was fouled over the back of the bleachers, the announcer put on records, one the sound of a rocket taking off, another of a window being smashed, and a third of a baby shrieking then crying. In the ninth inning ushers walked through the stands, handing out cards with the players' pictures on them. We had fun. Even Francis said he enjoyed the game, the first athletic event he has ever liked watching. During the game Eliza noticed a ball under the bleachers. Although a chicken-wire fence surrounded the stands and squeezing under the fence to retrieve the ball seemed impossible, the children set off at the end of the fifth inning on a "ball hunt." Up the right-field line behind the stands, Francis discovered a hole beneath the wire. After Francis and Edward enlarged the hole, Eliza crawled under the fence and retrieved the ball. Unfortunately, it was rubber.

Blue plastic post horns were sold as souvenirs. "Australians ought to sell didgeridoos," Vicki said; "the horns are too loud and American." Removing Edward from the United States did not remove the United States from Edward, and he asked me to buy a horn. I refused. Edward sang in the fourth- and fifth-grade choir at Nedlands Primary School, and I suppose music was on his mind. Once every two weeks school began with an assembly. The Friday after the game Edward's choir was scheduled to sing. That morning Vicki and I walked Eliza and Edward to school. Instead of gray shorts and a blue short-sleeve shirt, Edward wore long blue trousers, a white dress shirt, and a black necktie. The children assembled in a long narrow room with a blue carpet on the floor. While the choir stood in six rows on the stage, the rest of the school sat crowded on the floor in front of them, knees pulled close to chests, toes pressed against the bottoms of children in front.

Parents stood pasted to each other in the back of the room. Along the left wall ran a series of windows facing a courtyard paved with asphalt. Brass coat hooks jutted out from under the windows; to the left of each hook a child's name was printed in black letters on white tape. Above the stage two white crepe-paper pelicans flew toward each other through a cloudless blue sky. The right wall of the room opened into classrooms. The upper half of each door was made from glass panes, and mullions between the panes were painted different colors, on one door yellow, on the next light blue, on the next white, and on the rest dark blue. Behind the parents a green door opened into another classroom. Near the back of the room a rainbow curved down a wall. The ceiling was white, and fans turned slowly.

The assembly began with the Australian national anthem, *Advance Australia Fair*, the first time I heard the song. Mr. A., as he was known to students and parents, then led the choir through a medley of gospel songs. Mr. A. was a good music teacher and a lively school character. When Eliza's grade went to music class, he often greeted her with a song, "I know a girl that you don't know: Eliza Pickering." During the program Mr. A. complimented soloists and musicians profusely, introducing them as "the lovely," "the beautiful," and "the gracious." Before a girl played a tune by Debussy on the piano, one lasting, he said, three minutes and twelve seconds, he urged children to pay attention. "Listen carefully," he said; "you can play like this if you practice everyday. I want you ones, twos, and threes to behave and observe what is going on," he continued, "because it won't be long until you are up here, and we'll expect the same kind of discipline."

During the assembly those upper and junior classes that had kept their rooms neatest during the past fortnight received stickers, one winning class chosen from grades 5–7, the other from grades 1–4. Various teachers made announcements. After Mr. A. recognized teachers, the students said in unison, "Good morning, Miss. Weir," or "Good morning, Mr. Sampson." "Good morning, boys and girls," the teachers answered. Midway through the program two seventh-grade girls read "the injury report," one girl reading the account of the first week, the other girl that of the second week. During the first week five injuries were reported on Monday, none on Tuesday, Wednesday, and Thursday, and three on Friday. A teacher then stood and said she was concerned that the boys and girls were trying so hard not to spoil "The Injury Free Campaign" that they did not report their injuries and receive treatment. "Last week I saw a first-grade girl with an injury on the playground," one of the seventh-graders testified, "and when I asked her why she did not go to the office and report her injury, she said that she did not want to spoil the Injury Free Campaign." "Boys and girls," the teacher said, "I am pleased that you are trying to keep the school injury free, but if you have an injury, don't worry about the campaign. Please report the injury."

During the assembly the choir sang "Imagine" and "Drummer Boy." The sun was shining when Vicki and I left. Red and white roses bloomed in great cups by the front door. The assembly made us feel good, little things somehow mattering a great deal: the injury report and Mr. A's praising the children. As I age I find it difficult to distinguish the important from the unimportant. Matters I thought significant in youth, position and accomplishment, for example, now seem insignificant. Moreover with age comes the capacity to see other people's points of view, a condition that lessens fervor, not only undermining commitment to ideas but also reducing the stature of ideas themselves, perhaps making them those better things, incidentals, turning a clever theory into a brass hook, a new concept into a rainbow curving down a wall.

Of course being incidental does not necessarily decrease the capacity to annoy. In fact the things that irritate me most are usually small matters. Attached to the inner doors of men's bathrooms in Australian airports were signs reading, "Business or Pleasure. Pack Condoms." The meaning was clear. To avoid disease people should carry rubbers everywhere, not simply to board meetings and croquet matches, but to funerals, bar mitzvahs, and christenings. Although governments ought to be concerned about AIDS, the sign reduced all human pleasure and business to the copulatory. Whenever I noticed the sign, I muttered an obscenity, usually a short sentence with the F-word in the middle and in the past tense, to the left the two words "I'll be," to the right the three words "if I will."

Just as annoying was the sign that Qantas placed on the bulwark separating business from tourist class: "Business Class Only Beyond This Point Except in Emergency." On the other side of the bulwark no sign stated, "Tourist Class Only Beyond This Point Except in Emergency." The incidentals of flying provoke the democrat in my character. Almost as if I were reacting against altitude I become a leveler. Recently before flying from Sydney to Perth I bought Peter Mayle's *A Year in Provence*. I didn't finish the book. In fact I left it on the airplane. Although Mayle's meals stretched through interminable courses and silver services of cash, he rarely mentioned expense. Moreover he described trucks of workmen. The only people who know workmen well are workmen themselves and those people who employ them. Repairs to Mayle's house were endless; yet Mayle did not mention cost. "I would not mind swinging high on the grapevine myself," I thought, stuffing the book into the pocket of the seat in front of me, "but if I wrote about it I would at least say that I was so damn rich that money didn't matter a hoot in hell."

My irritation did not last beyond the flight. Landing brought me back to the earthy, sensible particulars of place. At home Eliza gave me a cone of firewood banksia. The cone was four inches tall and at its broadest point an inch and a half wide. Six follicles were open, each looking like a bill on a duck puppet. Resembling gray needlepoint, unopened follicles covered the remaining surface of the cone. The open follicles burst outward. When the cone lay on its side, it resembled, Edward said, the barrel of a cannon exploded by too big a charge of powder, the metal peeled back by heat. On my desk now is a cicada. For days I heard cicadas in the bushes around the house. Although the sounds were not so loud as those made by American cicadas, I recognized the calls. No matter how I searched I could not find one, however. Then on Sunday a small insect fell out of a sock Vicki took off. Not until I examined the insect with a hand lens did I know it was a cicada.

The Perth cicada resembled a model of the American insect, a metal creature made in Taiwan or South Korea and sold to children as a toy. Painted green and black, the model was half an inch long and a quarter of an inch wide. The workmanship was splendid, and a collection of such models would cost garages of Matchbox cars. Yesterday I hunted through shrubs, searching for another cicada. Although I heard several, I didn't see any. I noticed other things, however. Snails as big as knuckles pulled themselves across a brick wall. The leaves of lantana smelled rough and minty. Before they bloomed, the buds of lantana resembled small bow ties. Kookaburras ratcheted into laughter, and a magpie lark strutted across the yard.

Beside a neighbor's house jacaranda blossomed. The flowers bloomed in bunches, splaying out like bristles on brushes caked with gobs of blue paint. From a kaffir plum egg-shaped fruits hung down in clutches. Some plums were green; others were purple and ripe. The plums tasted sour and dry, almost pinched, not wet and soft, opening the mouth like the wild plum of the American west. Only a few blossoms remained on portwine magnolia. Smooth with red edging on the petals, the flowers resembled droplets of pink taffy. On black kurrajong sprays of translucent green bells dangled, ringing only to the eye. The edges of the bells scrolled back and up, five scrolls to each flower. Minute speckles of pink illuminated the scrolls and flecking the inside of the bells pooled around the tops of the clappers.

Along the street peppermint sifted out of flower, but brush box started blooming. The heads of the flowers resembled stars, the points fuzzy with stamens, each stamen a silver white stem with a round bundle of yellow pollen at the tip. I thought about counting the stamens on a blossom, but the number was too great. Instead I counted those spilling out from feijoa. The petals turned inward about the middle of the blossom. They had a doughy consistency and resembled minute loaves of bread sagging damp on trays before being pushed into an oven. The center of the blossom was the oven itself, from which the stamens erupted in a burst of red flame cooling out to yellow, seventy-eight stamens on the flower I counted. As the flower withered, the stamens blackened, resembling ash. Unlike feijoa a big Norfolk pine seemed chilled, the black lumps on its bark resembling small pails of coal, in another age potentially hot but now old-fashioned, an artifact, a decoration set beside an unused fireplace. In examining the bark of Norfolk pine I thought of Nashville and the coal fires of childhood. Thanksgiving was two weeks off, and although Vicki didn't make pumpkin and mince pies in Perth, the orange spikes of Ashby's banksia smelled like pumpkin.

Man is a pattern-finding, conclusion-creating animal. I observe the natural world because I want to be part of place and time. Despite knowing I'm a sojourner, I long for permanence, or if not permanence, the illusion of something lasting. Amid the little doings of life I imagine pattern and fashion meaning. I should not have criticized *A Year in Provence*. Enjoyment of the book depended upon illusion, the reader's imagining himself living in a house filled with finery and significance, far from meaninglessness and the fret of buying and selling. What really irritated me was not the cost of things but the meals themselves. I have strong appetites, and I was jealous of Mayle's sybaritic gourmandizing. Vicki and I are not bosom buddies or soul mates but table companions. Not love but eating shores up our marriage. After listening to the choir at Nedlands Primary, we went to Belinda's for lunch. We drank cappuccinos and ate smoked salmon and cream-cheese sandwiches. For dessert I ate French custard cake while Vicki ate lemon and passion-fruit cheesecake.

This past Tuesday we bought beach towels in Claremont. Afterward we went to the Astoria Café for a snack. Four towels cost twenty-four dollars. At the Astoria each of us ate and drank the equivalent of a towel, both of us having cappuccinos, Vicki bundling hers down with apricot ricotta, I munching a plum and almond tart. From the roof of the café a striped awning extended over the sidewalk. Beneath the awning sat four tables. Because the tables were empty, we ate inside. Behind Vicki a mirror ran the length of the wall. Overhead light seeped through a green fixture that hugged the ceiling and resembled the bottom of a flatboat. The pastry case was glass and stainless steel. A middle-aged man sat in a corner. He wore a blue yachting shirt and sipped red wine while he read a newspaper. Occasionally he looked up, a self-assured smile amiable as a wallet on his face. At another table a woman sat writing, three empty cups and a glass of water in front of her.

Behind Vicki was a couple. Dark-haired and foreign, the man spoke with an accent and was considerably younger than the woman across from him. The man wore green shorts and a sweatshirt advertising a health club. On the table in front of the woman sat a cup of coffee and two-thirds of a piece of cake. The woman had stringy blond hair and wore a black exercise outfit. The legs of the outfit were short, reaching just below the knees, and the back was scalloped and open. A stiff ruffle circled the waist of the outfit. The woman spent much time in the sun. Her skin was dried and freckled, and just under her shoulder blade was a brown growth the size of a dime. While talking she was animated and youthful. When her companion went to the lavatory, however, her expression drained into wrinkles and losing amiability and color resembled the craggy limestone cliffs bordering Freshwater Bay. The couple left before Vicki and I finished eating, he protesting several times that he wanted to pay the bill. Placing her left hand atop the bill, she ignored him. Even when he reached out to snatch the bill, she did not move her hand, leaving his arm to flutter weakly above the table.

After leaving the café, Vicki and I went to Claremont Fresh, a grocery store. While Vicki shopped, I looked at vegetables, and seeing several I did not recognize, took out pad and pencil and started taking notes. Chokoes resembled green peppers that had softened and begun to sag inward to moist bruise. While corgettes looked like okra in fancy dress, celeriac was down-to-earth, resembling a softball buried in mud so long that roots wrapped around it tightly and could not be peeled off even after the ball dried. "Excuse me," a voice said, "are you writing down prices?" The store manager stood at my side. He thought I was a spy from a rival grocery. When he learned I was not spying, he was embarrassed and tried to slip away. "No you don't," I said loudly; "you are not escaping so easily." I seized his elbow and leading him to a vegetable counter refused to release him until he told me how to cook six vegetables that I had not recognized. "That's the last time that man will approach anyone holding a pencil," I told Vicki later. "Approach," Vicki exclaimed, "the next time he sees a pencil he will run for the door. By the time you got to the fifth vegetable his eyes were wild. Military Police could learn a lot about crowd control from you."

In the incidentals of the morning lay story, or at least the makings of character. On a page detail is character, be the detail an object or a word. Although Proverbs Goforth barely knew Morris Hamper, he attended Morris's funeral, explaining that he wanted to see "the fellow who is going to be the richest man in the Carthage graveyard." "And what Proverbs said isn't the worst of it," Turlow Gutheridge told the lunch crowd at Ankerrow's Café. "It was raining, and Proverbs took his umbrella to church. The umbrella was new, and worried that somebody might take it by mistake, Proverbs kept it with him in the pew. The only time he put it down was when he viewed the corpse, and then he just laid it across the top of the coffin while he leaned over to get a good look at Morris. It's not true," Turlow said, pausing to swallow a spoonful of chocolate pudding, "that so much water dripped off the umbrella that it washed the makeup off Morris's face, staining his shirt collar. Only one or two drops fell on Morris's face, and they looked like warts. Most of the water fell on his necktie, and folks didn't notice it."

Rarely will the person who notices incidentals be bored. Moreover he will have fun and probably think his life remarkably successful. Sunday morning Vicki and the children and I went to the garage sale at Nedlands Primary. I stopped at the door and bought four lottery tickets costing two dollars. The prize was a basket of "gourmet food," a sign said. The food came not from a trendy café, but from a grocery store. Among items in the basket were two bags of potato chips, one seasoned with garlic, the other with salt and vinegar. While I puttered about among the used books, Vicki bought sweets: eleven date slices covered with coconut and costing $3.50; nine chocolate cupcakes with sprinkles on top for $2.50; then for $7.00 a chocolate fudge cake. Next she bought kitchen equipment so she could make her own cakes: a whisk, a mouli-grater, an eggbeater, and two mashers. All the utensils cost thirty cents apiece and were stainless steel with the exception of one of the mashers. By the back door of the assembly room were flats of petunias grown by Eliza's class. The petunias cost eighty cents apiece, and Vicki bought four. To carry them home she bought two straw baskets at twenty cents apiece.

I purchased only one item. Taped on a wall above a long table of books was a sign reading, "5–50¢ make an offer." I paid fifty cents for a book, *Meredith and Co.*, a novel about life in a boys' prep school in England, written by George Mills and first published by Oxford University Press in 1933. I could not resist the beginning of the book. "PERCY OLIPHANT NAYLOR GATHORNE OGILVIE, complete with nurse, red hair, and freckles, stood with his mother on the platform at Victoria Station. He was nine years old, an unattractive boy, fat and spoiled, and was being taken to a boarding school for the first time. 'Now, Percy darling,' said his mother, 'have you got all you need? Nice papers to look at and that box of chocs Aunt Agatha gave you, and that book of fairies we bought at the bookstall.'"

Aside from natural history and field guides I buy few books. My house in Connecticut is small, and the children are accumulators. Where once I had a library now rest collections of rocks, baseball cards, shells, ribbons, pencils, and bones. Each year I give away more books than I buy, those I review and those I am given, even books fulsomely inscribed by their authors. Giving away books autographed by friends makes me uneasy. Whenever I leave a carton of books at the Mansfield Library for the annual book sale, I imagine a friend perusing the dollar table and amid the claptrap discovering the book he brought to my house and presented to me a fortnight earlier. "I never give away inscribed books," my friend Josh told me; "suppose their authors found them at a rummage sale. That would be embarrassing, so instead of donating them to the library, I burn them. You'd be surprised how quickly a bad novel goes up in smoke and how long it takes to light a philosophy textbook." Most of my friends resemble Josh and either burn such volumes or throw them into the garbage that is buried in the town landfill. Aside from widows emptying shelves and clearing the old mate out before embracing the new, no one I know admits to giving away autographed books. In order to lessen the guilty twinges that ripple through me when I recall the presentation copies that I have dumped at the library, I search for kindred bibliophiles at garage sales, opening books to discover not knowledge or literary merit but inscriptions.

What first attracted me to *Meredith and Co.* was an inscription. On the flyleaf of the book, Joseph Craven *"Rector"* wrote, "Presented to Brian Horner St. Alban's Sunday School, Perth. December 1955." Before I noticed Percy, I speculated about Brian, wondering what we shared in common. I was older. In 1955 I was fourteen, six or seven years beyond Sunday school. Still, Brian was a comparatively old father like me. Because he donated the book to the sale, he had, I concluded, a child enrolled at Nedlands Primary, one who had outgrown Mills's book or, most probably, a girl not interested in Percy's trials at boarding school. I looked St. Alban's up in *Streetsmart*. St. Alban's was an Anglican church, and Brian had been raised an Episcopalian like me. The church was close, in Highgate at the corner of Beaufort and St. Alban's Avenue. After his schooldays Brian stayed in Perth, an indication, along with his being an Anglican, that he was satisfied and had done well, becoming, I guessed, some sort of professional, a doctor perhaps.

Certainly he wasn't a teacher, because teachers, Josh and me aside, don't usually prune their libraries but let shelves grow wild, books sending out runners like lantana and spreading musty fragrances throughout the house. No, I decided, Brian was a doctor. The book was a prize awarded to a hardworking, diligent academic child, one to whom a story about school appealed, a doctor in embryo. Moreover Brian had a daughter in Nedlands Primary because he married comparatively late, after completing medical school. "I wonder," I thought, "if Brian is listed in the telephone book." Here I stopped. I had, to paraphrase the old saw, come to conclusions before I reached an end. To have looked Dr. Horner up in the telephone book would have been intrusive, something not done by an Episcopalian. Consequently

I hung my deerstalker on the hat rack and put the magnifying glass back in the desk. Then I removed my hearing aid from the bedside table and, stuffing it down my ear, turned the volume on high.

If I could not sleuth through inscriptions in Perth, I could eavesdrop on conversations in Carthage. None of Loppie Groat's running mates drank wine in the morning or treated aerobic instructors to sweets after class. In Carthage life was simple. If a person was curious about a neighbor's doings, he asked a question. Not long after Loppie's cousin Clevanna Farquarhson had a baby, Googoo Hooberry met Loppie outside Read's drugstore. "Well, Loppie," Googoo said, "What did Clevanna have?" "Guess," Loppie replied. "A boy," Googoo said. "No," Loppie said; "guess again." "A girl," Googoo said. "Damn," Loppie answered, his brow furrowed in irritation, "who told you?"

After leaving Nedlands Primary, we dropped our purchases off at home, then I drove to Yanchep National Park, thirty-five miles north of Perth. As soon as we arrived we ate lunch: cheddar cheese, bread, apples, and oranges. We ate on the ground. Waterbirds strolled along the shore, and I brushed droppings aside before sitting down. After the meal Edward fed a raven, and Francis a black swan, then a swamp hen. A pelican flew overhead, and a family of wood ducks waddled through a gap in a stone wall. A pied cormorant dove under the water, and a musk duck paddled near the shore. Long-necked tortoises twisted around rocks at the edge of a dock, and Eliza dropped chunks of bread into the water for them. Just offshore in front of us were two small, reed-covered islands. Birds nested on the islands, and in front of each island a sign stuck out of the mud. "Sanctuary for Waterfowl and Tiger Snakes," the sign warned, discouraging children from hunting for birds' eggs on the islands. Tiger snakes were common around the lake, but they didn't live on the islands. A group of koalas lived in a compound at the park. Shortly after lunch we went to see them. Dozing in eucalyptus trees, the koalas paid no attention to us. A ranger, however, showed us an echidna that had been trapped in Perth and that he was going to return to the wild that evening. While the echidna's snout resembled a leathery black index finger, its bristles looked like slivers of wood, polished to bring out different shades of brown and gray.

The afternoon was full. We explored a limestone cave and toured the lake in a flat-bottomed boat. The children ate Wedges, after which we walked around the lake, a two-kilometer stroll. Bulrushes were thick along the shore. By the path swishbush was yellow with blossoms, and paperbark white. Dodder wound green through clumps of cut rushes. Before leaving the park, we walked up a gorge, formed when a cave collapsed. Above the path towered stacks of limestone, pits in their surfaces filled and softened by dirt, the stone flaking into plants. Beside the path stood grass trees, the leaves pushing up like green cowlicks. Smokebush grew along the top of the gorge, resembling wisps of white hair. Beyond the bushes glowed spikes of banksia, those of bull banksia orange and those of candle pale yellow and flickering.

Not far from Yanchep was Dizzy Land, the Disneyland of Wanneroo Road. Driving to the park I noticed Dizzy Land, seeing a Ferris wheel, a large sign saying "Kangaroos," and then in the center of the park a one-story, red-brick castle. I asked the children if they wanted to visit Dizzy Land, but they said they were too tired. "What we want to do," Eliza said, "is eat the chocolate cake Mommy bought this morning." Later Eliza got her wish. After the cake vanished, I answered a letter from Yerilla Station in Kookynie. The vice president of the Isolated Children's Parents' Association asked me to speak to the group when it met in Perth in February. "Many of us," she explained, live on isolated stations and teach children at home, contacting "their school teachers for about half an hour a day on the two-way radio." The association could not afford an honorarium. "I'll be glad to speak," I wrote, "but since you can't pay me, I want you to bring me samples of incidentals found about your stations, the sorts of things children collect: seeds, animal droppings, wondrous things of that sort." I mailed the letter at the university the next morning. At the Hackett snack bar I met Nigel. "Sam," he said, "did I ever tell you about the ranger who could identify wood by its taste? If you liked the story about the wine maker, you are going to love this one."

Australian stories are stronger than American stories. Even after their seasoning is diluted the stories remain hardy fare. Still, much as one ought to visit Scitech and Underwater World while in Perth, so one ought to listen to tales. Later he can do with them as he pleases, in my case wrapping them in words and sending them to Carthage. Dapper's still exploded and started a fire that cropped the tail of Long Dog Cove and singed four mountain ridges. As a result the government sent a ranger from Sevierville to supervise reforestation. On arriving in Carthage the ranger took a room in Morphett's Boarding House then hired a crew of men. Among those hired were Loppie Groat, Hink Ruunt, and Isom Legg, all the local ne'er-do-wells. Born in Biscuit, a small hamlet outside Chattanooga, the ranger was a democrat, not a man to let rank stand in the way of pleasure. At the end of each day's planting, he accompanied his crew to Enos Mayfield's "Inn" in South Carthage. There they drowned, in Loppie's words, "the heat what smoldered in our gullets all day." One night after they doused several inner fires, the ranger bragged that he could identify any tree just by tasting the wood. Moreover he said he could identify the wood blindfolded. Hink Ruunt did not believe the ranger, and a disagreement flared. To cool matters down Loppie suggested a wager. Hink was hot under the collar, and although he usually stuck to his money tighter than bark to ironwood, he bet a dollar and fifteen cents against the ranger. Loppie blindfolded the ranger with Isom's handkerchief then taking Enos's ax went outside the inn and chopped slabs of wood off trees. The ranger turned the wood through his mouth like hunks of tobacco, and xylem by xylem identified hackberry, dogwood, butter pecan, redbud, and shagbark hickory.

Hink couldn't bear seeing his money go up in smoke. After the ranger identified thorns from a honey locust, Hink went outside and tore a slat off an orange crate. After dropping his trousers, he ran the slat up and down his bottom, taking care not to jab splinters into himself. Then he walked back inside the inn and handed the ranger the slat, saying, "identify this by God." The ranger took a bite out of the slat and rolled the wood through his cheeks. His tongue first rested lightly on top of the fibers. Then like a corn snake hunting rats in a barn it began to poke at the wood, flicking the pith gently and pulling back suddenly then rushing forward to flick again. For a moment the ranger looked puzzled. But then just about the time Hink thought his money was safe from termite and carpenter ant, the ranger smiled, and leaning forward took the wood out of his mouth. Pinching the wad between his thumb and index finger, he studied it a moment, feeling it and resembling a boy holding a sourball. "Fellows," he said, "there ain't no doubt about it. This here is a shingle from off the shithouse roof."

Chances Are

Just a little flutter," I told Vicki. The Melbourne Cup was Australia's Kentucky Derby. Around the corner from the TAB, the state-run betting office, cars parked along both sides of Hillway. Inside the building people marked tickets then formed three lines in order to place their bets. So many people were betting that the lines stretched out the door, two trailing down the sidewalk beside Broadway, the third bending back up Hillway like an elbow. "Besides," I said, "a horse named Tennessee Jack is one of the favorites. I had to bet on him." "How much did you bet?" Vicki asked. "Ten dollars," I said, "five on Jack and another five on Dancing Lord." "Dancing what?" Vicki said. "Dancing Lord," I answered; "he's a long shot, but I liked his name. He sounds light on his feet and might promenade home." "A race is a round not a square dance," Vicki said; "to use an Australian expression, you have just pissed ten dollars out the window."

I did not tell Vicki that I bought tickets in two pools at the university. The dean's secretary managed the pools, and the two tickets cost four dollars. In one pool I drew Mercator. He finished third in the cup, and I won eight dollars. On the way home the next afternoon I stopped at H.J.'s Deli and bought Vicki and the children Magnums. "You only bought one ticket in the pool?" Vicki asked; "you are the kind of guy who would buy two or three." "Just one," I said, "and I spent the winnings on you and the children." "That's nice," she said, biting into her Magnum. "Then you only lost four dollars," she said, licking her lips before calculating; "you bet two at the office and ten at the TAB. That's not too bad."

I like taking the occasional chance. Much as I did not mention the second pool to Vicki, so she does not know about the stubs buried in the lower-right-hand drawer of the desk: at fifty cents each, four stubs for a raffle sponsored by the Friends of NGALA, a "family response center" in South Perth, then for a dollar a chance in the World Firefighters Games Raffle. First prize in the Friends of NGALA's raffle is a porcelain doll valued at four hundred dollars. Eliza wants a doll for Christmas, and the prize will go to her. First prize in the firefighters' raffle is a Toyota 4Runner, a four-wheel-drive vehicle costing thirty-eight thousand dollars.

After buying the ticket I thought about what I would do with the Toyota. For a time I considered keeping the car and visiting parts of Western Australia beyond the capacities of our station wagon, pushing north along the Batavia Coast past Carnarvon into the Pilbara. Sitting in the living room sipping tea, I imagined yellow gorges and limestone bluffs resembling teeth caked red by time. I saw horsemen herding cattle into bare yards and heard crocodiles slide into muddy streams. Afterward I wrote a book that people read on airplanes. Alas, I had less chance of writing a best-seller than Dancing Lord did of cantering into the Winner's Circle at the Melbourne Cup. As a result I decided to sell the 4Runner on December 12, the day after the drawing. The year in Australia has been costly, and the thirty thousand dollars I'll ask for the car will help me stay the course, insuring that I don't break down financially within sight of home.

Taking chances percolates slowly through my clogging arteries but pulsates rapidly through Edward's youthful veins. For three weeks a jar that once held 375 grams of Kraft peanut butter sat on the front porch. The jar was home to Edward's red-back spider, the most dangerous spider in Western Australia. A "bite from a Red-back" is, the Western Australian Museum warns, "highly venomous and can be lethal." Trapdoor, black wish-bone, window, and huntsmen spiders are also poisonous. Besides spiders, picnickers have to be careful not to set their baskets atop jumper ants, scorpions, and centipedes. The bite of a centipede, the museum notes, can cause "intense local pain and general symptoms." Avoid, the museum urges, kangaroo ticks, cup-moth, bag-shelter, and anthelid caterpillars.

"I'd like," Edward said last week, "to collect all the dangerous bugs in Western Australia. Will you help me, Daddy?" From the inclinations of childhood grow the occupations of adults. My naturalist friends spent their youths catching and collecting, turning homes into zoos and pesthouses. I didn't want to uproot Edward's interest in spiders.

Each summer I send the children to camp in Maine so that they can grow buggy, apart from the insecticide of manners and regulation. Many parents try to direct children's lives. A few attempt to mold their offspring in hopes that they will become the adults the parents dreamed of being. For me to have pruned Edward's days as if he were topiary would have been wrong. As I watched him examining insects, I imagined a life for him, days fertile with tumblebugs, hours spent outdoors under trees, not inside beneath fluorescent lights. I wanted him to hear the fledgling honeyeaters clamoring in the backyard. I wanted him to notice mats of fiber resembling burlap clinging to the trunks of cabbage palms. Nevertheless I didn't want him to keep a red-back spider for a pet.

"I'm careful," Edward said; "the spider hides in the leaves at the bottom of the jar. She only comes out at night. The chances of my being bitten are small." The danger that loomed in my mind did not lurk in Edward's mind. Because he was a child and I was an adult, we saw the world differently. Aware of the frailty of life the adult spends much energy trying to bar risk from his days. Unlike the child the adult organizes his doings. He excludes the random and organizes mind and hours so that chance does not tempt him. Exercising and dieting, he builds fences about himself in order to bar change from the door. Instead of increasing the number of his acquaintances, he decreases them.

As people age disease darkens lives. The fewer people one knows the smaller the chance of hearing a sad story. By banishing accounts of illness or unhappiness from thought the adult hopes to banish them from his conscious life. Not the youth but the adult demands cruise control on his car. The adult has yearly physical examinations and purchases a burglar alarm for the house. After her husband, Luburl, died, Arlene Haskins sold her possessions and moved to Florida. At the sale Slubey Garts bought two silver goblets and a roll-top dish for the altar at the Tabernacle of Love. Never before had the tabernacle contained expensive things, and Proverbs Goforth worried that thieves might break into the church. He worried so much that he installed an alarm. At Barrow's Store he bought three rattraps. He took them to the church and hid one behind each piece of silver. "Now," he told Slubey, "any thief who breaks in is sure to be caught."

Nowadays most adults want orderly, sterilized lives. Years ago in Carthage, folks were not so particular. Accidents simply happened. Lawyers had not convinced people that all mishaps were preventable and that someone or some corporation was responsible for every accident. Medicine did not promise and people did not expect miracles. People died suddenly despite the ministrations of Doctor Sollows. Chalkey Varnell owned four thin red cows. Every morning he milked them and set the milk out in pails by the end of the dirt road leading to his house. Passersby stopped and poured jars of milk, leaving money in Chalkey's mailbox. Chalkey was lazy, and his cows were covered with ticks as big as blackberries. When ticks fell into the milk, Chalkey didn't scoop them out. Neither did he cover the pails, and while the milk sat by the road, flies and grasshoppers tumbled into the pails and drowned. One Saturday, Coker Knox took the train to Carthage from Nashville in order to discuss politics with Turlow Gutheridge. The next morning while accompanying several men to church, including Hink Ruunt, Coker stopped by the road leading to Chalkey's house and poured himself a jar of milk. The morning was hot, and so many insects had fallen into the milk that it resembled rice custard. When Hink saw Coker peering into the jar, a green tinge spreading across his face, he spoke. "Don't let them bugs bother you none," he said; "the grasshoppers and flies don't drink much. As for the ticks just spit them out. They are fatter than watermelon seeds, and if you get your tongue up behind them, you can heave them a considerable distance."

Today most adults don't want life or milk raw. Instead they prefer pasteurized experiences, taking chances vicariously by reading books, watching television, or purchasing tickets for raffles. By providing the trappings of risk but not the substance, "adventure tours" appeal to armchair flutterers. On Monday I mailed a check to Camel Outback Safaris in Alice Springs, booking a tour in April. Tomorrow I will buy insurance so that if something comes up and we have to cancel the reservation I won't lose money.

Vicki thinks buying insurance silly. "Don't waste the money," Vicki said; "nothing will go haywire." Vicki is eleven years younger than me and does not worry much about consequences and possibilities. Moreover her temperament differs from mine. No longer do we watch television together. Whenever I see a mystery, for example, I think about the conclusion. I enjoy predicting plots and speculating about endings. Vicki resents my solving mysteries. Instead of flipping ahead of event and anticipating the conclusion, she prefers the gradual unfolding of plot. Perhaps I should not worry about Edward. He resembles me. When I read to the children, Edward interrupts to explain the story. He announces which characters will be sacrificed to grease the plot. The boy who recognizes why a character appears in a story and then predicts the character's fate will eventually see the danger of keeping poisonous spiders as pets.

Last week Edward's teacher quizzed me about education in the United States. She wanted to know if we taught courses that encouraged children to take risks. Some educators in Western Australia, she explained, thought that schools were shaping complacent children who would grow into selfish, unimaginative adults. If the teacher had talked to me before Edward caught the spider, I might have responded differently. "Risk," I said, "we don't have courses that encourage children to live dangerously. In fact we discourage risk. In kindergarten we warn children about AIDS and drugs of all kinds, including alcohol and cigarettes. In the United States the child who takes risks dies young."

This past weekend Eliza began a fairy tale. Invisible cloaks, seven-league boots, fairy godmothers, and red-eyed witches did not appear in the story. "Not long ago nor far away in the city of Perth there lived a modern princess," Eliza wrote; "Ms. Fiddlerum did not look or act like a princess, but she was a princess nevertheless. Her kingdom was a business building, and there she ruled. She sat at her desk all morning long signing papers. After that Ms. Fiddlerum walked to Hungry Jack's and got a whopper burger, only $1.50. When she went back to her kingdom, she signed some more papers then walked home. Squire Gordon always met her at the doorstep. He was her cat. Ms. Fiddlerum had only Squire Gordon. Except for him she was alone (pretty romantic, huh?). One Monday she decided to mount her trusty steed, in other words her airplane. She decided to go to the U.S.A. She kept Squire Gordon in the cockpit with her."

I would have locked Squire Gordon in a cage and stored him in the baggage compartment. If a mouse had jumped out of the control panel on the plane, the princess's flight would have been short. Of course risks taken with words are not chancy. On paper little is final. Apologies are easy to write. Later sentences can alter fortunes described by earlier sentences. The princess might have crashed in the Nullarbor and been rescued by a sand groper. She might have fallen in love with him and lived happily ever after, selling her business on St. George's Terrace and breeding with gusto amid sweet quandong, woolly bindii, crowsfoot, tall sida, and wire wanderrie grass, Squire Gordon no longer an aristocrat but just plain Gordie, purring contentedly by her bare, callused feet.

Taking a chance with words is less dangerous than keeping a red-back. In the telling poisonous words become less venomous. A thoroughbred paragraph drives several pages of brumbies out of mind, their cacophonous neighing and awkward kicking up of hooves soon forgotten. For my part I enjoy herding feral stories across pages. Shortly after Doctor Sollows removed a cyst from Clevanna Farquarhson's bottom, Turlow Gutheridge met Clevanna's husband, Newbern, on Main Street. "Newbern," Turlow said, "I heard about Clevanna's operation, and I trust she's doing well." "Oh, yes, Turlow, thank you," Newbern answered waxing medically descriptive; "Clevanna's doing just fine, although she can't sit on her tail yet. That cyst was almost as big as a honeydew melon, and though it won't quite so green, it was a lot lumpier. Dr. Sollows said he ain't never seen nothing like it. He chopped away at it for pretty near an hour. When he was washing his hands after he finished, he told me that Clevanna would be dandy although she'd have a scar that would be an eyesore as long as she lived."

Whenever anyone lashes my silly stories, I corral a pedigreed justification. Humans are foolish, proud creatures, and, I explain, I tell such tales to keep people from mounting high horses and, forgetting both their weaknesses and their fellowmen, galloping off into cold abstractions. The princess's plane smashed to earth with a lively thunk. The fall from abstraction is silent and more serious. Chalkey's milk, better yet a glass of milk with a spoonful of Hink Ruunt's honey stirred into it, might cure anyone suffering from the effects of such a fall. Hink kept beehives behind his tobacco shed. He ate most of the honey himself, but occasionally he sold some, setting jars out by the end of his road and like Chalkey trusting passersby to put the payment into his mailbox.

Coker Knox was fond of honey, and while taking a walk before breakfast, he bought a jar. On returning to Turlow's house, he toasted two slices of sourdough bread, basting them with sweet butter before blanketing them with honey. There, alas, his pleasure ended. The honey tasted terrible. As soon as it trickled onto his tongue, Coker staggered, his eyes rolling like lollipops. When Turlow came into the kitchen, he found Coker sitting on the floor scrubbing his tongue with a dishrag. Coker was so angry he went straight to Hink's house. Not bothering to knock, he banged into the kitchen, slamming the screen door behind him. Hink sat at the kitchen table. Heaped on a platter before him was a mound of okra, fried green tomatoes, and cornbread. "Hink!" Coker shouted, slapping the jar of honey down so hard on the table that an end of cornbread jumped off the platter and sliding across the kitchen floor disappeared under the sink, "this is the worst honey I have put in my mouth. It almost poisoned me." "Don't," Hink replied after fetching the cornbread from under the sink and pushing it over the table to sweep up a nub of okra that had bounced off the plate, "don't talk to me about taste. If a possum hadn't fallen into that batch of honey and drowned, I wouldn't of sold it. You were lucky to get what you got."

Society crafts laws to regulate behavior. By screwing lids on tubs of honey then putting them on the top shelf in the pantry beyond the reach of furry paws, planners try to create an orderly world in which rules, not whim or chance, determine action. Last week I walked down Bruce Street past the Nedlands Tennis Club. In front of the club Canary Island date palms stood like footmen. Behind the palms stretched a checkerboard of green courts, the rolled grass looking ironed. Pasted to the window of the clubhouse was a dress code. Appearance was not left to chance. Men had to wear shirts with collars. "Tracksuits, leisure suit slacks or similar garments (coloured or white) may be worn over TENNIS ATTIRE before play." Once the "hit-up" ended, players shed informal clothing. During cold weather, however, "an appropriate official" could approve the wearing of a tracksuit. Company or advertising logos on tennis clothes, the code stated, should not exceed two square inches or thirteen square centimeters. While only one logo could appear on each sleeve of a shirt or jacket, two were allowed on the front. Similarly two logos could appear on shorts, while one was permitted on each sock. If the rules governing dress at the tennis club mirrored rules governing Australian behavior, then encouraging children to take risks might be a good idea. The rules of society, though, are always only fabric deep.

Under the heading "Personal" eight or nine columns of advertisements appeared each day in the *West Australian,* touting not the talents of Mercator or Tennessee Jack but the skills of, as sociologists put it, workers in the sex industry. Kim, the paper recently informed people flying to Perth for "Business or Pleasure," was "Born to Perform." Mistress Zaina owned the "Best Dungeon in WA." From 10:00 A.M. to 10:00 P.M. one could drop his tennis attire into the hamper and "frolic with Lee" and "experience her French touch." For Anglophiles an "English Lady" offered the "Oxford Touch" from 10:00 A.M. to 9:00 P.M. For guys "Bad Boy Luke" misbehaved around the clock. Jamie, "Perth's newest toy boy," also kept unlimited hours. "Naughty but Nice," the Bi Twins were "hot to handle" and "totally shameless for your pleasure." With "fun-loving" Jessy, hackers could turn their "wildest dreams into reality." While Jessy wore "suspenders and stockings," double faulters could sport about in tracksuits, no matter the color. Between sets players bored with iced tea or lemonade could enjoy a "sweet interlude with Sharmy" or sample the "businessman's delight." After the match players who got a bit mussed could visit the "skimpy hairstylists with a touch of class." "Try the best," Candy suggested; "forget the rest," all that worry about the size and number of logos. "Hello, my name is Lucell," one advertisement testified, "I've just turned 18 and finished uni. I'm tall, slim but buxom and Mum says very innocent. Just started doing massage to earn some money for next year's uni. Please call me." The chance of meeting Lucell on a court at the university was slim. Great, however, were the risks of taking lessons from her classmates: Geena, Amber-Rose, Samantha, Rianna, Bruce, and Sebastian. Less dangerous was it to collect venomous insects than to "be captivated" by Allison's "slow gentle touch and warm personality."

Safer and more entertaining than either would be a visit to Carthage. Clevanna prepared lunches at Ankerrow's Café. For ten days after her operation she was weak and couldn't stand on her feet for more than fifty minutes at a time. So that Woody Ankerrow would not have to hire another cook while Clevanna recuperated, Newbern stood in for her at the café, taking orders, serving soup, and making sandwiches. Newbern was not swift, and making sandwiches stretched his capacities to the limit. Seeing Hink Ruunt eating okra and cornbread made Coker Knox hungry. The memory of the honey faded, and after leaving Hink's kitchen, he went to the café and ordered lunch. "I'd like a glass of iced tea and two ham sandwiches," he told Newbern, "one of the sandwiches with mustard and the other without it." Newbern took a pad and pencil from the pocket on the left-hand side of his shirt and wrote down Coker's order. Afterward he walked toward the kitchen. He didn't get there. Suddenly he stopped, and after taking out the pad and studying it for a moment, he returned to Coker and repeated the order. "Iced tea and two ham sandwiches, one with mustard and one without," he said, holding the pad close to his nose so he could read it better before asking, "Which of the sandwiches do you want without mustard?"

The nineteenth-century Romantic poets believed that taking chances could lead to insight. Most of the chances they took, however, were intellectual. Magical words intrigued them more than the "magic hands" advertised in the *West Australian*. Instead of toting their "fantasies" to Busty, they sought the muse. In contrast to the poets who chatted endlessly about insight, I think taking chances of the nonfleshly sort leads outward to observation. While insight focuses and can narrow, observation broadens vision and awakens appreciation. Despite knowing that the bite of a red-back could be lethal, I fed Edward's pet. Small moths clung to the side of the house. Cockroaches scurried across the back stoop, and millipedes lived under stones. A gray weevil inched along a twig.

As I prepared meals for the spider, I saw insects that had drifted across my vision each day like motes, practically invisible and unnoticed: cabbage butterflies spiraling above lantana; Australian admirals, night around their forewings, yellow sunrise seeping through and spreading before aging and running to dusky brown near the center of the wings; and common browns, orange washing up their hind wings to break against a shadowy headland, behind the headland boggy puddles of yellow. One morning I caught three cicadas and found a split pupal shell five-eighths of an inch long. Plastered to the house were light brown strings of egg casings, four or five casings in a string. Each egg was an eighth of an inch long. To hatch, insects dug holes in the lower end of the casings. Yesterday I looked out the kitchen window and thought I saw a centipede on the wall. A string of eggs had hatched. Small black insects stood on long stiltlike legs, yellow lines across their middles, their lower bodies resembling pillows.

Stuck to the wall outside Vicki's and my bedroom was a small geodesic dome constructed out of minute hairs. Bunches of eggs resembling little pearls clung to the hairs. The dome was raised over what seemed to be a pupal case. Silver and shaped like a small bullet, the case resembled an observation car on a passenger train. A furry creature grasped the lower part of the dome. "That's the mother guarding her eggs," Edward said. The insect remained on the dome until the eggs hatched. Gradually the eggs turned sandy. Yesterday wormlike larvae crawled out of the eggs, the head of each larva bulbous, silver hairs bristling on its body.

Last Saturday I bought Edward a Christmas present, a book describing common Australian spiders. One December when I was young, Father asked what I wanted to give Mother for Christmas. I said, "a cap pistol." Accordingly Father and I selected a pistol, one with a long barrel and a rotating chamber that held a circle of six caps. Much as I, not Mother, played with the cap pistol, so I will use the spider book more than Edward. Tomorrow while he is at school, I plan to spend the morning identifying spiders lurking about the house.

Two weeks ago I received a letter from Robert Colwell, professor of ecology and evolutionary biology at the University of Connecticut. Bob sent me an article in which he described being bitten by a fer-de-lance in Costa Rico. The fer-de-lance is one of the most poisonous snakes in the Western Hemisphere, and Bob spent nine days in the hospital, three of them in intensive care. Edward read the article. "Gee, Daddy," he said, "think what a great essay you could write if you were bitten by a tiger snake and lived." In the letter accompanying the article Bob described the chaparral pea, "a handsome bush" with waxy foliage, purple flowers, and long green thorns. The scientific name of the pea was *Pickeringia Montana*. "Named," Bob asked, "for some botanist relative of yours?" Francis also read the letter. "Daddy," he said, "instead of getting bitten by a snake, maybe you could discover a plant. To have a plant named after you would be exciting." The next day was Sunday, and Vicki, the children, and I took a picnic lunch to the John Forrest National Park in the Hills Forest, an hour east of Perth. After lunch we walked along the old railway track to National Park Falls. The day was hot, and Vicki and the children stopped at the falls. I continued on, leaving the track and following a path that wound through the bush alongside Jane Brook. "Every tropical biologist," Bob wrote, "watches for snakes." The path plunged through thick reeds and rushes, the habitat of tiger snakes, and although I kept alert, I was not so careful as I should have been. Figuratively the red-back had nipped me, the bite not causing pain but making me behave foolishly.

The brook tumbled through green pools, spun slowly, then bustled downward. Flat shelves of granite stuck out over the brook, the water seeming to resemble an electric bundle of nerves, the granite, disks, the forest's rocky spinal column. Round boulders settled into the hills above the brook. Sap oozed out of marri trees, gravity and heat pulling the sap like taffy into filaments incandescent in the light. On grass trees spikes were white with blossoms. Red sprays burst from cliff-net bush, and honeymyrtle was purple and yellow with pom-poms. Feather flower bloomed in pink bouquets. On snail hakea, fruit was sharp and green, and on rose-tipped mulla mulla, flowers blossomed in soft tufts. Heat made the walk difficult, and I sweated most of the spider's influence out of my system. When I returned to Vicki and the children, Vicki made me sit down. Then she went to the kiosk and bought me a Coca-Cola and a banana popsicle. "If you aren't careful," she said, "you are going to have a heart attack. You have a family. People who have families should behave responsibly and not take chances."

This morning I was responsible. I stopped writing and walked out on the porch and freed Edward's spider, dumping her into the fishbone fern behind the clothesline. When he comes home from school, Edward will want to catch something else dangerous. I won't let him. His days, and mine, of taking chances are over for a while. If I give him his Christmas present early, maybe identifying spiders will satisfy him. For my part I am going to copy Sawyer Blodgett of Carthage. Sawyer was a careful man, never leaving anything to chance. Each night before going to sleep he put two glasses on his bedside table, one full of water, the other empty. "The glass with water in it," he explained to Turlow Gutheridge, "is there in case I wake up in the middle of the night and feel thirsty. The empty glass is there in case I wake up and don't feel thirsty."

December

In Connecticut, Thanksgiving ends November, the last days of the month after the holiday seeming scraps, a hash of leftovers soggy and tasteless. We did not celebrate Thanksgiving in Perth, and December began on November 28, the First Sunday in Advent. That morning we swam at Cottesloe Beach. The sand sighed as we walked through it, and the water fizzed like seltzer. At first the light shimmered golden along the beach, but then the sun balled into strength and rolled searing across the morning. We ate lunch at the snack bar above the beach. Then I drove uptown to the Art Gallery of Western Australia to see an exhibition of aboriginal art. "The most comprehensive exhibition of Central Australian Aboriginal Art ever assembled in Australia," the museum catalog stated. "The show is wonderful," an acquaintance said; "study it. Afterward the world won't appear the same."

No matter where I travel, I remain in the United States. No matter how I struggle, I see other cultures through the filter of my background. Parked across the street from the Astoria Café in Claremont yesterday was a red Ferrari convertible. "What kind of person spends a fortune for a damn car," I said to Vicki; "I've a good mind to gump in the front seat." "A wealthy person," Vicki said, "and don't spit in the car. Australians wouldn't understand." "That's right, Daddy," Edward said; "Australians are about having a good time. The car is just a good time. It doesn't mean anything." In my mind the car was so loaded with meaning that it slumped off its axles like the uppers of old shoes bulging and sagging over soles. To purchase art, books, china, furniture, things exhibited in the privacy of a home, I explained to Edward, was acceptable in the society in which I grew up. But to squander money on a car was vulgar. "Daddy," Francis said, "Australia is different. There are traffic jams of Bentleys and Rolls-Royces here. Some of the people who drive the cars are bound to be nice." "I doubt it," I said.

Francis was right. To tell the truth I wouldn't mind an excursion in a Rolls once in my life, providing, of course, that the front seat was not slippery with anything other than envy. Still, the Ferrari across from the Astoria meant something to me that it did not to Australians. Similarly, aboriginal art conveyed meanings that I could not grasp. I tried to read the paintings, doing what I always do at galleries, selecting a favorite painting: *Bush Tucker Dreaming*. Nevertheless background determined what I saw and, more importantly, what I did not see. Soaked by rain, roots whirled across *Bush Tucker*, creating a green-and-brown study, an impressionistic mood, not the familiar yellow-and-blue mood of Monet, but a mood I could force into a recognizable mold.

I read the paintings much as I read medieval art, turning honey ants, rainbow serpents, yams, and dingoes into icons. Witchety grubs were not the stuff of Christian story, however, and my readings were contrived, the fabrications of a person far removed from aboriginal life and laboring to avoid admitting the show bored him. To help viewers appreciate the exhibition the museum staff pasted placards on walls next to individual paintings. The placards glossed the paintings. Not only did they provide information about aboriginal societies, but they also contained a fund of aboriginal story and lore. Only after I read a placard did I appreciate a painting, and then I did not enjoy the painting so much as the story, recognizable nouns and verbs, prepositions, adjectives, and adverbs. I wanted, for example, to learn more about the rainbow serpent. The creature lurked underwater during the dry season and emerged during the wet, unleashing the creative and destructive powers of flood and storm.

After wandering through the exhibition, I thought the claim that aboriginal art could change the way I saw the world was silly, the statement of a sentimental primitivist. Few people raised in conservative Western societies can really appreciate nontraditional art. Many people want to appreciate such art. Hankering for a simplicity that does not exist outside their own dreamtimes, they believe that they long to escape mechanized industrial cultural. Such people often assume that other peoples are closer to nature than they are. Moreover, they also assume that when artists appear unsophisticated the art produced is more honest and thus more powerful. "Plunging through the veneer of social life," a catalog might state, "such art taps the wellsprings of real emotion and splashes powerful and vital across the canvas."

On the second floor of the museum I explored galleries hung with late-nineteenth- and early-twentieth-century paintings depicting life in Australia. The artists were Europeans or descendants of Europeans, and I felt at home among their brush strokes. In imagination I hung Sydney Long's *The Hour of Romance* (1914) in my dining room in Connecticut. An aboriginal painting would demand attention, its dots gathering then exploding in dizzy swarms before the eye. In contrast *The Hour of Romance* would hang like balmy gauze on the wall, softening conversation and cooling evenings. At the left front of the painting two spindly trees tottered like long-legged waterbirds. Behind them stretched a shallow lake, the surface of the water reddish in the summer moonlight. On the far side of the lake a town clustered along the shore, lights flickering yellow and silver, over a chimney, a pillar of smoke rising like a column of dark sand. Just above the town the sky gleamed like slate. Higher in the air the sky turned purple. To the right of the spindly trees a bundle of rocks pushed out of the water. On the shore above them perched a wooden bench, a seat on which one could doze and dream, not of the rainbow serpent thrusting up cacophonous through the lake, but of a canoe slipping quietly along, neat pools rippling behind the paddle like buttons.

Late that afternoon I took Vicki and the children home. I changed clothes and then drove back uptown for the Festival of Lessons and Carols at St. George's Anglican Cathedral. Vicki and the children were too tired to accompany me. For eleven months of the year I rush through days like a car spinning down a superhighway. My eyes look forward along the asphalt, fitting vision to the road like an arm to a sleeve. In December I turn onto a dirt lane. Christmas approaches, and I loop backward, hoping to find a hint of myself amid the litter of bow and card, candle and bell. I went to the festival because I was far from home. Not being able to appreciate aboriginal art made me feel lonely. Amid the familiar Anglican ritual I knew I would sense community, not with the individuals at the service, for they were strangers and would remain so, but with the past, the old words evoking memories of people in Tennessee whom I had not seen for a long time but whom I missed, Mother and Father, Margaret Dortch, Katherine Ottarson, Bill

Weaver, and then places having little to do with religion but much with experience, Love Circle, Parmer School, the Onion Bowl, and Garth Fort's house on Jackson Boulevard.

A lattice of red jarrah beams supported the roof of St. George's. Beneath the rose window high in the back of the church was a new organ. Squads of silver pipes stood in ranks, rigid in wooden cases resembling closets, the wood winy yellow Tasmanian oak. Bricks used in building the church had been dug and fired locally, and they contained much iron. As a result the walls of the church were orange, and as candles tossed light over them they swirled with color. Not unlike, I suddenly thought, dots in aboriginal art. Anglican and aboriginal cultures were different, but the stuff of people's lives was similar. Europeans crafted an edgy rectangular world, and aborigines built with circles. The gap between the two was great. Common humanity spanned the gap, or so the December me wanted to believe as the light flickered over the bricks, swirling the stones in and out of shadows.

Fixed to the wall at the end of the pew on which I sat was a tablet. "To the memory," the tablet stated, of Reverend John Burdett Wittenoom, "under whose ministry amidst the struggles and privations of an infant colony, a scion of The Church of England was planted in a remote wilderness." For a quarter of a century until his death in 1855, Wittenoom had been "chaplain to this territory." I tried to imagine Wittenoom's life, but the choir stopped singing, and a cricket distracted me. I looked on the floor for the cricket and noticed that the twelve-year-old girl sitting on my right had taken off her shoes and was wiggling her toes. A clump of sand clung to her left foot just below the ankle. "What a full day she has had," I thought, adding, "what a full day I've had, too." The final hymn sung at the festival was Charles Wesley's "Lo! He Comes with Clouds Descending," the last line of which implores "Alleluia! Christ the Lord returns to reign." What followed the church service was not Judgment Day but the doings of family.

December is always children's month. Not only do Vicki and I embrace family tighter, but the children want us to do more with them in December. Vicki and I attended two Friday assemblies at Nedlands Primary. At one of the assemblies Mr. Martin described the success of the "Keep Australia Clean" campaign, urging the children to put "rubbish in the bins rather than around them." "Girls and boys," Mr. Sampson said before the school sang *Australia Fair,* "some of you are forgetting the words to our National Anthem." After the two Aussies of the Month were announced, Certificates of Merit were awarded. Measuring eight and a quarter inches by five and three-quarters inches, the certificates were made from thick, almost cardboard-like paper. Teachers wrote on the certificates with blue ink and pasted stickers around the edges. Cheery scenes appeared on the stickers: a goofy, smiling sun; a little girl skipping, blue ribbons bobbing in her hair, beneath her feet the name *Sweetie;* RIGHT ON stamped in the middle of a yellow bull's-eye, the O in ON being a red strawberry; and reclining in a hammock and reading a purple book, a pink koala. Students won certificates for a dreamtime of reasons: "for helping a friend," "for determined effort and happy smiles," and "for teamwork in social studies and science." Henry was awarded a certificate "for his kind handling of the baby guinea pigs," while Hannah won hers "for being cheery while her arm was in plaster" and Katy hers "for being kind to Hannah whose arm was in plaster." Both Eliza and Edward received certificates, Eliza "for adapting extremely well to her new school and for her valued input to the class" and Edward "for his high standard of achievement in language and mathematics."

At the second assembly the fourth grade staged a Christmas play in Japanese. Although shepherds and kings spoke Japanese, they wore the traditional costume of the elementary school Arab: sheets; bathrobes, one red and two blue; towels; and pajamas, most solid colors, but green stripes running across one and a school of blue fish swimming across another. In front of the stage sat kindergarten students wearing sheets. On their backs wings spread wide like cookie dishes. In a cradle on the stage slept a doll representing the baby Jesus. After the play Mr. Sampson shook the actors' hands, praising their performances and complimenting them for getting "these handshakes down." A skinny Santa Claus then placed a present in Jesus' cradle, after which parents and children sang "Away in a Manger," "Come Let Us Adore Him," and "Silent Night," hymns that would not be sung in Storrs for fear of offending people who were not Christian, provoking someone to sue the school system. Vicki and I haven't taken the children to church in

Connecticut, something that bothers me occasionally, not because I am a believer, for I am not, but because I want the children to belong to community, to be able to participate in rituals even if they do not believe the doctrines that once inspired the rituals. The carols appealed to heart, not mind, making me feel better about others and want to do better by them, no matter their faiths or the lack thereof. "Odd, isn't it?" Vicki said, "that we have to come ten thousand miles so the children can sing carols with kids their age."

Summer vacation began with the Christmas holiday. The special days that peppered the end of the school year in Connecticut in June occurred in December in Perth. Eliza's class ate a picnic breakfast on the shore of Matilda Bay. Francis's class went to Adventure World, an amusement park, and Edward's went roller-skating. Classes were canceled for the school pet show. Children brought a zoo of pets to school: guinea pigs named Wrinkle and Bubble; cats named Smoky, Ophelia, Tom, and Princeton; budgies called Blueberry, Cheep-Cheep, Feathers, and Max; and rabbits named Oops, Benjamin, Peewee, Goldy, and Long Tail. Nedlands Quality Meats presented a marrow bone to the dog with "the waggiest tail." A poodle wearing the bottom of a battered tutu won the contest for best-dressed dog, taking home a necklace made from dog biscuits. Other dogs did or tried to do tricks. A little girl pushed a small moplike dog around in a doll's stroller. When a boy blew his harmonica, a golden retriever sat on his haunches and looked happy. Only after the boy kicked him did the dog wag his tail. Another dog almost caught a yellow tennis ball thrown into the air by his young master.

A woman from the Department of Conservation and Land Management brought two orphans to school: a fourteen-month-old echidna and a fifteen-month-old kangaroo. I held both of them, the kangaroo like a baby, my arms wrapped around and under its back, the echidna swathed in a thick towel. The echidna's back resembled a thicket planted to deter wayward boys from taking shortcuts through a yard. Soft and hairy, the animal's belly rolled like Christmas pudding. A parent sat on a stone wall holding a nervous mutt. She got the dog from the pound four days earlier. "I believe in recycled clothes and animals," she said. "The dog already knows I am her mistress. In the old days stockmen," she explained, "forced dogs' jaws open and spat down their throats. That's how they imprinted themselves on the dogs. I did the same thing. Only I did it in a ladylike way. I spat in my palm and put my hand in front of the dog's muzzle. She licked the spittle off, and now she knows me. If ever you get a dog from the pound, spit in your hand and make her lick it off, and you won't have any trouble training her."

Eliza and Edward did not exhibit pets. Edward's new black house spider was dangerous, and he knew teachers would not allow him to bring it to school. Eliza wanted to show Albert, the big Australian cockroach I caught for her, but when she asked if she could bring it to the show, a teacher grimaced and said, "Ugh, how awful. Don't bring that ugly thing here." In truth cockroaches are beautiful. Albert's bullet shape was, as Francis put it, aerodynamic, and his black body gleamed. In place of George the dog back in Connecticut, we had insects for pets. Throughout December daddy longlegs hung in the corners above the front door. Whenever I touched their webs, they twirled like whirligigs, whipping the webs in order to snare prey. I studied the spiders trying to determine if they usually spun clockwise or counterclockwise. I'm not much scientist. After several days I concluded that they spun both ways, clockwise sometimes, counterclockwise other times.

Aside from ants who occasionally streamed in one side of a living room window and out the other, flies were the only insects that were nuisances. On hot days they hovered in clouds. Sometimes they were so numerous that I rarely stopped fanning them away from my face. On such days Perth seemed the world's friendliest city. In brushing the flies away everyone on the street appeared to be waving enthusiastically. In her room Eliza now has a shelf of jars crawling with insects. At the moment grasshoppers interest her more than any other bug. "If you behave this way for long," Vicki said to Eliza, "you'll be a grasshopper in the next life, and as soon as you start to hop about a big fat kookaburra will swoop down and eat you."

While Edward's favorite creatures are spiders, mine are cicadas. Although forty-five years have passed since I spent summers at Cabin Hill, my grandfather's farm in Virginia, I have not changed much, at least not mentally. At Cabin Hill I roamed July catching cicadas. On Melvista Avenue I catch several a day, dropping my pencil whenever I see one on the side of the house. In Carthage, Doctor Sollows said cicadas reminded him of lawyers, quarreling about things that "don't matter a hill of beans." Rarely do I disagree with anything Doctor Sollows says, but he misjudged cicadas. On every subject except cicadas Proverbs Goforth is wrong. But on cicadas he is right, calling them "sweet singers."

"If we could train a box of them to play 'Amazing Grace' and 'The Old Rugged Cross,'" he told Slubey Garts, "crowds would flatten the doors of the Tabernacle of Love on Sunday, and we could charge admission." Proverbs was so taken with the idea that when the Mighty Hagg Circus came to Carthage, he talked to the flea trainer. "It could be done," the man said, "but you know that in music education early is everything. You'd have to dig the little fellows out of the ground and start training them before they broke through their shells. Otherwise, likely as not, they'd play anything. Aside from the praying mantis, bugs don't naturally take to religion. What the maggot likes best on his dinner plate would clog the fan at a revival if some half-trained cicadas got six-legged and dirty and instead of 'Abide with Me' played 'Goober Grabbin' Mamma' or 'The Red Onion Stomp.'"

In December I thought a lot about Carthage. At Cottesloe Beach sunburn was dangerous. In Tennessee the weather was cold. Folks built big fires, and burning up was a danger. Lutille Jerdon suffered from dropsy. One winter night when she was asleep, her chimney caught on fire, killing her and reducing the house to ashes. "The fire was a humdinger," Proverbs told Turlow Gutheridge in Ankerrow's Café the next day; "there won't nothing left of that house but an iron stove, a crumpled pipe or two, then over by the hydrangeas an old bedspring that must have tumbled out of the attic. The amazing thing was," Proverbs continued, "that we didn't expect to find none of Lutille expect maybe a piece of that bridge of hers. But imagine the startlement when we found Lutille under a bunch of charcoal with hardly a sear on her hide. She looked as if she was dozing. The smile on her face was as broad as a turnip. Hoben Donkin says he reckons that the dropsy kept her moist and lubricated, and the fire didn't like the taste of all them buckets of water." This December, Proverbs himself suffered from water on the brain. He urged Slubey to preach about Christian adventurers. "Start with Brother Noah," Proverbs suggested; "he was the first man to sail around the world. During the flood all the land was out of the way, and he just kind took off, sailing west for forty days and nights until he come clear back to where he started from."

Early in December the English department at the University of Western Australia had a party at a vineyard in Swan Valley. I missed the party. While corks were popping, I was in a trailer at College Park, selling ice cream. The Nedlands Dodgers, Edward's baseball team, played in a tournament. I began the day cooking hot dogs. The last dog I cooked was shorter than the others, and I gave it to a little boy. "Tell your mother," I said, "that a nice American gave you this free." After lunch I switched to sodas and ice cream and spent three and a half hours handing out Twin Poles, Frosty Fruits, Billa Bongs, and Captain Cools. Instead of guzzling nectar, grape leaves in my hair, the aroma of, as the label on one bottle of wine put it, a "fresh ripe honeydew melon" wafting like a cloud around my head, I rummaged through a cigar box, searching for change, always nervous I would miscalculate and send a child back to his parents with less money than they knew was due.

The van was small, and I could not stand straight. Late in the afternoon, when I was tired, I forgot how low the roof was, and standing up to stretch, I jammed my head into the ceiling and shattered a fluorescent light. During my stint in the van I ate one of the Frosty Fruits, a popsicle, or as the manufacturers labeled it, an "Ice Confection," consisting of "Reconstituted Pineapple Juice, Sucrose, Reconstituted Passion Fruit Juice, Reconstituted Orange Juice, Gelatin, Food Acids (Ascorbic Acid, Citric Acid), Natural Flavour, Natural Colour (160e), Water Added." The confection sold for sixty cents, but I didn't pay for it. I was out of money. For the family I had already bought two hot dogs at $1.50 apiece, three chili dogs at $2.00 each, nine ice cream treats, and a carton of sodas.

Early in my tenure in the van I ran out of diet drinks, these last remarkably popular with skinny people. One man became irritated when in response to his asking for a diet soda I said, "We are out. Exercise is your only hope." From inside the van I could not see the games. When business was slow, I lay atop the ice cream freezer and stared into the distance, looking through the sugar gums planted along Bay Road. In the sunlight the white trunks seemed rinsed and buffed, the leaves clumped together to form wreaths at the ends of branches. The branches divided the sky into panes, forming a stained-glass window, an Australian window, tinted white and blue, fresh as the country itself, the picture not cluttered with icons from other ages and places, but clear, the observer looking through the window to dream, not at it to interpret.

Not just December, but all months are children's months. The children's Australia is the Australia that Vicki and I see. Only once in four months have Vicki and I been out by ourselves at night. During the last half of December I took the children to Cottesloe Beach almost every afternoon, including both Christmas Eve and Christmas Day. Not only did swimming tighten the loose hours of the summer vacation, but it also tired the children. Occasionally after a swim I watched the sunset, the sun resembling a red wafer slipping slowly down a flat surface to the ocean. On cloudy evenings the sky curdled then turned moldy pink and purple. Gulls hung in the air like kites. Rainbow lorikeets roosted in Norfolk pines south of the snack bar. Hurrying home in the evening, they turned through the air above Marine Parade like rudders, colors eddying in their wakes. Some afternoons Vicki swam, too. Afterward we drove to Fremantle and sitting by the harbor ate fish and chips.

During the vacation I thumbed the *West Australian* searching for entertainment. Not much was suitable for a family. On December 17, for example, musical groups were scheduled to play at eighty-five clubs, hotels, or taverns in and around Perth. Rude Emily appeared at The Superdome, Kiss the Fish at The Loft, Travelling Wheelbarrows at the Mirrabooka Tavern, and Seven Stories High at the Black Pearl. Age, not children, kept me far from such places. I'd rather have been in hell, as Turlow phrased it, with my back broken than to have spent an evening at Rockingham moaning to the rhythms of Rupture or howling with the Blue Healers at Riverton. I was too old to splash through beer at the Belmont Hotel with the Flying Piranhas, hop about at Kalamunda with the Fabulous Frogs, or drag arthritic through smoke at the Lone Star with the Bashed Crab. When Caligula, the Love Nazis, and Don't Call Me Shirley gather in the Backstage Bar and Get On Down, as one band called itself, I want to be high up, in a distant dress circle.

Unless a family paid dress-circle prices, escaping low culture could be difficult at night. For three and a half weeks in February and March, the Festival of Perth sponsored cultural happenings: plays, concerts, and dance recitals among other things. Tickets for *Measure for Measure* cost thirty-six dollars for an adult and eighteen dollars for a child. Admission to the Demon Dancers of the Lowlands from Sri Lanka performing in the Sunken Garden at the university cost twenty-six dollars for an adult and twelve for a child. In December, Vicki, the children, and I attended the first film in the Telecom Film Series at Somerville Auditorium at the university.

Somerville was an outdoor theater. A hill sloped gently down to a round pool. Beyond the pool was a big white screen. Many people brought picnic dinners to the theater and before the movie started sat on the grass and ate. Vicki made grinders, sliced vegetables, and baked chocolate chip cookies. I bought sodas for Edward and Eliza and chocolate milk for Francis. Vicki and I drank red wine. Seats in the theater were cloth lounge chairs, and if one tilted his head back, he could see the stars. A hedge of Norfolk pines surrounded the theater, smothering the sound of traffic on Hackett Drive. The great branches of the trees rumpled upward like blankets, and the auditorium seemed close and familial. Alas, among the fourteen films shown during Telecom's season, the first was the only one remotely suitable for a family. The rest of the movies were art films, some detailing rough doings on streets, others rougher doings in bedrooms. Why, I wondered, didn't the festival show films that families could enjoy together. Gore and casual fornication didn't interest me. But a movie about debonair koalas or a flying echidna would have appealed to both child and daddy.

On the second Sunday in December, Sotheby's auctioned sixty "Rare and Important Motor Cars" at the university. A white tent with translucent plastic windows was raised in the Great Court. Inside, the tent resembled a clean sheet of paper. Rows of folding chairs stretched like lines across the body of the page, and in the margin at the top stood an auctioneer's platform. For several days before the auction cars parked on the grass surrounding the tent. When the children learned about the auction, they wanted to see the cars, and so, despite my thinking automobiles simply utilitarian devices for shifting people about, I spent a Sunday morning walking around the Great Court. The collection of cars was a miscellany, ranging from a 1903 De Dion to a 1986 Lamborghini, Sotheby's estimating that this last would sell for $220,000. I thought the Lamborghini ugly and impractical, lacking space for suitcases and children. Moreover, the car was so low that any people other than the supple young would need hoists to drop them into and extricate them from their seats.

Eliza took three small finger-size dolls with her to the Great Court: Mandy, Lisa, and Wendy. Although they looked carefully, none of the dolls found an automobile to buy. "They want to have babies," Eliza explained; "these cars would be fun to ride in. They would be all right for going to the beach, but you couldn't pack a family into one and take a trip." Francis and Edward selected favorite cars, Edward choosing a 1959 Goggomobile Dart, its sale price estimated at $10,000. Francis has more expensive taste, and he chose two cars, a red 1955 Jaguar XK140 Roadster and a 1950 Jaguar MKV Drophead Coupé, both cars estimated to bring $85,000 in the auction. Buying was contagious, and after overcoming my initial disdain, I picked up a red "1934 Rolls-Royce 20/25 hp Sportsmans Coupé." A woman who had ties with the Mafia in Melbourne once owned the car. The backseat was expansive, and in Connecticut I planned to use the car to cart Eliza to ballet in Lebanon and ferry Edward and his teammates to soccer games. I looked at people almost as much as I did at cars, trying to pick out high wheelers. Two types seemed to be car folk: burly, red-faced men wearing Akubras and then slender, narrow-lipped men wearing trousers with deep creases. The wives of both sorts were thin and tanned and rarely smiled.

In the morning sun the cars shone. Light bounced off chrome in silver constellations, luring the eye and blinding reason. I squinted and for a moment did not see greasy, functional blocks of steel. Instead I steered through stories, verbs purring like heavy tires, my crankcase dripping adjectives and adverbs as sweet as frankincense. The mood was brief. A family of kookaburras lived in the tropical grove at the edge of the Great Court. Throughout the morning they called back and forth. Just when a car shimmered into poetry, awakening covetousness and dissatisfaction with the Fords of ordinary life, the cries of the birds rose wobbling and distracting, resembling bubbles building up in then exploding down a drain in a gust, splattering walls with sound and fertile brown sense.

The poetry of earth is raucous and does not lilt and flow like the carriage of a "1952 Aston Martin DB2 Drophead Coupé." The poetry of earth rattles and bangs. Handles fall off doors; mufflers clatter to the asphalt; headlights blear and die. "Daddy, listen to the kookaburras," Eliza said taking my hand; "Wendy wants to know what they are saying." "They are saying," I answered, "that it is time to hop into the Toyota and drive into the country."

The next day we went to Waylunga National Park. We ate lunch beside Waylunga Pool. A large Italian family pulled three tables together and ate next to us. Francis told me they came in Holdens. After lunch we walked in the park. Little black cormorants perched on snags in the Swan River. White-faced herons hunted frogs in the shallows. A flock of black-and-white cockatoos shifted through wandoo along a hillside. Edward caught a trapdoor spider, and Francis saw a gray kangaroo and her joey. From the remains of a kangaroo Eliza salvaged a thigh bone for a back scratcher. On the way home I stopped at a vineyard and for fourteen dollars bought a watermelon, green grapes, and a dozen red peaches. In the newspaper that night I read that the Lamborghini did not sell.

Maybe I was too hard on the cars and the people who purchased them. But December was our fourth month in Perth. I had grown so comfortable that I had the leisure to become irritated. Vicki suggested a remedy for the irritation. "Have a heart attack," she said; "that'll stop it." At times I criticized schools. Rarely were Eliza and Edward assigned homework, and what work they had seemed too simple, in the fifth grade, for example, looking at sketches of clocks and telling time. Both children worried about falling behind classmates in Connecticut. "At the middle school in Storrs, I would be using a computer," Edward said; "here the class goes at the speed of the slowest student." The dress code at Francis's school was rigorous, and the campus was so neat the grass appeared starched. Yet bullying was common, often occurring in the presence of teachers. I learned that Francis had taken the place of a boy whose parents withdrew him from school because of bullying. "I can handle bullying," Francis said one night at dinner; "I just wish lessons were more difficult." Tempering my worries about school, however, was the realization that both Edward and Eliza had more friends in Perth than in Connecticut. In fact Edward wanted to stay in Australia.

"I like the sports," he said, "and you could send me to a school that was really tough. Then everything would be fine."

Behind my concern lay weariness. In the United States I gave many talks. To control the number I asked large fees. I was a guest in Australia, and initially when asked to speak I did not mention an honorarium. "Being allowed to come here for a year," I told Vicki, "is payment enough." "You are a paying guest," Vicki said. "There is nothing wrong with receiving money for work." During my first months in Perth I fashioned honorariums out of oddments. In a hotel lectern in Fremantle I found the "Agenda" for Deanne and Piero's wedding reception. At 5:50 P.M. guests were steered into the reception room. By 6:00 they were seated. Grace, I read, was said "on behalf of Pastor Rocky and his wife who couldn't be with us tonight."

Speculation about the doings of the Reverend Rocky and his family occupied my mind for thirty seconds, not so long as a bottle of wine would have entertained my palate, especially one, as a label put it, "with hints of melon and grapefruit enhanced by light oak treatment." Alas, the Agenda was all the payment I received that night. The week before Christmas a flood of requests to speak swept through mail and telephone, jolting me out of the sentimental. I decided to refuse speaking engagements that did not pay. Because the English department had been generous, I made an exception for the university, deciding to accept invitations that benefited the school, addressing, for example, the Friends of the Reid Library.

This past summer, rain was plentiful around Carthage, and the harvest was good. In October, Slubey Garts preached a sermon on being thankful. The sermon ended with a prayer. "Lord," Slubey said, "I want to thank You for the sun in June and July and all that rain back in the spring. The pastures were green, and the crops were bountiful everywhere between here and Red Boiling Springs except in a few fields not worth mentioning." My months in Perth have been lush. Worries have been few and not worth mentioning.

After the death of his sixth wife, Hink Ruunt pocketed the insurance money and took the express bus to Nashville. He rented a room in the Andrew Jackson Hotel and stayed there until his money ran out. Folks in Carthage did not know how Hink spent his days in Nashville, and speculation ran high. "Hink," Turlow Gutheridge said on seeing Hink sitting on a bench outside the courthouse, "I've heard some mighty peculiar stories about you." "Oh, shucks, Turlow," Hink said, "don't believe everything you hear. You can't credit more than half the lies told about me." My mood changes as I write. What I believe one day I disbelieve the next. "Leaving Perth is going to be difficult," Francis said last night; "I am going to miss Marcus and Andrew." "What about your studies," I said. "I am going to take a course in computer graphics next term," Francis said; "and I hear it is exciting."

In Connecticut people wear corduroy trousers, mittens, wool shirts, down jackets, and lined L. L. Bean boots in December. In Perth I wore short-sleeve shirts and cotton shorts. Perth was so warm that I rarely wore trousers, certainly not more than a legful of hours a week. I spent much of December searching for season. Magnolias blossomed around the Great Court, and on cool nights their fragrance blew along the ground, forming drifts of perfume. Gum trees shed bark and looked scrubbed. White and yellow petals twisted out from the thick, drab limbs of frangipani. An Alleluia of red trumpets burst from white kurrajong. Blossoms flowered in clusters on jarrah and red-flowering gum, making limbs resemble arms laden with packages wrapped in red-and-white papers. Norfolk Island hibiscus slipped quietly into bloom, its pink flowers warm stars. Chains of blue blossoms hung down from duranta, and illawarra flame trees exploded in scarlet sheets of bells, color leaping like angels singing.

Kings Park rose above Perth like a soft crumbling altar, paths resembling aisles leading up toward Mount Eliza, the land beneath kneeling and filling nave and chancel with life. Spring was pagan. Wildflowers burst through the bush in streams, blossoms spraying out in liquid profusion. Perth was built upon sand, and by the middle of December the extravagant pools of color had drained away. Spring intoxicated the sight, and vision wandered like thoughtless youth, unable to settle and examine. By December walking in Kings Park was a more sober experience. Many blossoms had folded inward to seed, and stalks had thinned, color ebbing and leaving them silver or brown in the dry light. Like mythological creatures turning through grains of dreamtime or candles shifting shadows across the walls of a cathedral, the blossoms of December snagged vision. Now instead of bobbing smoothly through the bush on a milky stream of color, sight tumbled, catching first on a fringe lily, the edges resembling beaded blue strings of ice, next spinning around yellow flatweed and swirling through smokebush billowed high like foam, then finally bumping through blue shallows, some of the blossoms slaty and sharp like flax lilies, others like slender lobelia soft as an evening gown.

Pixie mops unraveled resembling stuffing pushing through frayed pillowcases. A yellow autumn lily branched into a candelabra of blossoms. Above the flowers the leaves of a grass tree folded out and down, in the sunlight the green jittery and electric. The stems of Australian bluebells twitched upward nervously while *Scaevola paludosa* crept unobtrusively along the sand. In contrast Prince of Wales feather stood straight and jaunty with an almost aristocratic abandon, its sepals slender white cockades. Although shorter than Prince of Wales feather, pineapple bush pretended to stature. Its striving came to little, however, for its flower heads were doughy dirty-yellow balls, the stuff of garages and parking lots, not the parade ground.

Sometimes in December I had to search for flowers. When I found them, I examined them closely. Particularly appealing were narrow leaf mulla mulla and *Anthoceris illicifolia*, a plant that flourished after a bush fire. From the flowers of mulla mulla purple splinters jabbed out, catching bits of yellow and snarls of white wool. The blossoms of anthoceris resembled minute ornamental caps worn by court jesters. The brims were yellow and molded into stars, the cloth being gathered and sewed to form five points.

Many wildflowers were small, and while examining them I saw other things: grasshoppers speckled with rust and resembling twigs, and a yellow dragonfly perched on a flower stalk, black bands running down and across its body like stays. A caterpillar resembling a fat sunburned finger humped across a path. The middle of the path was lumpy, and the caterpillar slipped in the sand and rolled over in a curve. I picked the caterpillar up and hid it in scrub beneath yellow starflowers, so a bird would not get it. I leaned against a candle banksia and listened to a rufous whistler, its call a long whistle ending in a thump and vibration. A family of gray butcherbirds foraged through the bush. A magpie pecked at a dead rodent. The head and chest of the rodent were missing. But the meat was red and fresh, and the magpie seemed pleased with his portion of hind legs and innards. Beside an orange mound of semaphore sedges I found a skull. The skull was three and a half inches long. At the end of each side of the lower jaw a sharp tooth curved upward. I pulled one of the teeth out; it measured one and one-sixteenth of an inch. I gave the skull to Eliza for her collection of bones. "This is the skull of a rabbit," Eliza said. The skull was not the only present I brought home. Clipped to a twig were two plastic clothespins, one green, the other blue. I gave them to Vicki. "Part of your Christmas present," I said, "a gift from the bush."

Christmas in Perth was different from Christmas in Storrs. In Connecticut days are cold and short. Trees are bare, and the ground is muddy or covered with snow. In Connecticut, Vicki decorates rooms, creating a garden inside the house. To warm chilly evenings I mix drinks heavy with cream and eggs, and Vicki bakes sweet cakes. The winter stops people from roaming and pushes families together. The Christmas tree blooms in a festival of light, forcing spring through the dank and, to some people, depressing season. Presents are not only gifts but also emblems of the warm months ahead, April and May when trees unwrap themselves and bloom in bows. In Perth houses were not cold but warm. School let out for summer vacation, and Christmas was a time not of emotional consolidation but of expansion. Instead of drawing into themselves families spun outward, breaking up with individuals wandering through the vacation.

Rather than nurturing a garden inside the house, people in Perth cultivated the outside. In yards near our house hibiscus and oleander grew in tall bushy racks. From a distance the blossoms glowed like the china department of a department store, the flowers settings of Wedgwood and Coalport, Spode and Royal Doulton. Sunlight rained into morning glories, filling blossoms with blue. Violent trumpet vine hung over walls, fragrance pearling about the petals like hints of spirits about the rims of liqueur glasses. In Connecticut people weave dried herbs and wildflowers into wreaths. In Perth the scent of gardenia and jasmine turned through trellises above doors. Coral blossoms burst from the branches of shotia. Tipu dropped petals, turning sidewalks yellow, and agapanthus floated white and blue above yards. Clinging to fences and garages bougainvillea resembled cut glass, the new leaves mats of prisms, purple at one street corner, red at another.

Many transients had rented the house in which we lived. The first Christmas card to arrive in the mail was sent to M. K. Yoneda from NGK Insulators in the "Shin Marunouch Bldg." in Tokyo. Across the top of the card five tall spruce stood like fence poles. The trunks of the trees were dark blue and the leaves gold. In the distance behind the leaves glimmered the white specters of three dead trees. In the background mountains rolled in blue currents, clouds sliding down their summits and seeping into valleys. Above the mountains towered a pink volcano, Mount Fuji I assumed. "Season's Greetings and Best Wishes for the New Year," the card stated, first in English and then in Japanese.

No card mailed to Storrs reached Perth before the middle of January, and the cards we received at Melvista were odd. A stranger sent a card to John Pickering. Inside the card the man asked if I would be "doing any public speaking," adding afterward, "I am writing to state how much your Work has effected and inspired me! It has ignited a Purpose-a-Code, and I must thank you." I had never heard of such a code and wondered if my correspondent sent the card to the wrong Pickering. Still Vicki included it and the one to Mr. Yoneda on the string of fourteen cards she hung across the front of the fireplace. Most of the cards were from the children's classmates, Francis receiving five, more than anyone else.

We did not have a tree. The mother of one of Edward's teammates on the Dodgers wanted to lend us the sixteen-inch plastic tree she erected in her playroom each year. The offer was generous, but Vicki refused it, explaining to me, "Christmas is going to be dislocating enough without having to worry about someone else's property." Outside the house were many Christmas trees. Strings of colored bulbs had been wrapped around a Norfolk pine in Claremont, and throughout scrubby lots the West Australian Christmas tree bloomed, the tips of branches exploding into orange blossoms.

I mailed several cards to the United States. On the front of one card koalas decorated a gum tree, one bear wrapping red ribbons around the trunk, another hanging yellow glass bulbs on the limbs. Several ornaments already dangled from the tree: a holly wreath, a silver angel with yellow hair, a red candle in a green holder, and a small Santa Claus. On another card Santa Claus perched atop a roof, a bag containing striped candy canes and presents, including a stuffed koala, swelling above his back. A blue-and-yellow butterfly fluttered beside him while a limb from a red-flowering gum rose above his head like an umbrella. Behind the house the bush spread in a checkerboard of green and white.

Bundled in red wool, Santa Claus was the product of an imagination nurtured on snow and cold. During the week before Christmas the temperature reached 104 degrees, hot enough, as Turlow Gutheridge might have put it, to melt candle flame, hot enough for imagination to strip Santa Claus and dress him in "bathers," douse him with sunscreen, then transform his reindeer into dolphins and his sleigh into a surfboard. Perth was too hot for Santa Claus. He was a creature of New England, of fireplaces and elm trees, of icy blue days, and of a home in which presents could be moved from under the tree and stored in children's rooms.

Gifts the children received this year would be left in Perth when we returned to Connecticut. Our suitcases bulged when we arrived in Australia, and finding space for souvenirs would be difficult. Consequently Santa did not slide down our chimney. Vicki did not bake cookies for him, and I did not slice carrots for his reindeer. The children no longer believe in Santa Claus, but Vicki and I wanted them to believe, and his vanishing from December has lessened our imaginative lives, not theirs. When I hear bells tinkling under the stars and reindeer prancing on the roof, I remember nine years ago when Francis tottered down the stairs and, seeing presents under the tree, turned to me, his face radiant with joy, and exclaimed, "He came." Next Christmas, in Storrs, Francis will be thirteen, Edward eleven, and Eliza nine. No matter how we struggle to delude ourselves, Vicki and I know that after this year Santa Claus will have lost not simply our address but also the snug place he occupied in our imaginations.

Not until December did I really feel as if I was far from home. Adjusting to life in Perth took almost no mental effort. People spoke English and even looked like me, "only the men are not so handsome," I told Vicki. "You mean not so fat," Vicki answered, rubbing hand cream into her palms, "you have gotten so big from eating cake that you ought to be called cellulite." Despite hearing kookaburras rather than sleigh bells and the white in Christmas being sunlight instead of snow, Vicki decorated the house. Edward shredded plastic bags and made a wreath by stringing the shreds around a coat hanger that he bent into a circle. He wove red and gold ribbons through the shreds and from the top hung a tin Santa Claus he bought at Aherns Department Store. On the sides of the fireplace Vicki taped two of Eliza's school projects. The first was a drawing consisting of two candles, two Christmas trees lit by blue and yellow candles, and two presents, one wrapped in red paper and tied with a green ribbon, the other wrapped in green paper and tied with red ribbon. The second project was the head of a bushranger made from clay, then baked and painted. The man had a black mustache, a red nose, and blue eyes and wore a green stocking cap. A deep cut scored his left cheek, thick stitches across it resembling the legs of a centipede.

For her babies, the gang of twelve with whom she slept every night, Eliza decorated the gas heater in the living room. Across the top of the heater she laid a bed of peppermint leaves. In the bottom of a small plastic tub she spread fishbone ferns. On top of the ferns she put the green-and-yellow leaves of brush box. Amid them glittered nine ovals of colored glass, bought at Fremantle at The Pickled Fairy and Other Myths. Sticking out of the hole in the end of a yellow barrel-shaped pencil sharpener was a bouquet of leaves from *Virgilia*, or tree in a hurry. To the left of the plastic tub rested a large limpet. Lined with leaves from the lilly pilly by the front door, the shell resembled a low couch, the sort of furnishing found in a spare Scandinavian home. Amid the leaves dozed an angel wearing a blue jacket and a black beret. Eliza made the angel from clay. While the angel's arms and legs resembled damp hunks of chewing gum, its wings stuck out like the cauliflower ears of a professional wrestler. To the left of the angel stood a second pencil sharpener, this one a Christmas tree, according to Eliza, polygala leaves sprouting bushy from its end.

Scattered about the trunk of the tree were presents for the babies: a red papier-mâché rosebud; two beaded bracelets that Eliza made last summer at Camp Wohelo in Maine; a gold star cut out of a magazine; a rubber ankylosauraus, pink, three-quarters of an inch tall and two and a half inches long; a scallop shell; and a souvenir key chain bought in October at Cape Leeuwin. Behind the tree was a pile of "scrunchies." By pushing a doll's hair through the center of a scrunchy and pulling the scrunchy tight, a child could give a doll a ponytail hairdo. "I gave them to the babies even though none of them have long hair," Eliza explained; "I'll just hang the scrunchies on their ears." The babies' big presents were four dolls, made from cloths removed from the tops of jam jars. After folding the cloths in quarters, Eliza cinched rubber bands around their middles, creating slender bodices and lower bodies that billowed out in skirts. The dolls lacked heads, arms, and legs. Nevertheless, the babies would be thrilled with them, Eliza said, "because they have never had dolls and have always wanted them."

In Connecticut, Vicki puts a Swedish angelabra in the middle of the dining room table. Villages of biblical figures spring to life on tables, some of the inhabitants from Advent calendars, others from the attic, remnants of Christmases past, still others made by the children during holidays. Mangers of animals tread windowsills, not simply camels and donkeys but birds and cats, even a troop of mice dressed like elves in green velvet suits and pointed red hats. In Perth decorations were simpler. At school Edward made two panes for stained-glass windows, each ten inches wide and thirteen inches tall. He cut designs on black drawing paper. Over the designs he pasted colored translucent paper. Depicted in one pane was a present wrapped in red ribbon and blue paper, the ribbon tied in the shape of a heart. In the other pane a yellow flame flickered above a white candle. The candle was decorated. From its right side two green holly leaves flared out like wings; beneath them bulged a big red berry. Vicki taped the panes to one of the dining room windows. On the other window she pasted postcards made by Edward and Eliza. On the illustration of one card colored glass bulbs hung from a white Christmas tree. Under the tree were two presents. Behind the presents stood a red brick fireplace. From a window a stream of silver moonlight shone on the fireplace. Printed in capital letters across the top of the card was "MERRY CHRISTMAS," *Merry* in red, *Christmas* in white.

Vicki covered the round table in the dining room with a square tablecloth. Forming a circle in the middle of the tablecloth were the words *Wildflowers of Western Australia.* Eighteen different flowers bloomed around the border of the cloth, among others, primrose orchid, leschenaultia, and Sturt's desert pea. In the middle of the table Vicki set two glasses of water. Floating in each glass was a candle shaped like a stopper for a bathtub, one of the candles green, the other red. In Storrs, Christmas lunch always stretches through an afternoon and a groaning board of food: ham and turkey, oyster dressing, sweet potatoes, mincemeat and pumpkin pies. In past years we ate to warm ourselves. Afterward in defiance of the cold we took brisk walks. Perth was too warm for a big meal followed by a walk. Custom dies hard, however. The absence of Santa Claus was change enough for a season, so Vicki cooked a roast and made Yorkshire pudding. For dessert she served a Yule log, and despite the heat we ate two helpings. Afterward we went to Cottesloe Beach and swam to cool off.

Breaking habit was not easy for Australians either. Before Christmas, Kings, the local butcher, put a sandwich board outside the shop. Listed on the board was a banquet of holiday specials: both "Old English Style" and "Kings Famous Champagne Hams"; rolled pork, "a boneless loin or shoulder of lean pork filled with fresh apples, apricots, prunes, fresh parsley, ground imported peppers and herbs"; and then a flock of turkey platters, the one I wanted to taste being turkey ballentine, "a free range chicken boned and placed inside a boneless free range duck which is placed inside a boneless turkey." All the cavities, the board declared, were "then filled with your choice of seasoning or your own tasty fillings."

Christmas day passed smoothly. After the swim I opened the game of *Scrabble* I bought the children and taught them how to play. Later Edward read *The Murder on the Links,* a Hercule Poirot mystery, Ed-. ward's latest book project being to read all Agatha Christie's novels. Francis started another of Isaac Asimov's science fiction stories, and Eliza retired to her room and shut the door. Later when I kissed her good-night, I noticed an infirmary by her bed, a shoe box containing the babies. Bound by a rubber band to some part of each baby—arm, leg, head, stomach—were bandages made from toilet paper. "They were playing follow the leader," Eliza said, "and Kitty tripped and all the other babies fell on her and hurt themselves. The doctor told them they have to stay in the hospital tonight. Tomorrow he will let them go home."

Because Santa's bag wasn't full this year, shopping was easy. I bought my present at the university bookstore, *The Heritage of Western Australia,* "The Illustrated Register of the National Estate." A large paperback, *The Heritage* cost $26.95 and contained pictures of places in Western Australia that have "aesthetic, historic, scientific, or social significance." At Creative Native in downtown Perth, Vicki bought herself two presents, one from me, the other from the children: a T-shirt across the front of which swam a crocodile and a big snake, then hand-painted earrings made from dried seedpods shaped like new moons. Vicki and I spent two days in downtown Perth. The shopping could have been accomplished in a morning, but since vacation had begun we needed to fill the children's hours. Moreover, because Storrs is small, we enjoyed being in the city. We ambled through shops and arcades. We sat on benches in the sun and watched buskers: a man on stilts manipulating a puppet, a boy playing a Chinese flute, a blind girl playing a piano, Salvation Army singers, and a jazz band composed of middle-aged men.

For their presents the boys selected books then shirts with Australian plants and animals printed on the fronts. In the Piccadilly Arcade, Eliza picked out a doll. She named the doll Clarabell. Clarabell has a porcelain head, blue eyes, and blond stovepipe curls. She likes clothes made from silk and lace and today is wearing a pale blue bonnet with a spiderweb of filigree around it. Her lips are big and red, and her nose turns up slightly like a ski jump. Despite her fashionable appearance, Clarabell is intelligent. Last night I found her standing on Eliza's desk facing the wall. "Clarabell is thinking about a story," Eliza explained, "and she does not want to be distracted. When she looks at the wall, she doesn't hear the noise the boys make, and characters in the story appear on the wall almost as if they were in a movie." "What is Clarabell's story about?" I asked. "Moon," Eliza answered, "an eight-year-old girl who is studying to be a witch. The story is about all the silly mistakes she made."

We munched through the two days downtown. Because children are more conservative than adults, especially in culinary matters, lunches and dinners were greasy, lumpy affairs eaten in food halls between the Hay and Market Street Malls. The second night the children chose to eat in Kentucky Fried Chicken. I missed dinner. In truth I did not need to eat. Once or twice each day Vicki and I parked the children in bookstores and raced off to cafés to drink cappuccinos and eat cakes. The second night downtown we saw a "nativity story" in Forest Chase, the large open plaza between the Post Office and Myers Department Store. The City of Perth sponsored the story. Students from the Johnny Young Talent School acted while the Perth Christian Choir and Orchestra played and sang. I bought the children ice cream cones, and we sat in folding chairs and watched the performance. The actors stood on a raised stage on the Wellington Street end of Forest Chase. Actually the entire plaza resembled a stage, shoppers themselves actors and the Christmas decorations the set. On the front of the Post Office hung five huge green wreaths. Suspended from the walkway behind and to the left of the choir was a giant Christmas card. On it a candle rose out of a mound of holly and red ribbon. To the right of the candle were the words *Seasons Greetings from Your City of Perth*. Attached to the lights that illuminated the plaza were big boards, some with Merry Christmas printed on them in gold, others bright with white candles on red backgrounds.

On the stage Joseph and Mary stood in a manger golden with straw. The production was a miscellany, blending the traditional and the new. Six goats drifted through the manger. A small army of Roman soldiers marched across the plaza. Diminutive Arabs gathered in garrulous knots, and the three kings appeared riding donkeys. Mary also rode a donkey, but her donkey balked at the steps leading onto the stage, so Joseph helped her into the manger. The choir sang "Little Town of Bethlehem," "The First Noel," "O Come All Ye Faithful," "Hark the Herald Angels Sing," and "Silent Night." While Joseph and Mary sang rock songs, dancers from the Talent School gyrated. A group from the school also sang a rap version of "We Three Kings of Orient Are," chanting " O star of wonder, / star of night, / Star with royal beauty bright; / Westward leading, / Still Proceeding, / Guide Us to thy perfect light." I liked the performance, and for a moment I imagined immigrating to Australia. I enjoy Christmas stories. I think all religions, including Christianity, to be superstitions, and superstitions when they are believed can be cruel, not just dividing man from man and shattering society but fragmenting the world itself. I was raised an Episcopalian, a church in which doctrine matters less than decorum. Never zealots and mindful of others, Episcopalians are social, not religious, creatures. In Forest Chase, though, I felt at home. Doctrine did not matter; community did.

Words, of course, do matter, more when they are spoken than when they are sung, however. Earlier in December, Vicki and the children and I went to "Carols by Candlelight," held in the sunken garden at the university. The congregation sat on the stone seats around the amphitheater. At the bottom of the garden were a small lawn and a pool of lilies. Above the seats a wreath of shrubs wrapped around the amphitheater. Families attended the carols. Some people brought hampers and ate dinner on the lawn while their children darted through the shrubs playing hide-and-seek. Volunteers from local churches handed each person a candle and a sheet of eleven carols. Nine of the carols were familiar, songs such as "Once in Royal David's City," "While Shepherds Watched," and "Good King Wenceslas."

The two carols that I didn't recognize were Australian. In one stockmen hailed Christmas morning as they rode on horseback. In the other a congregation sang hymns in a town in the outback, red dust blanketing houses, sparrows nesting under eaves, and the grass in paddocks brown and dry. I looked forward to singing under the stars of wonder. Unfortunately gusts of wind kept blowing out the candles, making the night silent not only when people tried to sing the Australian carols but also when they sang the less familiar third and fourth verses of old standbys like "Joy to the World" and "The First Noel." The wind was so strong that children turned keeping their candles lit into a game and paid little attention to the carols. "Not once," Francis said at the end of the evening, "did my candle go out. I put it on the ground between my legs and took my shoes off and built a wind break around it."

"Daddy," Eliza said, "the speaker wasn't very good. Twice he said, 'between you and I.' " In part the children spent the evening fiddling with their candles because the speaker talked down to them. He reduced religion to the vernacular of advertising and fast-food restaurants, making it seem unimportant. Christ, he said, "was no wimp." For some reason he tried to explain the concept of virgin birth. When Joseph discovered that Mary was pregnant, the speaker recounted, he considered divorcing her. "Oh, Lord," I prayed silently, "let him talk about goodwill and brotherhood, anything but virgin birth, even Santa Claus." My prayer was answered. "I am the last one to knock Santa Claus, but," the speaker began. At the beginning of his talk the man recounted an incident that happened to him during an earlier speech.

When he started to speak, he said, an insect flew down his throat, and he choked and was forced to stop talking. "Bugs," I muttered under my breath, "you are needed again." Like Isaiah I invoked a plague of bugs: roaches, grasshoppers, dung beetles, any of the larger orders would do. Alas, despite the wind the insect creation remained earthbound.

When I left the garden, I felt guilty. "Faith, hope, and charity," I said silently, "and the greatest of these is charity." "What happened to my charity?" I asked Vicki. "Buried under a thick sludge of everyday words," she replied. I wanted the children to experience joy. The carol service disappointed me, and so I led the family across Whitfield Court. Light shone on Winthrop Hall. The limestone resembled a honeycomb, gold dripping from it, flowing into the reflecting pool, rippling around two ducks, black as pearls. "Smell the magnolias," I said, as we walked past the Great Court; "if Jesus had been born in Virginia, one of the wise men would have carried magnolias to the manger rather than myrrh." "Yes," Edward said, "and if He had been born in Connecticut, the wise man would have taken baskets of daffodils." "In Perth," Eliza added, "the wise man would have carried boughs of banksia."

On December 23 I took Vicki and the children to the Festival of Nine Lessons and Carols at St. George's Cathedral. Aside from christenings the children had never attended a service in a church. I wanted them to hear the organ and see beauty in the bricks. I wanted them to appreciate pageantry and stained-glass windows. For my part I hoped that the festival would dull the edge of criticism and make me more charitable. I hoped the experience would replicate the Advent Festival. It didn't. Because I wanted the children to enjoy the ceremony I hovered over them. Instead of listening to the lessons I watched Eliza and Edward. When a tall man sat in front of Eliza blocking her view, I picked her up. When Francis stopped singing, I shifted seats and moving next to him shared his booklet of carols. Driving home that evening I realized that I had missed the festival. "Not only that," I thought, "I made the children nervous and ruined the service for them." "No, you didn't," Vicki said later, telling a Christmas lie; "the festival was beautiful, and we loved it."

In Connecticut excitement saps the children's energies, and on Christmas Eve they fall asleep by eight-thirty. In Perth with no surprises in store and no parents pretending to believe in Santa Claus, Christmas seemed but another day in the summer vacation. As a result the children stayed up late on Christmas Eve and watched a movie on television, *Ice Station Zebra,* a silly film about espionage and conflict in the Arctic. In Storrs the children play with their presents for days after Christmas. In Perth the day after Christmas also seemed ordinary, and the children moped about the house.

To fill the hours I took the family to Ascot. The Western Australian Turf Club Derby was being run. Neither Vicki nor I had been to a horse race before. We carried a picnic lunch and, sitting on the grass, ate bread and cheese, carrots, potato chips, radishes, and for dessert lumps of dark chocolate. Afterward we sat in the grandstand and watched the races. For every race the children selected winners. I bet a dollar on each of their selections, a total of three dollars a race. They picked horses named Fairly Ugly, El Cordero, Fianna, Regimental Tattoo, City Jewel, Gypsy Chimes, Serene Jungle, and What a Maze. I only bet once for myself, and that was on a horse named Sammy the Bull. He won, and I pocketed $3.20. In the last race the family won big. Francis's pick, Squeak, paid $6.70. At the end of the day our losses totaled $11.30, not much to pay for entertaining three children.

We spent the last week of December wandering bush near Perth. One morning we walked around Thompsons Lake. We planned to eat lunch by the lake, but the Department of Conservation and Land Management had set poisoned bait out for foxes. Along the water's edge we found two dead rabbits and five dead long-necked tortoises. Before we left the lake, the children draped the bodies on top of the sign warning people about the bait. We ate lunch near Fremantle in the park by Manning Lake. Afterward we played wood tag. The next morning Vicki's thighs ached, and she did not want to get out of bed. Yesterday I drove to Fred Jacoby Park in the Hills Forest. After a picnic lunch we hiked up the Portagabra Trail into the bush. Smooth grevillea, baeckea, and bluebell creeper bloomed. Jarrah blossomed, and grass trees shimmered in the light, greens and yellows flowing through the leaves then seeming to rise in hot halos above the plants. Along the trail hips of granite crooked out from the Darling Scarp. Amid the bush big boulders sat lonely, resembling massive balls torn from bone and socket and tossed randomly across the hills. Near the top of the ridge laterite speckled the ground turning the trail red. A splendid fairy wren hunted through grass in a dry streambed. In the heat the wren resembled a fist of cool water. A flock of New Holland honeyeaters chattered amid brush, yellow from their wings flickering between leaves like lights being turned on and off. A female red-tailed black cockatoo clutched a bare limb on a dead gum, her long tail a shutter of yellow and black bars. Crawling along Vicki's forearm was a kangaroo tick, big as the nail on my little finger.

After the walk I drove to Mundaring Weir Hotel. Built in 1898, the hotel clung like an outcrop of granite to a hillside above the dam. When we arrived, a bush band was playing country music, and a lamb turned on a spit. On a patio that dropped down the slope in steps people ate and drank: bikers in leather, grandmothers in light blue dresses, and families, the parents in shorts, partly because the day was hot but also because chasing children was easier in shorts than trousers. Fat dripped from the lamb, but the picnic lunch filled me. At the entrance to the bar inside the hotel a white-haired man sat behind a table. In front of him were fruit from his orchard and jam made by his wife. For three dollars I bought a cardboard box top rolling with peaches. For two dollars Vicki bought a bag containing thirty-eight apricots. She also bought jars of tomato relish, apricot chutney, and passion-fruit-and-peach jam, the three jars costing eight dollars.

From rambles in the bush I brought home a spicy assortment of inedibles. On my desk now are cones of bull and firewood banksia, the follicles gapping, sixty-eight on the bull banksia. Seed cones of Fraser's sheoak resemble small wooden casks. The surface of the cones is lumpy, and on the ground they resemble animal droppings. A seed lurks in each lump, spilling out when the lumps open like wooden shutters, a typical cone containing thirty-five seeds. The seeds are three-eighths of an inch long and are shaped like soft handheld fans. The handle of the fan is a swollen bundle of seed. Above the bundle trails a clear broad wing, a reddish strut running through the center. Dropped on white paper, a handful of seeds resembles a group of newly hatched tadpoles or a school of baby fish. The cones of dune sheoak are slender and more delicate. The shutters open in rows, and the cone appears cultivated, almost as if a salesman in a trendy store polished it. Only rarely does polish, social or educational, seep below the surface, and the wings of the seeds are shorter than those of Fraser's sheoak, making the seeds appear stubby and giving them the appearance of rude vitality.

Dark and warty with lumps of resin resembling fatty tissue, the cones of Rottnest Island pine seem nondescript until they open. Six valves compose each cone, and when they open like a tight fist being pried apart, crinkled red seeds tumble out. I counted sixty-four seeds in one cone. Stacked in a pile, the seeds resemble flakes of rock candy. From the sides of seeds, wings wrinkle out in waves. When the seeds are dropped from a height, the wings catch the air and the seeds twirl. Spilling into the bottom of a box on the desk are seeds from several common trees, large-fruited mallee and mottlecah among others. Marri seeds appear cooked, resembling minute red strips of jerky. The seeds of brush box curve like small yellow bananas. Spread across the bottom of the box, the seeds resemble spices, making days seem exotic. The heavy fruit of an illyarrie has just begun to open, a thin line splitting the bottom of the nut into a smile. Seeds have dropped out from the fruits of the Rottnest teatree, blowing into the web of a small spider living between the wall and the upper-right-hand corner of the desk. On a shelf lie pods from orange wattle and violet trumpet vine. Beside them is a twig cut from hairy yellow pea, the fruits resembling the egg sacs of spiders and almost translucent in strong light. A fruit from snail hakea lies on its side split into halves, each half an oval of black with an eyelash of white curving above it, resembling the eye of an Egyptian priestess painted on a tomb at Luxor. I can't explain why I brought the seeds home. They seem marvels. Nothing man has designed can match the lovely intricacy of a single seed. I suppose having seeds in front of me makes me imagine that I am part of the flow of life, not of traffic whispering along asphalt, but of December's vitality, of time's biological stream. I wish I could plant the seeds in Connecticut. Not only would planting them be against the law, however, but even if they sprouted, December would kill them.

"Daddy," Eliza said this morning, "why do you have all those seeds on the desk? Are you writing about them?" "Yes," I answered. "Daddy," Eliza continued, "do you think people will want to read about seeds, and you will become famous when you are dead?" "Yes," I said, "and how is Moon? Is she learning to be a witch?" "Yes," Eliza said, "although Moon is mischievous and sometimes upsets her mother, Wrinkle.

Let me read you chapter two." "One day," Eliza began, "Moon heard Wrinkle reciting some spells from *50 Spells* by Merlin. When Wrinkle was done and gone, Moon crept in and grabbed the book. She could hardly carry it, but somehow she managed to get it to her room. Thunder, her cat, was there as usual and decided to help Moon. Moon was having trouble with the first spell. With much difficulty she had gotten her feet invisible. Then her legs, tummy, arms, neck, and finally her head. Just then the bell rang for lunch. When she reached the dining room, Wrinkle had already sat down. 'Mom, what's for lunch?' asked Moon. 'Where are you!' shouted Wrinkle. 'I'm invisible,' said Moon. 'I am going to get you,' screamed Moon's Mom. It took her four days to catch Moon and one day to break the spell. So ends this experience of Moon." "Did you like it?" Eliza said when she finished reading. "I loved it," I said. "Good," Eliza said; "when I finish writing I am going to illustrate the story with pictures and give it to you as a late Christmas present." "Oh," I said, "what a Christmas. What a wonderful Christmas."

Waiting for School

Summer begins in Connecticut in June, and the children go to camp in Maine. In Perth summer started in December, and the children stayed home. "You should go on a trip," my friend Nigel said; "take the family some place exotic." "A trip!" I exclaimed; "this is our trip. I haven't come halfway around the globe to go somewhere else. I'll find things for the children to do in Perth." Discovering activities was easy. Keeping the children occupied, however, kept me so busy that carpe diem became coffee diem. In the morning Edward and Eliza took lessons at the Nedlands Tennis Club. Every afternoon all three children swam, sometimes in the community pool at the primary school but usually at Cottesloe Beach. During summers while I attended college, I was a counselor at the camp the boys attend in Maine. Rarely did Vicki accompany us to the beach. "This is a chance to regain your youth," she said one afternoon, settling into a low chair, shoes off, legs high on a stool, and newspaper in her lap, "seize the day." I bought the children boogy boards, diminutive surfboards three feet six inches long and twenty-three inches wide. While the children paddled behind waves, occasionally catching breakers, I bodysurfed. I imagined losing weight. I didn't. Only by eating could I keep up with the children, and so I ate mountains of soft ice cream, often "double chocs," scoops of vanilla ice cream dipped into hot dark chocolate, or "snowballs," double chocs rolled in coconut.

One afternoon I found a wallet in the surf. The wallet contained one hundred and five dollars, and I gave it to a lifeguard. We often find wallets. Just before we left Connecticut Vicki found a wallet in Eastwood Road. The wallet contained four hundred dollars. A woman put the wallet on the roof of her car while she unlocked the car door. She forget the wallet, leaving it on the roof while she drove to the grocery. Reaching the woman took a day, but we returned the wallet. Two weeks ago I took Vicki and the children to Bookland, so Francis could purchase supplies for the new term at John XXIII. I drove downtown with the passkey to the English department in my pocket. When I started to lock the car outside Bookland, I discovered the key. While I drove back to the university, Vicki found a wallet on the curb outside Bookland. The wallet contained a vacation of money. Vicki rummaged through the wallet and, finding a business card, discovered that the wallet belonged to the manager of Bookland.

When I returned from the university, Vicki stood waiting on the curb. In one hand she held a plastic bag full of Francis's books, in the other a brown sack containing a bottle of Andrew Garrett's N.V. Pinot Noir, selling for $14.95, I discovered that afternoon at the local spirit shop. "When I returned the wallet, the manager gave me the wine," Vicki explained; "I was embarrassed and didn't want to take it, but he insisted. I suppose it is left over from a Christmas party." "We'll drink it on your birthday," I said; "we will toast honesty and teach the children a lesson." Actually the children were extraordinarily honest. What they needed was not a lesson in honesty but one in appreciation, appreciation for the hours I spent filling them and their days with ice cream and swimming. Instead of courses in parenting, social agencies should teach "childing." Social workers should pound good manners into the little beasts and, instead of making children feel smug about their savage ignorance, teach them to make their parents feel good, giving parents, as educational philosophers phrase it, "positive self-images."

Surroundings influence mood. I would not be hard on the children if I hadn't talked to Nigel yesterday. Recently the Agricultural Protection Board released statistics on the feral animal "cull" for 1993. The *West Australian* published the figures. Above the article was a purple sketch of a "helicopter carrying marksmen in donkey shoot." In West Australia the board culled 412,711 goats, 28,318 donkeys, 4,448 starlings, 1,450 wild horses, and 455 camels. "Good Lord," Nigel exclaimed, "do you realize that is 1,130 goats a day, 47 goats an hour, 24 hours a day, 365 days a year with no time off for holidays or to eat, make love, or piss. Either administrators at the board are the world's biggest liars or they are maniacs diving out of the sky with machine guns blazing." "Well," I began, but Nigel interrupted. "Seventy-five donkeys a day," Nigel said, "and these dumbbells think they are accomplishing something. The real feral animals in this country are people. Think what a bulldozer can do in a single day at Mandurah. If the bureaucrats were really concerned about nature, they'd shoot bulldozers and leave camels alone. If you want to see what man has made of nature go to Kalgoorlie."

Once Nigel started, he was difficult to stop. "Go south," he shouted, "and see what is happening to the trees. Environmental experts are turning forests into sand dunes, shredding trees hundreds of years old into wood chips and selling them to Japan so the Japanese can print newspapers none of the ignoramuses in this country can read." "But," I said tentatively; "people can be educated to do better." "Humbug," Nigel said, "think about America. You have more universities than we have goats. Every dingo in the United States has a degree, yet what good does all that education do. While you wring your hands over the plight of rain forests in Brazil, politicians turn logging companies loose in the Pacific Northwest. West Australians are the new Americans. If a West Australian discovered a beam in his eye, do you know what he would do?" Nigel asked. "No," I answered. "Hellfire," Nigel said, pounding the table with his fist, "he'd wedge the beam out and sell it to Japan for lumber."

"Read this last paragraph," he continued, handing me the clipping from the *West Australian*; "it's a statement by the chairman of the protection board." "It is difficult to get to the last lot of breeding animals," the man said, "but it is important just to bring the numbers down." "The bugger is dead on," Nigel said, snatching the clipping out of my hand; "we'll never get the last lot of feral humans. But, by God, right-thinking people ought to try to bring the number of breeders down, using all means available, not just helicopters armed with howitzers. I am doing my part, trying to breed tiger snakes to kangaroos. If snakes in this country could hop, then the population would drop. Turn a few snakaroos loose in Dalkeith and Peppermint Grove, and all that tarty palaver about yachts and the America's Cup would dry up overnight." "How," I said, not sure where I should begin, "how is the breeding coming along?" "Pretty well," Nigel said, "for a while I tried to mate death adders and kangaroos, but the damn things kept coming out backwards with snake bodies and kangaroo heads and the nouveau-riche in Claremont wanted to buy them for pets. Now, though, I've got some really comely kangaroos and a pit full of handsome, vigorous tiger snakes, and things are looking up. Just yesterday a female kangaroo laid a batch of eighteen eggs."

Nigel lives in Perth, and city life may be responsible for his bite. Nigel would be happier if he lived in a smaller town. Perth is a beautiful and gentle city. Still, its influence on me has not been good. Storrs is not classless, but material differences between people are not so great as they are in Perth. Few houses are mansions, and shops are inclusive rather than exclusive. The wealth of Perth corrupts, not necessarily its possessor so much as its beholder. In January, Vicki and the children and I wandered the beach along the Swan River foreshore. Reddish crabs hid under stones, and jellyfish washed through seaweed in silvery plumes. Sails blinked like butterflies above windsurfers. In the sun limestone bluffs were buttery. Silver gulls bobbed in the water, and pied cormorants hunched like gargoyles at the ends of jetties. While walking I tried to look at the sand or out over the water. Often, though, I stared landward, coveting the big houses atop the bluffs. Not only were the houses above me, but they were also beyond my wallet, and I became resentful, quick to condemn owners as common. Instead of cleansing the spirit, walks along the foreshore soiled, making me long for a whiff of lemon-scented gum, feral donkeys or camels, anything natural to distract me from money and to interest me in goods more enduring than plaster and tile.

Resisting covetousness is difficult, particularly in a city where environment is manufactured, almost all elements of which are for sale. Instead of land stretching to the horizon, a house, something that one could conceivably possess, blocks sight. In the bush a person realizes he is small, no more than a sliver of bone or a tangle of root. He realizes that he is not so much the shaper of a life as a creature shaped by life, and if he is not a visionary, one of those deluded people blinded by partial truths, then he can escape the acquisitive self and become a steward. Then he can live richly, the walls of his mansion papered with sky-blue hovea, the molding white plume grevillea, and the lighting woolly orange banksia.

"Sitting in this room," Vicki said one day as the children banged in and out of the house, "is like sitting in a bus station." With the children stirring about like a crowd, I occasionally purchased a ticket to Carthage, a country place far from shore and mansion. Recently I arrived on Sunday. Slubey Garts was finishing a sermon at the Tabernacle of Love. Slubey had reached the peroration. His lips fluttered like lettuce. Sweat tumbled off his brow in itchy bales, and he thumped the pulpit, rumbling and gasping, sounding like a combine with rusty ball bearings. "These ain't paper words," he shouted; "these here are lung and tongue words, bone and groan words. If you don't listen to what I'm saying, you'll end down in that hot place where the birds carry jugs of water when they fly. When you open your mouth to breathe, your teeth will get sunburned. Listen to me because I'm bringing you cornbread baked in the oven of righteousness, baked from self-rising flour. What are you going to sop up with it, pot likker and damnation or the blood of the lamb and salvation? Oh, you wayfarers, you chickens of the church," Slubey continued, "you've got to know what you been pecking at. If you have been pulling up worms of sin, you are headed for the frying pan—drumstick and bosom, all of you is going to swim in the Crisco. To stop sinning you have to know yourself," Slubey said, pausing, his left eye shut and his right eye half-closed, the lower part of the eyeball fixing the congregation and glowing white like a scythe. "What I want to know," Slubey continued, suddenly slapping the pulpit, his eyes popping open wide as grapefruit, "is who do you think you are. Who are you?"

Just before Slubey said these last three words the door of the church opened, and a man and a woman and two children entered. "Why aren't you so nice to ask?" the man said, seeing Slubey gazing in his general direction. "I heard tell folks in Carthage were mighty neighborly. I'm Knuckly Royal, but all my friends call me Rime. This here to my right is my beloved wife, Sestina, and these two little sugars are our babies, the darling girl, Verse, and this sweet icing of a boy, Heroic Couplet, or H.C. as some of our friends who don't appreciate poetry call him. We've just moved to Carthage from Crab Orchard. I'm going to work as a clerk over at Barrow's Store, specializing in fruits and paper products. You come and see me, and I'll do right by you. Sestina is a fashion manicurist. If any of you fine ladies need work done on your lovely hands, just you come and visit. We've rented a house over on Chickadee. It ain't big or fancy, but it's our little dovecote, and we've hung some new pink curtains up in the parlor. There is always a place at the kitchen table for someone suffering from a hangnail. In no time Sestina will have you fixed up and tapping out 'Little David' on the Formica."

The appearance of the Royals and Rime's address ended the church service. Only once before had Slubey broken down in a sermon. During a storm a tremendous thunderclap exploded over the church rattling windows, knocking over the stand holding the American flag and so stunning Slubey that he lost his train of thought. He kept his wits, though. When the congregation settled back into the pews and looked up, expecting him to continue, Slubey raised his arms and said, "When God speaks, man must hold his peace." Two days later at the funeral of Maybird Barkis, Slubey redeemed himself, sucking, as Proverbs Goforth put it, all the stops out of his mouth organ. Maybird had flown the earthly coup prematurely, dying at eight years old.

"The Lord," Slubey said, "unraveled her thread of life so the pretty bud could bloom in Canaan in that garden with alabaster birdbaths, no fat naked boys on top of them spouting water out of their nasties, only angels flapping their silver wings, fanning zephyrs into lullabies. Maybird has gone," Slubey said, "with glory shining about her like the amber around that mosquito what most of you saw at the Mighty Haag Circus last week. She's walking barefoot on the golden streets, not worrying about hookworm. She's drinking nectar and eating turnip greens and sweet potatoes, not giving a thought to typhoid or pellagra. At the Male and Female Select School here in Carthage, Maybird had trouble with reading and arithmetic. Angels teach her now, and she's an A-plus student. She can figure the hypotenuse and square roots unto the third and fourth generations past the decimal point without counting once on her fingers."

Slubey was a religious entrepreneur. Not only did he own the Tabernacle of Love, Haskins Funeral Home, and the Pillow of Heaven Cemetery, but this past fall he began manufacturing pine coffins. Proverbs Goforth made the coffins, and Isom Legg painted them, not simply brown or black but "for the glory of God and the big white eyes of Jesus," as Proverbs put it. Customers specified what they wanted on their coffins. Maybird's coffin was simple. A pink lily bloomed in a dry, brown field. From the center of the lily six streams of yellow pollen shot upward, at the top of each stream a silver star.

For people not certain what decoration they wanted, Isom painted one of his standards. He had two favorites. In the first Jacob's ladder poked up through clouds from the top of a blue hill. Wearing the clothes in which he was buried, the deceased stood half-turned on the third rung of the ladder, smiling and waving good-bye with his left hand, his right holding an expensive leather suitcase. The second painting was more ornate. In a manger a baby sat upright in a crib, the manger, Turlow Gutheridge said, looking remarkably like Hink Ruunt's tobacco barn. While the child held a golden harp in his pudgy hands, wings unfolded from his back, stretching and drying like those, Turlow said, on a doodlebug that crawled onto a cattail and split its shell. Isom borrowed a photograph of the corpse before starting to paint, and the baby's face resembled that of the newly departed. Clustered around the crib were animals, not animals native to the Holy Land but good Smith County animals: a skunk frolicking with a possum, a squirrel tossing nuts to a raccoon, a rat balancing on one leg while standing on the back of a cat, then assorted pedigreed sheep and goats, and finally a mule, this last a dead ringer for Loppie Groat's Jeddry.

Despite the effort Isom put into the two paintings, most Smith Countians ordered personalized coffins. For his casket Boy Tupper ordered a portrait of his prize Angus bull, "Big Balls from Nashville." When her aunt Miss Mabel Campbell, the town librarian, died, Clotilla Jaxson ordered a coffin decorated with a picture of her aunt at work. Sitting at a reinforced table in the library, Miss Mabel mended the stone tablets on which the Ten Commandments were carved. She used gold to repair the tablets. By her right hand stood a mortar filled with yellow liquid, tiny angels fluttering over it like flies hovering above something unpleasant. On the shelf behind Miss Mabel's head was a row of books: volumes of Matthew, Mark, Luke, and John; four annual reports of the Eastern Star, accounts of the years during which she had been Corresponding Secretary; Sir Walter Scott's *Lady of the Lake*; the poems of Felicia Hemans and Lydia Sigourney; Hannah More's *Sacred Dramas*; and Miss Mabel's favorite children's book, Jean Webster's *Daddy Long-Legs*. Resembling barbells and holding the books upright were two busts: that of Isaac Watts to the right; on the left, Robert E. Lee.

Not long before she died Miss Mabel wrote me and suggested that I read *Daddy Long-Legs*. In January, I borrowed the book from the Nedlands Public Library. In the book an orphan wrote letters to a mysterious benefactor, a man whom she had seen once, from a distance noting only that his legs were long and thin. I read the book in a sitting. The story made me feel so good I read the book again the next day. The tale lifted my spirits, and as I walked to the university, I greeted strangers on the sidewalk. I whistled, and once or twice I skipped. If truth must out, I am tired of meaningful literature. Instead of making me appreciate life, such writing often horrifies and leads me to lock doors. "You don't need a big house," Miss Mabel wrote; "read *Daddy Long-Legs*. The story will warm the cockles of your heart and make you want to help others. When that low-down Slubey Garts climbs onto a stump and begins to preach about pagans and Catholics, I always quote Corinthians to him: 'though I speak with the tongues of men and of angels, and have not charity, I am become as sounding brass, or a tinkling cymbal.' If Slubey spent more time reading books like *Daddy Long-Legs*, he would be a better man. I doubt, though, that he would be such a successful preacher."

One day we spent a morning at the Sardine Festival on the Esplanade in Fremantle. Around the edge of the green, tents rose in colored waves: red, blue, orange, and white, making the park seem medieval, the host to a jousting tournament. A rope swayed upward, fifteen kites shaped like fish tugging it, the mouths of the fish open wide and air blowing through them. From a platform near the railway tracks the Fatts Band played rock and roll, the lead singer, Slim Jim, stopping in the middle of "I ain't got no satisfaction" to hold up a small boy and say, "Carlos, please claim your child." A clown with a bulbous nose rode a unicycle through the crowd. Another clown danced on stilts. He wore a black cap with earflaps, a yellow-and-green coat, a brown T-shirt, and red-and-black trousers. He painted his face white and his lips scarlet. Perched on his nose were sunglasses, the lenses narrow green rectangles. In the sky a stubby white airplane pulled a banner reading "Windsor Hotel."

A busker stood on the sidewalk beside Marine Terrace and played bagpipes. The sides of his head were shaved; the top was spiked and dyed blond; and a ponytail swayed down his neck. He wore green boots, black socks, a black vest, and a kilt, the design on this last the MacClaren plaid. A heavy sporran hung in front of the kilt. A big silver cross dangled from a chain around his neck. On his left wrist was a cheap digital watch. A tattoo flowed across his right shoulder and washed down his side and arm. Red goldfish with moonlike eyes curved through streams of green seaweed. Tattoos were common in Western Australia, and at the festival the children collected a menagerie: lions; tigers, one leaping from a rock onto a wildebeest, another tossing a ball in the air; panthers; eagles almost all with bunting in their mouths; crocodiles; snakes, mostly cobras and pythons; and one heavy rhinoceros, blue oozing out of his body, gradually turning him into a moldy lump of ink. The boy played the bagpipes well, and I gave him fifty cents after he played "Amazing Grace." Instead of shattered knights and lances, the tents along the Esplanade sheltered platters of food: yabbies, "W.A. Buffalo," rock lobster, "Gourmet Emu," trout burgers, bratwurst, mussels, octopus, "Seafood Pansatti with cream and chives," and arancini, dough baked in the shape of a pear with, in the middle, rice surrounding a muscle of chicken and peas. Francis, Vicki, and I ate sardine burgers, and Edward and Eliza ate ravioli.

One morning I returned two of the T-shirts Vicki bought the boys for Christmas. Stamped across the chests were ovals depicting *Xanthorrhoea preissii*, common in the bush around Perth and known locally as blackboys. The word *blackboys* appeared under the pictures of the plants. "The children," I told Vicki, "can't wear shirts with that word on it in Connecticut. They, or I, will be accused of racism. I'm not going to use the word in my book. Instead I am going to call the plants grass trees."

The children did not ride waves all vacation. We are a bookish, pencil-and-paper family. While Francis sketched computer circuits, Edward designed houses, "practical houses for real families, not like those along the river," he said. Eliza wrote stories, two of which were influenced by *Daddy Long-Legs*. One described life in an orphanage in London, and the other consisted of a series of letters written to

Clarabell, the doll she received for Christmas. "Dear Clarabell," the first letter began, "I love you so! Your voice is music to my ears. I have watched you from afar. Whenever I see your lovely face, I dance with glee. Alas, alas, I cannot reveal my identity. But here are some clues." The first clue was "my eyes are blue"; the second, "I wear a watch"; and the third, "I sleep near you." Eliza ended the letter by writing "With all my heart," followed by a question mark.

While Eliza wrote love letters to Clarabell, I fretted about money. In July, I wanted to take the family to the Kimberley. Plane tickets cost twenty-five hundred dollars, so I wrote Ansett offering to write an article for *Panorama*, the airline's magazine, in exchange for tickets. Only rarely do I have nerve enough to attempt to convert my little reputation into cash. Still, my fits of brassiness run in seams, and when a seam breaks the surface, I mine it until I collapse exhausted by embarrassment. In the *West Australian* I saw an advertisement for Cunard's *Crown Monarch*. "I have never been on a cruise," I told Vicki; "I am going to try to barter lectures for passage." "I predict you won't find the passage," Vicki said. To learn the name of Cunard's publicity director I telephoned Sydney. The telephone lines being busy, my call was put on hold, and I listened to a brochure of advertisements describing turquoise waters, emerald islands, and sun-drenched sands. Cunard "lets you lose yourself in the experience but not in the crowd." Later that morning I wrote a hotel in Sydney requesting complimentary accommodations in August. "Say that you heard about the hotel and want to write about it," Eliza advised, "but say that you have to have the experience of being in it." From the Australian National Railway, I requested tickets on the *Indian Pacific* in hopes of taking the famous three-day journey from Perth to Sydney. "Gosh," my final sentence read, "the trip is a great one, and I sure hope you like my proposal." "You wrote that?" Vicki said; "don't you have any shame." "Shame," I answered, "is something I can't afford."

Baseball started me writing letters. In November, I saw the Perth Heat play twice. At each game someone threw out the first pitch, a local basketball star or a visiting coach from a major-league team in the United States. "I'd like to do that," I told Vicki; "then the president of the United States and I would have something in common." That night I wrote a letter to the Heat and said that if they would give my family complimentary tickets I'd throw the first ball at a game. A week later Doug Mateljan telephoned and invited me to eat lunch with him and Don Knapp, the director of the team. Don wanted to see, I suppose, if I was nutty. We ate at Sardi's in South Perth. I had a shrimp salad, the same salad Don ate. The salad cost $17.95 and was the most expensive salad I had ever eaten.

That Saturday night I threw out the ball before a doubleheader with the Waverley Reds. I got to keep the ball, a Mizuno 100 made in China and used in batting practice before the game. I was also given a baseball cap, 100 percent wool and manufactured in Indonesia. The bill of the cap was red and the top blue. Stitched across the front were the words PERTH HEAT and the team's logo, a white baseball, red flames surrounding it and streaming out to the right as the ball burned a path through the air. Before the game I practiced throwing a tennis ball in the side yard. The practice went for naught. The pitcher's mound disrupted my motion, and instead of fizzing through the air, resembling, as a high school coach of mine once put it, "an aspirin going sideways," the ball looped upward, reminding me of the soft curve of a middle-aged man's belly. Edward was too embarrassed to say anything about the pitch. We sat in a box leased by Coca-Cola. At the end of the first game Doug sent us hot dogs buried under golden onions and chunky chips. For dessert the children ate double chocs. I heckled the Waverley Reds and embarrassed Edward again. One of the Reds was named Hubbard; I called him "old Mother Hubbard who couldn't hit a bone."

Man is a social creature. Rarely does an individual cut a path through either bush or life. Instead he treads established trails, following not inclination but signs emblazoned by education or convention. In Perth families traveled during December and January, many driving south toward Albany, others flying to Bali, or even farther afield to Europe or the United States. By the third week in January swimming had become dry and routine. The children were bored and quarrelsome. One morning I took the car to Brooking Mazda for a tune-up. The next morning we started north. "Everybody we know," Vicki said as she put the cooler in the car, "has gone south or east. They go north in September and October, not now." "I am not everybody," I snapped, suddenly seeing myself as an individual, not just another parent sagging under the strain of summer vacation. I drove up the Brand Highway toward Cervantes, 245 kilometers away. We ate lunch on a picnic table beside the gas station at Regans Ford. A woolly black-and-white dog joined us, and the children fed him purple grapes. A trucker strolled over. His truck broke down the day before, he said, and he had gone back to Perth to consult a mechanic. The man had been on the road for thirty-six hours, "not unusual for me," he added. Throughout the trip strangers talked to us: a man who quit his job, bought a motorcycle, and set out with his girlfriend to spend two years seeing Australia; a couple who had driven twenty-three hundred kilometers in four days. "Every chance we get, we go for a little drive," the woman explained; "we like to see things."

Distances that struck me as enormous didn't deter West Australians. "If you get to Kalbarri, go to Monkey Mia," the postmistress at the university said. "How far is it?" I asked. "About eight hundred kilometers round-trip," she said, "but the drive is easy. We got up early in the morning, spent the day at Shark Bay, and drove back that night." "The pressure of life in the United States," Nigel told me, "has driven Americans inward. Crime and social turmoil have made you retreat to small domestic plots. You convert homes into fortresses and are frightened to go out the front door. You send children to private schools and distrust strangers. The more miles you travel the more bad things you think can happen to you, and so you stay home, physically and mentally at home." "Horseshit," I said.

Nigel's remarks contained some truth. In West Australia when pressure built around a person, he could escape by turning outward. Instead of retreating inward to a small world cluttered with knick-knacks associated with a past or the present, the West Australian could easily wander away from the familiar, so far that he could imagine, and sometimes even create, a different future. Because he could leave tension behind him, the West Australian, I told Vicki near the end of the trip, was more relaxed and not so ambitious as the New Englander, who for want of other ways to rid himself of tension channeled his energies into a job. "Don't give me that frontier stuff," Vicki answered; "I've had it with the last frontier. People here can be too relaxed, at least about schooling. I have not met a single shop girl who can add. Besides, how do all those people in Perth building huge houses on tiny lots fit your scheme? They don't," she continued, answering her own question; "leave pop psychology to faith healers and write a straightforward account of our travels."

Travel and ideas loop about each other, thoughts making straight roads seem curvy. Despite my reservations about Nigel's assessment of the American imagination, I don't enjoy driving long distances, not because I fear something evil will occur but because I don't trust automobiles. My grandfather never kept a car for longer than a year. Each spring he bought Mother, Grandmother, and himself new cars, saying, "The surest way to commit suicide is to keep a car longer than twelve months." Australian highways were bumpy, and until I locked the car and stretched out on the bed at night, not only did I dread but I expected a breakdown. South of Cervantes lay Nambung National Park, famous for the Pinnacles, yellow sand dunes out of which stuck hunks of limestone, some resembling tombstones, others jagged, resembling the weathered, fallen walls of a lost city. To reach the Pinnacles I drove seventeen kilometers on an unpaved road. The surface was corrugated, and the car thumped and rumbled like iron being dragged over wrinkled tin. Kestrels hung above the road, and emus and kangaroos pushed through the bush along the shoulders, their heads bobbing. Vicki and the children saw a circus of animals. I did not. I clutched the steering wheel so tightly that my hands became creased and my fingers tingled. When we stopped at the entrance to the park, Vicki said, "This jaunt has been quite educational. I am sure the children will never forget the word *shit.*"

We spent the first night in an apartment in Cervantes. Twice a mouse scurried across the kitchen floor. For dinner we ate fish and chips at the Ronard Bay Tavern. On the wall hung a picture of a racehorse named Always Thinking. Ten people, including the bartender, owned Always Thinking, each paying part of his upkeep, the total being eight hundred dollars a month. The horse's winnings went for his keep. As a result some months the owners did not have to put up money. "How has Always Thinking done?" I asked. "Not so well," the bartender said; "we have leased him to a fellow for five years. He takes care of the expenses, and if the horse wins any races, we get a little bit."

Children and adults are not good dinner companions. In Dongara the next night the only food Eliza and Edward would eat was pizza. We ate in a small café, and I ordered the Dongara pizza, a mélange consisting of cheese, onions, ham, salami, shrimp, pepperoni, mushrooms, tomatoes, capsicums, and pineapple. I only sampled the pizza. We sat at a white plastic picnic table covered with pink oilcloth. Against the wall to my right stood two video machines, the first "Terminator 2 Judgment Day." The machine was red. On the front was a picture of Arnold Schwarzenegger. Half his face was missing, making him look as if he had just risen from a nap in a grave. The second machine, "Mortal Kombat," featured tiffs between, among others, Sonya, Goro, Scorpion, and Sub-Zero. Goro had four arms and was half-human, half-dragon. "His specialty," the owner of the restaurant said, "is ripping out spinal cords."

I drove less the second day than I did the first. Swimming that bored me in Perth now became exercise for the children. We swam and played tag at Green Head. Edward sliced his big toe open on coral, but he forgot about the cut when a seal swam close to us. At Leeman we ate a picnic lunch. Afterward I drove to Dongara, following the shore road. Wattle grew on the sand plains, pressing against the road and resembling a heavy fur collar. Squatters' shacks were occasionally visible, hunched behind dunes near the ocean. They were made from bits of wood and corrugated iron and asbestos. A television antenna stood atop every shack. Snapped by wind, the antennas twisted over roofs. Black against the sky, they resembled branches of old socks grevillea, bent and fibery with dry seedpods.

In Dongara, I explored Pickering Drive. The first part of the street was paved, but then, curving over a rise, the road ran to dirt and bush. Six houses had been built on the street, "a start," Francis said. We stayed in a motel that had a swimming pool. The room was small, and Eliza slept on a cot four inches above the floor. Many rooms in the motel had been rented to "Dynamic Satellite Surveys." Employees drove white four-wheel-drive Nissan Patrols, and strewn across the automobile bays outside their rooms were tires, lengths of pipe, and cardboard boxes. We got up early and ate breakfast at the Coffee Tree restaurant, sitting under a Moreton Bay fig. The food was good, and Francis fed crumbs to a magpie lark. While we ate, a cleaner sprayed our motel room with insecticide. The mist was so thick our eyes watered and we sneezed.

I planned to spend the next night in Geraldton, but the town was big and busy, so after a swim and fish and chips, we drove to Kalbarri, 170 kilometers north on the coast. Kalbarri was a resort town. "Do you think we will be able to get a room," Vicki said; "after all this is school vacation. Suppose we can't find a room. What are you going to do?" "I don't know," I said; "let's just count foxes." During the trip we counted seventeen red foxes dead on the shoulders of roads. The hills beyond Geraldton rolled like Middle Tennessee, and I drove slowly. Windmills stood in fields. Printed on the rudder behind the vanes of almost all the windmills were the words *Southern Cross.* "I could live in this country," I said; "Grandfather Pickering had a windmill in Carthage." Vicki did not answer; she was asleep.

By late afternoon the children were swimming in the pool at the Kalbarri Beach Resort. "Last week," the clerk told me; "we turned away six families a day. You planned well." We had a two-bedroom unit with a kitchen and a combination dining and living room. Built near the mouth of the Murchison River, the resort was white and at first glance smacked of Greece and the Mediterranean. Although Kalbarri was peaceful, travelers with children rarely rest. The next morning at six-thirty we boarded a bus for Kalbarri National Park. Six hours later we returned to the resort. To reach the most spectacular sites in the park one traveled thirty-one kilometers on unpaved roads, simple stuff for a four-wheel-drive but not for a Toyota with 56,000 miles under its belts.

The Murchison River wound through the park, cutting deep gorges through the sandstone, exposing layers of color: red, orange, yellow, white, and brown baked deep and immobile into the land, but simultaneously flowing under bluffs like syrup. At the bottoms of gorges white sandbars gleamed, and pools were green. Kangaroos grazed on the edge of the bush. Feral pigs rolled about like barrels, and kids bawled, sounding human. Birds called, the sandstone softening their songs, so that the notes didn't slice the morning air but instead seemed to float liquid through the gorges, here and there the melody snagging and twisting on a shrub. On the flatland above the gorges, sand-plain woody pear bloomed, the flowers creamy white and the fruits gray and chunky, shaped like spinning tops.

Scheduled on the tour was a descent to the bottom of Z Bend. The trail pitched sharply downward. Amid the rocks golden orb weavers spun webs large as serving platters. The spiders themselves were bigger than my hand. Their silk was gold, and the webs glittered like mirrors. Near the bottom of the gorge river gums clung to ledges. In the effort to pull themselves out of shadow and into light some of the gums resembled white knots that had frayed, their trunks and branches twisted, resembling loose threads. I caught a small gecko and sat down and examined him, not because I was curious about him but because the descent was difficult and I wanted to rest. At the bottom of the gorge people on the tour swam. I paddled away from everyone and floating on my back looked up through the gorge. Rocks jutted out from walls in loose bales bound together by weight. A crack here, a loose boulder there, and the bluffs would spill out in ledges like heavy clots of hay.

"Average health and agility," the brochure of the tour company stated, "is required to descend to Z Bend." The children managed well, Francis not noticing the difficulty, Edward mastering his fear of heights, and Eliza skipping behind the guide. Vicki and I suffered. "I hope," Vicki said later as we sat soaking in the hot tub at the resort, "that you won't be getting us up early again. This is supposed to be a vacation." Two mornings later we were canoeing down the Murchison at six-thirty. Vicki had not paddled a canoe before. For a while the trip went easily. The river was low, and we stopped frequently to walk the canoes through shallows. Pelicans stood on sandbars, and a sea eagle flew above us. For breakfast the guide made tea and sandwiches, stuffing bacon, eggs, and beans between toast. I ate three sandwiches. Unfortunately we paddled into a head wind after breakfast. Because Eliza and Edward were a good team and Francis drifted instead of paddled, I made Francis my bow man and put Edward and Eliza in Vicki's canoe, hoping they would make the going less difficult. They didn't. "I cried when you disappeared around the corner ahead of us, Daddy," Eliza said; "but I stopped because I didn't want to discourage Mommy and her shoulders hurt so much."

The next day while I followed an osprey along the bluffs south of Kalbarri, Vicki and the children swam at Nancy Beach. I climbed past Red Bluff and Rainbow Valley to Pot Alley and Eagle Gorge. The sea swept inward in white rushes, and from a distance the cliffs resembled red slabs of rotten wood. I wanted to walk to Layer Cake Gorge, but I worried about leaving Vicki and the children by themselves on the beach, so I hurried back. Behind the toilet in a changing house Edward found a goanna. "Catch him, Daddy, and take him outside," Edward said; "somebody might kill him in here." I picked the goanna up and, after the children rubbed its hide, carried it a hundred yards into the bush and turned it loose under a big wattle.

I told Vicki that I booked the tours in Kalbarri so the vacation would give the children memories. That won't happen. I remember almost nothing of my childhood, and once school starts vacation will slip from the children's minds like water rippling under canoes on the Murchison. I will remember the tours, however. I booked them so that Vicki and I would have memories. When Francis was a baby, he and I lay side by side on a red rug in our apartment and made cooing sounds. The sounds started low and climbed higher until we both laughed. Francis is now taller than my shoulder, and we have probably spent more time together in the past than we will spend together in the future. I cannot speak the languages he uses. I know little about computers or quantum physics. Electricity is a mystery to me, and I don't read science fiction. But I delight in him, and I love him. When the time comes for him to vanish from my life, to appear only at the occasional holiday, I want to have memories. I want to hear him groan while paddling a canoe. I want to see him lever himself up a rocky chimney, his white shirt streaked red by sandstone, the sun rushing orange off his hair, the freckles on his face seeming to grin.

In Kalbarri the children jumped on trampolines and played miniature golf for the first time. Edward shot 62, making a hole in one on twelve, and Eliza and Francis shoot 82 and 83 respectively. Eliza wanted to visit Fantasyland, "the House of Four Museums," as a flyer labeled it. Outside the house two white plaster seals perched on top of a stone birdbath. Two green frogs sat on the edge of a wishing well decorated with seashells. Fantasyland resembled an attic. By the door was a collection of bottles and ironstone jugs, containers once full of Heath Beverages, Bonningtons Irish Moss, Bengal Chutney, and Scotts Emulsion. On three shelves stood eighty-nine bottles containing animals in formaldehyde. In one bottle four blue octopuses twisted together like a ball of twine. In another was a braid of pygmy pythons. A Stoke's sea snake resembled a length of worn rubber pipe. A banded sea krait looked like a necklace, black and silver rings circling its body like a string of polished shells. At the end of one row was a small bird's nest resembling a stale cupcake.

A stuffed red squirrel scampered up a branch leaning against a wall. In an aquarium a yellow breasted boatbill spread its wings and defended its nest against a four-and-a-half-foot crocodile. Clamped to walls were dried fish. Mouths open and teeth protruding, the fish resembled gargoyles atop ancient cathedrals, smog corroding their features. A moray eel lay on a shelf, and the stiff tentacles of an octopus leaned against a table, appearing rooted in the floor and resembling the dried stems of weeds. A teddy bear slumped against a big starfish. A yellow light shone on the "Coral Grove," shells and corals arranged so that they seemed to bloom. Two plastic lovebirds, one blue, the other green, kissed while perching on a brass swing. The head of a doll sat atop an arrangement of scallop shells. The head had blond hair and blue eyes. Painted pink and blue and then sprayed with silver glitter, the shells flowed out from the head forming a long, formal gown. Beside a garage of toy trucks and cars stood a tricycle and a motorcycle made from paper clips, their wheels red caps removed from bottles of Emu bitter.

While trolls gathered in the shadows near the wall on one shelf, Mrs. Santa Claus kissed Mr. Santa Claus. Nearby, a wooden aboriginal mermaid sat beside a mountain pool, a nugget of gold in her hand. A washboard leaned against a display case. In the case were "Dolls from the Bridal Cars of Penny and Dennis Ceru, who were the first couple married in the Church at Kalbarri." While Penny wore a glittering white dress, Dennis wore a blue coat and black striped trousers. We stayed at Fantasyland for an hour and a half, Francis studying gemstones, Edward the animals in bottles, and Eliza the dolls. "Did you see," she said as we left, "the doll from Germany that had three faces? One face was smiling, one crying, and I couldn't see the third."

After leaving Fantasyland I drove to Rainbow Jungle, an aviary bustling with parrots and cockatoos. The owners planted palms around the buildings, and near the trunk of a tree, Edward found an orange-and-black centipede. The centipede was as broad as a belt and as long as my foot. Although I dislike seeing birds in cages, I enjoyed the Jungle. The cages were large, and the parrots were beautiful. I walked through the gardens twice, and we stayed two hours, looking at eclectus, regent, red-rumped, orange-bellied, king, and princess parrots. When the parrots flew, colors shimmered around them like mist. My favorite parrot was the northern rosella, its head black, a blue band under its neck, the back feathers silvery with black margins and appearing scaly. If we were changed into birds, I decided, we would be cockatoos: Edward, a pink-and-white galah; Eliza, a sulfur-crested; Vicki, a gang-gang; and Francis, a glossy black cockatoo. For my part I would be a red palm cockatoo, a red dimple on my cheek and my hair curving up in black spikes.

Vicki and the children bought souvenirs at the Jungle: Edward and Francis postcards, and Eliza two "Blue Moon Cards," laminated cards the size of placemats, both depicting Australian animals. On one card animals gathered in and around a big gum tree. A striped goanna circled the trunk of the tree. Sitting on a limb above the goanna a koala chewed leaves and looked beneficent. On the other card two wallabies sparred, the limbs above them serving as a grandstand for spectators: koalas, possums, then three azure kingfishers, their chests resembling orange sunsets, their backs blue nights. For her birthday Vicki bought a mug decorated with parrots and two dish towels, galahs stamped on one, rainbow lorikeets on the other. I did not buy anything. When Vicki and the children buy souvenirs, I worry about money. Although the amount spent is always small, Vicki says I become grim as soon as the family enters a shop. Rather than float like a dark cloud across their sunny moods, I usually stay out of shops. While the family bought souvenirs at the Jungle, I wandered through the palms, finding another centipede then a wolf spider with legs two inches long.

Not once did we eat pizza in Kalbarri. Every morning we ate cereal in our kitchen. For lunch we had sandwiches at little cafés. Four nights we ate dinner at Findlay's Fresh Fish BBQ. Findlay's had been the town ice works then a fish factory. The restaurant was an awkward shed, constructed mostly from corrugated tin and resembling an adolescent whose arms and legs grew at different rates. Wooden picnic tables and chairs sprawled across a dirt yard. Strings of colored lights sagged above tables. In the middle of the yard two round stone fireplaces glowed like eyes. Occasionally a customer sat on a log beside a fire and played a guitar.

Many restaurants in Western Australia did not serve alcohol, so people brought drink with them. I stuffed six beers into my backpack, and while waiting for the meal I drank and watched the sunset. "It's always apricot," Edward said one night. From the lip of the roof covering the main part of the shed hung a thick screen. Suspended on the screen were decorations, mostly tools: among other items, lanterns, two-man crosscut saws, and a monkey wrench four feet long. Stoves and a low counter lay behind the wire. Rocks had been plastered into the side of the counter facing the courtyard. The cook put meals on top of the counter. The cook himself wore a blue Greek sailor's hat with a small black bill. He had a ponytail, his nose curved like the beak of a hawk, and he wore shirts blossoming with flowers. On the end of the counter stood a wooden prospector, a bedroll on his shoulders, a felt hat crumpled on his head, and a mangy feist between his legs. The prospector was toothless, and his face, sharp and pinched, resembling one of the fishes nailed to the wall in Fantasyland.

The menu was written on a blackboard in colored chalk. Barbecued snapper cost $7.50; snapper with chili sauce, $8.00; sweet-and-sour backbones, $6.00; barbecued prawns, $12.00; fish ribs, $6.00; deep-fried dhu fish, $10.00, and a half-dozen oysters, $7.00. If a person ordered a main course, he could eat as much salad as he wanted. For $5.00 children could have fish or steak and chips. Damper bread cost fifty cents a loaf. We ate through the menu, my favorite meal consisting of a half-dozen oysters Kilpatrick, two loaves of damper bread, and the leavings from the children's plates, usually snapper.

From Kalbarri I drove straight back to Perth. Driving was easy except when I met a road train. The big trucks lumbered down roads like clots, trailers swaying, threatening to cause an aneurysm and slam us into the asphalt in a spray of blood. Road trains terrified Edward, and when he saw one approaching, he begged me to pull off the highway until the train passed. I wanted to spend a night in the guest house at the Benedictine Monastery in New Norcia, 132 kilometers from Perth. Everyone else in the family wanted to push on to Perth, however, and when I stopped at the Monastery, the guest house was deserted. Eliza and I explored the guest house, and I rang a bell beside a registration desk, but nobody answered. Pasted to a door leading into a courtyard was a sign saying, "Please Shut the Door so the Flies and Goannas

Can't Come In." Eliza and I searched for goannas in the courtyard, but we could not find any.

We arrived home at six-fifteen. During the six days I drove 1,586 kilometers, and the car did not break down. Waiting for me was a packet of Christmas mail forwarded from Connecticut: cards from a real estate agent at Century 21 and from Mike, Joe, and Deirdrea at Econo-Clean who washed our windows this past June. Esprit Travel sent a calendar containing pictures of Thailand, Japan, and New Zealand, but not Australia. During our absence from Perth, a kitchen cabinet, eight feet long and three feet high, pulled free from the wall, crushing a shelf underneath it, smashing a telephone and a radio, and shattering every glass in the house. While Vicki swept up the shards of glass, I walked to Broadway Pizza and bought two family-size pizzas, only pepperoni on the one for Eliza and Edward, for Vicki, Francis, and me, the Broadway Gourmet loaded with Adelphi ham, artichokes, sun-dried tomatoes, mushrooms, olives, garlic, and herbs. That evening when I kissed him good-night, Edward said, "Daddy, when are we going to Adventure World? You promised to take us before school started."

This morning we went to Adventure World. We arrived when the gates opened at ten o'clock. Immediately the boys raced go-carts. I told Eliza she was too little to race, and so she and Vicki and I drove Bumper Boats. Afterward we rode toboggans down Thunder Mountain and climbed through Dracula's Castle. Vicki and the children splashed down water slides. Because I thought I might hurt my back, I stayed dry and watched. For lunch we drank Coca-Colas and ate chunky chips and cheeseburgers. Immediately afterward Eliza and I peddled a car along the Sky-Rail. Then all of us went to the Animal Park and petted kangaroos. Next we took the Chair Lift up Thunder Mountain, and the children rode the roller coaster. At four o'clock the boys wanted to ride the go-carts again, and Eliza asked if she could drive one. I wanted Eliza to do the things her brothers did and have the fun they had, so I let her drive a cart. Eliza was eight. If she had been a boy, I would not have let her drive the cart. I would have told her she was too young. On the first curve she lost control and crashed into a pile of tires, banging her head against the steering wheel, slicing both her lips open and loosening her front teeth. "It's not your fault, Daddy," she told me tonight; "I wanted to ride in the cart." School starts tomorrow. Eliza's lips are sore and swollen; she won't be able to say much in class. I am glad that summer vacation is over and she and her brothers will be back in school. They may not learn much, but they will be safer.

Another Day in Paradise

At seven-thirty in the morning the men's locker room at the university pool was social. The men who swam early were middle-aged. Exercise tired them, and they dressed slowly, buttoning sentences and resting while tying shoes. "When the alarm buzzes," a visiting professor from Oregon said, "I don't groan like I do at home. Instead I look out the window and think 'whoopee, another day in paradise.'" In February, Perth was still a garden, if not quite Eden. Breezes paddled through gums, catching and turning leaves so that their undersides curved upward in quick, silver splashes. Smoke from bush fires eddied in slow currents, seasoning the air, smacking of thin bark and rust-colored staves. From mottlecah, blossoms hung like pink grapefruit. On Burdett's banksia flowers resembled chunks of vanilla ice cream dipped in orange sherbet. Showy banksia was lemony, and southern plains banksia, yellow. From beds of red down, the lobes of scarlet feather flower rose into chalices, the insides orange froth, a long style leaning out to the side of each blossom, floating like a swizzle stick forced upward by heavy liquid. Small orange fruit burst on corkwood, spilling yellow seeds. Rosemary grevillea curled into flower, the blooms resembling minute pink harps. Rainbow lorikeets bumbled loudly through marri, knocking bouquets of white blossoms to the ground. Illyarrie was heavy with bud and flower, the buds first green then bright red, creased and resembling soft bundles wrapped in paper, twine cinched tightly across them, pulling them into four lobes.

After being expelled from paradise, man was forced to work, in the process losing leisure, time in which to meander and appreciate. Although I walked through Kings Park occasionally, I missed much of midsummer. Instead of wandering February, I planned my departure from Australia. The details of leaving so cluttered days and thought that weeks passed almost without my noticing. For Ansett Airlines, I agreed to write an article about the Kimberley. In return the airline arranged to fly us to Broome and put us up at the Cable Beach Club. Once the flights were set, I booked a twelve-day trip through the Kimberley. Next I told John Allison, our landlord, that we would leave the house on July 8. I wanted to save the rent for the sixteen days that we would be in the Kimberley, and I talked to Mrs. Trivett at university housing and reserved an apartment from July 24 to August 1. Then I agreed to speak in Perth on July 31, to a convention of "delegates from all local governments throughout Western Australia." The fee paid for our room and board during the last week in Perth. Last, I booked passage on the *Indian Pacific*, on the train leaving Perth on August 1 and arriving in Sydney on the fourth. Because Vicki and the children had not seen Sydney, I reserved a room in a hotel for the fourth, fifth, and sixth of August. My plans resembled a jigsaw puzzle, one that I cut as I progressed, sawing new pieces so they would fit the old.

Making plans for family travel was not easy. Several times I tossed the puzzle into the waste can and taking out a new board started over. I wrote letters, talked on the telephone, and sent faxes. I kept a pad and pencil by my bed. Often I awoke in the middle of the night and jotted down details that I neglected during the day. On the telephone I was unable to make reservations for the flights back to the United States, no flight seeming to have five seats left in our class. As a result I went to the Qantas office in downtown Perth, where an efficient woman quickly booked the reservations. Concern about reservations kept me up almost an entire night. So that I would be alert when I went to the Qantas office, I drank two cups of coffee, giving myself the fidgets, thereby ruining the rest of the day. On the trip back to the United States we were allowed one stop. I chose Fiji. I was too tired, though, to decide where we would stay.

The journey home filled only a corner of the puzzle. Scattered about waiting to be sanded were weeklong speaking trips to Papua New Guinea and New Zealand, three days at a convention in Queensland, and a two-day trip to Sydney for an appearance on a television show. In addition I agreed to make several talks in Western Australia. Just today I received invitations from Caulfield, Victoria; Monteagle, Tennessee; Melbourne; and, from within Western Australia, Kojonup and Mandurah. The top of my desk looks as if a rat family took possession and tossed papers in all directions to build a homey nest, a Dalkeith nest complete with a wraparound veranda, swimming pool, and tennis court. Yesterday a radio show in Sydney interviewed me over the telephone. This morning the producer of a program in Melbourne rang and asked me to go to the ABC studio in downtown Perth on Thursday for an interview. Last week I spent thirty minutes at ABC recording commentary for the Verity James Show. That afternoon I wrote two articles, one thousand words for *Insight*, the educational supplement of the *West Australian*, and three thousand words for *EQ Australian*, a magazine for teachers.

Despite receiving many invitations, I spoke only once in February, that being to the Isolated Children's Parents' Association, the group of rural parents who taught their children at home. The woman who asked me to speak wrote from Yerilla Station in Kookynie. The place-names intrigued me, and since the association's meeting was held only two miles away from our house, on the Claremont Campus of Edith Cowan University, I agreed to speak. My honorarium, the common stuff that I asked the children to collect, is now stacked along the floor of the bedroom, enough matter for a small natural history museum. Hanging from molding above my bed is the golden brown skin of a dugite, six feet seven inches long, the scales on the underside of the skin resembling marks left in mud by tires on mountain bikes, the treads deep and thick, capable of pulling the snake quickly through scrub. Pinned in boxes is a summer day of insects: dung beetles the size of thumbnails; cockroaches; wolf spiders, legs crinkled under their bodies but here and there a leg jutting out like a dark, thin twig; moths; crickets; grasshoppers; and praying mantises. The wings on one grasshopper are four and a half inches long. Barbs on the legs of some grasshoppers are so sharp that I have sawed through writing paper with them.

Brown kangaroo droppings fill a small paper sack. To keep the droppings from spilling out a child crammed a handful of gray bird feathers into the mouth of the sack. Seeds and pods fill a cabinet of plastic bags: pods from curara resembling fried noodles; from hop mulga, pods looking like snow peas; and bowgada, its long pods pale and streaked with orange, the dark brown seeds inside resembling fat ticks. Out of the nuts of large-fruited mallee, seeds spill like cinnamon.

My favorite seeds are sweet quandong and sandalwood, both round and the size of gumballs. When the outer shells are removed, however, sweet quandong is yellow and crinkled like brain tissue while sandalwood is smooth. When crushed, the sandalwood smells, Vicki said, "like old furniture." The owners of Meeune Station at Mount Magnet sent an album of pictures that almost made me want to leave Perth, and Storrs: fields white and yellow with wildflowers, in places pink everlastings rumpling like comforters; charred loaves of damper bread cooking in coals, beside them billy tea simmering in black buckets; a red bluff resembling a slab of wood; a monitor lizard speckled orange and brown and big as a suitcase; a small girl wearing a white straw hat kneeling on the ground and holding a thorny devil in her left hand; and last, a little boy standing in a sheep shed, the window in front of him silver with spiderwebs.

Suddenly in midsummer the mail bloomed. One or two items were fragrant. The manager of a hotel to which I wrote offering to barter publicity for accommodations sent a form letter. "Whilst we believe this to be a very worthy cause," he declared, "I regret to advise that budget restrictions prevent us from assisting on this occasion." "Better to be thought a worthy cause than a hopeless case," Vicki said. From Connecticut the couple taking care of our house mailed a packet crammed with tax forms and letters from the Internal Revenue Service. Neither the tax packet nor the letter from the hotel manager required replies. Other letters did. Several parents wrote me. After describing problems their children experienced in school, they asked for advice.

An after-dinner speech is evanescent. Words recorded for radio are more sound and mannerism than sense. I replied carefully to the letters. I was not qualified, I explained, to give advice. But the lessons taught in schoolrooms, I said, were always limited, and I suggested that the parents encourage their children to become interested in things outside school. On my desk lay a cone of coastal banksia. The cone was white, I wrote, and looked as if it had been dusted with powder. The follicles were open. Resembling lipstick, a dark red line ran around the inner edge of the follicle. The wood inside the follicle looked like polished cherry, grains of orange and red seeping through it in creases. Perhaps, I wrote, schools would serve society better if they encouraged students to appreciate the rich world outside the classroom. Perhaps the poor speller or stumbling mathematician could learn, I said, other languages, "that of the shoreline, waves green and tossing with life, or that of trees, birdsong slapping through the leaves in bright arrows." I told parents not to be discouraged. "Once your child finds what he likes," I wrote, crossing the middle and index fingers of my left hand while penning the words, "he will succeed, not always in ways that schools or teachers will recognize, but in ways he can be proud of."

Summer vacation ended early in February, and education was on my mind. In contrast to what I wrote anxious parents, I wanted more English and mathematics for my children. Instead of lessons teachers emphasized the presentation of lessons, requiring that precise lines be drawn down margins and around problems, in many cases drawn over lines already printed on the paper. Vicki spent two evenings making covers for the covers already on notebooks, "wrapping wrappers," as she put it. So that the boys would not find themselves behind their peers when we returned to Connecticut, I taught math. Before dinner I gave Edward sixty problems involving fractions. With Francis I studied algebra, after dinner working through a score of pages in a ninth-grade textbook. In high school I was a good math student. Although I had not used algebra in thirty-five years, I remembered how to solve most problems. Processes had not changed. What was different was the presentation. Words rather than numbers filled books, making simple solutions complex. Instead of just showing Francis how to solve a problem, I had to make certain that he, and I, could define "the multiplicative inverse of a number."

Although I was uneasy about the lack of difficult homework, I was not dissatisfied with the children's schooling. If they had not had to return to the competitive system in Storrs, I would not have worried. Indeed schooling everywhere seems wrongheaded. Only in classrooms did I use algebra, and I suspect that Francis will rarely use it once he leaves school, this despite his interest in science. The common defense of mathematical studies is that they "train the mind," the argument once used by people who wanted to keep classical studies central to school and university curricula. Many activities train the mind, at least in the baggy, nonintellectual way educators discuss training the mind. Man knows little about his mental workings, and I suspect mowing grass or catching spiders trains the mind about as well as an hour of mathematics four times a week, thirty weeks a year.

School curricula ought to be revised. By making schoolwork so easy Australia has in effect erased traditional curricula from classroom blackboards. Now Australians should cover boards with something better. Instead of lessons that go no deeper than statement, the "Just say 'no'" campaign against drugs in the United States, for example, health should be a real subject. Students should learn the effects of disease and chemicals on tissue and organ. In my ideal school languages both foreign and domestic would be taught from first grade through secondary school. All children would learn enough math to buy groceries or compute taxes. For students interested in studying mathematics intensely, small classes would be available. Reading well and thinking clearly are more important than writing well. Instead of assigning children folders of themes, something not done now in most schools, I would make them learn at least one practical skill in which they used their hands to repair or create, carpentry, for example.

Computer education should begin in first grade, at least until another technology becomes necessary to living in an urban environment. Central in my curriculum would be ecology, taught not by sentimentalists like me but by people with backgrounds in biology. Initially students would learn the names of plants and animals. Then they would study what we think are the relations between different things. Since man's knowledge is partial, students should have opportunities to explore and develop unconventional interests. Finally, I would teach history. Peoples' histories vary greatly. Because the first American historians were New Englanders, Thanksgiving celebrates the landing at Plymouth Rock in 1620, not the earlier colony at Jamestown, Virginia. In my school students would be encouraged to explore the history of their families, not in order to celebrate their family or group as different from or superior to others but in order to know themselves and their world better.

The snake was the first teacher, his reasoning coiling deceptively and teaching man pride, so much pride that he thinks himself capable of revising educational practice in a paragraph or two. Although I often wished they had more homework, the children were happy in school. At dinner Edward entertained us with accounts of his days.

Mr. Buntin liked his room quiet. "Tim was humming in class today," Edward said on Monday. "Mr. Buntin heard him and said 'stop that humming.' The room was quiet for a couple of minutes. Then Tim forgot and began humming again. When Mr. Buntin heard him, he slammed his book shut and said, 'whoever is humming had better stop or this class is in trouble.' There wasn't a sound. The room was as quiet as a grave," Edward said. "Suddenly Mr. Buntin shouted, 'stop that humming. If it continues I won't let you go out to recess.' The room was absolutely silent," Edward said; "for five minutes no one moved. But then Mr. Buntin jumped up and said, 'All right, I told you to stop humming, and you disobeyed me, so the whole class will have to stay inside for the first ten minutes of recess.' What Mr. Buntin heard," Edward said smiling, "no one else heard, but we stayed in for ten minutes of recess."

Last year Eliza's teacher won an award for being one of the best teachers in Western Australia. Despite having thirty students, she kept the class happy and interested. At home Vicki drilled Eliza on the multiplication tables while at school Eliza wrote stories. When Kitty caught chicken pox, Eliza decided to teach her to spell. The first lesson consisted of a series of easy words, including, *am, me, the, like, man,* and *day.* Unfortunately Kitty didn't feel up to learning, so she asked Eliza to write stories for her. "Once upon a time in the land of Jolum playing meant a lot more than it does now," the first story began; "mice played with cats, and lizards played with rats. The King and Queen were always playing. In fact everyone played except a certain frog in a certain pond. All he did was eat flies. He ate millions of them. His name was Frank. Frank grew very fat until one day he popped, and all the flies he had eaten flew out of his belly. Then everyone in Jolum had to stop playing and start working. They are still swatting flies and counting their bites." Eliza really liked her teacher. Pinned to a cork bulletin board in Eliza's room yesterday was a bundle of paper. On the papers Eliza wrote descriptions of, among others, "A Good Wife" and "A Good Mother." The top sheet described "The Ideal Teacher, Mrs. P. Odgers." "Always calm and responsible," Eliza wrote, then added, "makes you drink a lot of H_2O (Water)."

Once school begins parents rarely awaken to visions of paradise. Instead they rush to kitchens and fix breakfasts and pack lunches, all the while shouting "hurry" to children in distant parts of the house. During afternoons and on weekends parents become professional drivers frequenting circuits with pit stops named ballet, tennis, swimming, baseball, and soccer. On the second morning of the new term Vicki and I accompanied Eliza's class to Matilda Bay. While parents sat on blankets drinking coffee, children swam, Eliza distinguishing herself by collecting more jellyfish than any other girl.

Three days later I attended a meeting of fourth-grade parents. I sat at Eliza's desk. While Mrs. Odgers discussed the class, I behaved much as I did when I was in fourth grade. I drew a portrait of Eliza on a scrap of paper. I drew a little girl with goggle eyes and braids sticking out like worms. The girl had snaggleteeth and a chin as big as an elephant's bottom. She had more warts on her face than Nambung Park has pinnacles. On the top of each wart sat a bug, some bugs with hairy nostrils, others with fangs curved like swords. Above the picture I printed "PORTRAIT OF ELIZA." Under the girl's chin I drew an arrow pointing down. I folded the bottom of the page up. Beneath the fold I sketched a heart. Inside the heart I wrote, "Love, Daddy."

When the meeting ended, I left the picture on Eliza's desk, pinned down by the *Oxford Dictionary of Australian English*. That night when I pulled the bedspread off my pillow I found a piece of paper. Drawn on it was a picture of "DEAR DADDY," a man whose face resembled an acorn squash. Shaped like minnows two brown eyes swam across his face, their heads bumping into each other, making him cross-eyed. His nose was a cliff, and his nostrils flaring like caves while his mouth resembled the front of an automobile involved in a fender bender, the grille and most of the chrome knocked askew.

Four days later I was back in Eliza's class, listening to a man describe the Gould League, a club for budding naturalists. Yesterday at eight-fifteen in the morning I was in Edward's classroom, listening to plans for the class trip, a five-day jaunt north to Monkey Mia scheduled for the fourth week in May. Friday we go to the "Bush Dance and Sausage Sizzle" at Nedlands Primary. The Mucky Duck band will play, and hamburgers and hot dogs will be sold. For dessert we can eat Fairy Floss. The night is bound to pump up my cholesterol. Since February I have been enduring, not a diet, but "controlled eating." I have sliced bread and snacks out of my day, and I get only one dessert at night. When we go to Fremantle after swimming at Cottesloe Beach, we avoid the harbor and fish and chips. Instead I trudge through a paddy of rice at a Thai restaurant. In four weeks I have not lost a pound. "Not an ounce," I told Vicki today. "That's true," she said, "but if you had continued grazing they way you did during summer vacation you would have given birth by now."

Once school began the children's days also filled, and they had little time or desire to explore the bush with me. One Sunday, though, we revisited the zoo. Another day we went to the Museum of Childhood on the Claremont campus of Edith Cowan University. Although the museum was small, we stayed three hours. Artifacts in a model classroom dated from the late nineteenth century. A leather satchel hung from a peg, and a dunce cap leaned against a chair. In a cupboard stood slates, a box filled with pens, and an abacus.

In the teacher's desk was the *Punishment Book* of the Armadale Government School. On February 2, 1900, John Alexander, age thirteen, received "6 strokes with rod" for "misbehaving on way to school." On April 6, 1901, Lionel Law received "1 stroke with cane" for "carelessness." Lionel, the teacher wrote under *Remarks*, was "a very lazy boy." On February 14, 1901, "a very bad boy," Keaton Davies, received "2 strokes on hand with cane" for "stealing fruit out of orchard." On February 19, 1907, "for throwing stones at a small girl on the way home," John Walsh and Edwin Meedrum, both eight, received "6 strokes on the buttocks." The punishments were not severe and seemed to be, as a teacher wrote after caning Roy Turner in April 1903, the "last resource." In 1901 only four entries appeared in the *Punishment Book*. During the next three years just nine entries appeared.

Hanging on the wall in the back of the classroom was a large print. Standing at the dinner table with her eyes shut and hands folded in prayer, a little girl said a blessing. The girl's father, mother, and little brothers sat around the table, their eyes also closed. Next to the table a baby dozed in a wooden cradle. A black cat lapped milk out of a saucer. In a corner of the room sat a bushel basket red with apples. On top of the table were a round loaf of bread, a brown teapot, and a yellow pitcher full of milk. The door to the room stood open. Outside a dove fluttered through sunlight. Beyond an old stone wall sheaves of wheat leaned together golden and promising. Printed under the picture was the blessing repeated by the girl. "Thank you for the world so sweet. / Thank you for the food we eat. / Thank you for the birds that sing. / Thank you, God, for every thing."

At the end of the nineteenth century, life in Western Australia was not always so gentle. In another part of the museum bereavement cards announcing the deaths of children hung on a wall. "Another precious gem in heaven," one card declared. Near the cards hung studio photographs of dead children. Photographers took pictures of the corpses. Later they superimposed the dead children's faces on the bodies of healthy children, creating memories of what could have been or what once might have been.

A class of second graders visited the museum the same time I did, and I stopped reading the bereavement cards when I heard the teacher say in a strident voice, "She wrote a book, probably boring to you, but interesting to grown-up people." "That's not the way to get the children's attention," I thought and walked toward the area in which the class was gathered. I looked through a doorway. The children clumped together silently on the floor. "Stay seated," the teacher shouted, not noticing me; "the next person who stands up is going to stand up near the door for five minutes." So far as I could see not one child had moved. "I hope no one hums," I thought.

Museums with tracts of open space don't appeal to me. I like cramped museums that resemble basements, places in which one can poke about. I spent time looking at games and toys. The Butterfly Hunt was a "new and exciting game of skill." Across the right side of the illustration on the box a portly man in a boater, spectacles, a red vest, and white trousers chased a white butterfly. On the left side of the illustration the man tumbled over, turning like a rolling pin while the butterfly skipped away on the breeze. I remembered playing with Tinker Toys and recognized regiments of lead soldiers: Coldstream Guards, Beefeaters, the Black Watch, and Royal Bengal Lancers. I studied the heads of dolls owned by children in West Australia at the end of the nineteenth and beginning of the twentieth centuries. Most of the heads were bisque, but others were made from wax, wood, tin, and glazed china. Two pudgy koalas hopped across the cover of *Billy Bluegum or Back to the Bush*. The koalas looked thankful to leave the turmoil of streetcars, gaslights, and horseless carriages. They were eager to get back to a world in which butter came from a churn, not a store, and where eucalyptus oil came from leaves, not bottles.

In February I spent many hours in Reid Library. I foraged through the stacks, hunting stories, not trying to trap narratives thick with lessons or social realism. Instead I searched for tales that occurred before the Fall. After being expelled from Paradise, man was forced to study and interpret in order to attain the Kingdom of Heaven. The simple became complex. Actions that had been meaningless because they were natural became full of meaning, for acting naturally, even determining what was natural, became difficult. Stories now "meant" and became instructive. In my essays Smith County was a garden soggy with shallow talk. Winesap apples grew across the hills. Children stole them from the trees by the bushel, but no teacher caned them. The sharp, tart flavor didn't burn innocence from lives. Instead the flavor made people gasp and smile. Sometimes people even said, "Whoopee."

In beating through books I flushed out all sorts of creatures. From a paperback copy of H. Allen Smith's *Lost in the Horse Latitudes* published by the Invincible Press fifty years ago fluttered a ticket for the "W. A. Govt. Tramways." The ticket cost four pence and was two and three-eighths inches long and one and three-eighths inches wide. Printed in green ink on the back was an advertising jingle: "Always fight a Cough or Cold / Before it takes firm hold, / Get your WOODS' GREAT PEPPERMINT CURE / By Chemists and Stores it's sold." Along with the ticket I bagged a covey of stories, a couple of them describing the doings of Proverbs Goforth's cousin Piety.

A native of Pancake, a flat spot at the foot of Bucket Hill on the road to Red Boiling Springs, Piety was cut from the same intellectual quilt as his cousin. According to Turlow Gutheridge, Piety entered the Carthage library only once in his life. Piety wasn't a reader. After going into the library he didn't know what book to look at, at least not until he noticed the bust of Andrew Jackson staring down from the top of a bookcase. On a lectern in front of the bookcase and in what appeared to be Jackson's line of vision lay a copy of Noah Webster's dictionary. "What's good enough for Old Hickory is good enough for me," Piety thought and, walking over to the lectern, began reading. He did not read long. "The dictionary," he told Loppie Groat later, "just don't make satisfactory reading. It changes subject too often."

Loppie told Turlow that he didn't think Piety could read a single word, much less a dictionary, calling him "the most ignoramus man what I've ever met." Once when some of the boys from the school for the afflicted in Buffalo Valley were in Carthage on an outing, they found an almanac on the street. They were sitting on a bench outside Read's Drugstore trying to read it when Piety happened along. "Mr. Piety," one of the boys said, "this book says that farmers ought to plant a lot of corn next spring and plow the fields a lot because there's a load of droughts coming on, and we wondered if you could tell us what a drought is?" Piety stopped. After taking a toothpick out of the top pocket of his overalls, he probed behind the first bicuspid on the left side of his upper jaw, digging out a spool of soggy tobacco before he spoke. "I haven't done a lot of studying about droughts," he said; "but I believe they are germs what have got loose from the Research Station over at Oak Ridge. I'm not sure but I think they are a kind of graft between a coon and a grizzly bear. Anyway they sure is hell on corn, particularly golden bantam."

Despite his Christian name, Piety was a full-bloodied pagan when it came to drinking. One morning after a week of sipping Dapper Tuttlebee's moonshine, Piety appeared at his cousin's house. "Proverbs," he said, "you've got to help me. Last night I dreamed I was a possum. Now that I am awake I don't know whether I'm a man who dreamed he was a possum or a possum who is dreaming he's a man." Piety's dilemma lay beyond Proverbs's expertise, so he took Piety to Slubey Garts. "Piety," Slubey said after Proverbs explained the difficulty, "your teeth are sharp and yellow, and you've got thin lips and a sickly smile like a possum. You don't wash much and you smell rank. Your shanks are long and skinny, and your hair is knotted up like that of a possum. But," Slubey continued, "you don't have no tail to speak of. In fact your trousers hang down off your backside like the udder on a cow with a ruptured bag. No, you ain't a possum. You're just a poor sinner." "Oh, thank you, Lord, for making me a sinner," Piety shouted, raising his hands toward heaven; "praise King Jesus."

Like me, Slubey was busy in February. Instead of organizing a departure from Australia, he tried to interest people in planning their exodus from the earth. He preached in the small communities in the hills above Carthage: Sugar Chest, Quack, Shinbone, and Shoe.

Proverbs Goforth attended receptions after the sermons and handed out cards describing the virtues of patronizing Haskins Funeral Home and the Pillow of Heaven Cemetery, both of which Slubey owned. "Welcome mats on Heaven's stoop," Proverbs called the businesses. "The bristles are strong," Proverbs said, "and when a fellow wipes his traveling shoes off on the mats, his sins fall away and the door to Glory swings open." In his sermons Slubey dug all the knots out of the stump. He poured, as Proverbs put it, "a mighty grist of rain" on luxury and fashion. "Don't set fire to the roof of your house and go back to sleep," he warned congregations. "Have you killed the fatted calf and sold the farm for a peddler's pack of nets and snares?" he asked. "I'd rather be a gold-finder in the outhouse of the Lord," he testified, "than sleep on satin sheets in the tents of the damned." "The woman who puts silver on her head pours lead into her heart," he declared. "Adam and Eve didn't wear no clothes," he said, "until the serpent rattled in Eve's ear. Then they run out behind the barn and started hanging tobacco leaves over themselves, hiding their shiny trinkets so they couldn't sparkle in the rosy light, casting a broad gleam over the waves, showing the way home to some poor shipwrecked soul."

"The fumes of that tobacco," Slubey continued, "got under the skin and that's what makes people stink. Before the fall man smelled as sweet as a rasher of bacon cooking on a cold winter morning. Later folks draped themselves with the hides and pelts of savage beasts. Before the serpent rolled his tongue around words, folks were as smooth as looking glasses. As soon as that fur touched skin, it took hold, sent down follicles, and spread like crabgrass. You could spend all day sliding down a black locust, and you wouldn't even begin to scratch that hair out. Nothing that comes in a bottle or a tube can barber that hair off.

"No matter what you scrub your mouth out with," Slubey continued, "the stink of sin will stick to your breath like a cocklebur. But open your heart to the Lord and your teeth will shine like shorn lambs, and a wind of heavenly words will wash over your lips smelling like Beulahland. But if you eat donkey, you'll bray. No number of high-falutin' elocution lessons can change an ass into a thoroughbred. But let the Lord into the saddle and you'll high-step it right on through the Pearly Gates into Glory. You might as well try to shoe the goose as try to sneak into heaven without repenting. Don't repent tomorrow. Repent today. Water in the creek down by the pasture ain't going to put out the fires of hell. Use the well by the back door. Pour that water on now when you are dirty. Mix it with gall and vinegar. There ain't no short cut to Canaan. If you kill the freshened cow and plant the carcass in the garden and sprinkle lemonade on it every day, a milk tree ain't going to grow. If you thirst after glory, you are going to have to pull udders, and pull them morning and evening until that golden chariot with the diamond wings and amber wheels slides down through the clouds and carries you beyond the stars."

Slubey was not prejudiced. "Slubey don't know the difference between a Catholic and a Buddhist, nor yet even an Arab," Loppie Groat once said. Slubey did, however, think Smith County his territory and himself the Lord's agent, a heavenly manufacturer's representative wholesaling salvation, selling eternal holiday packages, including accommodation, transfers, portage, and the services of an expert personal guide. Slubey did not take kindly to poachers trying to lure his lambs out of the fold. When he heard that a priest had been seen near Gospel, he preached a sermon, as Proverbs put it, "bilious with righteousness."

"All these Romanists do," Slubey said, "is dip a wishbone into a bucket of creek water. Afterward they empty the bucket into a silver jug and call the pourings holy water. Then they put the bone on a cushion and carry it way out in front of them like it was something that smelled bad. They forget Thanksgiving and the turkey that donated the bone to the incense pot. Instead they tell people that the bone was took from the right hand of Saint Dolly the 95th or some such number. And do you know," Slubey continued, shaking the pulpit until the boards came loose, "that some of these prittle-prattle Christians believe them? Why some of the malt-worms hereabouts are so gullible they'd swallow a fat man if you greased his head and pinned his ears back."

"Sam," Vicki said, after I told her about Slubey's latest doings, "I thought you were writing a book about our year in Australia. Do you think people in Perth are going to understand Slubey or whatever it is you are getting at?" "Probably not," I said, "but if some reader shouts 'whoopee' that is good enough for me. Besides," I continued, "misunderstandings are often more educational than understandings."

Just last week Wesley Junior Scraggs enrolled in the Male and Female Select School in Carthage. Wesley was from Defeated Creek, the most isolated and backward place in Smith County. Wesley boarded above Read's drugstore. Thinking Wesley might be homesick and hungry, Quintus Tyler gave the boy a banana after his first day at school. "I've never seen one of these before," Wesley said. "That's all right," Quintus said; "you just eat it tonight and tell me what you think at school tomorrow." "Well," Quintus said the next morning after class, "did you like the banana?" "No, not much," Wesley answered; "it was mostly all cob, and once I threw that away what was left was bitter and hard to chew."

Dorky

Mr. Pickering," the boy said as I entered the library, "you are looking particularly dorky today." I didn't know the boy, but I knew what he was talking about. A week earlier an editor at the *West Australian* asked me to write an article for *Insight*, the newspaper's educational supplement. The school year was about to begin, the editor explained, "and we would like a thousand words from you welcoming new students to the university." Rarely do I write short essays. Form determines content, and the short essay does not provide space for wisdom or foolishness. The best one can do is plant old chestnuts, spread story over them, then hope that a word or two takes root in a reader's consciousness. In the essay I said nothing original. I urged students to work hard and to participate in university life. "Study your surroundings," I wrote, "so that you become part of the university and of that larger community, Western Australia. If you appreciate this place," I said, "the sand heaths of the north and karri forests of the south, then your understanding will grow. Not only will individuals begin to interest you, but you will like people more." I advised students to wander books and places in hopes that they would become men and women with gumption enough to tell others, "I'm not doing that because it is wrong"; people strong enough to say, "I'm sorry."

Unlike the long essay that blossoms slowly into idea, paragraphs unfurling like petals, color and tone changing as words flow over a signature of pages, the short essay blooms and blows on a single sheet. Instead of being nurtured through seasons of bulb and bare stalk, the short essay resembles a potted plant. Bought fully grown at a garden center, the short essay does not bud but blossoms garishly in the first paragraph to catch the reader's eye. Printed above my essay in letters one-half to three-fifths of an inch tall was, "Importance of Being Dorky." I expected the headline, for I began the essay with an

157

anecdote to attract attention. "Daddy," Edward said some nights ago after I embarrassed him again, "why you are so dorky?" "Because of education," I said; "I seized my opportunities." *Dork* was slang. Students understood, though, that a dork did not belong to popular groups. He was usually an outsider, the odd person, sometimes inept, other times cranky. For my purpose a dork was an individual, the person who studied life and who roamed far enough intellectually to be opinionated. I concluded my essay by urging new students, "Do well in your studies. Be an active member of the university. Learn to appreciate other people. Become tolerant, not of those things that are intolerable, but of different ways of living. Then dare to be a dork. Good luck."

In a box printed above my essay the editor wrote, "At the start of the academic year, a visiting American academic offers the unorthodox advice that university students should dare to be dorks." The editor got things slightly wrong. Although using *dorky* as a compliment may have been unconventional, my advice was orthodox. "You are not going to change the world," I wrote, "but you can better your lives and the lives of others. When you graduate, know your subject and yourself, so that you can become that fine person: the responsible son or daughter, mother, father, aunt, uncle, friend or neighbor."

"Wholesome treacle, stuff you have ladled out before," Vicki said that morning. "But," she continued, "what is different is that not just two hundred people are listening to you in a lecture hall. A quarter of a million people will read this piece and think you King of the Dorks. Carpe dork." By dinner Vicki had mellowed. "If you dredged all the dopey wisdom out of your essays and clumped the muck together in a book called *Helpful Thoughts of a Dork*," she said, "you could sell a million copies. Put one thought on each page. Print it in big type, and don't use more than two or three sentences to explain it."

In the English department Brenda said the essay made her laugh. Sue said a man telephoned the department and asked if she knew the other meaning of *dork*. "I told him I didn't want to know," she said, "but he wouldn't hang up and insisted on telling me. In fact he told me twice just to make sure I understood." The next day I received a letter in the mail. The letter consisted of a single line. "You really are a dork," it said. That afternoon Eliza brought me a note from her teacher. "We loved your article in the *West Australian,*" she wrote; "congratulations on being such a super dork. Please come and talk to our class so that we can all learn to be *real* people, viz. dorks!!" The article appeared on Tuesday. By Thursday eight schools had invited me to speak. On Wednesday morning Sophy wrote Eliza a letter and put it in the class mailbox. Across the bottom of the page she drew four blue violets and three red tulips. A green tree grew up the left side of the page. The letter floated above the tree like a cloud. "Dear Eliza," Sophy wrote, "I think that you are so lucky having a famous Dad. I just wanted to tell you how much I like you and mostly I love your accent." That night at dinner Francis said students at John XXIII teased him about the article. "What did they say?" Vicki asked. "Nothing interesting," Francis responded.

By Friday morning the article had vanished from conversation. That night Vicki and the children and I went to the sausage sizzle at Nedlands Primary. Along with classrooms of other parents we danced the chicken and the hokeypokey, the same dances parents wiggle through at school picnics in Storrs. The moon was full, rising succulent and pink over Perth when we arrived at the sizzle. By the time we left, it floated far above the city, shrinking and drying pale yellow like a lemon dangling from a tired brown limb. The next night we went to the family barbecue at John XXIII. We arrived early. While I cooked hamburgers on a grill, the sun set, the skyscrapers in Perth absorbing light, shedding the gray humdrum of business hours and transforming themselves into golden bars.

The next weekend I spoke at the Fremantle Sailing Club. The Education Department of Western Australia sponsored the talk. Teachers and principals attended. A bush fire burned south of Thompsons Lake. Acrid smoke blew over the ocean, the sunset glowing below the dark like an orange hem tacked onto a thick, coarse skirt. Rows of boats were docked at the club, their masts rising white from the water like jagged remnants of a sunken forest. As I stood on the balcony of the club looking at the boats and watching the smoke twisting in the distance, I imagined saying something startling in my speech. I didn't. Instead I told stories and explained that I did not have a philosophy of education. "Real philosophy is complex," I said, adding that I did low things to interest students and to keep myself awake. "To elevate my doings to the abstract would," I declared, "diminish me and mislead people. The extraordinary and the high are beyond most of us. What is not beyond our grasp is the ordinary. Examining the ordinary closely," I preached, "brings joy to life and transforms the everyday into the extraordinary." "Not only are you dorky," Vicki said later, "but you are also the apostle of the mundane."

Fall began the day after I spoke, and I spent the morning walking the streets around Melvista, looking for signs of a different season. I didn't notice any. Yards were still gardens. Hibiscus hedges were garish with blooms, cameo queen still yellow and white. Plumbago was blue, and the trumpet-shaped flowers of Mediterranean heather bloomed in clusters of red, the tips yellow and brassy. Petals of the blossoms were gluey, and minute insects that perched on them stuck and died, almost, it seemed, from a surfeit of brightness. No hints of rain or chill were in the air. Beside a wall great sunroses opened like yellow cups, the red triangles near the bottom of each petal dregs of a sugary spring drink. Illyarrie blossoms smelled buttery, and tufts of white blossoms hung on paperbark. Resembling the ends of medieval bludgeons seared black by fire, old fruits clung to the limbs of bald island marlock. Amid the leaves, though, new fruits blossomed, the stamens spilling out in a rush of green.

"Most good teachers," I told the audience in Fremantle, "love life. They look at flowers and birds, pick gum nuts off the ground and, after turning them through their hands, stuff them into their pockets." Speeches are verbal equivalents of short essays. Audiences react to speeches spontaneously, much as readers do to articles in newspapers. Like comments made after the appearance of my essay, the small talk that followed the speech was more vital than the speech itself. Such talk was particular rather than abstract. "For a man you aren't bad," a woman said to me. "I had a tough time in class today," a lively and comely young teacher said; "my knickers kept getting stuck in my bum, and I had to tweak them out." "You have a beautiful inner being," began a teacher who had left Plato and Aristotle behind and embraced the new age. "I want to see your soul. Speak from the heart and reveal yourself." "No," I said. "Why didn't you bring copies of your books to Australia?" another teacher asked. "Stuffed animals took shelves of room in our suitcases," I explained.

Yesterday I spoke to second- and third-year students studying creative writing at the university. My topic was "The Uses of Experience." Because the audience was young, I warned them that many experiences destroyed not simply writing lives but lives themselves. I quoted Tennyson's poem "Ulysses," noting that when the hero said he would "drink life to the lees," he did not write for a deadline or have to drive home in a car. Much as I had done in the *West Australian*, I urged students to examine their worlds, whether they were sitting in Reid Library or pushing a cart down an aisle in a grocery in Subiaco.

"Details furnish paragraphs," I said; "without the right details your paragraphs will fail, and you will write abstractions. You may be profound, but your prose will be duller than ditch water." After I finished the talk and was stuffing my notes into a manila envelop, a man approached me. "Come outside," he said, "there is something you must see." On the grass below the steps to the Arts Building, two ravens shredded the body of a dead rat. "Look at the way that bird jerks the rat's tail then shakes his own head back and forth," the man said, pointing to the raven on the left, "that's a detail you wouldn't want to miss." The next morning a note appeared in my mailbox in the English department. The note described the clothes I wore while I talked: a black leather belt, khaki trousers, a blue-and-white-striped shirt, and a "flambouant red tie."

Big things lurk in small talk. "There are no bright kids in my class," Edward said last Monday; "the teachers won't let anybody be bright. Everybody has to learn the same things at the same pace, and it doesn't matter if somebody wants to learn more. The teachers won't give him a chance." Last night Francis typed 55378008 on his calculator. Then he turned the calculator upside down. The numbers read "BOOBLESS." "Where did you learn that?" I asked. "I learned it in camp in Maine," Francis said, "but kids were doing it at school today. Things get around." Yesterday was Edward's eleventh birthday. "I would have preferred," he said, "to have remained ten," adding that "ten is neutral." At ten, he explained, a boy could have "lots of fun without much responsibility."

"The way I write stories," Eliza said after I described the lecture, "is that I just open my head up and write about what comes into it." Eliza's most recent story, "What Tommy Grasshopper Saw," was short. "When

Tommy Grasshopper jumped he saw fields with horses running over them, trout swimming in rivers, a fox playing in a pine forest and an eagle circling round a mountain. He saw a lot in just one glance before he fell."

In essays I tell silly stories. Characters in the stories are dorky. In part I tell the stories simply because I like them. I also include them because I don't want readers to take my writing seriously. The ideas in my essays are not so important as the thoughts of people reading them. By changing tone I disrupt the flow of words in hopes that readers will pause and examine the ordinary things about them, their own thoughts or knickknacks on a bedside table. Some people, of course, shut my books and don't open them again. "I'm sorry, Sam," Vicki said recently when I read an excerpt from one of Slubey Garts's sermons, "I like a different brand of tea. You serve Lipton, and I prefer Twinings." As soon as Vicki stopped talking, I poured her a big pot of Lipton, stirring tablespoons of one-liners into it like sugar. "I couldn't commit suicide," Loppie Groat said the other day to Turlow Gutheridge, "not even if my life depended upon it." "Regular work tires a woman," Hink Ruunt said, indirectly explaining why he married seven wives, "but it flat out wrecks a man." After Hink's tobacco barn burned down, Sheriff Baugham investigated. "Hink," he said, "this looks like the work of an incendiary." "Incendiary, hell!" Hink exclaimed, "if this fire won't set then the raccoon can chew my rectum."

One cannot know the effects of writing upon readers. The product of mood, letters written to authors are unreliable. I know only one person whose behavior has been influenced by my essays: me. More and more I behave like someone from Carthage. Wednesday morning I wore a T-shirt to the swimming pool. On the front of the shirt a green frog peered through a red triangle. In his left hand the frog waved an American flag. Printed in white letters under the frog were the words *Toad Suck Daze—Conway, Arkansas.* Where did you pick up that shirt?" John asked me in the locker room. "The organizer of a crafts fair in Arkansas gave it to me," I replied. "For free?" John asked. "Yes," I said. "Well, you can't beat that," John said. "No," I said, "even if I had bargained for two or three hours, compliments dripping off my tongue like honey, I probably couldn't have gotten a better price."

John Locke said people were born blank tablets. Experience marked the tablets, shaping character and determining moral and financial success. When Ulysses said, "I am a part of all that I have met," he echoed Locke. I told students in the writing course that what they did or saw, heard, read, or imagined was matter for their tablets. I did not say that years of observing detail might mark that other tablet, personality. This past Friday, Vicki, the children, and I went downtown to buy presents for Edward's birthday. We roamed Perth for three hours. Crowds clotted streets. But I didn't really notice them; they were too large and anonymous. Instead I saw small things.

In the window of the Chokeby Road candy shop in the Piccadilly Arcade sat a chocolate Humpty Dumpty. He was four and a half feet tall and weighed 130 pounds. Perched on the side of his head was a sailor's cap made from white chocolate. On his feet he wore slippers, also made from white chocolate. He had fat lips and a bumpy, happy nose. This Humpty Dumpty was wide awake, not the careless sort liable to fall from his seat and break into bars. The whites of his eyes were chocolate, and the dark pupils soft nougats. While I looked at him, three people handed me vouchers. At the Bar Espresso in the Plaza Arcade I could get "two coffees for the price of one." At the Perth Town Hall, Revival Centres International staged a "Bible Prophecy Display." Admission, tea, and coffee were free. "Present this coupon to receive a FREE Big Mac with the purchase of another," the last voucher instructed, adding "valid only at McDonald's City Stores."

Ulysses exaggerated when he said he was a part of all he met. Like the crowds throbbing through Perth, much of life passes unobserved. Occasionally, however, a person notices details. From the gradual accumulation of detail comes awareness of both place and self. As the writer who does not describe carefully often loses readers, so the person who is unaware of detail is liable to be dissociated from place and community. He is likely, as Tennyson put it, "to rust unburnished, not shine in use." For my talk in Fremantle the Educational Department printed a program. On back of the program was Robert Herrick's poetic advice, "gather ye rosebuds while ye may." One flower leads to another, the rose to the cape daisy, the cape daisy to blue fanflower, the fanflower to a richer life. I quoted Tennyson to students because Richard Brantley, a friend from graduate school days at Princeton, recently sent me his latest book, a comparison of the writings of Tennyson and the American philosopher Ralph Waldo Emerson. "An open letter to Sam Pickering from his friend," Richard wrote on the title page.

After reading Richard's letter, I borrowed Tennyson's poems from Reid Library. A decade had passed since last I read his best-known poems. *In Memoriam* took three days to complete. Often while reading, I stopped and pondered. "Our little systems have their day," Tennyson wrote; "They have their day and cease to be." Societies, and sometimes philosophers, have systems. Rarely, though, do individuals think systematically. Instead people wander, roaming places and ideas and, as in my case, ladling out treacle. Every morning Vicki and I accompanied Edward and Eliza to school. In the afternoon we walked home with them. On the walks we studied the houses and gardens on Kingsway. Because real estate values were rising rapidly in Nedlands and because homes were exempt from capital gains tax, people invested savings in houses. "When the time comes for me to sell," Nigel told me, "I should make a bundle." Two days before, Carina builders started putting a tin roof on the big new house around the corner. The lot beyond the next house was vacant. Six weeks earlier, builders tore down a wooden house and hammered a sign into the yard reading "An Exciting New Development." Across the street a fence had been built around another house. Made from broom, the fence was seven feet tall. Vicki thought it resembled a hair shirt. To me it looked like a high starched collar. Three lots farther down the street a carpenter had just torn a rotten porch from a brick house built in the 1920s.

Vicki and I did not know the people who lived along Kingsway, but we knew their tastes, and we improved their houses, adding windows, pruning gardens, and converting shadowy garages into airy family rooms. We also knew their pets. The old black dog who was almost blind barked furiously at passersby when he was confined behind the fence that surrounded his yard. When he lay in the sun on the grass next to the curb, he wagged his tail. Although I walked along Kingsway at least twice a day, the walks never bored me. Yesterday bees swarmed on a peppermint tree. Beside a white gate berries hung so thick from duranta that they resembled a veil decorated with orange beads.

On Saturday, Vicki packed a picnic lunch, and we drove to Mersey Point at Rockingham. A small, flat-bottomed ferry took us around

Shoalwater Bay before dropping us at Penguin Island. The water was green, and a thatch of sea grass covered the bottom of the bay. Pied cormorants beat low straight lines over the water, and bridled terns spun around limestone outcrops, their flight patterns cutting silver swirls through the air. On the beach of Seal Island sea lions basked in the sun. From a distance they resembled boots, Wellingtons swept off the deck of a fishing boat, the rubber swollen in places, filled with sand, in other places rotting and collapsing in on itself.

Penguin Island was not quite forty acres, and after eating lunch under a Norfolk pine, we wandered about. Webs of orb-weaving spiders hung in tatters, the shreds yellow in the light. Under wattle were remnants of birds' nests, gray down clinging to twigs and lumping together in dusty mounds. Bones stuck out of the sand in white shards. King's skinks pressed themselves flat on the ground. They resembled stubby hunks of wood, but when they moved, they looked like soles ripped from the bottoms of shoes, the edges curling up in the heat. Banded rails rushed across a grassy plot behind a picnic table. Silver gulls bent over and hunching their necks forward bullied each other, yapping in irritation. Bridled terns bobbed on top of the scrub covering dunes, their long, low bodies slipping through the wind like outriggers sliding across waves.

We spent the afternoon swimming on the western side of the island. Near the shore waves spooned over the rocks, pulling off mouthfuls of stone. Chitons and limpets clung to the rocks while green crabs hid in crevices. Limestone reefs lay just beyond the beach, and the children and I swam over them, following fish as they turned through little canyons. Resembling a small, knotted rag, a blue-ringed octopus hurried across the edge of my vision then fell out of sight. At four o'clock the ferry took us back to Mersey Point. We bought Magnums and ate them, sitting on the grass. "What a great day," Edward said. "A super day," Francis added, a strip of chocolate falling onto his white T-shirt. "Yes," I answered, recalling "Ulysses," "we have touched 'the Happy Isles.' "

*From left to right: Edward, Francis,
and Eliza in their school uniforms.*

Francis, Eliza, and Edward at the foot of a giant tingle tree near Denmark, Western Australia.

Francis, Eliza, Vicki, and Edward at Green's Pool, near Denmark.

Christmas morning at 12 Melvista, Nedlands.

The Pickerings strolling through the Pinnacles in Nambung National Park, Western Australia.

Sam aboard Sammy, near Alice Springs, Northern Territory.

The base camp of Camel Outback Safaris, near Alice Springs.

Andrew saddling up at the base camp.

Rainbow valley, near base camp.

Ghost gum and camel riders.

Ayers Rock, or Uluru.

Francis and Sam atop Ayers Rock.

Vicki and Sam in the Olgas, or Kata Tjuta.

Edward, Eliza, and Francis in the Olgas.

Peter Murray of Kimberley Safaris.

The safari vehicles stopped beneath a boab in the Kimberley.

Shaving on safari.

Flowering wattles in the Kimberley.

Termite mound and Vicki.

Preparing to sleep "outside the prince's castle."

Sam at a swimming pool in the Kimberley.

Edward and Eliza waving from the Bungle Bungles.

*Outside the Wilgena Hotel in Tarcoola
during the journey to Sidney.*

Peering out the train window.

Price Waterhouse

In June," the woman said, "Price Waterhouse of Malaysia is sponsoring a management conference in Perth. One hundred and twenty account executives are flying from Kuala Lumpur. They will spend two days at the Burswood Resort. During mornings and afternoons they will attend lectures. We would like you to be one of our facilitators." I was in an office on the seventh floor of a building on St. George's Terrace. Over the chair in which I sat brown leather flowed seamlessly, resembling paint sweeping along the contoured fenders above the wheels of a Bentley or a long sleek Jaguar, a roadster from the 1950s, an arrow poised on the string of flight. The leather was so polished that when I crossed my right leg over my left, my trousers lost purchase, and if I had not jammed a foot into the rug, I would have slipped out of the chair. In front of me an oblong table stretched like a highway, yellow inlay cutting through the jarrah like lines marking lanes. Across the table from me a small woman wearing a blue suit sat on the lip of a chair. Behind her was a rectangular window. Clouds were not visible, and the window pressed against the sky, flattening distance, ironing wrinkles out of the day.

"Workshops at the conference," the woman said, "will explain the firm's new mission. We want managers to have a vision and to understand the firm's values. Here are our objectives," she said, handing me a sheet of paper on which she listed five goals. "By the end of the workshop," I read, participants will "be convinced of the power of vision and of the importance of values • understand what change is and why it is both necessary and vital • be able to manage themselves in an environment of change and will feel positive about it • be able to influence their subordinates so that the latter are equally receptive to change • and feel motivated, excited, and positive about the prospects of introducing the firm's vision, mission, and values."

181

In companies in which turnover of employees was rapid, motivational speeches were popular, forming part, as one "human resource director" told me, of "rest and recreation days." Bubbling with carbonated words like *creativity* and *flexibility*, motivational talks were snake oil. At best they resembled Grandmother's remedy for a cold, a teaspoon of sugar in a shot of bourbon. Sweet and palatable, such talks may intoxicate for a moment and actually clear worries from the head for an hour. By the end of a morning, however, the congestion of chore and responsibility invariably returned to plug the day. I had given motivational speeches. Money, not words, motivated me. Corporations paid so well that despite believing the speeches ineffectual I was willing to don the top hat and swallowtail coat of platitude and to hang a sandwich board of advice from a lectern like the rankest huckster swaggering from the rear of a wagon in some backwater alley. Still, I didn't like to think myself a charlatan. When asked to speak, I warned personnel directors that the effect of my performance would wear off as soon as I left the stage.

"Instead of having them listen to me," I told the woman, "why don't you order your managers to swim through a pool of strawberry ice cream? The ice cream will cost less, and the managers will never forget the experience." Despite the suggestion the woman urged me to send her a proposal for the conference. I agreed. My financial condition was not A-1. After six months in Perth the balance sheet on my interim report was beginning to tilt. Operating expenses in Australia had been high. No revenue was coming in, and trips to Alice Springs and the Kimberley loomed as future liabilities. If I could not trade upon intangible assets, I would have to write off our last month. Without amortization our fun would sink, a fiscal matter I could not explain easily to the minor shareholders sitting around the conference table in our dining room.

"One hundred and twenty Chinese accountants," Vicki said after I described the interview at Price Waterhouse. "Not one will understand your accent, much less your goofy stories. How do you plan," she continued, "to change the pattern of a thousand years of thought in a single speech? Only a swindler would even consider the talk." I wrote an honest letter to Price Waterhouse. "Your response may reduce the cash on hand," Vicki said, "but with me you will have credit for residual integrity."

Change and vision, I wrote, needed to be defined in detail. Was Price Waterhouse simply restructuring? I asked. "Companies seem to restructure every ten or fifteen years. Despite the upheaval competent employees adjusted. Does the change you mention imply that Price Waterhouse is swimming into financial straits it has avoided in the past? Or does change mean that Price Waterhouse wants employees to become involved in, say, community in ways they have not done before?" In the letter I urged the woman to flesh out *vision* and *mission*. For most people, I said, Price Waterhouse was a financial institution, a report printed on glossy paper sent to shareholders or a tall building with opaque windows staring over busy streets. Did Price Waterhouse, I asked, want to appear humane? In the United States many corporations attempted to change their public images, if not their substance, by seeming to become "eco-friendly," making contributions to environmental organizations. Did mission extend beyond sloganeering? Did mission involve "more than platitudes or 'showcasing' glitzy programs depicting Price Waterhouse as a responsible and concerned corporation?" Most people thought accounting hard and statistical, the poetry of numbers cacophonous, not rising through quatrains singing, but instead sinking, slumping against a dead bottom line. Did mission imply that employees would be urged to stray outside asset and liability columns? Beyond the page, I said, life was not clear, the best-kept books rarely balancing. Aside from reliability, what values did Price Waterhouse want associated with the firm's public image? Accounting for actions in this world was very different, I wrote, from accounting for money in a ledger.

Asking questions was easy. Answering was difficult. I knew the woman could not respond to the questions I posed, and I asked them as much for myself as for Price Waterhouse. Although motivational speakers talk much about values, they think little about them. Performance does not lend itself to deep thought. Likewise a business letter was not the forum for a discussion of values. Consequently I did not push *mission* about until the word grew sodden. Instead I skipped to the easier topic of the conference itself. "I suspect," I wrote, "that what Price Waterhouse really wants is for employees to be enthusiastic and energetic." Two years ago I talked to the personnel director of a company whose employees came and left like morning breezes.

The man asked me to chat about enjoying ordinary life. After my speech the director scheduled play. In one activity people shot water balloons at bull's-eyes, using catapults placed on opposite sides of a football field. The personnel director labeled the day "psychic rejuvenation." I doubt that psyches were rejuvenated, but employees had fun. At conferences, I wrote, pleasure was more important than education. "Avoid a rigorous course of meetings," I suggested; "too many lectures tire people and drain the spirit." I also warned the woman not to have high expectations. "No matter what speakers say, many long-term employees won't want to change their ways. After all they achieved their positions within the existing corporate framework. In contrast change may excite newer and lower-paid employees because it offers opportunities for advancement." My letter was commonsensical plain fare. "If you really want employees to become more creative and enthusiastic, encourage them to enrich their lives. The living room opens into the office. Private life influences public life. The concerns of the home often determine both the manner in which an employee accomplishes tasks and the satisfaction he finds in his job."

On paper I was a moralist, or at least a worrier. "Sending employees to Burswood Resort and *Casino*," I wrote, "is a mistake. For the person who loses a bankbook of money gambling, the conference will be a failure, no matter who speaks. Instead of feeling 'motivated, excited, and positive' about values, he will lament the value of the money he lost. The next time Price Waterhouse sends accountants to Western Australia bundle them off to Rottnest Island for a long weekend. Hire bicycles and prepare picnic lunches for them. Urge them to spend the days exploring the island. Don't try to accomplish much. Ideas blend nicely with coffee after breakfast and with dessert at dinner. They don't go down so well during the rest of the day. No matter the cook stirring the lesson, ideas curdle by ten-thirty in the morning."

I told friends in Storrs that I was going to Perth to refurbish my larder with zesty words and tangy scenes. I had written so much about Connecticut that I worried about paragraphs failing to rise. A pinch of yeasty eucalyptus and a basting of black swan might, I hoped, make my sentences swell fresh and appealing. While writing Price Waterhouse I examined the year in Perth not in culinary metaphors but in terms of yields and acquisitions, equity and obligation. The words were different from those I used in Storrs, and I was not comfortable with either the financial language or the financial doings. "What's against nature," as the old saying puts it, "just can't be did." Consequently I concluded my letter to Kuala Lumpur by asking an outrageous fee.

One Saturday, Slubey Garts sat in the reception room of Haskins Funeral Home writing a sermon on yellow paper. Proverbs Goforth walked into the home and seeing Slubey looked over his shoulder at the sermon. Across the top of the first page was written "Miracle of the Loaves and Fishes or Feeding the Five Hundred." "Slubey," Proverbs said after studying the page, "the gospel says the loaves fed five thousand folks, not five hundred." "Hold your tongue, Proverbs," Slubey responded, "people in Carthage may be gullible, but they aren't stupid. As it is I'm going to have plenty of trouble convincing them that five loaves fed five hundred people without a street of boardinghouses donating several hogsheads of bread puddings." Unlike Slubey, who tempered miracles in order to increase "inventory" at the Tabernacle of Love, I inflated my fee beyond market value in hopes of driving down my appeal. "You asked for seven thousand dollars!" Vicki exclaimed. "Nobody will pay that much."

The night after I mailed the letter to Kuala Lumpur, I wondered if I had acted impulsively. Price Waterhouse would probably have paid thirty-five hundred dollars. The money could have been put in escrow, in Vicki's hands, to pay for the five-day layover I scheduled in Fiji on the flight back to the United States. Shrugg Lovelace bought an insurance policy on his house in South Carthage just before burning it to the ground. "Shrugg," Sheriff Baugham said after stirring through the ashes, "did you have time to get the furniture out before you set the fire?"

Like Shrugg I acted hastily, my letter turning opportunity into smoke and doing so without the benefit of insurance. By the next morning, however, Price Waterhouse had drifted out of thought. At nine o'clock I was at College Park. Edward's baseball team played a game, and my turn had come to erect the dugouts, tents that sheltered children from the sun. From College Park, I drove to the Nedlands Library and returned twenty-four books. Then I went to Martineau's and bought five chocolate croissants. Afterward I rushed home, and Vicki drove to the grocery. At eleven o'clock I was back at College Park. In his last at bat, Edward hit a home run, his first of the season.

When the game ended, I took down the tents and carried them into the storeroom. At one-thirty Vicki, the children, and I were downtown. At five-thirty the children and I were swimming at City Beach. Vicki was in the living room at home, sipping tea and eating her croissant, the evening news on the television. We stayed at City Beach until after sunset. The waves tumbled endlessly in heavy, doughy rushes, and at dusk the sky was frothy. Streaks of color sprayed upward, swaths of pink, orange, and purple whisking across the horizon like confectioner's sugar in a mixing bowl. Later the horizon settled into icing, buttery and layered, binding evening to night. I was tired when I got home. The boys and I had a contest to see who could stand longest in the surf without getting knocked over.

People and corporations blunder through existence. Annual statements deceive. Financial and personal doings are not so clean and orderly as printed pages. According to an old Circassian tale angels never stumbled. Angels had eyes in their toes and were surefooted morally and physically. Always seeing what lay ahead, they did not step on honeybees or bang shins against temptation. That night when I pushed my chair back from the dinner table, pain jumped like the letter T across my lower back and up and down my right side and leg. While shopping Vicki bought sparklers for the children. Bending over so much that I resembled a safety pin, I shuffled to the stoop and watched the sparklers. My flame went out with the sparklers, and I spent the next four days flat in bed. Being down in the back, I told Vicki, was only a short-term liability. Although I did not say so, the liability was a sign that eventually I would be a long-term loss. "You can plan your life all you want," Slubey Garts said, "but finally life plans you."

While in bed I missed several things. A herpetologist visited Eliza's class. While children sat in a circle around him, the man held up a Gould's snake, then a dugite and a tiger snake. "The snakes were used to being handled," Vicki said after I asked if the children were close to the man when he held them. "Suppose the dugite had bitten him, and he dropped it," I said; "what would have happened then?" "Don't be a worrywart," Vicki said; "the snake didn't bite him, and he didn't drop it. People are more relaxed in Australia than in Connecticut." "But," I began, turning toward Vicki to emphasize the point I was going to make. I got no further. Pain dug into my hip like fangs then twisted venomously down my right leg.

The days spent in bed were not a complete write-off. I read, mostly books, but other things also. In the newsletter from Francis's school the chaplain lamented the declining number of young men studying to be priests. "Perhaps," he wrote, "if all our families prayed for an increase of priestly and religious vocations at Sunday Mass, God would bless us with many more." For his English class Francis unearthed a "Confidential Watch List" purportedly published by the CIA and describing ten spies wanted by the Interstellar Federation. Most wanted was Aaron C. Morgan, a graduate of Massachusetts Institute of Technology, the university Francis dreams of attending. Also listed were Genghis T. Stevenson, Ujalambo G. Harrison, and Sir Reynolds Busch-Wellington. The books were a mixed lot, being not simply those in the house but those I could reach when I was alone: Albert Facey's *A Fortunate Life*, published when the writer was eighty-eight, an account rich with detail and sentiment describing growing up poor in Western Australia at the beginning of the twentieth century; *Birthday*, a children's book Eliza read and left on the bed, the story describing a friendship between a boy named Samuel and Benjamin, a one-legged cockatoo; then two of Raymond Chandler's mysteries, *The Long Good-Bye* and *The Playback*, Chandler's detective Philip Marlowe avoiding, to use an accounting term, liquidation only through luck.

The book I enjoyed most was Charles Dickens's *Little Dorrit*. The last time I read *Little Dorrit* was twenty-six years ago. Although I have aged considerably since then, the book remained fresh, its narrative spine firm, its theme and structure limber, not like me creaking and crumbling under the weight of time and pages. What a person reads colors his thought, especially when he cannot change his position and thereby see different things. "How not to do it," Dickens wrote, describing a bureaucracy established by the government, "was the great study and object of all public departments and professional politicians all round the Circumlocution Office." Australians addressed one another by their Christian names. Sometimes the egalitarianism seemed just salutation deep. "When it comes to political doings," Nigel said, "boards and councils make decisions behind closed doors, excluding the people they are supposed to represent. Studies are commissioned and written but never released to the public who paid for them. Here the government won't tell citizens how they have not done it."

Nigel was outspoken. Occasionally, though, he seemed right. A study of education in Western Australia ranked secondary schools on the basis of graduates' results on university entrance examinations. To get a copy of the study a local television station was forced to sue the state government. Educational studies always distort. A school in a poor district, for example, may be accomplishing more educationally, and socially, than a school in a wealthy district. Yet because of the children's lives at home and countless other factors, students from the wealthy district may score much higher on standardized tests than those from the poor district, creating the superficial impression that the school in the affluent area is far better than that in the poor area. Simply because surveys distort, however, Circumlocution Offices should not forbid the public from examining them. From mulling, from analysis and talk, not silence, comes awareness. "What West Australia needs," Nigel said, "is a Sunshine Law that opens meetings to the public. No matter what politicians say, a muddy pit produces water, not wine."

Bed rest helped my back and gave my entrepreneurial instinct opportunity to regain strength. One night an editor from *National Geographic* telephoned from Washington. He was writing an article entitled "Searching for Walt Whitman," the kind of piece that frees one to scavenge across an eccentric landscape. When the writer turned over a newspaper column, I scuttled out. We talked for some time about poets, not simply Whitman but Wordsworth and Tennyson, too. The man asked me to send him "a couple of pages" describing both me and the room in which I wrote. I agreed and then asked him to look at *Trespassing*, a collection of my essays just published in the United States. "You will like *Trespassing*," I said, adding that if he included anything about me in the article I'd appreciate his mentioning the book. I have never made more than three thousand dollars on a book. "Maybe *Trespassing* will make the best-seller list," I said to Vicki when she brought me dinner in bed; "then the cost of Australia won't bankrupt us."

The day after I got out of bed Vicki drove me to the office, and I sent the man two pages. I filled the pages with detail, the kind of clutter that makes articles and, in another form, mission statements entertaining. I described the railing outside my window where Fred the kookaburra perched. I said I wore cotton shorts; running shoes, the heels of which were slipping down over the soles; and short-sleeve shirts, the sort of shirts worn by nice boys raised in the 1950s, stripes of yellow, green, and blue encircling the bodies in big bands. Instead of describing my physical appearance I said I resembled Daddy, the father often seen sitting in a folding chair in a drafty auditorium waiting for a daughter to finish a ballet lesson, the father who umpires a son's baseball game and misses half the calls, none of the other parents getting very irritated at him, however.

In Perth the University of Western Australia Press was publishing *Trespassing* in April. The press bought on to the run of books published in the United States. While the press got the books cheaply, the American publisher was able to reduce his "per-unit cost." The more books printed, the less each cost to print. For my part I received about fifty cents royalty per book, for a total of two hundred and fifty dollars, money for pizza and croissants. The press was kind to publish the book, and I wanted to sell the printing for them. When I left Australia, I hoped good memories, not a warehouse of unsold books, would linger behind. Consequently, ten days after hurting my back, Vicki, the children, and I spent an afternoon off Point Walter Reserve walking along the sandbar into the Swan River.

Scores of spotted jellyfish were snagged on the sandbar. In the shallows they resembled green cabbages. The children picked them up and carried them to deeper, flowing water. Birds bustled about us. Near the boat ramp ring-necked parrots rang loudly. Silver gulls quarreled under a fig tree, and pied cormorants perched on the jetty. An Australian pelican flew overhead, its wings arching across sight. A black-winged stilt hunted along the shore, its long thin legs maidenly and too fragile for the throb of motor and the heavy wash rolling behind cabin cruisers. When the stilt flew, its legs trailed behind its body, resembling lengths of twine caught in a wind and blown straight. Black ducks paddled lazily through rocky pools. Terns hurried overhead: fairy, Caspian, and crested. Occasionally one fished and wheeled by, a silver minnow in its bill. In flight the wings of terns bent back sharply like staples, the long feathers at the end of each wing pulled to thinness by speed, making the birds seem faster than they were. Over the sandbar flew small flocks of red-necked stints, red-capped plovers, and pied oyster catchers, the bills of these last brighter than the skin of ripe tomatoes.

Birds were not our only companions on the sandbar. Accompanying us were two photographers from *Who* magazine. The day before a writer interviewed us in the living room at home. Many articles in *Who* described people whose public lives seemed only private parts. I agreed to be interviewed because I thought an article might sell *Trespassing*. The woman who interviewed me was pleasant, and the article she wrote was familial. To check her facts she read the article to me over the telephone. Only one fact was wrong. She said I hurt my back surfing. Surfing sounded more romantic than getting up from the dinner table, so I did not correct the writer, thinking paper truth an improvement upon actual event. Strangers do not acknowledge each other when they meet on the street in Perth. When spoken to, at least by me, people set their lips in straight lines and look down at the sidewalk or into the distance where I don't exist. After I hurt my back and had to hobble along sidewalks, people became friendlier. In two days, four strangers greeted me like a cousin from the proper side of the family, saying, "Been surfing, have you?"

Although four weeks have passed since I hurt my back, I cannot bend over or turn my hips quickly. On the other hand my entrepreneurial instinct has recovered completely. Two days after leaving bed, I wrote *Holiday*, "Australia's Own Travel Magazine," in hopes of bartering an article for the cost of a camel trek in the Northern Territory. Recently the superintendent of schools in the Kimberley asked me to visit several schools. Not many visitors see the far north of Western Australia. Unfortunately travel cost so much the superintendent could not pay an honorarium. *Holiday* did not answer my letter, and I worried about money again. "Let me think about this," I said to the superintendent. The next morning I called the Education Department and suggested it pay me a modest fee. "That way," I said, "I could justify being away from family for four or five days." That night I received a telephone call from the Graduate School of Management at the university, asking me to speak at a dinner for employees of Western Mining and Alcoa. The employees were completing "a seven-day residential management education programme," one that contained a healthy dose of recreation and motivation. "We can offer you two hundred dollars," a man said on the telephone. "I'll speak for five hundred," I said. "Done," he said.

I spoke at the dinner during my second week out of bed. I spoke four times that week. For talking to eleventh and twelfth graders at John XXIII and to seventh graders at Wesley College, I did not ask a fee. For giving a keynote address at the Joondalup Literary Conference, I received one hundred and fifty dollars and two bottles of wine. The woman who introduced me at Joondalup mentioned the essay I had written for the *West Australian* on the importance of being dorky. At the end of her introduction, she turned and gesturing toward me said, "And here he is. Let us welcome Professor Dork." "She labeled you correctly," Vicki said later, adding, "anyone who speaks twice in one week for nothing and then a third time for a couple of trips to the grocery is a simpleton. To become a good speaker you have incurred twenty years of development and production costs. When Western Mining and Alcoa sell their products, they charge for their costs."

For a week after getting out of bed I hobbled. Last year in Connecticut, after I hurt my back shoveling snow, I walked with a cane. In Perth, I leaned on a wooden mop handle. The handle was four feet long. Attached to the end of the handle was a swivel then a plastic rectangle, three and a half inches wide and eight and a half inches long. Resembling a week's growth of beard, thick Velcro bristles covered the side of the rectangle farthest from the handle. When Vicki mopped the kitchen floor, she pushed the bristles down onto a red sponge. When I limped about, I held the mop bristles up and jabbed the end of the wooden handle into dirt and cracks in the sidewalk.

Despite tottering I tried to maintain my "productive capacity" and collect raw material for essays. I stumped through our neighborhood. Although I did not know many people, the streets above Melville Water were familiar. I walked along Bruce past the Nedlands Park Croquet Club then the Nedlands Bridge Club and finally the Tennis Club. Across the grass courts, sprays of water swished like soft silver feathers. From the tops of Canary Island date palms, fruit spilled through the fronds in damp orange streams. On the ground surrounding the trunks of the trees, dates spread like tablecloths. Galahs bobbed pink and white through grass along the bluff overlooking Melville Water. Above them swallows tobogganed through the air.

Spotted doves hurried into flight, their wings squeaking and resembling rusty cranks jerked into motion. While a pair of red wattlebirds gargled in a banksia, magpies strolled about, appearing self-assured and almost disdainfully formal in black and white. The yellow spikes of slender banksia glowed. At first glance the old cones were not noticeable. Gray and hairy they lurked amid the leaves, resembling trolls wary of light. Acorn banksia also flowered, orange blossoms sweeping up the white spikes. Firewood banksia was swelling toward bloom. Green bundles shaped like arrowheads thrust outward from deep within the cone. Once in the sunlight they expanded, unraveling the gray-and-white patterns that seemed to bind the cones into needlepoint.

By the entrance to the Nedlands Yacht Club at the foot of the bluff a sheoak bloomed. Twisted around small stems in silver braids, the flowers hung down, turning the tree pastel and drawing a hive of bees. Because pain forced me to walk slowly, I saw more than I did on faster walks, for example, the Gallop House built in the 1870s. With wrought-iron railings and a tin roof, the house resembled an ornate stone shoe box. Below the house the foreshore opened into a field. At the edge of the field stood a sign reading, "City of Nedlands Teeing Area. 6:00 A.M. to 10:30 A.M. Monday to Friday Only. Permit required for Golf Practice. Replace Divots." The last phrase on the sign, "Beware of Cyclists and Pedestrians," seemed an afterthought.

Pedestrians mattered little in Western Australia. Rarely did drivers slow cars to allow people to cross streets. Each day when Vicki and I walked the children to school, we crossed Princess Avenue. Never did a driver slow down and let the children cross safely. Cars not people had the right-of-way in Perth. Even when the children had clearly been standing at the corner of Kingsway and Princess for a long time and were just starting to cross Princess, a car inevitably hurried down Kingsway, ran the stop sign on the children's right, and turning left brushed the children back onto the curb. When I approached the teeing area it was after ten-thirty. Practicing golf on the foreshore was not without drawbacks for the golfer. While a slice could disappear into shrubs and high grass along the bluff, a hook splashed into the water. One morning while counting white saucer jellyfish I saw a man wading in the water, searching for balls. He had little luck, so I found two balls for him.

On my walks time was not, as accountants phrase it, money, but flowers. In yards honeysuckle, daylilies, lantana, hibiscus, and golden guinea blossomed. Amid the scrub below the bluff granite kunzea bloomed in scarlet fist-size bunches. Yellow horns reared upward from tree tobacco, almost as if the twigs were jazzmen blowing blossoms toward the clouds. A hedge of plumbago softened a corner. Petals dripped from frangipani, and from a mound of veronica blossoms shot upward in small blue jets. Along the roadside, flatweed was yellow. In gardens roses grew angular and sharp, the leaves coppery and poisonous, but the blossoms soft puddles, breezes drawing fragrance from them like the sun pulling dew from a wet field.

My walks were circular, ending at home where they began. They made my back feel better, though, rejuvenating not a psyche but a lumbar region. I got exercise, looking up at trees as well as down at flowers: Norfolk Island pine, branches rising above one another in circular layers like plates on a lazy susan, and Mediterranean cypress, narrow and bringing accounting to mind with its thin world of lien and ledger. The yellow blossoms of illyarrie smelled like angel food cake, "store-bought not homemade cake," Vicki said. Fruit hung in purple bunches on lilly pillys. Crunchy and mildly sweet, the fruits were full of water. Umbrella trees blossomed. Red flowers clung in bundles to spikes spinning around each other like spokes on the wheel of a bicycle. Gungurru bloomed, stamens spraying out liquid from the white cups. From coral gums buds stuck out like sharp nails protruding from the knucklebones of an ancient bird. Before the flowers bloomed, the buds expanded and the caps fell off, the stamens then rising frothy out of the buds, for a moment turning the buds into soda glasses bubbling with crimson.

I spent much time between Birdwood and Waratah, roaming Carroll, Browne, Wavell, and Throssell. A pug followed me up Sadlier, snorting and grunting. Twice I fetched him from the middle of the road. A Chinese man parked a BMW in front of a house that was for sale then walked around the yard. On Hobbs, I found a house for us. "A Tudor style home" with "five bedrooms, two bathrooms, dining room, lounge, family room, television room and pool," as an advertising weekly described it; the house sold last week for $775,000 at auction, a price beyond even the most larcenous regimen of motivational speeches.

The collection of houses in the neighborhood resembled an architectural cocktail, each house being a section from a different fruit: mandarin, plum, orange, and pomelo. On one side of a French provincial stood an English cottage, on the other side a Tuscan villa. Below the prow of a stucco-and-glass ship squatted a red-brick that I associated with childhood in Nashville and air cloudy with smoke from bituminous coal, not with downtown Perth rising in the distance clean between marri trees, the buildings blue columns drawn on white graph paper. The children's favorite house was number 27 on Birdwood. Two stories tall, the house had white columns and high windows surrounded by green shutters. "Although not as big," Edward said, "it reminds me of a southern house." "I like the house," Eliza said, "but it is strange to find such a place here." Despite limestone walls, red tiles, and tin roofs, many homes reminded me of elsewheres, and despite the auctions, ordinary elsewheres, of Moline and Orlando, Paducah and Wytheville. "Everything is jumbled," Edward said after a walk, "but I would like to live here in a house with large windows and a tennis court." "And with a big yard," Eliza added, "so George could run around." "We would also need a Land Rover," Francis said; "then we could travel in the bush." "What does a new Land Rover cost?" I asked. "Almost a hundred thousand dollars," Francis said. "Living here would bankrupt me," I said, feeling a twinge in my back, "and I would die in the poorhouse."

"A man called from Malaysia," Vicki said when I returned home one afternoon from a walk. "I told him you were out, and he said he would call again tomorrow afternoon at four o'clock." Despite being handsome, many of the houses on Birdwood Parade seemed gilded cages, their bars forged not from iron or steel but from the harder, and sometimes invisible, amalgams of receivables and mission statements. At four o'clock the next afternoon I defaulted. When the telephone rang I was not home. That morning I agreed to speak to an eighth-grade class for free. I spent the afternoon at the university looking at banksia: lemony Wallum, orange hairpin, and southern plains, the flowers of this last resembling mugs, yellow flowing out of them brighter than coin.

Loony with April

"Ice is still melting on Davis Road," Ellen wrote from Storrs. "The winter was wonderful and stormy, and there was plenty of skiing. But now it's time for spring. The snow was a good blanket, and I'll have a huge poppy crop. The cat, loony with April, dances for us during dinner in the field outside the dining room windows." In Perth, March waltzed into April, the temperature dipping in the early morning but hiking upward by midafternoon. Kookaburras clattered at daybreak, and small flocks of honeyeaters squeaked through the bushes in the backyard. Ring-necked parrots reappeared and hung upside down in the gum trees. The water in the Nedlands community pool cooled, and leaves from coral trees floated on the surface in brown mats. Cones fell from the white cypress behind the pool, the valves thrusting outward to disperse the seeds, the wood seeming to explode, the cones resembling minute brown soccer balls pumped too full of air. Fruit fell from lilly pillys and stained sidewalks, resembling purple ground beef.

In four months we flew back to Connecticut. At night Vicki and I discussed leaving. Our moods varied. Some nights we speculated about what we would miss when we were in Storrs. "Probably nothing," I once said; "I will be so busy figuring taxes, preparing classes, and driving the children to soccer and ballet that I won't have time to miss anything." Other nights I regretted not looking for a job in Australia. "If I were offered a post here, I'd probably take it," I told Vicki, "but I don't have the initiative to find a position on my own." Teaching had been so comfortable that I was not as resourceful as I was when I was younger.

At the beginning of April, I stepped mechanically through days like a student in dancing class, doing what I had done many times before. On the first of April, I drove the family to Jarrahdale. Vicki packed a picnic lunch. We ate beside a small stream then spent the afternoon walking in the bush along Darling Scarp. At the falls, water rolled over a rocky lip and, twisting into a white ribbon, fell into a green pool. Above the pool red granite walls rose like the sides of an old pot, a kettle set in charcoal and used for boiling tea. From a hole in the bottom of the kettle the river dribbled away over rocks. Along the bank scarlet robins flashed through trees, the red crowns on their heads gleaming against green leaves. From a hillside gray with marri, two-leafed hakea, and rock sheoak, a flock of black-and-white cockatoos called, their cries nipping at the edge of sight but the birds themselves invisible. Butter and salmon white gum grew along the scarp, the new bark on this last flush with pink and orange.

A fire had seared the scarp, and near our path stood a sign reading "Serpentine National Park Boundary." The back of the sign was black with ash, and the letters had blistered. The fire had burned away one of the two legs supporting the sign, so that it resembled a flag blown taunt by wind. Beside a dark rock seeds tumbled out of zamia. An inch and three-quarters long and surrounded by a damp orange rind, the seeds were pale yellow and resembled heavy knucklebones. On the walk we startled gray kangaroos. Ants' nests spread across the trail like scars, no plants growing near them. Holes pocked the nests. When Edward skipped a stone over a nest, ants boiled out like black steam erupting from under the lid of a pot hot and thumping atop a stove. We hiked until our thighs ached. Then we started home. At the edge of the park I stopped at a small store, the Jarrah Joint, and Vicki bought $17.80 worth of breakfast goodies, a jar of banksia honey and five pots of jam: plum, peach, nectarine, ginger and fig, and lastly sweet amber, a blend of melon, lemon, and ginger.

Although everything in life is fleeting, both failure and success, even the family one fathers and nourishes, confronting evanescence isn't cheery. Man lives almost as much by fiction as by bread. Imagining conclusions to life that are not conclusions, he transforms endings into beginnings. He dreams that some mark he scratched will endure into time. Thoughts about leaving Australia brought mortality to mind. The year in Perth was an emblem of life. Once I left Australia, I would not return. Place and person would sift out of recollection, much as my parents vanished from my thought, leaving a scribble here, an image there, lightwood to flare for a moment in another generation's memory before becoming ash.

Repetition creates the illusion of continuity. The morning after our trip to the Serpentine National Park, I repeated the day, driving to Lake Leschenaultia. Vicki put some of the jam and the remnants of the lunch we took to Jarrahdale into the cooler. At a roadside stand near Chidlow we bought fruit. After eating on a patch of grass above the shore, we walked six kilometers around the lake. Moorhens scratched amid reeds at the edge of the lake, sounding like bigger animals. Once we left the shoreline, the day dried. Green grass disappeared, and small balls of laterite rolled underfoot. I recognized many plants: wandoo, parrot bush, grass trees, and harsh hakea. I wondered how soon they would wither out of memory. Bound to place, they would not transplant to Connecticut. I looked at bull banksia. The leaves resembled blades on a double-edged saw, each tooth rounding up to a point, giving it the appearance of a flattened eggshell. I picked a cone off the ground. The cone was six inches tall and three inches broad; forty-six follicles were open. Jarrah shimmered across a hill, its stringy bark resembling slats on picket fences, the color gray but turning blue the longer I looked.

The first days of April passed smoothly, and I shuffled easily through them. Easter morning I got up early and hid twenty-one eggs in the yard, something I do every spring in Connecticut. So that crows don't find them and spoil the children's Easter egg hunt, I hide the eggs in hollow logs and beneath rocks. Because red-back spiders lurked about the house in Perth, I hid the eggs in the open, wedging them in the crooks of trees and tying them up in vines, weaving creepers about them like gloves. Because April is often rainy in Connecticut, Vicki puts the children's baskets in the garage. In Perth she put them in the laundry room. The contents of the baskets were the same, however, a mound of chocolate eggs in a grassy nest of shredded green paper. Guarding the eggs were three ten-and-a-half-inch chocolate rabbits. Dressed in shiny tinsel, two rabbits were soldiers and wore red caps with black bills. The other rabbit was a geisha girl. She wore a frilly pink jacket and held a silver fan in her right hand.

For lunch Vicki cooked a roast and baked a chocolate cake. After lunch I drove to Scarborough Beach, and we bodysurfed. The waves were smooth and tall, and rides lasted longer than my breath. Swimming tired us, and after changing clothes, we bought waffle cones at the Great Australian Creamery. I ate two scoops, Jaffa atop ginger swirl. The following weekend I took Edward to a baseball dinner. Instead of singling out the best players for awards, the coach bought trophies for all the boys, telling them teams played together, not as individuals. The next morning Edward played his first soccer game, his team, Subiaco, beating the Infant Jesus 3 to 1 with Edward getting two assists.

On Friday I went to the assembly at Nedlands Primary. Eliza received a certificate of merit. Mrs. Odgers spent hours on her certificates, putting seventeen stickers on Eliza's card, including, among others, a pink horse, a yellow-and-blue butterfly, a blue whale, and two teddy bears sliding down a rainbow. Mrs. Odgers's students loved her, and several nights arguments between Edward and Eliza disrupted dinner, Edward, whom Mrs. Odgers had not taught, declaring that she could not be as good a teacher as Mrs. Titchen in Storrs, and Eliza, who never had a class with Mrs. Titchen, maintaining that no one could teach as well as Mrs. Odgers. Mrs. Odgers knew her students well. Eliza received her certificate, Mrs. Odgers wrote, for "being an outstanding class member in all areas throughout the first term and for being a responsible and innovative vice-treasurer for Red Cross, Exemplary behavior, Excellent story writing, Super 'Save the Whale' letter to Prime Minister Keating, Excellent endeavour with swimming, Enthusiastic Gould League member, Enthusiastic astronomer at Star Gazing" and "Magical music maker." "Remember," Mrs. Odgers wrote at the bottom of the card, "it's O.K. not to be perfect all the time."

Shortly after the assembly odd notes began to ring through days. From Brisbane a woman wrote, inviting me to speak at a conference in November. She said sponsors of the conference would pay for my travel and accommodations, adding, "We do however ask that you waive any speaker's fee that you may normally charge when attending such an event." The flight from Connecticut to Queensland took thirty-six hours one way, or three days round-trip. The conference itself lasted four days. "A week," I replied, "is a chunk out of the life of a middle-aged man, too big to give away."

While waiting for a prescription at a drugstore, I read *The Combantrin Guide to Worms*. The thread worm, the guide stated, was "the most common parasitic worm affecting Australians." "With thread worms it doesn't really matter how young or old, how clean or careful, how rich or poor you are. The fact is that sooner or later someone in your family is likely to catch thread worms." Not only could people become infested by eating infected food but they could also simply inhale the eggs. Once in the stomach the eggs hatched. "At night," the guide explained, "the female thread worm lays thousands of eggs around the outside of the anus" (afterward referred to here as the you-know-what).

"The 'glue type' substance used to stick the eggs to the you-know-what causes the person to scratch, thereby transferring the eggs to the fingernails, back to the mouth, and continuing the cycle." Suddenly I began to itch, not simply at the place so often mentioned in the guide but between my ears, under my toes, and around my belly button. To discover if one had worms, the guide suggested that a person use a flashlight and "look for moving worms around the you-know-what at night." Only a contortionist could use this method without the aid of a companion, and Vicki being less than expert with a flashlight, I ruled out this method of detection. For that lone person who lived without benefit of a friend with medicinal insight, the guide suggested that before bathing in the morning "press a piece of sticky tape (sticky side out) over the you-know-what. Any eggs will adhere to the tape."

The doings of a day often resemble colored threads bound together only by hours. Matters that itch in the morning rarely stick to the brain at night. In hopes of discovering a book on parasites I hurried from the pharmacy to the university bookstore. Piled by the cash register was a stack of flyers announcing a lecture entitled "Inside the Eye of the Storm, Coping with Stress More Effectively." Reading the flyer purged worms from my system. Admission to the lecture cost twenty dollars. "For free," I said aloud; "I'd teach people how to cope with stress for free. My talk would be short, too," I said, addressing Thryza at the cash register. "And I would be clear. I wouldn't mention mystifiers like 'adaptive energy' or 'dynamic stillness.' I would come right to the innards of the matter, dividing my speech into five parts." "What parts?" Thryza asked. "One," I replied, "aiming the gun. Two, the decorous use of arsenic. Three, the rope, the noose, and the drop. Four, from the high dive into the empty pool. Five, the pharmacist as undertaker, or getting tablets from Pilljerk Peter."

"Parasites," I muttered, leaving the bookstore, "people who promise to cure the ills of personality feed on weakness and unhappiness." "This kind of talk," I said later, showing the flyer to Nigel, "gives me a royal pain in the ass." In the mail that afternoon I received a copy of *Trespassing*, my latest collection of essays. "Here is the new book," I said to Vicki when I walked in the door. "Sam," Vicki said, "I want to read it, but I am awfully wound up in *Anne of Green Gables* right now."

Vicki has not read any of my books. Still, whenever one is published I urge her to sample a page. "Writers now imitate me," I said; "they find my books inspirational and write essays like mine." "Inspirational," Vicki repeated, raising an eyebrow; "chronicling the doings of our days is not inspirational. What do they write?" she continued, fashioning a sample paragraph. "I got up at six forty-five and had a crap. It took four minutes and fifty-eight seconds. Then I went to the kitchen and found half an English muffin left over from yesterday's breakfast. There wasn't any margarine in the house, but I ate the muffin anyway."

Although months may turn to the rhythm of the spheres, the mind works by association. The egg that enters the body through the eye eventually hatches and wiggles into view. The next night I spoke to the Friends of the Reid Library. Recent speakers discussed art and philosophy with the Friends, "Light and Shadow in Seventeenth-Century Italian Painting," for example. I began my talk conventionally. "Friends of libraries," I said, "are always wonderful folks. They are quirky and nice, very different from Advocates of Learning Resource Centers, these last being people with whom one can mate surreptitiously but with whom one must never be seen breaking bread." A therapeutic lecture followed the introduction, not "Inside the Eye of the Storm, Coping with Stress" but "Inside the Bowel, Coping with Flatulence."

Twenty years ago I spent a summer reading sixteenth-century herbals, searching for causes of and remedies for the wind colic. I intended to write a breezy scholarly article on such matters in the eighteenth-century novel. Although I did not write the article, I kept the research in my library thinking that it might come in handy someday, much as Australians keep Combantrin in the medicine cabinet. The Friends of the Library were middle-aged, just the audience to benefit from a dose of my research. The talk was a success. "Breaking wind," one woman wrote the next day, "is a major activity in our house. We talk more about farting than almost any other subject. Yet last night was the first time I ever heard a lecture devoted to this common and most interesting of human activities."

April had become a jitterbug. The morning after the lecture I flew to Sydney. The next day I appeared on *Mid-Day*, a television show. Immediately after the program I returned to Perth. Traveling was tiring, and I told friends I made the trip to publicize *Trespassing*. I really made the trip for that most frivolous of all reasons, just to say that I had done it: flown across the continent and back for an interview lasting eight minutes. I spent the night in Sydney in the David Bath suite in the Sebel Townhouse. The suite consisted of a bedroom, sitting room, bathroom, and two foyers, one of the foyers inside the entrance to the suite and the other outside the bathroom. In the suite were two television sets, two videocassette players, two desks, four telephones, and two big bathroom sinks, one of these in the foyer. That night I watched *Rising Sun*, a movie about crooks in businesses owned by Japanese in the United States. When I travel, I don't sleep well, and I watch movies that I wouldn't bother even to read about at home.

I ate dinner in the Encore Restaurant in the hotel. For an appetizer I ordered roast pumpkin and coconut soup with a crab samosa for $7.00. For the main course I ordered a "Medley of Seafood on Avocado, Roast Capsicums and Mesclun Salad drizzled with Roveill." The salad cost $18.50, setting a new record for the most expensive salad I had ever eaten. Although the television program paid for the meal, I felt guilty about spending so much for dinner. Ordering made me feel as if I was a conspicuous consumer, and I wanted to fade into the wallpaper, not that of a chic restaurant but that depicting a simpler, less expensive time and place, a wallpaper decorated with ricks of hay; a heavy wagon with wooden wheels pulled by a tall horse, in the seat a shepherd dog gray around the muzzle; nearby a slow creek flowing over round pebbles; and then under a bushy oak, a stone cottage, buckets heavy with butter standing by the door.

Anonymity did not last. "I think you are much better looking than Robin Williams," my waiter said. Three months earlier the waiter heard me talk about the movie *Dead Poets Society* on the radio, and he remembered the sound of my voice. I have been interviewed on radio and television many times in Australia, and strangers occasionally recognize me. "You!" a woman shouted as I hurried into the terminal at the Sydney airport on the way back to Perth; "I just saw you on television. I stayed home to watch. I worried that I might miss my plane. But here you are." "Yes," I answered, "here I am."

By becoming an observer a person escapes identity. In the restaurant I took out a pad and pencil and faded out of personality, if not into the wallpaper. "I put ten dollars on it on Saturday," a bald man said discussing a horse race, "but I didn't follow it up." A Spanish couple with a teenage daughter sat near me. A waiter mixed a Caesar salad for them. "This is very special," he said, "for my new friends from Spain." "Okay, darlings," another waiter said to two middle-aged women, "how are you going?" Laughter fluttered through the room sounding like thick crisp bills being shuffled. A waitress wandered from table to table grinding pepper. I ordered an espresso. Six candies accompanied it, two chocolate bonbons, two fruit tarts, and two small bars bumpy with nuts. I decided to eat only two of the candies, but eventually I ate all six. The salad was not large, and if Vicki's leftover muffin had appeared on the table, I would have eaten it also.

I got up early the next morning. After eating eggs Benedict, I walked up Elizabeth Bay Road to Kings Cross. In October, I spent four days in Sydney. One night I explored Kings Cross. The "sex industry," as reporters dub prostitution, struck me as not only seedy but soiling, and I was happy to return to Perth. By day I thought Kings Cross might look different. Along side streets wrought-iron railings bent around buildings. From a garden a gum tree rose straight and muscular, the new bark blue in the morning light. The fountain in Fitzroy Gardens resembled the seedhead of a silver dandelion. Sprayed in black along the back of a red wooden bench were the names Cindy and Ted. A backpacker with stony calves sat in a white plastic chair outside a café drinking a cappuccino. A greengrocer sold grapes to an old woman wearing a red shawl and pushing a handcart.

I was tempted to wander more, but then I noticed teenagers slumped in doorways. Their eyes resembled old marbles chipped and ground out of luster. Their arms moved stiffly like limbs on trees dried by winds. They seemed rotted, not by the age that comes to everyone, but by the absence of vitality, as if some parasite had bored into their beings and gnawed their quickness into brown granules. Suddenly I remembered the first sentence of Edward's latest story. "I relaxed," he wrote, "and gazed at the endless sea of stars." Kings Cross seemed like old night, dark and without stars, or hope.

Thirty minutes later I arrived at channel 9. I was early, so I went to the waiting room and drank a soda. Also in the room were a doctor and her two-year-old son. While the doctor sat on a sofa and read a script, her son played with blocks. On a landing pad outside the window sat a helicopter with a green propeller. "That helicopter brought me here," I said to the boy, "but I didn't travel inside. I stood on top of the propeller." When the boy looked intrigued, I told him that sometimes I stood on my hands and that once I did a back flip. The boy and I were busy building a helicopter with the blocks when the "segment producer" appeared to talk to me. The producer was nervous, and she lectured me, explaining how I should behave "on air." I became irritated. "Sugar," I said, talking like one of the rougher characters from Carthage, the sort of person whom I do not allow off backstreets into my essays, "stop worrying. I don't say *turd* on television unless folks preach to me beforehand."

A daily television show resembles a thick sandwich, each guest being an ingredient: a snippet of lettuce, a slice of tomato, or a handful of bean sprouts. I did not meet the host until I stepped onto the set. After a woman dusted me with powder, "to cut the glare," she said, I waited backstage. The audience was live. To keep them enthusiastic, a heavyset man with a pigtail jollied them along during advertisements, telling jokes and getting them to play children's games. The itsy-bitsy spider climbed up the garden wall while I waited offstage. Near the end of a segment of advertisements a woman wearing a headset stepped from behind a television monitor and counted loudly, saying "eight, seven, six," until the she reached "one." As the advertisements ended and the cameras focused on the host, the comedian signaled the audience to clap. Before I appeared, a group of black singers sang moral rap music.

An advertisement for the Kings Collection of Demtel Knives followed next. The collection consisted of ten cutting knives, eight steak knives, a two-piece carving set, and sundry kitchen aids, all for $49.94. Cutting knives were the showpiece of the advertisement, and I watched them slice though tomatoes, potatoes, and an old shoe. The knives, the advertisement implied, were a steal. Two days ago on the Hay

Street Mall a man crouched on a low seat selling perfume. Between his knees was a big cardboard box packed with smaller boxes containing perfume. "Four different perfumes for twenty dollars," the man said, "this is your chance to buy stolen property. The perfume goes in the front of a store in the morning and comes out the back at midnight." Like the knives slicing and trimming on television, the man's voice never stopped dicing and paring. "With the perfume you get a free pair of earrings," he said, reaching into another box and pulling out a shiny bauble, "and for four dollars more you can have this gold necklace. Last night it was locked under glass, but now, darlings, it is yours."

I was on the set for eight minutes. I sat on a high metal stool, the sort placed in the corner of schoolrooms and occupied by dunces. A group of students sat in the audience. When the host recognized them, they asked questions, reading them from a monitor. I talked to the host only when I was on the set. Seven minutes after my words had been spread through the middle of the day like mayonnaise I was in a taxi riding to the airport. Traveling on the same plane to Perth was a singing group. "Do you know who they are?" the woman sitting next to me said, gesturing toward the group, the closest member to me being a forty-year-old man with long hair and wearing baggy green shorts. "No," I answered, "who are they?" "The Hoodoo Gurus," she replied. "Oh," I said.

Shortly after returning to Perth, I appeared on the *Jenny Seaton Show*, a morning program on channel 7. I cannot recall what I say on radio and television. Printing stamps life into words, giving them bodies, albeit frail ones. On radio and television words are electronic, impulses glowing for a moment then vanishing. I remembered little about appearing on channel 7 except that while adjusting my necktie in the men's room I slipped and almost fell into the urinal. The next day I was interviewed on the radio, a producer calling early in the morning from Melbourne. The producer telephoned six minutes before the interview took place. While waiting for the interview, I listened to the end of a discussion of clothes. "People over sixty-five," a man said, "don't buy many pairs of jeans." Four days after I returned from Sydney, the University of Western Australia Press sponsored a party celebrating the publication of *Trespassing*. Bob White spoke and said things that would have made Mother blush. Alas, thread worms and huckstering still curled about in my mind. "I don't know how *Trespassing* stands as literature," I said after Bob spoke, "but I guarantee that it is good for what ails you. A paragraph every evening will cure acne, sinus, athlete's foot, and cholera morbus. A page at breakfast, and stress will vanish from your day. Two pages in the evening will rejuvenate your love life. There is not much this book won't help. Appreciative readers have testified," I said, "that if used in the proper way in the proper room in the house a single essay will cure piles, even those left unmoved after a regimen of chain gangs and sledgehammers."

In November, I had booked a camel safari for April. "A week riding camels strikes me as a little long," Vicki said. "No," I answered, "it is barely enough." Enjoyment takes energy. Speeches and appearances on radio and television tired me. By mid-April a week on a camel struck me as a little long. Still, I had paid my money. The children were excited about the trip, and I had to ride the course. Accordingly, on the sixteenth we boarded a plane for Alice Springs at six o'clock in the morning. We stayed at the Desert Rose Inn on Railway Terrace. For two days we explored Alice Springs. Belts of leathery ridges circled the town, red boulders bulging and hanging over them like fat. Ghost gums gleamed like soap, their white trunks resembling handles and their leaves gathered in yellow mops. Along the Todd River, Port Lincoln ring-necks bustled through red river gums. Long-leaf corkwood clung to Anzac Hill, the trunks of the trees bent into snarls and the bark black and crevassed. At the bottom of the hill stood a metal sign. Printed on the sign were the words *Urban Enhancement Program*. Sprayed on the sign, once in red then again in black, was the word *fuck*.

Scattered about the legs of the sign and spreading over the hillside, resembling patches of melons from a distance, were empty wine coolers, most having once contained four liters of Coolabah Moselle. Across the illustration on the front of the cooler a man rowed a boat over a still pond. A woman leaned dreamily against the bow. The man wore a straw hat while the woman lounged under an umbrella, flowers cascading from her bonnet. Behind the couple a cool mist fell green and yellow in the sunlight. Reality was harsher and dryer. In the bed of the Todd River aborigines sat in circles drinking, babbles of noise rippling out from them. Staggering in the streets they begged, one seizing my arm and asking for four dollars. To be rid of him, I gave him two and felt lousy, knowing that he would buy drink. "This is the first time," Edward said, "that I have ever seen really poor people. Why are they so poor?"

I had read books describing aboriginal cultures and the problems of aboriginal peoples in Australia. In Perth the Kadaitcha man roamed bedtime stories, wearing emu feathers on his feet while he stalked victims. In the living room I would have had an easy answer for Edward. Above the riverbed I was too ill at ease to be glib. When the children swam in the pool at the inn, two small aboriginal children stood at the fence and stared, their fingers pushed through the wire mesh. "They made me uncomfortable," Eliza said, "and I didn't want to look at them. Do you understand, Daddy?" "Yes," I said. Of course I didn't understand. Australia was not the segregated south in which I grew up. Like us the aboriginal children were staying at the inn.

When a person travels with a youngish family, most meals are "encores," not dishes smacking of restaurants in Sydney, but meals that could be eaten anywhere. The first night in Alice Springs we ate pizza. The second night I bought takeout at a Chinese restaurant named Chopsticks: fried rice, spring rolls, chicken and almonds, and braised beef and vegetables. At Woolworths, I purchased milk and a tray of Lamingtons. Vicki did not want milk with her meal, so I walked across Railway Terrace to Red Rooster and bought a large bottle of Coca-Cola.

The second day in Alice we walked up the Todd River to the old telegraph station. Opened in 1872, the station lay midway between Darwin and Adelaide along the Overland Telegraph Line. The stone buildings had been restored, and in the barracks we drank coffee and ate scones. Although scones and drink were priced at $2.50 a person, the woman baking the scones charged us a total of $7.00, the price for a "nice family," she said. The woman grew up on a station outside Alice and said that when she was young, people often drove eight hours for a picnic. As we started to leave, she opened the oven and, taking out a pan of hot scones, offered us more.

The walk to the station was three kilometers. A red kangaroo broke cover and crossed our path. A black-footed rock wallaby bounced across a ridge. Galahs rattled noisily, and a pied butcherbird called, his cries belling then breaking like hard silver bubbles. A white-plumed honeyeater foraged through scrub, his yellow head bobbing. A flock of gray-crowned babblers wrinkled through bush, one dropping to the ground in a straight line, another jerking into a ghost gum, his breast a red stain on the white bark. At the telegraph station we rested under a peppercorn tree. On a branch above us two crested pigeons huddled against the trunk. Small white blossoms with pale yellow centers dangled down in streams, and the hum of bees lapped about us like water ebbing slowly across a flat beach. Paddy melons grew in the dry riverbed. Green with yellow blooming over them in splotches, they were the size of softballs. On the other side of the river black kites perched in river red gums. Occasionally they swirled upward and rode thermals before falling back into the trees. I counted thirty-six kites. Their wings bent back in V's, and Francis said they resembled paper airplanes.

I asked a ranger if he liked his job. "I can't think of anything else I'd rather do," he said. We climbed Trigg Hill above the station. The land crinkled about us, stretching through hard flats then rising into sharp ridges and red saddles cut by shadowy gaps. I imagined hiking the Larapinta Trail from the telegraph station to Simpsons Gap, a journey reaching through twenty-three kilometers and lasting two days. Instead I returned to the buggy shed, and the children bought souvenirs: postcards and handkerchiefs. In the middle of each handkerchief was a map of the Northern Territory. Around the edges were sketches of tourist sites: Katherine Gorge, Palm Valley, and Standley Chasm among others. Vicki bought a cardboard sign for the upstairs bathroom in Connecticut. A black stick figure swam across the middle of the sign. A red circle curved around him. Through the circle and across his body sliced a red diameter, the sign warning people not to swim. Beneath the circle were the toothy head of a crocodile and the words *Northern Territory.*

From the telegraph office, I sent a message to the English department in Perth. "Am covered with flies; please advise." Small bush flies buzzed about us like black dust, and we bought fly nets for the camel trek. Without nets, riding would have been impossible. On the camel trek we wore nets from breakfast until dusk. I also wore a yellow sweatshirt when I rode. Stamped in blue on the front of the sweatshirt was JOHN XXIII COLLEGE. On the rest of the shirt were flies. One morning I counted more than two hundred on my left arm alone. When I took the net off to eat or drink, flies swooped for my eyes and mouth, and during a day I ate five or six. "If you scooped the fly droppings off the back of your shirt at the end of a ride," Vicki said, "you'd have enough shit to fertilize every garden in Dalkeith for a year."

We spent six hours at and walking to and from the telegraph station. Returning to the motel I was tired, and weariness influenced mood. Along the opposite side of the riverbank from the path, aborigines camped in battered tents and makeshift huts, these latter large strips of black plastic, the sort used to make garbage bags, draped over a board or a low limb. I felt uneasy, and I was glad to reach the motel and the swimming pool with the fence around it. The next morning at seven-thirty Noel Fullerton drove us to his place at Stuart's Well, ninety kilometers south of Alice Springs. In his sixties with a white beard, he resembled a gritty Santa Claus. Energy and anecdote cracked through his conversation. He reminded me of Francelia Butler, a teacher at the University of Connecticut, a person so bursting with idea that she was the delight and occasionally the bane of those who knew her. Seeing the image of a friend domesticated a foreign experience. Although I read about Noel Fullerton and Camel Outback Safaris in a guidebook, I did not know what to expect. For seven days of riding and six nights of sleeping and eating, I paid twenty-seven hundred dollars, seven hundred and fifty apiece for Vicki and me, five hundred for each of the children. Because I booked the trip directly instead of through a travel agent I received a 10 percent discount.

By nine-thirty I was perched on Sammy and had crossed the Stuart Highway into Orange Creek Station. Nine of us rode together, not behind one another but in a fan: the five Pickerings, a woman from Melbourne and her two teenage sons who had signed up for three days, then leading the group Noel's nephew Andrew. The camels had names and personalities. Twenty-two years old, Vicki's camel, Sandy, was the oldest and slowest. At nineteen Edward's Moses was a veteran of treks into the Simpson and Great Western deserts. Heidi, Francis's camel, was fifteen and headstrong, forever pulling Francis aside in order to munch mistletoe or witchety bushes. Eight, the same age as Eliza, Charcoal was lively, at day's end winning races back to the base camp, victories resulting as much from Eliza's as from Charcoal's personality. Eliza had the best seat in the family. One afternoon Eliza chased me for miles, catching me near the camp only when I started to slide through a sharp gully. Instead of slowing down at the gully Eliza thundered through, Charcoal snorting and Eliza laughing. Although Eliza's hat flapped over her back and her right arm whirled as she thumped Charcoal's flank with a length of green hose, her bottom was stitched to the saddle, the seam between leather and cotton invisible.

Sammy was a gelding, seven years old and weighing thirteen hundred pounds. A racing camel with white legs and a tuft of hair on his neck, he was worth thirty-five hundred dollars, nine hundred more with his saddle. "He is a little skittish," Andrew told me, explaining that he had been broken by brutish people who ripped the plug out of his nose and beat him with an iron bar. I was not sure what skittish meant. I found out. To make a camel kneel so the rider could dismount, one said, "Hoosh." To remount a kneeling camel the rider pulled the reins over the camel's head, put his left foot into the stirrup, swung his right foot across the camel's back, and after inserting it into the stirrup said, "Walk up." Or so matters were supposed to go.

After riding for two hours I "hooshed" Sammy down. This first part went according to direction. Remounting did not go smoothly, however. After I put my left foot into the stirrup and was swinging my right over the saddle, Sammy bounded up. I fell backward, my left foot catching in the stirrup. Sammy then panicked and bolted, dragging me on the ground. By the time I twisted free, my watch was broken and a hand lens in my breast pocket smashed. While running, Sammy kicked me in the head, and I chipped a tooth. My lower lip resembled hamburger, and a long cut sliced down the backside of my ear. Blood washed down my neck, and shoals of flies immediately wallowed in it like tadpoles fighting to submerge themselves in a mud hole fast shrinking in the sun. In rolling off Sammy I landed in a mound of three-cornered jacks, turning my hands into brier patches. That night when I removed the gray sweatpants in which I rode, I discovered that my legs resembled a map of Wisconsin. Instead of lakes, though, bruises pitted the terrain, most small but three or four large, Lake Superior swelling up the inside of my right leg, Lake Michigan, storm-tossed, yellow and brown, down my left calf.

"Are you all right?" Vicki said when she saw the blood. "Yes, of course," I answered, embarrassment at being the center of attention sharper, for the moment at least, than pain. When I remounted, the jacks in the back of my sweatpants stung like hornets whenever I sat on the saddle. We rode more than twenty miles a day, one hundred and fifty miles during the safari. By the end of the week I handled Sammy well. He remained quick to walk up, and so when I mounted I repeated "hoosh down" until my feet were firmly in the stirrups. Sammy responded immediately to the reins. He was fast, and I enjoyed racing. I rose in the stirrups, leaned forward in the saddle, and hunched over his neck until my thighs ached and I slumped back into the seat. Neither tooth nor ear bothered me, but a canker sore developed on the corner of my mouth then spread halfway across my bottom lip, still drying and cracking into blood eight days after the safari ended.

Riding a camel was blood sport. Hours in the saddle sandpapered the skin over my tailbone, and every day after riding the upper part of my underpants was brown with blood. Bleeding from the lower region did not last so long as that from the upper. The bottom lands, if I may call them that, dried three days after the safari ended. Did we enjoy ourselves? You, to use an expression popular in Carthage and thematically appropriate to the trek, bet your sweet ass we did. We had a glorious time, even Vicki, who after dismounting at the base camp after the first day hissed, "Damn you! Why don't you ever ask anyone what they want to do on a vacation? My female parts are ruined."

After three days Vicki took the camels into the corral at night and removed the reins from their nose plugs. Every evening she treated Sandy to orange peels and apple cores. Together we stood at the corral and studied the animals. We rubbed their necks and ran our hands over their heads, marveling at their soft eyes, long lashes, and the hard bumperlike bones protruding behind the pupils. We examined their small tufted ears and soft floppy lips, the whiskers on their lips tickling our fingers when they took treats out of our hands. "Don't you wish we could take some camels back to Connecticut with us?" Vicki said the last morning; "what a sight you would be riding to work on Sammy."

Before eight every morning we left base camp. We returned around five in the afternoon. Some days we rode through Rainbow Valley, slipping between sandstone bluffs and rambling across plains and claypans toward the rail line connecting Alice Springs with Tarcoola. Other days we drifted south toward the Hugh River. Always we looped through canyons and crossed stony ridges. Color seeped through the cliffs of Rainbow Valley, red iron in the sandstone having been dissolved and pulled to the surface, leaving the inner rocks bony and leached. Red, orange, pink, purple, and white shimmered like bands of heat, floating and breaking. In shadows color trickled down rocks like thick preserves sweet with peach and nectarine, strawberry and plum. Bluffs fell off suddenly into boulders, the rocks at first rumpling hard like red-and-white scarves pulled tightly around necks but then tattering and billowing over the plains in threads. Walls of stone had peeled from ridges, and in places the white inner rock seemed scalloped and gleamed like dried joints from which arms and legs had been torn.

Desert oaks and blue mallee stretched between ridges, this last tree silvery in the sun and almost damp looking. Spinifex grass grew in circles, forming sharp spiny compounds. Parakeelya bloomed in low purple patches. After I rode Sammy for half an hour in the morning, his nerves settled, and he ate bales of blossoms. Only a few flowers were blooming, though: pussytails; yellow buttons; and thick amid the acacias, another of Sammy's favorites, maiden's mistletoe, the blossoms dangling in thready green clusters. Buckbush dried and tumbled across flats, catching on spinifex grass and piling against rocks. On banks above dry creekbeds, wild orange bloomed. The stamens spilled over the compact green trees like showers over mossy rocks. On silver cassia a handful of yellow flowers bloomed late. Above the Hugh River bloodwood blossomed, the pink flowers high and not so bright as the trunks of the trees, the bark red and gray and appearing inlaid.

Cattle grazed through the low vegetation along the riverbank. Their hooves crushed much of what they didn't eat, compacting the soil. As a result the sides of creeks eroded. In the rain small indentations in the soil became sharp channels, pulling banks down into themselves before flushing them out broken into the channel. Cattle don't eat colony wattle, and in a field above the river the wattle thrived. Instead of outlining twig and trunk, the white bark eddied through definition, and the field shimmered, resembling a sand dune, the shape of which shifted as the sun rose and fell. After I rode for a couple of days, trees and shrubs became familiar and almost intimate: salt bush; mulga;

whitewood, its seeds resembling those of a maple; rattlepod grevillea; plum bush; and ironwood, drooping like a willow. Beefwood was my favorite tree. The leaves jutted out in vital, startled clutches, and on the dark trunk red sap dried into black tunnels.

Early in the mornings we startled euros feeding on flats beneath rocky outcrops. Occasionally wallabies bounded across ridges. In the dust around base camp were tracks of dingoes, feral cats, and perenties. In mulga, apostle birds built deep nests resembling mixing bowls. The nests of processionary caterpillars hung in acacia. The caterpillars buried themselves in their droppings, and the nests were heavy, bulging and reminding me of socks stuffed with loose dirt. Fairy martins plastered the undersides of sandstone ledges with their nests. The martins roosted in colonies, and the nests resembled small wine jugs. Once while sitting under a ledge I watched a wedge-tail eagle stitching across a ridge, riding thermals up and then sliding back like a shadow. Aside from birds, though, I saw few animals. Most desert animals were nocturnal, and feral cats and foxes had reduced many to endangered species.

"When the only animals left in Australia are feral," Nigel said, "life will be interesting. A few years ago a feral cat mated with a feral goldfish. The result was a cish, an animal with a cat's head and a fish's body. Unfortunately the creature did not live long. The head was greedy and couldn't resist the oily aroma of fish. One day after a long swim the cish ate two cans of cat food. Unfortunately the cish was still hungry, and being partly Manx didn't think much of its finny tail, so the head turned around and gobbled up its own body. After that the creature wasted. Scientists at the University of Sydney tried to save the poor thing.

"For a while," Nigel recounted, "they fed it intravenously through the eyeball, but that blinded it, and since the cish didn't have a stomach, the liquid gushed out past the retina. They tried to plug it with Agarol and Parachoc, thinking the vanilla and chocolate flavors might appeal to the head. But no matter what they tried nothing stuck to the creature's ribs. Everything just shot through the head licketysplit, though there wasn't much for the head to lick. Still," Nigel continued, "the head took fifty-six days to die. Scientists at Sydney wanted to send pictures of the head to *Life* magazine, but the president of the university wouldn't let them, saying that the Royal Society for Prevention of Cruelty to Animals would pounce on them with all fours, claws unsheathed."

We broke the riding twice during the day, at eleven in the morning for tea and then later for lunch. Usually Andrew led us up a watercourse or into a draw seamed with ledges and caves resembling broad, gapping pockets. Traces of aboriginal life lingered everywhere. Carved into boulders were the tracks of dingoes, emus, and kangaroos. Handprints and drawings of snakes and lizards curved across the walls of caves. Broken arrow- and spearheads, scrapers and grinding stones gleamed in the sand. Stone chips from cutting and scraping shone from hillsides near creeks. Chips were so thick on one hill that they resembled wildflowers, small hard violets blooming white, orange, and red through the seasons.

Teas and lunches were leisurely. Afterward the children had time to explore. Francis and Eliza once wedged themselves through a chimney and climbed to the top of a high, steep ridge, much to their delight and my terror. Heights frightened Edward, and while his brother and sister climbed, he and I explored caves and ledges, hunting drawings and arrowheads. Wallabies and euros rested in the caves, and we always found buckets of their droppings, that of the euro shaped like a cube, the wallaby's smaller and tapered, often with a point resembling that of a thick pencil at one end.

Riding made me thirsty, and at tea I drank four or five cups, black without the powdered milk the other riders stirred into their drinks. On the front of my saddle was an aluminum canteen holding two and a half liters of water. Soldered to the end of the canteen was a metal loop that slipped over a spike sticking up eight or nine inches from the saddle. The canteen was heavy and didn't bounce when Sammy galloped. I could not hold Sammy's reins and at the same time lift the canteen, at least not without worrying that if Sammy bolted I would not be able to react quickly. Consequently I drank only after I dismounted.

Andrew packed lunch into his saddlebags. Most of the food was canned. We spooned the food out of the cans and dumped it onto paper plates that we burned after the meal. A day's lunch consisted, for example, of creamed corn, corn kernels, mushrooms, beetroot, julienne carrots, "tiny taters," tropical salad, and bean and corn salad, the two salads sold by Masterfood, the rest by Edgell. Andrew also sliced onions and opened a loaf of bread. On the bread we spread canned meats: Fray Bentos's Corned Beef or Plumrose Deli Ham or Light Chicken. Rachel, Andrew's wife, joined him at base camp, and she helped with breakfast and dinner. At breakfast I drank coffee and ate a bowl of cereal, cornflakes usually, followed by four pieces of buttered toast. For dinner we often ate meat cooked outside on a flat iron grill: steaks, sausages, or lamb chops. I didn't eat much lunch, but at night I ate heartily in hopes that digesting would made me drowsy and I would sleep soundly.

My riding outfit consisted of gray sweatpants, bought for thirteen dollars at Fossey's the week before we flew to Alice Springs, jogging shoes, a T-shirt, the yellow sweatshirt, and an orange vest, the kind worn by men working on the shoulders of highways. The vest had nine pockets. In them I stuffed eyeglasses, the broken hand lens, my wallet, a notebook, and a ballpoint pen. I also wore a backpack. In it I carried binoculars, extra pens, and two guidebooks. In a zippered pocket in the backpack I stored our airplane tickets and three thousand dollars in cash. Sunglasses dangled from a yellow string around my neck. Over my head was the fly net. Atop the net and cinched tightly around my neck was a sun hat bought from the Australian Cancer Society in Perth. At least twice a day the strings tangled. When I wore the binoculars things got so snarled that occasionally I had trouble breathing. Red dirt stained my clothes, and I changed socks and underpants three times during the week. I changed my T-shirt twice. The rest of my clothes I wore every day.

After lunch, riding was more arduous than in the morning. Not only was I tired, but my back ached. In the morning before the earth absorbed the shadows, breezes drifted through draws and around ridges. Afternoons were still. Even the flies stopped moving and clung to the sleeves of my sweatshirt and the front of the net like sticky ashes. Not only did heat press down like an iron, but it also rose from the ground, oozing in hot grains out of the sandstone. Every day after lunch I calculated the number of hours remaining that I had to sit on Sammy and wondered if I would hold together. By late afternoon, though, my mood changed. Shadows and breezes reappeared, and

Eliza inevitably ranged alongside, whacking Charcoal with her length of hose. As we raced across the pans, I felt cool, the ghost gums leaning over the gully near the base camp shining like ice.

At the end of the day I tied Sammy to the hitching post at base camp, after which I removed his saddle and put it in a small shed. In the morning Andrew saddled the camels. For the first two afternoons I stripped the five camels we rode. By the third day Francis removed his saddle from Heidi, so I only stripped four camels. Made from quarter-inch steel piping and leather, usually cattle hide, each saddle weighed thirty-five pounds. Three leather straps bound it around the camel's belly. To remove the saddle I undid buckles on the left side of the camel, pitching the loose ends onto the body of the saddle itself. Then I walked around to the camel's right side and pulled the other halves of the straps from under the camel's belly, occasionally having to lean against a camel and rock it back and forth as it knelt on the ground. Behind the camel a thick rope formed a half circle starting at the left side of the saddle, running under the animal's tail before turning back up to the right edge of the saddle. Before removing the saddle, I shouted "tail," after which I pulled the camel's tail up then forced it back down inside the rope, freeing the rope so the saddle could be lifted off.

I removed the saddle from the right side of the animal and stood it on end in the shed. Under the saddle were two blankets. These I laid flat across the top of the saddle so they would dry before morning. After a day of riding, removing five saddles was difficult, and I felt middle-aged. Built to fit around the camel's hump with thick pads on the animal's back and haunches, the saddles were cumbersome and sturdy. From a distance they resembled fortresses, castles of knights forced by finances to eschew towers and turrets. Thick steel struts supported the joints where the steel bars had been soldered together. The rider sat above the camel's back legs. Behind the rider was a tall steel support, surrounded by a leather pad and resembling the base of a small chair tilted backward. Unlike those on a horse, the stirrups on a camel were short, enabling the rider who wanted to gallop to stand and lean forward over the animal's neck, much as a jockey does in a horse race.

The base camp lay in a rectangle across the mouth of a draw. At the western end barbed wire surrounded a corral. Beyond the corral the ground buckled into a low red ridge. A dry creekbed twisted through boulders at the foot of the ridge then ran out along the south side of the camp. On the bank above the creek stood two privies, one a curtained-off outhouse, with a hole dug beneath it, the other a portable lavatory, complete with a plastic toilet seat. Vicki and I did not use either, preferring to relieve ourselves in the bush. Next to the privies and close to the corral stood the small metal saddle shed. Open on the side facing away from the creek, the shed did not have a door. Directly in front of the shed and within the rectangle were the hitching posts, three logs pounded into the dirt and linked by plastic twine. On the opposite side of the rectangle or yard stood a metal toolshed the size of a closet. Although the shed had once been green, red dust had melted into the paint and turned the shed brown. Beside the toolshed stood a bigger shed. Piled in one half was hay, mostly sorghum. After the day's ride Andrew broke up four bales and tossed them into the corral for the camels.

In the other half of the shed were a sink and two showers. Attached to the right front of the shed were a mirror and a shelf. Below the shelf was a water faucet. Each evening I took a shower. There was not much water, so the shower was brief. Most of the holes in the showerheads had rusted shut, and the water tumbled out in a slow stream. On the roof of the shed was a water tank. During the day the sun heated the water, and the shower was warm. There being no well at the camp, water was trucked in. Parked beside the shed was a long, flatbed, ten-wheeled truck. The cab of the trunk had been painted black and white. Attached to the bed of the truck was a blue tank capable of holding twenty-five hundred liters of water.

Every morning I shaved using the mirror outside the shed, rinsing my razor off in water from the faucet. Two pans sat on the shelf below the faucet. When the pans were full of water, from people's shaving or washing their faces, the water was poured into a blue bucket and taken into the portable lavatory where it was used to flush the toilet. We brushed our teeth outside the shed. Although we rinsed toothbrushes off at the faucet, we did not spit into the pans but on the ground. By the end of the week the ground beneath the shelf looked whitewashed. Inside the shed were planks forming not floors but places on which to stand before the sink and in the showers. Scattered about the yard were three-cornered jacks, the largest with thorns a quarter of an inch long. Because of the jacks we never walked barefoot. Above the showers another ridge rose upward resembling a red loaf. Farther along what was in effect the north side of the camp stood two picnic tables. An ironwood hung over them like an umbrella. Rarely did I sit at the tables. Not only did ants use them for highways, but the tops of the tables had rotted into splinters, and the boards that formed seats pulled off exposing rusty nails. Behind the tables a slab of iron rested on small boulders forming a grill.

Across from the picnic table and running along the south side of the rectangle was the camp's main structure, a green metal trailer. At the end closest to the saddle shed was a room with two sets of bunk beds. Here people stored duffel bags and changed clothes. The rest of the trailer was a combination kitchen and dining room. After dinner Andrew and Rachel unrolled a rubber mat and slept there. The camp was not electrified. A generator ran the refrigerator, and bottled gas the stove. The kitchen was the size of two desks placed side by side, and a long table covered by a red-and-blue oilcloth filled the dining area. Placed around the table were worn green folding chairs, the sort often seen when schools host tag sales. A small gecko lived in a hole in the ceiling above the dinner table. Every night he crept out of the hole and moved silently over the wall, hunting insects.

Attached to the trailer at the end of the dining area was a wooden addition. In it were stored food and bed frames. We ate by oil lamp, and the talk was gritty, like the long rides. Handling camels was strenuous work, and Andrew was tough, cutting through conversation much as he sliced open a boil the size of a cereal bowl on Charcoal's cheek. In the trailer Andrew was in his territory, and he exuded confidence, his know-how and way with animals making him outspoken and giving him a hard charm. He told callused tales about days spent as a truck driver and as a bouncer. "Daddy," Edward said one night as I zipped up his swag, "are those stories Andrew told at dinner true?" "Yes," I answered, "they are true out here."

Vicki, the children, and I slept on the east, open side of the camp, our heads facing across an open plain toward Dingo Mountain. We slept in swags, thick sleeping bags placed on metal bed frames six inches above the ground. Above us the sky seemed to stretch to infinity, and at times I longed for boundary and border, a closed place whose walls I could touch. Bats squeaked above us, and shooting stars fell across the horizon, some turning like wings, reminding me of white doves. Others with glowing tails seemed to scratch the sky. I slept poorly, always getting legs, pajamas, and swag knotted together. While the first part of the night was warm, early morning was chilly. If I lay on my back, the Southern Cross was on my left. I watched it through the night, eventually falling asleep when it crossed the sky and disappeared behind the ridge and ironwood on my right. I studied the Milky Way, not knowing what I was looking at or why I was looking at it, frightening myself by imagining what would happen if the sky fell. I was always awake when the sun rose. Ridges and tall gum trees resembled cutouts, black against the yellow sky. Later as blue coursed into the morning the edges of things disappeared, and tall trees collapsed back into the landscape.

On our last day we followed the Hugh River and stock route back to Stuart's Well. The day was long. We drank tea in the riverbed, sitting under a big river red gum. Burls hung off the tree, and the roots turned through and across themselves like great hunks of wicker. Flies were bad. At lunch scores got stuck in the open cans. "Out of my peas," Eliza said, "I picked fourteen flies." We reached Stuart's Well at four-thirty. At six Noel dropped us at the Desert Rose in Alice Springs. After bathing and tweaking a tree of splinters out of my hands with Vicki's tweezers, I went to Chopsticks and bought takeout again. At Woolworths I purchased orange juice, bananas, and cornflakes for breakfast the next morning. For dinner I bought a big bottle of Coca-Cola and a chocolate cake, this last reduced in price because it was stale. We didn't finish the food because we were tired and sad. The safari had been arduous, but we enjoyed it. "Maybe I can get an American magazine to sponsor me on the fourteen-day trip," I said to Vicki before falling asleep; "I'd really like to see Palm Valley and explore the Finke River Gorge."

The end of the safari did not end the month's travels. Two days later at eight-thirty in the morning I was driving south on the Stuart Highway toward Yulara, or the Ayers Rock Resort, two hundred and seventy-five miles away. "If we are going to Alice Springs," Vicki said in November, "we have to see Ayers Rock. The rock appears on the front of every book about Australia, and friends at home are sure to ask it we have seen it." I drove fast, over a hundred miles an hour, slowing only when a road train approached shimmering back and forth over the pavement like a poisonous centipede. On either side of the road cattle grazed, and signs warned drivers to "beware wandering stock."

Collisions between cattle and cars occurred, and twice on the shoulders of the road I saw dead Herefords, their bodies bloated and resembling cords of wood, their upper legs sticking out like logs. When I stopped for gas at Erldunda, the man operating the pumps said, "Be careful at dusk. Up the road last night a man hit a steer and was killed." I am not sure why I drove so fast. At home I never drive faster than fifty-two miles an hour. In part the Northern Territory influenced me, not simply drawing me through the open spaces but somehow making me less conventionally responsible. In part I drove fast because the car was new and rented. Rental cars were expensive in the Northern Territory, and I wanted my money's worth, the Mazda I drove costing $590.75 for five days.

Two weeks earlier I booked a room in the Outback Pioneer Hotel and Lodge, the cheapest of the three hotels at the complex at Yulara. Prices vary, not only within resorts but also over the telephone. Some years ago when a receptionist at a hotel in Boston quoted the rate for a room to me, I said, "Gosh, that's too much. I'm poor and can't afford that." "Are you really poor," the man asked. "Yes," I said into the phone. "Well, then," he said, "let me see if I can find you a better price." The rate he found was half the original rate and included free breakfasts.

At the Visitors Center at Yulara I read the list of accommodations and discovered that a two-bedroom flat in the Emu Walk Apartments, part of the fancier Desert Gardens Hotel, cost less than the single room I booked in the Outback Pioneer. Not only did the apartment include a kitchen, a dining area, and a sitting room but it was only a two-minute walk from drugstore, post office, takeout restaurant, bookstore, tavern, and grocery. I changed the reservation. We spent four nights at Yulara. Usually we ate in the apartment, buying takeout food or shopping in the grocery. At the Tavern bottle shop I bought Coopers Sparkling Ale. Screwed to the door of the bottle shop was a white sign with blue letters stamped on it. "It is at the request of the Aboriginal people," the sign stated, "that the tavern may not sell takeaway alcohol to anyone who is a resident of or is traveling through any

Aboriginal community in the region. Please respect the wishes of the local Aboriginal communities and do not purchase alcohol on behalf of individuals from our communities."

One night we did not eat in the apartment. Instead we walked to the Pioneer Self Cook Barbecue, and I cooked steaks on the grill. "I know you," a man cooking hamburgers next to me on the grill said; "I know your voice. I heard you on the radio." Gardens had been planted throughout the resort. Emu bush and lemon-flowering gum were yellow with blossoms, and for the first time I saw Sturt's desert pea, pictures of which appeared on almost as many book jackets as Ayers Rock. Flies did not bother me as much at Yulara as they did in the Rainbow Valley. For tourists who had not spent a week riding camels, however, flies were a terrible nuisance. "And I came halfway around the world for this," I heard a woman exclaim as she hurried along the walk behind the apartments, all the while fanning her face furiously with her right hand.

What she and Vicki and the children and I came for was the Ayers Rock or Uluru of tourist brochures. Commonsensical with feet pressed into bedrock like stones into conglomerate, we did not anticipate wonder or delight. But wonder and delight were what we experienced. The afternoon we arrived I drove to Uluru. Rising abruptly from the plain the rock was red against the blue sky, resembling a giant loaf of bread, Eliza said, or a blind cave mole, Francis said, its skin sunburned and peeling, or maybe, Edward added, "a huge cocoon, in which an ancient, primitive creature is sleeping." Since 1965 twenty-five people had died climbing Uluru, most suffering heart attacks, but a few falling off the rock. Uluru was sacred to local communities, and aborigines asked visitors not to climb the rock, a request I learned about too late to honor. Because the industrial revolution has given people legs that run faster than a hundred miles an hour and wings that carry one from Perth to Alice Springs in two and a half hours, humility does not come naturally to contemporary man. Many people travel widely and shift homes several times during their lives. As a result they often lack both a sense of place and in the larger natural world a sense of their place.

Climbing Uluru restores lost perspective for a moment. Atop the rock a man realizes how small he is, a grain of sand on a steep slope, his existence precarious, depending on forces beyond his control. As one looks out from the top of Uluru, he may, if he is fortunate, also look inward and realize that he is part of a fabric of being. Perhaps instead of urging tourists not to climb Uluru, aboriginal communities might be better served if people were encouraged to climb, at least for a few steps.

Uluru was 348 meters high and 3,600 meters long. Climbing was arduous. A link chain ran up the initial steep portion, and as people ascended they held on to it, or I did, using it to heave myself up. Francis went first, climbing at a gallop, pulling the rest of us after him. Vicki, Edward, and Eliza followed close after Francis. I brought up the rear, carrying water, binoculars, our tickets, and cash, and serving as a backstop in case someone slipped. The sides of the rock sloped steeply away from the chain. If a person nervous about heights looked away from the chain, he could become frightened. Halfway up the chain Eliza became terrified and, soldering her hands to the chain, started crying. I brought her down, one slow backward step after another. By the time we reached the bottom, Edward and Vicki had turned back also. Francis had vanished.

Driving from Alice Springs tired me, and bringing Eliza down was nerve-racking. However, Francis's traipsing across the rock by himself so worried me that I set off after him. Two-thirds of the way up the chain my heart pounded, and I could not stand straight. The rock fell away steeply, and I became a white-knuckle climber, thinking that if I lost my grip I would stumble and roll to eternity. The chain ended at a cup-shaped saddle. I sat in the saddle and drank. When I looked out from the rock at the landscape, I became dizzy with fear. The better part of the climb lay ahead across the surface of the rock.

Resting beside me was George Rowlands, a man my age. If he had not pushed on, I might have gone down. But when he started, I followed. Two-thirds of the climb remained, and I clambered over ridges and pinched my way along spines. Francis was waiting beside the monument at the top. Graffiti covered the monument, most of it Japanese. George took a picture of Francis and me, and I smiled in relief. We descended slowly. The surface of the rock was mottled, gray patches under a lace of red, formed when feldspar oxidized. Sometimes the surface sliced upward bony and sharp, other times it tumbled and formed bowls and saucers. Along the edge of a small pool shield shrimp sunned themselves. Forty kilometers to the west the domes of the Olgas or Kata Tjuta rolled purple out of the plain. Below on the ground a tour bus stopped, and people clambered out resembling white ants.

The next morning we walked around Uluru, the path flat but the distance nine kilometers. In the backpack I carried apples, oranges, and four liters of water. From the ground the surface of the rock resembled velvet brushed both with and against the nap so that some patches seemed to glitter and stand upright while others collapsed dull and lifeless. Dimples and caves pocked the surface. A sheet joint sliced under a rounded extension of the rock. In a cave hard arkose turned over us in a rocky wave. Walking pushed my eyes down to the path rather than up. Although the rock was close, I did not notice it unless I forced myself to look up.

A native fig sprawled through a gully. I picked a handful of black plums and ate them. On hopbush, leaf beetles gleamed like drops of oil. A green lizard clung to a ledge, resembling a piece of expensive jewelry pinned on a stiff collar. Cassia and mulga bloomed yellow, and ruby dock was red, adenoid in shape and color. Yellow-throated miners rummaged through flowering bloodwoods. In the shade lantern flowers glowed like warm candles; in the sunlight Australian bluebells flickered like bits of feather.

Until I read a guidebook I had not heard of the Olgas or Kata Tjuta, massive rounded domes of conglomerate. Rising from the plains, they resembled, Vicki said, huge scoops of ice cream, some firm and cold, the others melting and sliding. The largest dome was 168 meters higher than Ayers Rock. We spent two days wandering the Olgas. One morning we walked through the Valley of the Winds, an eight-kilometer trek across plain and through canyons and over ridges. Again I was the family's beast of burden, carrying the usual four liters of water, then lunch, this last including sandwiches, apples, carrot sticks, and bars of Cadbury's dark chocolate.

Cattlebush was blue with blossoms. On Mt. Olga wattle, small fingers of blossoms were yellow. Azure butterflies the size of fingernails wrinkled across red rocks. Zebra finches dropped from a river gum into the bush, black-and-white tails flicking like semaphores, pink cheeks glowing. Corkwood unfurled into flower, the blossoms loosening like yarn. From the canes of spearbush white flowers dangled, resembling trumpets hanging from a rack in a music store. "A little affection would not be out of place here," I said to Vicki as we walked through a soft spot in a green canyon. "Sam," she exclaimed, "how tacky!"

A kangaroo bounced across the path. Above us holes as big as rooms gapped in the walls of a canyon. "The caves would make good jail cells," Vicki said; "put violent criminals in them, and society would not be bothered by them for long." Vicki and I sat at Lookout Point for ten minutes, trying to press the landscape into memory. On the point stood a cairn of rocks. We each added a rock to the pile. On the way back to Yulara, I stopped at the Kata Tjuta "viewing area," and Vicki fed the remains of our lunch to two orange dingoes. On the thirtieth we flew back to Perth, arriving at our house at ten o'clock at night. Amid the mail waiting for us were letters from Connecticut. "Your descriptions make it sound like you are never coming back," Frank wrote; "don't forget you are missed here." "Well," I said after reading the mail, "that was a good trip, but I'm looking forward to going home." "You are just tired, Daddy," Edward said, "a week from now you will think of somewhere else to visit, and you will want to stay in Australia."

Room 668.7

In middle age a person realizes that the future repeats the past and that the new is the old. Days spin like records on turntables. Life resembles a phonograph needle and traces a circle. Occasionally something causes a bobble, but even when the needle skips loose, it soon drops back into a groove, any scratch made adding only a small click to the repetitive melody of existence. In November the United States Information Service arranged a speaking tour for me in New Zealand and Papua New Guinea. The tour was scheduled for May. Because May was distant, the trip existed in a haze. Instead of thinking clearly about New Zealand and Papua New Guinea, I imagined them, envisioning days rich with golden new experiences. As May approached, the haze lifted, and I saw coppery past trips: dressing in hotel rooms with pastel ceilings; evenings spent scrubbing socks and underwear with bath soap; nights chasing sleep across strange beds, never corralling it, the covers twining into lengths of fence, the boards falling to the floor in splintery lumps; and finally gray mornings roaming streets, becoming an urban hunter-gatherer searching for a reasonably priced breakfast.

Fifteen years ago Vicki and I spent the first year of our marriage in Syria. We were the only native English speakers in the town, and we filled scrapbooks with exotic memories. Afterward we mused about spending other years in, from our suburban point of view, faraway places. But then children appeared, and we changed. Comfort and safety now appeal to me more than thrill. One evening in February, Vicki and I looked through Francis's atlas and selected countries that we wanted to visit. The list was short, consisting only of nations in which English was the native language. "Are those the only places you want to go!" Edward exclaimed. "When I grow up, I want to travel all over the globe. I want to go everywhere and talk to everybody."

"What about the solar system?" Francis asked; "don't you want to travel through space?" "You bet I do," Edward said. "Going to Papua New Guinea will be great," Edward said the night before I left Perth on the speaking tour. "Yes," I answered, "I will have fun." In truth I wanted to stay home and watch the Ruth Rendell mysteries on television with Vicki.

"I bet you make a lot of new friends on this trip," Eliza said. "Yes," I said, "I will." Although I would meet pleasant people, I knew that I would spend more time with and know more about the author of the books I read on airplanes than anybody I met during the trip. Before starting a book I always write my passport number on the title page so that I do not have to dig through backpack or suitcase in the middle of a flight in order to fill out a form for Customs. In May I wrote "150320565" in Patricia Cornwell's four books: *Post-Mortem*, *All That Remains, Body of Evidence,* and *Cruel and Unusual*. Cornwell's mysteries had become popular, and during the tour I noticed that while biographical sketches in her first three books said she lived in Richmond, Virginia, the sketch in the last book stated, "She divides her time between Richmond and Malibu."

I tried to bounce myself out of the past. In hopes of seeing anew, I recorded the numbers of the rooms in which I stayed. I spent three nights in airport hotels, two of the nights in Sydney and the last in Cairns, the numbers of these rooms being 625, 934, and 429. I spent four nights in New Zealand, the first two in a room numbered 810, the last two in a room numbered 920. I stayed three days in Papua New Guinea, all three nights in a room numbered 413. Added together the numbers totaled 6,687, those rooms in which I spent more than a single night being counted twice or thrice depending on the length of my stay. When this figure was divided by ten, the number of nights I spent away from home on the trip, the result was 668.7. "That quotient," I told Vicki later, "is the average number of the room in which I stayed, not a matter I have thought about before." "Yes," Vicki said after sitting quietly for a moment, "many travelers fill books with numbers describing the heights of mountains or the lengths of rivers. You have calculated something original, a fact reviewers are bound to notice."

My trip began on May 2, two days after Vicki, the children, and I returned from school holidays in the Northern Territory. I spent the first night in the Sheraton at the Sydney airport. The American government paid lecturers modestly. In New Zealand and Papua New Guinea, I received an honorarium of one hundred American dollars a day plus a living allowance. Adjusted to local standards of living the allowance paid for room and most board. During the three days I traveled between countries I received only a living allowance, a total of $459 Australian. The hotels in which the government booked me for those nights cost $397, leaving me $62 for departure taxes, meals, and transportation to and from airports. I spent carefully and returned to Perth with $364 Australian, making my wages $36.40 a day. The workday usually lasted ten or eleven hours. Rarely was I offstage. Even when treated to meals, I performed, laboring to make conversation and to be cordial. When figured on the basis of a ten-hour day, my wages were $3.64 Australian or $2.62 American an hour. The first night in the Sheraton I did not eat dinner. On a mahogany table in the hotel lobby sat a silver bowl filled with fruit. I removed two grapefruit, stuffed them into my backpack, and later ate them in my room. In order to stay within the travel allowance I got up early the next morning, so that I could eat breakfast at the airport. The "Australian Breakfast" at the hotel cost $23.50. In the terminal I bought a cappuccino for $2.00 and at McDonald's ate a bacon and egg McMuffin costing $2.10.

Auckland was the first official stop on the tour. I arrived on the afternoon of the third. The director of the American Center met me at the airport and carted me to the residence of the consul general, where I was, I then learned, to address a group of literary folk. There not being time enough before the gathering for me to register at a hotel and change clothes, I opened my suitcase on the sidewalk outside the residence and digging through it pulled out a blue sport coat, deodorant, brown shoes, and toothbrush and toothpaste. In an upstairs bathroom in the residence I brushed my teeth, rubbed on deodorant, changed shoes, and put on the sport coat. Introductions did not include biographical sketches, and I did not realize that some of New Zealand's best writers were at the residence. Only later in Wellington when I saw their faces on the jackets of books in a store did I learn to whom I had spoken.

The party lasted an hour and a half. At its conclusion an embassy official dropped me at the Regent Hotel, warning me not to pay more than $160 for my room. I paid $180, the extra $20 being government tax. For dinner I walked across Albert Street and ate at Food Alley, an arcade of oriental restaurants. Dinner cost eleven dollars, six for a bowl of Thai noodles, chicken diced on top, two for a beer, and three for coffee and pastry, this last a cinnamon bun sprinkled with raisins. Breakfast at the Regent cost twenty-five dollars plus a government tax of 12.5 percent. The price making a mockery of the living allowance, I got up early the next morning and wandered downtown Auckland until I found a food arcade. There, at the Baron Supreme, I bought a full breakfast of eggs, toast, bacon, tomatoes, and coffee for $5.50. At a greengrocer's stall I purchased a bag of Granny Smith apples for $2.50.

At nine o'clock the director of the American Center drove me to the University of Auckland, where I talked to teachers. At eleven-thirty the hostess of a radio program interviewed me. "What do you think of Shakespeare?" she asked. "I like him," I said. The producer of the program telephoned five minutes before the interview began. While waiting for the hostess to come on the air, I listened to an advertisement for the *Milford Wanderer*, a local cruise ship. "Majestic sky and land, waves lapping on the hull, and lunch, ah, lunch," a man said rhapsodically. After the interview ended the director of the center took me to the Auckland College of Education, where I addressed students and faculty for an hour. I ate lunch with the English department. Actually I sat at the table while they ate. For my part I sipped coffee and nibbled half of a chicken sandwich. Instead of eating I worked, trying to turn conversational crumbs into a three-course meal. Later that afternoon I ate two apples.

At seven-thirty that night I spoke at the Auckland Museum. I saw more of the room in which I talked than of Auckland itself. The room resembled a large box, and a rust-colored rug lined the floor. I stood at one end of the room on a stage. The floor of the stage seemed to have been made from pressed wood, the color resembling that of ground orange peels. White folding chairs stretched across the room in rows in front of me. The doors opening into the room were green, and the walls were white. Black boxes containing amplifiers jutted from the walls. In front of me just above eye level a square black rig of lights hung over the audience. In addition to the rig's four metal sides, two metal girders ran parallel through the middle, making it seem heavy, not a tool of stage and concert hall but one of construction sites, part of a crane towering over rubble. When I arrived, the woman organizing the talk said, "I wish I could take you out to dinner. Usually I take speakers to dinner, but tonight I cannot." After the speech I ate in the Food Alley. The next morning at six-thirty I took a taxi to the airport, where I bought a cup of yogurt and ate the rest of my apples for breakfast.

Although one day had spun into another and I was in Wellington, the present was the past. An official from the embassy met me at the airport and drove me to Scots College, a private secondary school for boys. A television crew waited for me. I opened my suitcase on the front steps of the college and took out a clean white shirt, a necktie decorated with red and blue stripes, leather shoes, and then the blue jacket, deodorant, and toothbrush and toothpaste. I changed clothes and brushed my teeth in a faculty bathroom. Then I went upstairs to an English class, and while the television crew filmed, I pretended to teach. Afterward the headmaster invited me to have morning tea with the faculty.

After tea the embassy official took me to the James Cook Hotel, where he left me, saying I had an hour to eat lunch. Hurriedly I registered and deposited my suitcase in my room. From the concierge I got a map of Wellington. Then I rushed onto Lambton Quay to search for a sandwich shop. At the Fresco Espresso Café I drank a cup of coffee and ate a sandwich stuffed with apricots, sliced chicken, cottage cheese, lettuce, bean sprouts, and alfalfa. The only seat available was at a table occupied by a tall man in a gray suit. I sat down, and we talked, initially about our sandwiches, neither of us ever having eaten a sandwich spread with apricots.

My lunch companion was Tony Spite, the accounting and administrative manager of the Pharmaceutical Society of New Zealand. I explained that I was a college teacher in town to speak that night to the New Zealand–American Association. Lunch was so enjoyable that I did not want to return to the hotel. For the first time in New Zealand I was not performing. At one o'clock the features editor of a newspaper met me at the hotel. We rode the Kelburn Cable Car from Lambton Quay to the Botanic Garden overlooking Wellington, where the reporter interviewed me beside the Carter Observatory. After the interview the embassy official bundled me off to a second television interview, this one also held at a private school, but in a dining hall, not a classroom. On returning to the hotel I found a message. Tony Spite had called all the tourist hotels in town until he located me. He invited me to dinner. When I returned the call, Tony was out of his office, so I left a message accepting the invitation and inviting him to my talk. I then showered quickly, shaved, put on a gray suit, and rushed off to speak. Tony got my message, and after the talk he and his wife, Jenny, took me to the Wellington Club.

At the club, Pembroke tables shone like mirrors. Molding swirled about lintels and mantels, and red and brown leather chairs clumped together comfortably in corners. Through sherry and whitings in eggs, sherbet, bluenose dripping with Hollandaise sauce, syllabubs, and broccoli and carrots, conversation flowed like smooth wine. We talked about traveling and family. I did not want the evening to end. In bed that night I imagined spending a year in Wellington. The city huddled along the shores of Port Nicholson, houses pinching themselves into hills that rose dark into the sky. Perth appeared friendly because it was roomy and open. In contrast Wellington seemed friendly because it was cluttered, resembling the parlor in a Victorian cottage, the home of a great aunt, every table and wall a collage of memories.

I slept well. The next morning I got up earlier than usual and after eating breakfast roamed downtown. I wandered along Lambton, Featherstone, Johnston, Brandon, Panama, Customshouse, Grey, and Hunter. Modern buildings in the city center were ugly, some drab slabs of glass and metal, others follies of the mechanical age, resembling radiators, batteries, and ball joints. Streets were narrow. The smell of gasoline twitched through the air in cold currents, catching for moments against the trunks of London plane trees, but eventually lapping over and sweeping toward the harbor. A cement mixer churned past; delivery trucks rattled like tin matchboxes containing children's collections of nuts and screws. Doors of buses hissed, and tires jabbered brittlely along the asphalt. Schoolboys holding satchels and wearing red and gray blazers hunched in doorways, sheltering themselves from the cold. Women in business suits switched briskly along sidewalks. Men moved more erratically, their dark suits seeming to catch in doorways and on windows, causing the wearers to stumble and stagger sideways.

As the sun rose higher, shards of light melted into pools, around their edges scraps of paper suddenly noticeable.

On curbs small sandwich boards appeared. At Pete's Leather one could purchase "Belts and *Things.*" "Just ask for Kylie," the Diplomat Men's Salon instructed, and get a haircut for ten dollars. The Body Shop was "Open." At the dental offices of John Burton, Tina Godbert, and Jane Pairman, a person suffering from a toothache would find "a relaxed and friendly atmosphere." Afterward one could go to Shannon's Electrolysis and Beauty and have a red vein removed for twenty-five dollars. By the time the vein vanished the filling would have hardened, and he could stop at Home Made Takeaway and sample a toastie with two ingredients for $2.30. Medical insurance often suffers from financial underbite, and before leaving Wellington a person could stop in at State Insurance and see if his coverage paid for dental work, not to mention red-vein removal. Most probably the insurance paid for everything, for State Insurance cared about its customers, declaring, "our policy is working for you." The tooth having been paid for, one might have a little extra cash in his pocket, enough, perhaps, to stroll through Rowlands of Christchurch and examine "fine clothing" or more exotically "come up to level # 1," as a sign put it, "and talk turkey" at Zingana Oriental Rugs and Kilns.

After breakfast I talked through the day. I recorded a radio interview and chatted at lunch with members of the English department at Victoria University. Afterward I addressed a lecture hall of students. A writer for a magazine interviewed me. The photographer for the magazine wanted to return to Scots College. She had arranged for a class of primary school students to meet us. "I want," she explained, "you to lead them dancing across a field. Pretend you are the Pied Piper." I was chagrined. I did not want to inconvenience staff and students at Scots College again. "No," I said to the photographer. "The children who followed the Pied Piper vanished. The Pied Piper was a mass murderer if not a pedophile."

The next day was Sunday. That afternoon I flew back to Sydney and spent another night in the Sheraton at the airport. The morning in Wellington, though, was free, and I treated myself to four and a half hours in the Botanic Garden. In gardens I meander silently along paths. I escape public personality: the mouth braying, the wit twisting sentences in order to startle, the concerned teacher plastering over people's doubts about education, shoring up tired institutions with words like *duty* and *commitment, stewardship* and *community,* not because I always believe in the words themselves but because I think they occasionally invigorate others, making them hope that what they do in life and in classrooms might enrich someone's day for a moment, maybe even shine a healing light into a shadowy corner of a mind. Alone I shed the burden of concern. Instead of being a person from whom others seek answers I become someone beyond questions, an observer thrilled by bush and tree.

I am not always alone, however. "Have you seen a professor walking around?" a young man said to me on Wakefield Way. "What kind of professor," I asked, "a botany professor?" "I don't know," the boy answered; "I heard him on the radio this morning, and the man talking to him said that the professor could be found in the garden." After recording the radio interview on Friday, I chatted with the host of the show, saying that I was going to the Botanic Garden on Sunday. When I said I was the professor for whom he was looking, the boy said, "I'm studying to be a teacher and enjoy it. Do you think I am doing the right thing?" I talked to the boy for ten minutes. After he left I started up the Camellia Path. Buds were swollen, and the waxy green leaves shone like water.

"Excuse me," a man said, "are you the Sam Pickering I heard on radio this morning?" The man gave me a copy of *P/S,* a newsletter published by the New Zealand Poetry Society. He invited me to the society's next meeting. On learning that I could not attend, he recited two haiku poems he had written then left, wishing me "all the best." Not long afterward I walked into the Education and Environment Center. A volunteer and a gardener stood in the main room talking. "Mr. Pickering," the volunteer said when he saw me, "welcome. We have been expecting you. We are pleased that you came to our garden."

Their pleasure in my presence did not match my enjoyment of their place. The garden rumpled across hills, some flowing softly into lawn, others collapsing into sharp creases. On Mamaku Way green rose in a cloud. Tree ferns stood like whisks, and silence beat the air, the sky above blue as a porcelain bowl. Trails in the garden resembled poetry: those winding through bush free verse; the formal ones heroic couplets, flowers in beds crisp as verbs. Not having the leisure to linger I did not read entire poems. Instead I saw fragments of planting and metaphor: the leaves of native beech, painted fingernails; strips of bark twisting slowly around Japanese cedar like an alexandrine; black butt thick as a wall; and a white peppermint, leaning at an angle and resembling a partially eaten candy cane in the hand of a child, the old gray bark licked into shreds, the bark damp and yellow underneath. Maritime pines stood atop Druid Hill, dark red currents running between slabs of bark, the tops of which had peeled off, making the remnants resemble flat rocks, silver with spray in the sunlight. On the ground scarlet mushrooms as big as softballs thrust through damp, khaki pine needles.

The base of pohutukawa reminded me of a rough planter, limbs sprouting up and out like fence staves, ferns reaching up green around them like hands. With a black marker someone had written "L.R. + I.W." on the back of a bench. The ink had faded, and I wondered if the love was an annual, blooming for only a season. I chewed Mexican sage in the herb garden. In the teahouse beside the Lady Norwood Rose Garden, I ate a piece of chocolate cake and drank a cappuccino. Two English sparrows scratched under tables searching for crumbs. In Anderson Park below the rose garden boys in blue shorts and blue shirts practiced soccer.

Each of "the 106 formal beds," a brochure stated, represented a different variety of rose. The garden was circular, beds spooling out from the center. I threaded my way through the garden, noting individual roses: Moulin Rouge, pink and purple, resembling confectioner's paste; clean yellow friesia; whiskey, its fragrance fermented and orange as the blossom itself; pink, aristocratic Brandenburg; and Katherine Mansfield, the open petals turning brown like the life of the writer herself, but the swelling buds tight and full of clean, blue words.

In Sydney the bowl in the lobby at the Sheraton still bulged with grapefruit. This time I did not eat any. Instead I called room service and ordered a pot of coffee, a slice of walnut cake, and a hamburger thick with lettuce, tomatoes, and onions. My flight for Port Moresby left at eight-thirty the next morning. On the way the plane stopped in Brisbane. It was Francis's thirteenth birthday, and I telephoned him from the airport. In Port Moresby I stayed at the Travelodge, a tourist hotel built on a hill above downtown. The public affairs officer at the embassy met me at the airport. Before leaving me at the hotel, he warned me not to wander the city, explaining that crime was epidemic.

An hour later I was roaming the city with two engineers who had also arrived on the flight from Brisbane and who were traveling to a mine in the highlands the next morning. Signs of crime were everywhere. Battalions of security guards strolled the grounds of the hotel and patrolled the streets surrounding buildings downtown. They wore black shirts and trousers, knee-high military boots, and carried Billy clubs. Topped with barbed and sometimes sharp concertina wire, fences surrounded houses. In front of the Travelodge the hill dropped sharply off to Ela Beach, not a place, a guard advised me, to stroll at night

Beyond the beach the Coral Sea opened like a hand, soft hills rising behind palm trees like green knuckles. Reading influences vision. When I looked down the coast, I saw a page written by Joseph Conrad, a tramp steamer sailing down the margin, print smeared like a thin wisp of smoke. Between lines I stood cramped, wearing a soiled white suit. Beside the Travelodge, Hunter Street ran like a ledge down to the beach. Along the road blossoms exploded from yellow oleander. Above the road houses stuck precariously to slopes. Bougainvillea grew thick about the houses, tying them to hillsides in red and purple snarls, not tight enough, I thought, to keep a heavy rain from washing them to board and plaster. Beside the road trash formed thick clots, lumpy with cans, wet paper, and plastic bottles. Flowers bloomed on frangipani in rough bundles, big as wheels.

In the other direction Hunter Street slanted down toward Fairfax Harbor. Modern buildings appeared screwed or at least plugged mechanically into the hills. Little effort had been made to fit the buildings to the land, and they seemed temporary and replaceable, fuses easily removed from sockets. From a distance the buildings looked like stacks of air filters, the kind used in automobile engines. Individual floors with long expanses of windows resembled separate filters. Tucked between floors were concrete gaskets, both dividing and binding the floors together. When first built, the buildings had been white. Rains and humidity changed their appearance. The gaskets leaked, weeping down sides of the buildings in thick streams, staining the buildings brown and red, the color of the surrounding hills.

Beyond the buildings lay the harbor, a coastal freighter a dark smudge in the distance. Anchored nearby were fishing boats and a tug. The tug resembled a whirligig beetle, and the fishing boats, water striders, antennas and poles spidery over them. Stacked behind a high fence resembling insects wrapped and stored at the corner of a spiderweb were metal shipping containers, paint flaking off them like hunks of flesh: blue, red, and green. Behind another fence tires jostled together in mounds, some tires larger than small trees, the whole yard appearing black with monstrous round droppings.

The engineers and I walked along Champion Parade. Small buses loaded with people and spewing white exhaust fumes rattled past us until we were opposite the Royal Papua Yacht Club. Windows on the third and top floor of the building were open. I looked up and saw two men in shorts drinking. "Those men," I said, "have been there forever." Suddenly the men waved and invited us up. We joined them, sitting on stools at a long, narrow table. They were drinking South Pacific Lager. One of the men had lived in Papua New Guinea for more than thirty years, the other for ten. We sat with them for an hour looking out over the harbor. Conversation was difficult. For the men, sitting seemed entertainment enough. Masts of sailboats stuck up like dull pins. Beyond them cruisers dozed in the water or lay beached, their sides fat and the same muddy color as the hills. Gray storm clouds formed in the distance then broke up. Nothing happened in the harbor while we watched. Over our heads ceiling fans turned so slowly that I expected them to stop. Finishing a sentence became almost as difficult as finishing a beer.

The first night in Port Moresby the political action officer took me to the Ela Beach Bistro for dinner. The ambassador and his wife and other embassy officials also came, and we ate pizza, the "House Special," loaded with prawns, capsicums, avocados, and tomatoes. The next morning I ate in the hotel. Breakfast was dear, fruit, cereal, toast, and coffee costing ten and a half kina, about eleven dollars American. I did not try to find a café in which to eat breakfast. Amid the swarms of dark men I would have felt uncomfortable. "Walking is OK in some areas during the day (ask for advice) but never at night," an embassy publication warned; "keep everything secure and yourself alert at all times. Avoid large crowds, being alone outdoors, and scenes of confrontation." Eating in the hotel was not stressful. From a vase in the middle of the table a purple orchid with a green center leaned toward me. The orchid looked sleepy, and I relaxed and ate two bowls of five-corner and passion fruit.

Afterward I walked outside. Guards smiled and waved. On a field below the hotel children dressed in red shorts and shirts ran wind sprints. I picked a Pepsi can off the ground and put it into a garbage barrel. Then I walked down Mary Street. Scattered around the trunk of a tree were okari nuts. The nuts resembled miniature coconuts and were small enough to fit into the palm of my hand. I borrowed a hammer from a hotel repairman and sitting on a curb crushed a small basket of nuts. The outside of the nuts was soft and purple and tasted like fruit salad, heavy with banana. The inside was hard and tasted like coconut.

I spent days in Port Moresby much as I had done in Auckland and Wellington. One morning I taught three classes at the University of Papua New Guinea, each class an hour long. Reporters interviewed me, and I gave a public lecture one evening at the university. Graffiti covered signs, walls, and the bottom stories of most buildings in Port Moresby. Before lecturing I went to the lavatory. Sketched above the urinal was a dragon. Wings flapped over his back. His body was a thick tube, and his head was broad and heavy, his eyes smiling. Printed under him in capital letters was the label, "The Flying Dick." The last graffiti I noticed in Port Moresby was above the urinal in the men's lavatory in the international terminal. "God loves You," I read, "He cares '4' You."

I appeared on television in Port Moresby, and just before I boarded a flight a security guard approached me. "I saw you on television," he said; "you said good things." The man told me about himself. He was a "mixed breed," he explained, his father and mother belonging to different clans. Some seven hundred languages were spoken in Papua New Guinea. People in one valley spoke a language different from that spoken by people in the next valley. Loyalties, I was told, were to family and clan. In Port Moresby family groups composed neighborhoods. To move into a neighborhood one had to belong to the family. When a member of a family prospered, his responsibility extended beyond wife and children to distant relations who were not prospering, even those who made no attempt to find jobs.

Jobs were scarce in the city, and unemployment was high. Six or eight men and boys sold newspapers at every traffic light, one man following another to a car window even though the seller preceding him didn't sell a paper to the driver. Behind the crime lay unemployment and dislocations brought about by city life. Travelers rarely see clearly. Most of what I heard I heard from westerners. Several people told me that life in Papua New Guinea was difficult for women. "The sounds one hears at night in a village," one man said, "are not wild creatures or birds calling but the sounds of women being beaten." A businessman who had lived in Papua New Guinea for forty-five years sent his daughters to Australia, explaining that although he loved the land, "this country is not kind to women." Nor was Papua New Guinea a place in which to break a leg. "For a month last summer," a man told me, "there was no material on which to take X rays in Port Moresby." "Before that," someone else said, "the only X-ray machine was broken for six months."

Papua New Guineans themselves talked a lot about the environment. They did not worry about an abstract environment but about particular places, a river, for example, butterflies and family stories rising above it in sprays of words. History was bound to place. When place was so changed that landmarks vanished, family identity vanished. "Chinese money is ruining everything," a man told me; "it is pouring in from Malaysia, the Philippines, Singapore. Politicians are being bought right and left." For an hour I was interviewed on the radio, the host of the show steering conversation toward environmental topics. As words slipped glibly from my mouth, I wondered how Papua New Guineans could save their forests if Australians were unable to do so despite the political power of the "Green" party. I started to become gloomy, but then the host broke into the interview to insert a public service message urging people to drive carefully. "Oh, my God!" a man exclaimed after a clatter of brakes followed by an explosion of metal; "is she all right?" "She's dead," a woman answered.

One afternoon the embassy driver and the assistant to the public affairs officer drove me to Sogeri, a plateau forty-five kilometers from Port Moresby. In part because the government prohibited the construction of houses more than one story tall, Port Moresby sprawled through suburbs: Three Mile, Boroko, Korobosea, Sabama. Painted on the sides of many businesses were advertisements for cigarettes: Benson and Hedges, black letters on an orange background; Winfield 25s, white letters and yellow numerals against red; then Spear, a local brand, dark letters against a yellow background. Many signs were written in pidgin. The first word of Yumi Kitchen meant *you me*, not yummy. Written in black letters above Christian Book and Videos was "Kaikai Bilding Tingting," which roughly translated as "food for thought."

Outside Port Moresby the road curved through a landscape that seemed blue, yellow, and green, this last color often so bright that it seemed yellow, too. The road wound through sharp hills, the trip making my stomach queasy. Many curves resembled hairpins; posted before them signs urged "Sound your horn." Bananas grew on flat terraces, and dogs wandered through the scrub, most of them females, their nipples sagging and their bellies jagged in profile. Black-and-gray bluffs thrust through the green like the remnants of ancient temples. Along the plateau the road ran beneath raintrees spreading wide like lacy green umbrellas. A river swirled red then pitched down a valley, white flushing up in feathers as water spilled over boulders.

In villages women and children sat beside rickety wooden tables. On top of the tables were bunches of bananas and peanuts. I bought some of each. The bananas were stubby and sweet, and the peanuts white and raw. The excursion to Sogeri tired me, however. While on the tour I worked hard at being gracious, and even on the drive I felt obliged to make conversation by asking the embassy employees about life in Port Moresby. The men found my accent difficult to understand, and as a result I repeated every question at least two times.

Early on the morning of the fourth day the public affairs officer took me to the airport. We planned to fly to Goroka in the Eastern Highlands. There I was to lecture at the university and visit with faculty and staff. Heavy rains, however, had started the night before, twelve, fourteen, or eighteen inches falling in twenty-four hours, the number of inches depending on the source. The bottoms slipped out of roads, forming potholes as big as tubs. Water swept down the hills pushing rocks into the streets. Rain also fell in the highlands. Clouds hung over the mountains, and to land in Goroka the pilot had to trust radar and twist blind through mountains and ridges keener than knives.

When we took off, the rain was so thick that I could not see the tips of the plane's wings. To every god I could think of I prayed that we would return to Port Moresby. Suddenly halfway to Goroka the plane slipped to the right. The pilot explained that the air pressure was not working correctly, and he was headed back to Port Moresby for repairs.

The air pressure seemed fine to me. Even finer, though, was the return. "Now," I prayed, "let the repairs be so thorough that the lecture will be canceled and I won't have to fly into the jaws of death again." Sometimes prayer is answered. The day of the flight was the last day of term. Rescheduling my talk was impossible, and so when the plane vanished into a hangar, I changed my ticket. At five o'clock that afternoon I boarded an Air Nuigini flight bound for Cairns. Most passengers were westerners: a skinny boy with luminous eyes who looked as if he belonged to the Peace Corps; two couples who looked like missionaries, the wives patient and soft, the husbands middle-aged and flabby but men in whose faces features seemed set, their eyes not ranging in search of something but satisfied and knowing. Also on board were a score of workers from the Chevron oil rig on "The Ridge." Big-bellied men with laughs that thumped, they looked taller than they were. After working a twenty-eight-day shift, they had twenty-eight days off. All wore large belt buckles, and several, cowboy boots. Most were southerners, old hands from oil patches in Texas and Louisiana, and they were flying back to the United States.

At the airport in Cairns I changed my ticket again, booking a flight that left at six o'clock the next morning, arriving in Perth, after stops in Brisbane and Sydney, early in the afternoon. In Cairns, I checked into a hotel on the Esplanade. I telephoned Vicki and told her to expect me. Then I showered, after which I put on clean clothes and walked along the Esplanade to Barnacle Bill's, where I ate a seafood dinner. For a moment I regretted not visiting Goroka. The regret passed. During free moments in Papua New Guinea I met pleasant people: a man, three of whose relatives had been killed by black snakes; another man who said, "Some Australians are good"; then a man studying to be an Anglican priest who when I asked him the names of plants explained that he, like many people in Port Moresby, was a "foreigner" who came from a distant village and did not know the names of plants in the city.

The nationals had quick smiles. "Quick to smile and quick to stab," a hard man said.

Papua New Guinea was a country of masks, personal and ceremonial. I spent part of one morning in PNG Art, a dusty warehouse cluttered with artifacts. I bought a gable mask three feet tall. Cowry shells surrounded eyes as big as knotholes. Red paint swam down the nose like a snake sliding across a river. Out of the mouth crawled a crocodile. The tusks of a pig curved up like new moons from the side of the nose. "The people who made this are different from us," Vicki said when I showed her the mask." "Yes, I know," I said, "but I am not sure exactly how different they are. If I had stayed in Papua New Guinea for years I would not have found out." "Anyway, I am glad you are home," Vicki said, "did you stay in any nice hotels?"

Green Ants

When the superintendent of schools in the Kimberley telephoned in March, I was in bed with a bad back. "Would you be interested in coming up and talking to teachers in May?" he asked. I had been flat for three days. Any proposal that included the word *up* sounded magical. After hobbling about for a week, though, I thought the trip arduous. Unlike my first months in Australia, during which I rarely left home, the last weeks of the year had become so cluttered with engagements that Perth itself slipped almost from sight, the city being reduced to an airport. Instead of dropping into the English department and stirring words slowly about at tea, I had my longest conversations with taxicab drivers as they pushed swiftly through dark mornings taking me to Ansett and Qantas—Mounts Bay, Riverside Drive, and the Great Eastern Highway, roads that once took me places in and around Perth, now trailing off like dangling modifiers, going nowhere. "I am tired," I told an official at the Education Department, adding that only a draft of financial tonic could buck me up enough to undertake the trip to the Kimberley. Saying that she thought money could be unearthed for an honorarium, the official said she would dig about then confer with the superintendent. When she failed to obtain funds, I assumed the trip was canceled.

"Assumptions are always dangerous," Vicki said as she packed my suitcase. The day after I returned from Papua New Guinea, having spent twenty-four out of twenty-six days away from Perth, the superintendent called. "Everything is arranged," he said; "I'll send you an itinerary on Monday." "That's splendid," I said, turning my mind back through days like someone flipping through a desk calendar in hopes that a name or address would jiggle recollection. "This is good news indeed," I continued, papering the gap in my mind with words, "very good news." Suddenly I remembered March and the telephone conversation. "I really look forward to seeing the Kimberley," I said, exclaiming, "what a treat! Few visitors have such an opportunity." "Did you really say that?" Vicki asked, "didn't you ask about a fee?" "I couldn't," I said; "the message about money didn't reach the superintendent, and I have to go no matter what."

At six-ten in the morning on May 23, I left Perth in a cold drizzling rain. Three hours and forty-five minutes later the plane landed at Kununurra. The day was bright. From the bark of ghost gums, light radiated outward, white nearest the trunks then spilling yellow and blue, tie-dyeing the landscape. I stripped off my sweater when I stepped off the plane. Later I put on short pants. The teacher who met me at the airport drove me to Kelly's Knob, a lookout above the town. Kapok bloomed beside the road. The yellow petals bent backward, almost as if they were nervous about appearing showy, the pinched limbs of the trees inhibiting them, reminding me of evangelicals narrowed by doctrine into fervor. Kununurra was a new town. Streets spun in circles around Coolibah Drive, a road resembling a well-trimmed thumbnail, rising from and turning about a straight cuticle, Ivanhoe Road. Beyond the town stretched newly plowed fields, the dirt resembling heavy black work cloth, irrigation ditches slicing through it in thick depressed seams. I sat on a bench at the top of Kelly's Knob. Painted on the back of the bench was "Katie & Susie 93."

At Kununurra District High School, I ate lunch with teachers. In Western Australia chances were good that a teacher's first post would be in the country. Only after spending time in, for example, the Kimberley or the wheat belt could a teacher transfer to Perth. As a result many teachers I met in the Kimberley were young. A large number were unmarried or did not have children, and building a conversation was often difficult. About the table in Kununurra talk was youthful and hormonal, focusing on athletics and parties, subjects in which I was no longer able to feign even ironic interest. When I addressed groups, older members of the audience almost always responded quicker than younger. While the faces of older teachers wrinkled into understanding, those of younger teachers remained smooth, resembling dough not yet cooked in the oven of life.

After lunch I talked to twelfth-grade students. Neither they nor their teacher knew much about me. "Why did you write that book? What is its name?" a girl said, thinking about the movie *Dead Poets Society.* For an hour I cast remarks into the placid classroom, making them skip lightly in hopes of getting someone to rise to a response. I wasn't successful. "Life in Kununurra is easy," a teacher said to me later, "and students don't work hard. Two or three," the woman added, "plan to sit the tertiary examination in order to qualify for university or technical school." Throughout Australia demands made upon students in primary and secondary school were so few that children often lost interest in school and thought education not only boring but a matter of little consequence. "I am not allowed to give homework," a teacher in Queensland told me, "not even when students ask me to assign it." "My sons have become Australian," lamented a university professor born in Canada. "Both are in university, but neither cares if he does well. They just want to have fun. I was ambitious," the man continued; "life in Australia is too easy. Ambition and ease are not compatible mates."

In Kununurra, I stayed in the Quality Inn, room 522, this despite the motel's consisting of a single story and a handful of rooms. After the class I walked to Hidden Valley National Park, a kilometer from the inn. Limbs twisted out of the tops of boab trees in knots. Woollybutts leaned sideways, the lower portions of their trunks scuffed and brown, resembling unwashed fingers. Beside trails in the park spinifex grass grew in prickly tussocks. Water lilies bloomed in a green pool. From the scrub a bird called, its voice bouncing off rocks in silver ripples. Above me rose sandstone formations resembling red cupcakes. The edges of the cakes were nibbled and broken, and slabs lay tumbled at the base of the formations like big crumbs. Rock figs ground themselves into cracks then leaned out from bluffs in heavy green brushes. That night I ate dinner in the Quality Inn. Painted on a wall in the dining room was a mural of Hidden Valley, the sandstone formations yeasty and tattered with shreds looking like strips of carrots. After dinner I spoke to eight teachers. "The number is small," a man explained, "because an agricultural expert is talking at the Rotary Club about sugarcane. Around here sugarcane is money."

I don't belong to the frequent-flyer club of any airline. I can't relax on planes, and the words *frequent flyer* frighten me. Until the trip to the Kimberley, I had never been in a small plane. On the morning of the twenty-sixth I left Kununurra for Kalumburu Mission on a plane chartered from Alligator Airways, the logo of which depicted a cross-eyed alligator wearing a pilot's cap, his jaws spread and his teeth glinting. The plane was a single-engine Cessna 206, nineteen years old and capable of carrying a pilot and five passengers. The only passenger, I sat next to the pilot in the right front seat. To reach my seat I climbed through the door on the pilot's side of the plane, there being no door next to my seat. Piled on the two back seats were cartons loaded with groceries for teachers at Kalumburu Mission.

The plane was white with blue and red patches. In black letters under the left wing was VH-ERM, the first two letters identifying the plane as West Australian, the next three giving its call name, Echo, Romeo, Mike. The panel in front of me resembled a serving tray, the gauges and dials stains left by hot dishes and wet cups and saucers. I watched the gauges carefully, and whenever a pointer drifted toward hot, my internal temperature rose. Pasted to the tray was a "Fuel Calibrator." When the plane bumped through a current of air, I studied the calibrator. Both wings, I soon memorized, held 144 liters of fuel. When the dials showed half empty, each wing contained 70 liters of fuel. When the dials showed three-quarters and one-quarter full, however, differing amounts of fuel remained in each wing, 89 liters at the three-fourths mark and 45 at the one-fourth mark for the left wing. For the right wing the figures were 82 and 35 liters respectively.

I had the same pilot for three days, Ian Pearson, son of Ron Pearson, principal of the school at Kalumburu. Ian examined the plane carefully before we left Kununurra, and I felt reassured, at least until the engine turned over, clattering like the motor on top of a lawn mower, the bolts of which had been loosened by summers of banging rocks and chewing up vines and sticks. Takeoff was quick. The plane hopped into the air so suddenly that I missed being frightened. Ian flew at 4,500 feet, and the flight to Kalumburu lasted ninety minutes.

Ian grew up in the Kimberley, his father being principle at a series of schools, most of the pupils of which were aboriginal. Scattered among young instructors in the Kimberley were older teachers like Ian's father who had devoted years to the region. Such people stood out, glowing and vital. The glow came from inside, generated not simply by experience but by their delight in life and their love for the Kimberley. Ron knew plants and animals as well as people. For him the Kimberley was not barren but infinitely various.

After lunch Ron and Margaret, his wife, drove me about in an OKA, a lumbering four-wheel-drive vehicle raised so high off the ground it could lurch through trenches that gutted the sand roads leading to and from Kalumburu. By road the distance from Kalumburu to Kununurra was over five hundred kilometers. At Kalumburu one didn't hurry around the corner to the grocery; he drove for twenty-four hours. About the only place one could dash out to was the bush, there being little in the settlement other than school and mission.

Behind the school, though, straw-necked ibis strode through high grass, and a flock of masked plovers beat quickly into flight. Rainbow bee-eaters sat on a wire, yellow in the afternoon light. A flock of little corellas squabbled through a grove of river paperbarks growing on the banks of the King Edward River. In the trees the birds resembled crowns of flowers, at first bleached buds but then fluttering blossoms, their feathers white petals streaked with yellow. Over a bend in the river draped a curtain of freshwater mangroves. Clumps of fruit clung to the branches of stem-fruit fig. From a distance a Leichardt pine swam shadowy through sight, its leaves thick and layered, resembling dark green scales. From the tops of tall, thin pandanus palms foliage sprayed out in loose round batches. Resembling needles, the leaves seemed to be in motion, spinning and puncturing the blue sky, much like a cultivator tilling hard ground.

North of the mission, the river dug a gorge through stone, the rocks on either side of the watercourse resembling orange bales of petrified hay. A red-winged parrot sat on a limb, and a double-barred finch clutched a twig. Beside the road stones clung together in gray bundles almost as if they had been dumped out of huge paper sacks, some bundles towering like the remnants of keeps and castle walls, others resembling battered sculptures, the face of the sphinx and headless torsos of primitive Davids. A startled quail beat low across the road while a blue-winged kookaburra hardened immobile on a branch. Nests of green ants hung like ripe grapefruit from gum trees. Ron handed me an ant. "Hold the head between your thumb and index finger," he instructed, "then bite the bottom off." The flavor nipped like lime and numbed my tongue slightly. I liked the taste and ate twenty more ants. Later, along the shores of Napier Broome Bay, I smashed oysters against brown rocks and sucked out the animals.

Cultures change rapidly, making people feel dissociated from time and place. Behind myths of better, usually simpler, ages lies the hankering for permanence. Fundamentalisms appeal because they promise stability, proffering truths that ostensibly exist impervious to time. Change is clamorous and disturbing. By denying the benefits of change, fundamentalisms block out clamor and, channeling life into narrow certitude, enable weak people to function, if not in general society, at least within a group. As people age and see the world in which they grew up alter, even vanish, they often feel uncomfortable and become conservative, unthinkingly condemning change and so romanticizing the recent past that it becomes a fiction, a story of a better time alongside which the present seems crass and corrupt.

These dislocations felt by middle-aged people in western cultures are probably insignificant when compared to those experienced by many aboriginal peoples. Kalumburu resembled a Band-Aid. At one end of the Band-Aid were the mission and the houses of teachers. At the other end was the aboriginal community. The extremes were remarkably different. Stuck to the first end were well-kept houses and neat gardens. Nothing and everything adhered to the other end. Houses had been battered out of function. Instead of vegetables and flowers, litter grew in yards, not simply crops of small things like tin cans and plastic bottles but trucks and automobiles. Between the two ends of the Band-Aid lay the absorbent center of Kalumburu, the school binding teachers and children together. Neither able to live the wandering lives of their ancestors nor able to adjust to modern Australia, many aborigines seemed to stumble between cultures, spending their time, children told me, gambling. Adults so neglected children that the youngsters seemed to be rearing themselves, not ideally like Caddie Woodlawn but amid parasites and dietary deficiencies. Hookworm was epidemic in Kalumburu, and the state nurse in the community battled it constantly. At school each day students received vitamin and iron supplements.

Seven teachers taught at Kalumburu. Most had recently completed teacher training and were energetic and well-meaning. Their students were young, the majority seeming twelve and under. Students studied in family groups rather than grade levels. In the past when students were taught according to grade level, fights between children of families who were quarreling in the community disrupted school. I visited classes. In one room I sat on the floor behind a screen and played a game with three boys. The game taught addition. We sat in a circle. In the center of the circle was a small box filled with wooden cubes, each cube a quarter of an inch on a side. We passed around a red die. When the die reached a player, he rolled it onto the floor. If the side with four dots appeared faceup, he took four cubes. Once a player amassed ten cubes, he traded them for a piece of wood the length of an index finger. Notches divided the piece of wood into ten sections, the equivalent of ten cubes. The first person to collect a hundred cubes, or ten pieces of wood, won the game. I did not win. When the game ended, I had eighty-four cubes.

In another room a class played bingo. A young girl assisted the teacher by pulling printed cards from a box. Printed on the cards were the alphabet and alliterative phrases, on *Jj*, for example, "Jellybeans jumping," on *Cc*, "Caterpillars coughing," and on *Qq*, "Queens waiting quietly." I read phrases aloud, and the children giggled. In another class students wrote paragraphs describing a recent holiday. Earlier in the year the class adapted "The Three Little Pigs" to the Kimberley, changing the title to "The Three Little Lizards." After completing the writing exercise, the class recited the story. The first lizard built his house out of grass; the second, from twigs; and the third, out of rocks, on the top of which he laid a thick roof made from sticks. The villain in this version of the story was a snake. "Little lizard, little lizard, let me come in," the snake hissed; "I want to come visit you." I enjoyed the classes. The children's eyes were bright, and they asked questions. "Do you live in New York," a boy asked. "No," another boy responded before I spoke, "he's a cowboy. Listen to him talk. He talks like a cowboy."

Kalumburu was familial. Each teacher prepared a dish of food, and we ate a potluck lunch. Ron pushed three tables together, and conversation flowed easily. That evening I spoke in the same room, the tables having been removed and chairs arranged in a circle. Twenty people attended the talk: the teachers, the nurse and his wife, the man appointed by the government to help aborigines manage the community, and four nuns from the mission, these last born in the Philippines. No aborigines attended. A fight erupted that afternoon, and people stayed out of sight.

Ian and I got up early the next morning. Two days earlier a car carrying an eighty-year-old priest broke down in the bush. Instead of remaining in the car the priest walked off. Although the man had spent forty years in the Kimberley, people worried about him. Just before Ian and I left to search for the priest, we learned that he reached the mission late the night before. I was relieved. I would not have seen much from the airplane. Every time the plane banked, I would have shut my eyes. Still, I was getting better. The flight from Kalumburu to Fitzroy Crossing lasted two hours. Ian flew at 6,500 feet at 156 miles a hour. I spent the time peering out the window. Rocky outcrops erupted upward, stones flaking and peeling from gorges like clumps of dry skin. Salt flats shimmered, their surfaces white as pearls. Rivers wrinkled across the land, in places running shallow to crow's-feet, in other places cutting deep creases, bluffs shaggy above them like brows. Shadows oozed blue from under ridges. Gums pricked valleys, the trunks resembling small white toothpicks, the green leaves visible when I concentrated but quickly seeping out of sight again into the red soil. When Ian landed at Fitzroy Crossing, a dust of kites blew up, whirling brown around us before they slipped back along the runway.

From the airport I went to Muludja, a small aboriginal community. The woman who drove me slid through dirt roads at ninety kilometers an hour, making me long for the airplane. Because the Margaret River often flooded, the school and houses at Muludja stood on stilts. Consisting of a principal and three young teachers, the school was small and happy. I visited classes and talked to children. Afterward I shot basketballs, missing every shot. The principal then took me to Fossil Downs Station. For a moment I thought myself on Grandfather's farm in Virginia. White buildings gleamed across a trimmed green yard. Although place transformed Virginia's magnolias into gums and boxwood into dwarf poinciana, I felt at home. Mrs. Henwood, the owner, served tea and familiar conversation. I drank two cups of tea and ate a slice of fruitcake. A green tree frog flattened itself along the top of a sliding door. The size of a child's fist, the frog was larger than those I caught in Virginia. Still, I knew the animal well. When

I mentioned that Vicki and the children and I were returning to the Kimberley in June with Peter Murray, Mrs. Henwood said, "Tell Peter to stop here. I think your family would like Fossil Downs."

From Fossil Downs, I went to the District High School at Fitzroy Crossing. I repeated the first day of the tour, eating lunch with teachers and afterward visiting a class of twelfth graders. I longed to be behind a screen throwing a red die with third graders. No student rose to the ideas I tossed through the room. For an hour I worked against the silence, changing lures, casting upstream and down, but I didn't hook a word. "English," a teacher said later, "is not the students' first language. When students talk in class, often teachers can't understand them." The principal and I chatted in his office. Problems confronting schools in the Kimberley were as much medical as pedagogical. "None of my students," a woman told me, "will continue their studies after high school. What we teach about books is not so important as what we teach about health. Venereal disease is epidemic, and I am frightened for my students."

I stayed overnight at the Fitzroy River Lodge. After visiting the high school, I changed clothes at the lodge, putting on shorts and walking shoes. Then I bought a Boomy, three bearing-size balls of frozen fruit juice arranged along a wooden popsicle stick, lemon on the top, strawberry in the middle, and orange on the bottom. Ian and I spent the afternoon walking through the shallows of the Fitzroy River. A white heron stood beside a pool, and two sulfur-crested cockatoos squawked in a gum tree. The vines of stinking passion fruit scrambled through mangroves. Fruits were yellow and the size of apricots. I plucked a handful from the vines and biting through the rinds sucked out the innards. Aside from one that had dried dusty and brown, the fruits were seedy and sweet. That night at the lodge I spoke to sixty teachers, some of whom had driven a hundred and fifty kilometers to hear me. The next morning Ian and I flew to Broome. The air was still, and Ian asked me if I wanted to fly the plane. I declined. At the airport in Broome, I rented a car, and Ian and I separated. I was sorry to leave him. I liked him and his family. In Broome, I ate lunch with faculty at the Senior High School, then I visited two classes, one a twelfth-grade class, the other a ninth-grade class. The ninth graders were lively and as soon as I stepped through the door tossed questions at me.

When school ended, I drove around Broome. I enjoy wandering through graveyards, and when I saw the Japanese cemetery on Port Drive, I stopped the car and got out. Nine hundred and nineteen people were buried in the cemetery, many losing their lives in pearling operations. Hacked out of sandstone the old markers in the graveyard were bony and rough. The Japanese letters drawn on them resembled shadows of birds fluttering red over time. Broken markers were re-placed by stones cut from black granite. Smooth and scrubbed, the new stones reflected changes in Broome, "the town," as a tourist brochure put it, "on the move," polishing itself into a holiday resort.

Next to the Japanese cemetery was the "Muslim Section." Instead of tombstones, rocks and shells marked graves, the people buried remaining anonymous. A lizard scurried across the grave of a child. Three ravens bawled in a bloodwood. Atop two graves plastic Coca-Cola bottles lay on their sides, stems of flowers sticking out from their mouths. From the Muslim Section, I roamed out into the rest of the graveyard. Wooden crosses stood at the heads of many graves. Several of the crosses leaned at crazed angles. Painted in black letters across the center of a large number was "RIP." Some graves had sunk. Others rose in small red dunes, shells encircling them resembling the detritus left behind by a high tide: cockles, occasionally a turban, conches, and clams, some of these last large, their edges wrinkled like paper. Color leached out of gardens of plastic flowers: carna-tions, roses, and tulips. On a rock above a grave was chiseled "our little girl."

I had a sore throat. I was not sure what caused it, perhaps air-conditioning in the lodge at Fitzroy Crossing. Most of the children at Kalumburu had runny noses; maybe I caught a bug from them. Whatever the cause, I decided to swim at Cable Beach and gargle saltwater. On my way I stopped at Malcolm Douglas's Crocodile Farm. I watched the crocodiles being fed, after which I ate two ice cream cones, the first mango, the second blueberry. That night I spoke to fifty teachers at the Roebuck Bay Resort. They sat at tables in a garden, and I stood on steps, a lectern in front of me. Each word scraped my throat like sandpaper. The next morning I drove to Derby, 236 kilometers northeast of Broome. Because I was supposed to arrive at the Derby District High School at ten o'clock, I drove fast, and the landscape passed in a blur, all except termite mounds that pushed through the bush like the tops of brown peaks poking above clouds of earth.

Max Clarke, the principal of the high school, resembled Ron Pearson. Like Ron he had spent years in the Kimberley, eighteen in Derby. "Max is a piece of work, not to be trusted," Ron said fondly; "he stole my basketball court." "Did Ron tell you I stole his basketball court?" Max asked. "Yes," I said, "and lots of other things, too." "That's Pearson for you," Max said; "he has been talking about that court since 1978." Communities in the Kimberley were far apart, but community among people existed. Life in the Kimberley was paradoxical. Less could be more. The lives Ron and Max enjoyed in the Kimberley were more various than those they would have lived in Perth. Getting about a city used time and sapped energy, reducing not only opportunities but also capacities for pursuing interests. Because people often lived in different suburbs, activities that required a group were difficult in a city, depending more upon scheduling than upon inclination. In a small town like Derby with a population of four thousand people the immediate was close. In a city the immediate was often far away, strapped to distance by a tangle of conversations and telephone wires. In Derby, Max owned and published a weekly, magazine-size newspaper, the *Boab Babbler*. He was host of a sports program on the local radio station. He belonged to a singing group, specializing in western songs and known for its colorful appearance on stage. "Yes," a woman said, "that and much more. Max is also a very fine town crier."

Few people who drove to the school arrived on schedule, and Max had not expected me until later. To fill time he showed me the school. The grounds and buildings, like those of all the schools I saw in the Kimberley, were spotless, providing examples for the children and from which adults could also learn, roadsides often resembling scrublands next to landfills, plastic snagged on twigs, rusty cans, bits of white enamel gleaming, here a smashed television, the tube cloudy with glaucoma, there a washing machine lying on its side, the door open and swinging like a detached retina.

In shop, students built a miniature metal windmill. In third grade a girl introduced herself and said her name was Pickering. The art teacher was accomplished, having exhibited his own work in many places, including Boston. Like Max he had spent years in the Kimberley, and as place determined the texture of his days, so it colored his canvases. In October he was exhibiting his and his students' work in San Francisco. Drawings and paintings hung from the walls. On a tray lay decorated boab nuts. After the nuts dried, students rubbed the fuzz off and colored the nuts ocher, after which they carved designs on the surfaces, fish and crocodiles swimming up white through the inner wood of the nuts. Much of the art was good. "Many aboriginal students are fine artists," Max said; "most, though, will never have regular jobs. From school they sometimes get things to make their lives more satisfactory."

Would that I could have stayed longer in Derby. But after lunch and a talk to the teachers, I boarded a plane bound for Broome, Port Hedland, and Perth. Port Hedland was an industrial town, the port and nearby mines thriving. The terminal at the airport was a modern box of blues and silvers. Unlike the building the people inside were not polished. Tattoos covered skin like graffiti, appearing almost, it seemed, at random on necks, calves, anywhere and everywhere. Passengers filled the plane at Port Hedland, mostly miners traveling to Perth for the weekend. When the men first boarded, they were quiet. During the flight many drank, and by the time the flight landed, the inside of the plane reverberated with noise, sounding like a pond busy with mallards, all drakes, ebullient and boisterous, the F-word, as the children put it, rattling loudly. The man seated behind me used it or a variation of it six times in eleven seconds, for an average of one F-word every 1.833 seconds. Australians use the F-word more than Americans. "Today," Edward reported, "I heard the F-word used nineteen times at school."

I did not remain long in Perth. The following Thursday at 12:05 in the morning I took the red-eye to Sydney. I arrived at Coolangatta on the Gold Coast at nine. There I addressed teachers attending a conference on early childhood. I stayed at Sea World Nara Resort. My speech was not until early evening, so I explored the hotel. Gardens folded around buildings and a kidney-shaped swimming pool, this last more inclusive than kidney, however, including bulges for spleen and liver. African tulip trees were orange with blossoms. The flowers trapped the sun in cups, streams of light beading then slipping over their brims.

Golden trumpets wound yellow and green through a trellis. Scarlet powder puffs spilled shimmering out of calliandra. While leaves of clock vine were thick and dry and almost rattled when shaken, the flowers were white and blue, their textures soft as cloud. So purple were the blossoms on princess flower that they absorbed the shadows and colors about them, making the world one-dimensional. Black ducks bobbed in a wading pool. Three superb blue wrens, a male and two gray females, bounced through a thicket hunting insects. Unlike the splendid wren in Western Australia whose breast was blue, broken only by a necklace of black, the male superb wren seemed in formal dress, a stylish black bib hanging beneath his bill and down his chest until it reached a starched white waistcoat. "What is the name of those wrens," I said to a reporter who interviewed me. "I've seen them all my life," she said; "how do I know what they are?"

The room in which I spoke was long and narrow. At one end was a platform with a lectern standing on it. Watercolors painted by elementary school children hung in a border around the platform. Birds flew through the pictures in flocks of dark M's. Trees grew like lollipops, and houses resembled tea caddies. In front yards twiggy people picked bunches of lettucelike flowers. In the background suns beamed like headlights. Before I spoke an administrator welcomed the teachers. He urged them "to network." "What comes out of networking," he said, "is that you have an internal locus of control." "Where I come from," I said to the woman sitting next to me, "networking produces mittens and socks, or if a person is really good at it, a sweater." The Kimberley seemed far from the room. But, of course, it was not. To know one place a person must know other places.

Early the next morning I walked the beach then meandered through Philip Park, a green fringe of sheoak and bush separating the beach from Sea World Drive. In the distance hives of hotels and apartments seemed papery, not clinging to ledge or eave but tumbling haphazardly and brokenly, the rooms empty cells. A middle-aged man wearing khaki shorts and a red sweater walked confidently toward me, his stride firm as new money. The tide was low. A father and his two sons stood at the edge of the water and collected worms for fishing bait. A black dog with a curly tail splashed through shallow water, his master several paces farther out and pushing a surfboard shaped like the pod of a snow pea. A young woman jogged past. When she ran, her knees practically touched, making her resemble an X. She wore a pink cap, reflecting sunglasses, and form-fitting shorts that stretched to her knees. Except for two pink triangles that rose up from her knees along the inside of her thighs, the shorts were black. She also wore a sweatshirt. On the front was a square pool of blue water. Through the pool dawdled a school of fat yellow fish.

At the edge of the sand near the sheoaks a bodybuilder paraded. He wore a baseball cap, dark sunglasses, and tight bikini shorts. He did not wear a shirt. He was on show, "trolling," as Nigel would put it, for attention and perhaps affection. A Japanese couple walked on the beach. They wore sneakers and were careful not to get their feet wet. Around the neck of the man hung a camera. I volunteered to take the couple's picture, using the man's camera. After I took the picture, the wife indicated that she wanted to take a picture of me. I did not let her. Instead I took a second picture of them. Suddenly a white airplane with pontoons flew low along the beach. Sounding like an angry gnat, a helicopter followed it.

I turned and walked into the bush. Only then did I hear the ocean thumping and pulling. Honeyeaters sang, and wrens chattered. I searched for them but could not find them. Blossoms flickered like candles on coastal banksia. Butterflies bobbed about me, one or two lemon migrants but most blue tigers. When the tigers basked in the sun, soft droplets of blue trickled wet along their wings. At four o'clock I made "some closing remarks" to the conference. Later, as I left the hotel, I noticed a young teacher sitting on a bench, *Trespassing* in her hands. "I hope you don't mind," she said when she saw me, "I'm just dipping in and out of your book. Last night I tried to read from the beginning, but there were just too many words."

The Great Deep

A teacher to whom I spoke in Queensland pressed an envelope into my hand as I left Sea World to go to the Coolangatta airport. "Read this on the airplane," she said. Inside the envelope was a piece of white paper, eight and a half inches wide and eleven long. Written diagonally across the page in black capital letters was "KEEP SEEKING YOURSELF," followed by two exclamation points, these in red and twice as large as the letters. The teacher misunderstood my talk. Personal essayists are often misunderstood. Because I write about immediate matters and describe hours as I bump through them, people, especially those nurtured on motivational books, assume my verbal meanderings are parts of a pilgrimage winding toward self-knowledge. In truth I usually examine things in order to escape self. Because the distant and the abstract cannot be seen clearly, the mind often pieces them together, using the familiar as building blocks. As a result distant objects often lose their particular identities and become reflections of the observer's mind. In contrast the immediate impresses its concreteness upon the senses, making it difficult for an observer to create the object out of his imagination. "Yes," I said aloud as Ansett passed high over the Great Australian Bight and I balled up the letter, "the better I describe the nearby, the more I escape self."

In imagining me and probably others as seekers, the teacher envisioned life as linear and most likely progressive, the seeker striding ever outward through experiences, all of which taught lessons and which would eventually lead to a dawn radiant with awareness. My life is repetitious and turns through circles, or so I thought in June. Winter had returned. August fast approached. Once the occasion of arrival, the month now marked departure. The ends of our year in Perth pinched together like a bracelet pressed tightly around a wrist. The morning after returning from Queensland, I walked through Kings

Park. Once more capeweed was yellow and stinkweed orange with blossoms. Again flowers splattered native wisteria, gleaming like purple drops of water. The red-and-white blossoms of pearl flower tapped in the breeze, once more resembling minute wing-tipped shoes. A flock of yellow-rumped thornbills bounced out of brush beside a path. I looked up and saw a rufous whistler clinging to the side of a gray branch. Rarely do I look upward, however.

Later that day when I stood beside the War Memorial and stared out over the Swan River, my vision did not reach the blue haze near Darling Scarp. Instead it floated downward catching on jetties and tumbling to the ground near the red roofs of the university. "If I could look higher and be inspirational," I said at dinner that night, "maybe my books would sell better." "Daddy, don't worry," Eliza said, "you are not as unpopular as you think." "Yes," Edward added, "you are one of the minor essayists." "What you have to do," Eliza continued, "is make more paragraphs, so people can take a breath once in a while. Then they will look up and dream, and you can write about anything."

Seekers find gazing upward easy. For my part, at least when I was not imagining selling a road train of books, I looked down. Things I noticed one August resembled things I noticed the next. Throughout the year I studied my mail. "I am writing to thank you for attending the dinner for Arts students who live in the Hall," a dean wrote early in June; "the students enjoyed the evening and appreciated the opportunity to talk to a visiting academic in relaxed circumstances." The dean was gracious in the extreme, for I was not at the dinner. When the first course was served, I was wading through shallows in the Fitzroy River two thousand kilometers from Perth.

In the past I criticized sports in American universities, stating that semiprofessional athletic programs corrupted learning and trivialized education. For ten months in Australia, I had not thought about American universities. In June, however, as the end of the year in Australia spun closer, my mind skipped into worn grooves. One morning at the Hackett coffee shop I read the *Pelican*, a newspaper published by the student guild. On the sports page the University Basketball Club solicited new members. The club, a member wrote, "caters for a wide range of experience and competence, from our Premier teams in the Senior League Division for both men and women to the lower grades where a player will take eight steps with the ball and wonder what is wrong when a 'travel' is called."

The club hoped to send teams to the Australian University Games and had begun raising money to pay their expenses. "If you see us selling choccies make sure you buy one from us for only $2," the member wrote, adding that "a second legendary cake stall is definite. No one has died from our last cooking effort, so we are hoping we'll be lucky a second time." Boys and girls cooking fudge cake, I mused, this is the way athletics should be, the basketball stadium a half mile from my house in Storrs and the classrooms of dollars spent each year at the University of Connecticut on intercollegiate athletics nagging at me. My spirits sank, and for a moment I dreaded returning to the United States.

The mood did not last. Low vision brought the immediate into sight and led, if not to high spirits, at least to entertainment. At dinner Eliza handed me a sampler of her writings: fiction, poetry, and biography, writings, she noted, that allowed people to breathe. Among the poems was "White Fairies." "On a cold winter's day," she wrote, "you can see the white fairies falling, falling from the sky. / On a cold winter's day you can see the white fairies resting, resting where they lie. / O delight with them as they run by! / But shiver and shake afterward 'cause the white fairies are the Winter Lords." Eliza's longest piece was a biography of Kitty, a small stuffed kitten and the family's most sentimental, maybe even most valuable, possession. Kitty has accompanied us on our travels and has been the subject of a miscellany of dinner and bedtime tales.

"Kitty," Eliza wrote, "is an eleven-year-old cat doll. She lives with her nine-year-old mistress in a house on Hillside Circle in Storrs, Connecticut. Kitty is really alive because she speaks to me everyday. She is the leader of a doll gang; some of the members are Elmer, Fuzzy, Clover, Bubble, and Cowboy. Nobody knows where Kitty came from at the beginning. One day when my older brother was just born, the postman came by and gave her to him. That was a big mistake. For the next two years Kitty suffered every kind of punishment, from being thrown against the wall to being stepped on continuously by my brother when she had done nothing at all. But then I came along. Mom and Dad immediately gave her to me. At first she wasn't much better off because for the next ten months I completely ignored her. I can just imagine poor Kitty crying and crying. Naughty me! Soon after that I became inseparable from her. I used to curl up with her at night sucking my thumb. On an average I lost Kitty about eight times a week, and there were long unhappy nights spent without her." When Eliza was young, I searched for Kitty so often that I had neither energy nor time to think about things so trivial as athletics. Now, as the children have grown older and become more distant, I occasionally ponder abstractions. As a result my days and paragraphs have grown longer.

Not only did Eliza's writings make me feel better, but when I finished reading them, I thought about the gang that wandered my essays: Googoo Hooberry, Hink Ruunt, and a toy shop of country characters living in Carthage, Tennessee. Much as Eliza once ignored Kitty, so I had ignored my gang for some time. I wondered what they were doing. Turlow Gutheridge had booked passage on the *Queen Mary* and was about to visit England. The biggest boat Turlow had ever been on was a rowboat, and he was apprehensive about steaming across the Atlantic. When Turlow picked up a prescription at Read's Drugstore, Googoo Hooberry asked him if he was sick. "Not really," Turlow said, "my diverticulitis has been acting up. But the truth is I'm nervous about venturing out on the Great Deep." "If that's all that's bothering you," Googoo responded, "you don't have to worry. This here has been a dry summer, and I imagine that the great deep is running pretty shallow right about now. The creeks hereabouts are so low that the catfish have got freckles."

My subconscious resembled Dunphy's Pond outside Carthage more than it did the great deep. Instead of billowing and swelling skyward, exotic creatures curling up from dank caverns far below the surface, my subconscious was still, home to thick green patches of algae, carp swimming in loose S's just below the surface, and then fishermen in shadows, stretched out like logs, at the ends of their poles rows of dozy dragonflies, their wings opened wide, catching the heat and resembling ribs. Turlow's queasiness about his journey mirrored my own concerns. In ten days Vicki, the children, and I were flying to Cairns to begin a two-week cruise through the Solomon Islands and along the coast of Papua New Guinea on Cunard's *Crown Monarch*.

In February, I read an advertisement describing the *Crown Monarch*. Vicki and I had never been on a cruise, and I wrote Cunard offering to barter lectures for passage. I didn't expect to receive an answer, and when Cunard bit on my proposal, I was startled. Although Vicki and I received free passages, the trip was expensive. Passage for two people in a stateroom on the Coral Deck where our cabin was located was $6,940. All the cabins on the boat had not been booked, and after leaving port I discovered that during the week before the cruise Cunard sold cabins on a two-for-the-price-of-one basis, or, on the Coral Deck, passage for two for $3,470. Despite receiving a complimentary cabin, I paid $700 for our gratuities and "port and handling charges." Next door to us, the children shared a cabin for three. For each child I paid $1,940, or a total of $5,820. The cruise lasted two weeks. During that time we incurred additional charges of $1,483, of which $1,367 was for tours taken when the *Crown Monarch* visited ports. If Vicki and I had been alone, we would not have taken many tours. Instead we would have explored on our own. Children don't explore well. Wandering markets and tasting "crackling" pulled from flying foxes does not appeal to them. Of the remaining $116 of costs, $66 was for laundry, almost all the rest being for soft drinks the children drank by the pool.

I did not drink anything alcoholic during the cruise. "Salt and spirits don't mix," I told Vicki. For her part Vicki had only two drinks, the first a sunset-colored mango concoction when we sailed. The second she drank at the end of the first week after a discussion of how our trip had become the children's trip. When I observed that we had not drunk wine with dinner, Vicki said, "It's not drink I am after. It's romance." Shortly thereafter she got drink, a brandy Alexander, just the sweet thing to sip while making sure the children brushed their teeth.

For the trip I paid Cunard $8,003, each of the three lectures I delivered costing me $2,667.67, or if figured on the basis of forty-five minutes a lecture, $59.28 a minute. There were other expenses. The *Crown Monarch* sailed from Cairns. Before leaving Connecticut, I bought air passes for flights on Qantas within Australia. Ten passes were left, enabling us to fly from Perth to Cairns and back without purchasing more tickets. We spent three nights in Cairns, one before the cruise and two after, these last two because Edward said his year would be ruined if he did not see Cairns and the Great Barrier Reef.

We stayed at the Holiday Inn, a four-star hotel built around blue fountains and hanging gardens. I reserved a suite at "the government rate." During earlier trips I noticed that the United States Information Service booked rooms for me at the government rate, a charge usually the same as the business rate but occasionally lower. "But you don't work for any government," Vicki said, "what will you do if the hotel asks you for a government identification number?" "Give them one," I responded; "of course the number will get garbled in the sending." The hotel didn't ask for my number, and on our arrival a placard in the lobby greeted us, saying "Welcome Pickering Family," our names being sandwiched between similar greetings to two groups of Japanese tourists.

Cairns, a brochure claimed, "caters for your every need." Tourists swarmed through the center of the city, and cafés, restaurants, and eating halls clustered along sidewalks in fragrant, inviting hives. In broad windows owners of souvenir shops draped clothes iridescent with color. We fluttered through the downtown, not simply along the Esplanade and Pierpoint but across and along Abbott, Lake, Grafton, Sheridan, Spence, Shields, Aplin, and Florence. In Cairns we gathered pollen for our suitcases: sweaters with *Cairns* stitched on the fronts, each letter a different color, the *i* the green trunk of a palm, a yellow coconut dotting it and leaves pouring out above; and T-shirts, across the chest of one a coral trout lumbering, resembling a speckled orange boulder.

Souvenirs in Australia resembled those in the United States, consisting primarily of clothes, particularly sweaters, pullovers, baseball caps, and T-shirts. In Cairns, however, at the House of Ten Thousand Shells, Edward bought a cowry shell for $2.50. Pasted across the top of the shell were decals depicting a butterfly fish and the words *Cairns Great Barrier Reef*. For $4.50 Francis bought an inflated puffer fish, spines sticking out all over him in eyebrows, making him look like an aging college professor. Although I rarely bought souvenirs, I purchased an Akubra hat, not to wear in Australia but when I returned to Connecticut. I bought the Oxley. "The hat makes you look as if you own the whole plantation," Vicki said. People who owned plantations didn't waste money. I paid $64.50 for the hat, buying it in a clothing store several streets from the city center. Prices of Akubras varied, and once I saw the Oxley priced at $89.90.

We arrived in Cairns at ten-thirty at night on June 14, having left Perth at seven in the morning and changed planes in Melbourne and Brisbane. The flights were uneventful. Between Perth and Melbourne a stewardess spilled milk in my lap. During the year stewardesses on Qantas dropped a lunch of meals on me: for drink, milk, soda water, and Coca-Cola; for the main course, scrambled eggs and an end of sausage; for dessert, a lump of trifle awash in a yellow custard sauce. I think the sauce contained coconut, although I didn't sample the trifle when it suddenly catapulted onto my right thigh.

At two o'clock on the fifteenth we boarded the *Crown Monarch*. Comparatively new, the *Crown Monarch* made its maiden voyage in December 1990. Four hundred and ninety four feet long and sixty-seven wide, the ship displaced 15,271 tons of water. The boat was a metal island. From our cabins, numbers 360 and 358 on the port side and opposite one of the two major staircases, I wore a series of paths. Up a single flight of stairs and to the rear of the boat was the Palm Dining Room, where we ate dinner. Climbing three flights of stairs took us to the Ocean Terrace, where we ate breakfast and lunch, serving ourselves from the buffet. At four o'clock in the afternoon we returned to the Ocean Terrace, Vicki and I usually having tea and a biscuit while the children ate cakes and ice cream. From the Ocean Terrace, I walked forward along the port side of the boat until I came to the saltwater pool. Early in the afternoon we gathered there about a table on the port side of the boat, Eliza and Edward ordering sodas. When the children finished their drinks, we swam. Vicki and I ran circles through the water and imagined that we were exercising.

I trod the same paths every day. Only rarely did I walk along the starboard side of the boat. Several times a day I climbed the single flight of stairs to the Crown Deck and walked forward, passing the casino and Treasures Boutique, a souvenir shop, on the way to the Crown Cabaret. Sometimes I went through the cabaret and entered the library just beyond in order to get books for the children. Usually, though, I stopped in the cabaret to listen to a lecture, to play bingo, or at night to watch the floor show. I always sat near the back of the room on the left side. When the boat arrived in a port, I watched docking from the sundeck. Sometimes after dinner I went to the sundeck just to look at the moonlight sliding like silk over the water. Rarely did I stray from my paths. Although I explored the boat with the children, I did not return to any of the three lounges once I saw them.

Passengers on the metal island inhabited two villages composed of those who ate dinner at the first and second seatings, the first village dining at 6:15, the second at 8:15, the population of both villages totaling 332, two hundred under the *Crown Monarch*'s capacity. Clustered outside the villages were several small clearings in which people from both sittings met for communal activities: in the Crown Cabaret for bingo or at the Splash Bar beside the swimming pool. Although the island was small, one saw more of the people at his sitting than of people at the other sitting. Each night entertainers staged two shows, one lasting from 7:30 to 8:15 for early diners, the other from 9:30 to 10:15 for people who ate late. We ate at the early sitting and saw the first show. Every night I was in bed by 9:15.

By the end of the two weeks faces of passengers were familiar. Most were middle-aged or older. The children gave some people nicknames, Madame Sparkle, for example, who wore a different dress to dinner each night, all the dresses constellations of sequins. "How many trunks did you bring on the trip?" I asked Madame Sparkle. "Only two," she said, "but they are big." Rumors about passengers blew through the villages like smoke from cooking fires. According to the first version of a rumor, Jane was taking her sixth consecutive voyage on the *Crown Monarch*. In the second version she had been on board for six months, having inherited eighty-six million dollars in November. The final version said Jane inherited eighty-seven million dollars, adding that she was from Chicago.

Aside from Francis, Edward, and Eliza, only two other children were on board, a boy aged six and his infant brother. People's occupations ranged widely. One man had recently retired after serving thirty-seven years on the police force in Perth. After selling the dairy he owned for thirty years, another man became director of a funeral home. People were quietly pleasant, and I did not see any drunkenness. During the cruise many people complimented the children on their behavior. "Sometimes I wish," Vicki said two days before we disembarked, "the children would misbehave and shock everybody, including us."

Few passengers gambled. Only twice did I notice people playing blackjack. Never did I see anyone playing roulette, and dealers stood idle, their faces stiff with boredom. One afternoon a croupier amused himself by trying out a system on a roulette wheel. "After I leave the boat," he said, "I'm going to test the system in the casino at Brisbane." The croupier was in his early twenties, one of many young Australians I met during the year who were traveling for a time before settling into place and a permanent job. "I'll do this for five years," the croupier explained, "and see a little of the world. Then I will go into real estate. Do you think my system will work?" he asked. "No," I answered; "they never do." "You are right," he said, "but now I am winning against myself."

Racks of poker machines surrounded blackjack and roulette tables, eighty-seven machines, Edward told me. Four and a half feet tall, the machines had colorful names: Lucky Bug, Heat Wave, Monkey Business, Lion's Share, Rebel Yell, and Apache Gold, among others. A red ladybug with seven black spots puttered across the front of Lucky Bug, while a fuzzy golden lion smiled beneficently from Lion's Share. Waratah bloomed in red goblets across the left side of Wild Flowers, while yellow wattle flickered on the right. Resembling Batman, Captain Combo stood atop a tall building, gold coins raining about him and a sign reading "CLUBLAND" pasted to the side of the building. At any time during the day one or two people could be found playing the machines. The players were women. Pinched between their thighs were plastic tubs filled with tokens. The women played only the nickel machines. In the middle of each machine were fifteen windows. Under the windows were twelve buttons, each with instructions printed on it. I could not figure out how to play the machines. When I asked a woman to explain the workings of a machine, she said, "You don't want to learn."

At the cabaret the first night the captain sang "Welcome to Our World." The 230 members of the crew resembled the indigenous fauna of an island in the temperate zone. Aside from the tour director, a handful of entertainers, and Robby, the waiter who served us every night and who taught Eliza to fold napkins so that they resembled candles, trussed-up chickens, and the boots of elves, I hardly noticed the crew. Occasionally the crew noticed us, especially a comedian who played with his audience. "Kids, I've thrown a handful of dollar coins into the deep end of the pool," he said to the children during a performance; "go get them." "Kids," he said another time, "do you want to play with a propeller?" "I have a story that you can tell your teacher when you go back to school," he said to Edward during one show. "Ask her if she knows how to catch a polar bear. If she doesn't, you tell her to cut a hole in the icepack then scatter peas around the hole. When the polar bear comes over to take a pea, kick him in the icehole."

I was part of the entertainment staff. Immediately after the lifeboat drill, I attended a meeting of the staff. Twenty-six people sat around tables in a lounge: singers, dancers, musicians, and tour guides, most young and American. Before the meeting started, they chattered. One girl retrieved a packet of photographs left in Cairns in May. She passed snapshots around. "That's a cute picture of Jennifer," a boy remarked. "Ooh, look at the sweet kangawoo," a girl cooed. "I can't tell those twins apart," a girl said examining a picture of two members of the orchestra. "That's not hard," a boy said; "Zack has crinkly ears." "Hey, Justine," another boy said, "how are you?" "None of my friends wrote," Justine pouted, "only my mother."

Raising the average age of the staff were the amateurs: a woman who taught bridge, a painter who conducted classes, and five lecturers, including me. A middle-aged woman lectured on stress. One morning I walked past the room in which she spoke and heard her say, "If you are talking about suicide, then suicide is on your mind." A doctor, himself slipping down the slope of life, lectured on "How to Prevent the Aging Process and Improve Your Sex Life." A financial planner discussed money matters, and a minister who had lived in Papua New Guinea gave history and geography lessons. The director of entertainment instructed us to write the titles of three lectures on a small yellow card and give it to him. The director did not tell us when we would lecture. Only when *The Chronicle*, a leaflet describing the next day's activities, was delivered to the room at eight at night did I discover if I was lecturing the next day. My lectures were: "Living with the *Dead Poets Society*," "Seeing the Extraordinary in the Ordinary," and "Writing My Days into Books." Fifty people attended my talks in the Cabaret Room. The audience was faithful, most people who heard the first lecture attending the other two as well.

Aside from me, the lecturers were seasoned mariners. The minister had sailed the cruise-ship circuit for years. The *Crown Monarch*, he assured me, had better food and accommodations than any other ship that toured the seas around Australia. Having sold his practice in Wisconsin, the doctor and his wife were taking their seventh cruise in less than a year. Next, he wanted to take a boat out of Hong Kong or Singapore. Although this trip was the first cruise on which he had lectured, the financial planner had invested heavily, signing on for three consecutive cruises lasting for a total of thirty-five days. I liked my fellow lecturers, particularly the doctor and the financial planner, both of whom were gracious and attended my talks, a courtesy I did not return. I did not get to know anyone on board well, acquaintances never passing beyond the stage of greeting and casual question. As in Perth, family doings filled the hours.

Vicki and I had a standard stateroom, consisting of 140 square feet and containing a private bathroom, twin beds, and a square double porthole. Although the space was rectangular, the living area resembled a keyhole, the left side of the rectangle nearest the door pinched in by closets, the right by the bathroom. The bathroom was small. A curtain and a step separated the shower from the rest of the room. The shower resembled a milk carton. Turning to adjust the nozzles was difficult. Like clabber I stuck to the side of the carton and without thrashing about could not wash. The walls of our room were cream; the rug, blue and gray; the bedspread and curtain, blue with gray flowers whirling through them like waves.

High in the left corner of the wall where the room widened beyond closets and bath was a television. Although two movies were shown during the day, the first four times and the second three, I never watched a movie. Beneath the porthole and along the walls at the end of the room farthest from the door were our beds. The steward volunteered to convert them into a double bed, but Vicki said she would be more comfortable in a twin. Between the beds was a night table with enough space on top for a book and a basket of apples. Against the wall at the foot of Vicki's bed was a shelf with a chair in front of it and a mirror above. At the foot of my bed stood a small table. Next to it was a little cabinet with three drawers. From the wall above the cabinet the television stared down, the picture tube resembling a thick, dark fog. The children's room was similar except that a third bed pulled out from one of the walls.

At night water pushed against the boat, sounding like wind blowing through grain, the stems vibrating, sometimes almost whistling. On rough nights the boat creaked, and seams pulled and whined. The trip from Cid Harbor in the Whitsunday Islands off the Australian coast to Honiara in the Solomon Islands was 1,132 nautical miles. During this part of the cruise seas were choppy, swells sliding toward us in pillows. We did not get sick, but a few people became ill, one or two so ill that they remained in their cabins for the entire cruise. Occasionally I suffered from headaches and nausea. The crew kept the ship spotless, forever waxing and polishing, scraping and painting. Fumes from cleansers, I suspect, caused the nausea. Inside the boat, escaping fumes was impossible, and every day, no matter the weather, I sat on the sundeck, just to breath air less clean and polished.

Staterooms resembled huts. Before going to meals we gathered in our rooms. In being the struts around which the cruise day was raised, meals kept us disciplined, forcing us to schedule activities and preventing us from drifting into slovenliness and boredom. Breakfast was served from seven until ten on the Ocean Terrace. Unless we left early on a tour, we ate at nine. Lunch ran from noon until one-thirty. We ate at twelve-thirty. If we slipped off schedule during the day, dinner forced us back on. In the Palm Dining Room we sat at table fifteen. The table was at the end of a row on the starboard side, the head waiter probably assuming that three children would be disruptive.

The dining room and table appointments shone. Formality fostered anonymity. After a day of sight-seeing we looked forward to dinner with flowers on the table, the passengers in dresses or coats and neckties, and the meal, five courses, one following smoothly and predictably after another. Arranged carefully on the plate the food looked better than it tasted. Fruits were often grainy and dry and desserts too creamy. Instead of being jerked thrashing from the great deep that morning, the "Catch of the Day" had been hauled frozen out of the depths of a refrigerator.

From Cairns the *Crown Monarch* sailed south in order to refuel, allowing us to spend a day in Townsville. After breakfast we took a bus to the center of the city. Flowers interest me more than buildings, sometimes I think more than people, and herding the family before me I walked to the Queen's Gardens. Near the entrance annuals bloomed in long beds: snapdragons and cleome, the blossoms of this last pink and white, reminding me of gardens in Connecticut. To wash off the aroma of the ship's cleansers, I rubbed my hands through the cleome then massaged the lemon fragrance into my hair. From limbs of banyan trees bundles of roots spilled groundward, the smaller resembling stacks of beanpoles, the larger banks of organ pipes. Across a lawn in front of a mango tree four white ibis followed a magpie lark. Because ibis wobble when they walk, the ibis looked aged. "The lark," Francis said, "is a guide from the ship; the ibis, the passengers."

Castle Hill towered above the garden. Although my sight sagged whenever I looked toward horizons, hills attracted me. "That's where we are going next," I said, pointing to a knob atop the hill. "Not me," Francis said, "I climbed Ayers Rock." Twenty minutes later I started up the cliff face, or goat trail, as locals dubbed the path. I was alone. Vicki and the children took a taxi to the Great Barrier Reef Aquarium. Blue lichens grew in splatters on rocks bulging out of the hill. From shallows in rocks grass grew in stubbles, and knots of figs wedged themselves into crevices, making the hill resemble the face of an unkempt old man. The path wound between boulders. Thick mats of white webs clung to boulders, swelling out from the surfaces like varicose veins.

A lemon migrant butterfly wavered in the sun just before the path dropped into a cove green with palms. Higher along the path cattle-bush bloomed. The walk tired me, and when I looked at the cattlebush, it seemed weary, too, its blossoms drooping, the stamens bleached and stacked around the pistils, almost as if they were protecting them from heat. From the top of Castle Hill, fuel storage tanks in the harbor resembled spores, clustered on the bark of a rotting log. Railway tracks crossed a plain then reaching the yard split like veins running through a leaf. Most new buildings in the town resembled computer chips, replaceable and indistinguishable from one another, windows stapled across floors in dark ranks.

To the north lay a graveyard. At first I thought it an abandoned airfield, the tombstones strips of pavement peeled back by heat. Two fighter planes roared inland from the sea, the noise loud but the planes only irritating midges. Down the hole of an unused privy spiderwebs spread in tissues. A beer bottle lay on the roof of a pillbox, the box constructed, I assumed, during the World War II. On the ceiling of the pillbox dirt daubers built nests. In a corner was an empty red Pepsi can. Balled up next to the can were four napkins, KFC and the face of Colonel Sanders printed on them. On a wall someone had scraped "Minty NZ," digging through a layer of cream paint to expose an earlier coat of blue. I stayed on Castle Hill only long enough to catch my breath. I climbed for the sake of climbing, not for sight of the ocean opening trimmed like a blue lawn at the edge of the land. I took a steeper, quicker route down, one that led directly into the city. On Flinders Street I looked back. Castle Hill seemed screwed into the landscape like a red doorknob, on one side of the door a wide plain, then the forests of tropical Queensland, on the other side Flinders Street with its Edwardian buildings and wrought-iron railings.

I hurried to the aquarium. Guessing that I would appear, Vicki bought a family ticket. "You must be Mr. Pickering," the woman behind the counter said when I tried to purchase admission; "we have been expecting you." I found Vicki and the children on a terrace eating ice cream cones. When the children finished the cones, they went to the souvenir shop while Vicki returned to the aquarium with me. Inside a tank was a small coral reef composed of over one hundred and fifty corals and sheltering two hundred different species of fish. When we left the aquarium, we caught a bus back to the *Crown Monarch*. The entertainers had gone shopping. At the Sheraton Casino a singer got on the bus carrying a new red dress. "What a nice frock," a dancer exclaimed. Although bright, the dress was dull when compared to the fish that slid through the reef like winged rainbows.

At seven-fifteen the next morning a catamaran took us to a platform at Hardy Lagoon on the Great Barrier Reef. Binoculars changed my view of birds; hand lenses, of flowers; now snorkeling changed my view of fish. I snorkeled for two and a half hours. When the time came to return to the *Crown Monarch*, I was the last person out of the water. As a child I raised tropical fish in aquariums. Now I was in an aquarium. The day was overcast, and other passengers became cold. My interest boiled, and I hardly noticed the temperature. Lizardfish lay still amid rock and sand; a spotted moray eel sank into a crevice. Rock cod hunkered on ledges. A school of golden trevally turned in unison like a silver wave. Fusiliers hurried past, their yellow tails waving. A giant Maori wrasse drifted into deeper water, his big body a dark cloud beneath me. Anemones waved like corn, bright and heavy with ears in a late summer breeze. Through the shucks rode anemone fish, some orange and white, others black with white dots. Above them a school of angelfish banked, their color flowing from green into silver and blue as the fish rippled through bars of light.

Black-and-white scissor-tail sergeants bustled out of sight when I approached. Blue-and-yellow damselfish sank into small holes. A parrotfish tumbled under a platter of plate coral then slid away through a shadow. From the surface I watched two bannerfish as they swam beneath a bridge of coral. Butterfly fish and angelfish drifted through staghorn coral like leaves falling from trees, twisting slowly toward the ground, many yellow, others yellow and black, still others yellow and blue. How little I had seen in my life, I lamented as I floated above the reef. I regretted spending so much of my youth playing, not simply on field and court, but in the classroom, where instead of learning to read land and sea, I studied insignificant matters. Of course the cruise itself was trivial, an amusement for older people on whom time hung lightly, passion and ambition no longer riding them high on the neck, urging them past a series of arbitrary markers toward a finish line that forever receded.

The old saw that children keep parents young is wrong. What happens is that parents keep children young, if young can be equated with active. From Hardy Reef to Cid Harbor in the Whitsundays was forty-two nautical miles. The *Crown Monarch* anchored at Cid Harbor at one-thirty in the afternoon. Squalls of wind and rain blew through the islands in dark banks. Waves rolled like sand dunes then collapsed and slid out to foam. As soon as the boat stopped, we boarded a rubber raft with an outboard motor at one end. The raft took us to the *Gretel*, a twelve-meter yacht, once Australia's representative in the America's Cup, now turned into an excursion boat. The man sailing the *Gretel* raised the sail only three-quarters up the mast. In the heavy weather, that was too high for me. Waves gushed over the bow, and despite wearing a yellow slicker I was soon soaked. We sailed four hours, and Francis helped fold sails. Although I helped once, I spent most of the afternoon clutching railings and spars, hoping I would not be swept overboard.

At the end of the excursion one of the crew exclaimed, "That's the first good sail I've had in a long time." Vicki was so cold her hands looked like purple claws. "Thank God!" she exclaimed as we stepped back into the *Crown Monarch*, "Thank God that you will be tied to teaching next year and won't be able to get up to any of this nonsense." A hot shower and dinner improved Vicki's mood. "Sign up for another one," she said when the cruise ended; "lecture on whatever it takes to get us on the high seas again."

For the next three days we sailed across the Coral Sea to Honiara and Guadalcanal. While Vicki and the children read, I thought about characters in my essays. One morning a young man got off the Greyhound bus in Carthage and asked where Horace Armitage lived. That afternoon Horace withdrew five hundred dollars from his savings account, or so LaBelle Watrous reported after standing in line behind him at the Smith County Bank. That same evening the young man bought a ticket on another Greyhound, this one bound for California. "Horace has done some misbehaving in his time," Loppie Groat said, rubbing his chin and looking pensive before he continued. "The black snake knows the way to the chicken coop. Ten to one that young fellow was the probable son come looking for the fattening hog." "I don't know," Hoben Donkin said; "there appeared to be a good deal of human nature in that boy, and there ain't much in Horace." After reading, the children played bingo, five games costing ten dollars. The children liked the phrases the staff attached to numbers and often repeated them at dinner: "B-4, not after, but B-4"; "I-22, two little ducks, quack, quack, I-22"; "N-44, dollies out of the cage, hubba, hubba, N-44"; and "B-6, if you don't take your Dramamine, you will B-6."

Historical memory is short. Names that rang like fire bells through the mind of one generation quickly become faint echoes. My children have never imagined the pop of minié balls and cold mornings hot with smoke at Stones River and the Wilderness. Neither they nor Vicki had heard of Guadalcanal. I stood on the sundeck when the *Crown Monarch* arrived in Honiara. Lashed to the dock were tramp steamers and freighters. Rust blossomed like lichens across the sides of the *Mawo II*. Near the stern an awning sagged between four poles, the wood on the deck puddles of brown and black, resembling the gritty surface of a parking lot. Clumped along bow and stern were barrels of fuel, some clusters silver, others brown. Tied to the dock beside the *Mawo II* was the *Ligomo IV*, a top-heavy black steamer, its motors jangling, the crew tilting red barrels on edge, spinning them along the deck until they rested against the bridge. Piled on a concrete dock and resembling a huge sandpile were brown bags bulging with copra. Behind the pile stretched long tin sheds. Inside the closest shed a yellow forklift spluttered in and out of sight. Along the shore above the docks storage tanks with MOBIL and SHELL painted on them hunkered down, resembling mushrooms the caps of which had begun to slump into black decay. Gasoline fumes seeped through the air, occasionally the smell of coconuts scrubbing the breeze like soap.

Signs were painted on the sides of buildings in the town: ANZ, 7UP, Super Mini Cinema, Victoria Bitter, and Joy Supermarket, on this last sign blue letters against a white background. Above the town rose a pudding of green hills, some bare, vegetation pouring down others like sauce. Appearance deceived. The hills were actually steep, distance rumpling ridges into soft folds. After breakfast we boarded a bus for the Tambea Resort. The trip lasted seventy-five minutes. The road was bumpy, and fumes from the exhaust billowed into the coach.

By the end of the trip the children's faces were white, and Vicki was nauseated. The bus drove through coconut plantations, the trees spilling over us like silver water. Beside the road hibiscus bloomed red and yellow. From cocoa trees fruit hung down like footballs. Black pigs scampered into brush, and children stood outside gray huts and waved. Sensitive plant grew in low mounds along the shoulders of the road, the blossoms resembling scraps of purple fluff, shredded trash tossed from the windows of passing cars. Breadfruit towered above the road, its leaves resembling big green gloves. Buried in the sand along the shore were remnants of war: a landing craft, red and so weathered it resembled coral broken by a storm and tossed into shallows, then in front of a hut facing the sea, a propeller stuck into the ground as decoration and from a distance looking like a wooden wagon wheel.

At the resort I swam. The water was green and marbled, and I floated on my back and watched black-and-yellow butterflies shake through trees above the shore. Across the road from the resort was Tambea Village. On the shoulder of the dirt road leading to the village I found a page torn from a religious tract. "Bible Teaching 8" declared "JESUS

WILL COME AGAIN!" His coming, the tract added, "Will be Glorious." "For *as the lightning* cometh out of the east, and shineth ever into the west; *so shall also the coming of the Son of man be.*" A creek ran beside the village and emptied into sea just above the resort. Garbage littered the banks of the creek. A woman who swam at the resort cut her leg in the water. Her leg became infected and two days later turned as purple as an eggplant.

Employees at the resort cooked a pig in stones and leaves, and for lunch we ate pork and an assortment of local foods: papaya, starfruit, bananas, cucumbers, spring onions, breadfruit, and yams. Afterward we sat in a semicircle under raintrees. Atop the limbs grew birds' nest ferns, making the trees resemble huge planters. Philodendron wound into palms, its yellow-and-green leaves hanging down like shields. Nine women in grass skirts and shell necklaces danced for us. A man wearing blue shorts stood beside them and directed their steps. After the women finished dancing, they put on western dress: skirts and blouses. Then a group of men danced. Later that afternoon, before the *Crown Monarch* sailed, a group called the Pan Pipers danced on the dock. All men, they wore grass skirts and beat drums and played wooden pipes. When they finished, they changed clothes in a shed, appearing afterward in cutoff jeans and T-shirts.

The *Crown Monarch* left Honiara at five in the afternoon. The boat sailed across Iron Bottom Sound, named for the ships sunk there during World War II. As the sun fell, the green hills of Guadalcanal turned blue. Along the shore white ribbons of smoke curled up from cooking fires and then, tattering into gray, vanished. Evening turned sky and sea silver, the light collecting on the water in platters, the waves resembling marks left by the hammering of a smith. Later sunset gilded the water, and the platters turned gold. As the boat left, children scampered along the shore, whistling and waving. I waved back, but I felt alien. If I had wandered more, learning the names of plants, butterflies, and birds, I would not have felt out of place. Because I bought natural history books soon after arriving in Australia, I rarely felt alien. Indeed I learned to recognize so much that at times I thought Australia home, not the United States.

The *Crown Monarch* sailed through New Georgia Sound, along the Solomon Sea, and through St. George's Channel, some 587 nautical miles, arriving in Rabaul, the capital of East New Britain, at eight in the morning two days later. Rabaul was the first of three stops in Papua New Guinea. Once the center of a volcano, Simpson Harbor resembled a bowl of water. Around the top of the bowl buildings formed a lip, for the most part white but here and there chipped and stained gray by warehouses. A glaze of humidity hung over the shore. Above the town volcanoes rose blue.

I booked a tour of Tavurvur, a small but still active volcano. At eight-fifteen we boarded a bus. As we drove through town, I read signs. Many were in pidgin. Haus Laplap sold rungs. Next to gasoline pumps at a Shell station a sandwich board commanded "Noken Simok." A grocery sold "Hot and Cold Bia." Native roses wrapped fences in pink ribbons. Hedges were red with hibiscus, and in yards frangipani blossomed white and yellow. At the edge of town stood the Frangipani Hair Salon. At Matupit Village we climbed into dugout canoes, each with an outrigger on the right side to provide stability. I paddled bow in a canoe, and Eliza sat in the middle. A villager sat in the stern. The canoe leaked badly, and the man paddled little. While I pulled us across a lagoon, he bailed water, using the lower half of a plastic bottle as a bucket. Water in the lagoon was still and brown, and plastic bottles bobbed slowly about, from a distance resembling waterlogged buoys.

The climb up the cone of the volcano was short and steep, winding through banana trees and coconut palms near the shore then turning almost straight up a ridge. Spools of vines tangled across the path. I asked a guide the names of flowers, a blue pea and then a bush, yellow blossoms erupting from the top in spires. The guide could not identify the plants, but he said sap from the bush cured ringworm. Humidity made the hike difficult, and Francis, who was the best climber in the family, wilted and turned red in the face, almost collapsing when he reached the top of the cone.

From cracks in the volcano steam blew upward, spreading in plumes like fronds on tree ferns. Sulfur stained rocks around the cracks yellow, the color running up rather than down. The damp air absorbed the fumes, and breathing resembled drinking mineral water. Edward gagged. On the floor of the volcano tourists had piled rocks into letters spelling their names: Gus, Roy, Nixo, Maya, and G. Bone. A guide tied a thick rope to a tree and threw the loose end of the rope over the top of the cone so that it dropped through rocks along a steep path. I let myself down the rope slowly, and Edward and Eliza followed. At the bottom Edward and I collected rocks and spelled UCONN. Next to us Eliza spelled KITTY.

When we returned to the lagoon, guides opened coconuts. The children were so tired they only sipped the milk, but I drank the contents of two large coconuts. On the way back to the boat the bus drove through a coconut plantation. The road wound between craters dug by bombs during the war. Like shards of pottery scattered about the ruins of an ancient city, parts of airplanes lay amid the trees. The wreckage of a Japanese fighter and bomber lay tossed, it almost seemed, in a clearing, the bomber having dug a trench as it slammed into the ground, the rising suns under its wings still visible.

The clearing resembled a bowl turned upside down, the planes seeming refuse floating on the surface. In contrast the green fronds of the palms appeared woven, curving through each other to form the bottom of the bowl. The air below the palms and above the planes was as clear as water. Through it floated blue butterflies, their wings as big as hands and shining like stained glass. I took out my binoculars, but before I could focus I was interrupted. "This is betelnut," a guide said, holding out a handful of green oblong fruits as long as my index finger and as round as the circle formed when the tip of my thumb touched the tip of my middle finger. People in Rabaul chewed the nuts almost like tobacco, combining them with native mustard or building lime in order to release the fruit's mild narcotic. The combination of nut and lime turned lips, teeth, and sidewalks red, these last so splotched they resembled splatter ware.

After hurrying through lunch on the boat, we walked along Malaguna Road to the open market. After morning excursions Vicki and I explored markets in Madang and Alotau in Milne Bay, the other two ports of call in Papua New Guinea. Heat tired the children, and they did not accompany us to these last two markets. Instead they stayed in their room, reading and playing cards, usually "war." Because we had been the only westerners at the market in Rabaul, the children were uncomfortable. "Everybody stared at me," Edward said afterward, "and I couldn't relax." So that I would feel at home, I ate raw peanuts or bananas, thirteen bananas in Alotau. Most of the merchants were women.

They were friendly and smiled when they saw me eating. Sheltered by sloping tin roofs, the market in Rabaul resembled long sheds. The floor of the market was concrete, and women piled food on wooden tables: peanuts, tomatoes, starfruit, onions, bananas, dried tobacco, and coconuts among other items. Atop leaves from the breadfruit tree merchants stacked betelnuts, laying the string bean–shaped mustard across the nuts.

Women wore cotton dresses dyed bright colors, and in Madang, Vicki bought Eliza a dress that she wore to dinner on the *Crown Monarch*. On a bank just beyond the gate to the dockyard in Honiara, merchants spread quilts. On the quilts they displayed souvenirs: reed trays, necklaces made from shells, painted face masks, and carved wooden animals. On returning to the boat, passengers walked through an avenue of merchants. Vicki and I did not buy anything in the Solomon Islands. In Papua New Guinea, however, we bought so many souvenirs that in Alotau we had to buy a suitcase in which to pack them. In Madang alone Vicki bought seventeen necklaces, most made from cowry shells or seeds from Indian walnut. In all the markets in Papua New Guinea, Vicki bought reed bags. In Alotau a woman dumped bananas out of a bag before she sold it. She wasn't thorough. On board the ship a cockroach scurried out of the bag followed by a hairy black spider.

In Madang we bought carvings produced in the Sepik River area of Papua New Guinea. My favorite was a wild woman with bright eyes made from cowries. Dressed in beads and a grass skirt, she leapt high in the air, legs and arms akimbo. From the tip of her bottom to the top of her head she was seven inches tall. The span from the tip of her left hand to that of her right was thirteen inches. "That," I told the children, "is how your mother behaved when I asked her to marry me." "Wasn't Mommy wearing more clothes when you proposed?" Eliza asked. "Yes," I answered.

Going to markets was an excuse for roaming together: strolling, for example, around a pond in Madang, its still surface an oilcloth green and white with lilies. Vicki and I did not buy expensive souvenirs, spending a total of $340 Australian, including the price of the suitcase. "So long as I didn't get sick," I told Vicki; "I could live in Rabaul or Madang." Malaria was epidemic in Papua New Guinea, and when I stood under a banyan tree in Madang, mosquitoes fell upon me like a shower. "Not me," Vicki said, "I don't like the way men look at me."

As the cruise steamed toward the end, I stayed on deck longer. The night we left Rabaul and sailed through the Bismarck Sea toward Madang a dark island shaped like the cone of a volcano appeared on the left side of the boat. As we passed, the boat seemed to slip and drift toward the island. For a moment I imagined that the island was sucking us toward it and we would be wrecked. How, I wondered, would I get Vicki and the children out of their rooms before the boat sank? Early the next morning flying foxes spotted the sky over Madang, their heads shaped like arrows, slicing through the blue sky and pulling their bodies behind them like remnants of night. Later Vicki and I walked past sheoaks in which they slept. They hung down in bundles, resembling small hams wrapped in thick brown paper.

In both Milne Bay and Madang we went on tours after breakfast. In Milne Bay a truck took us to the village of Halowia, where we snorkeled. We sat on wooden benches in the back of the truck, an awning over our heads. The truck crossed seven bridges and forded nine streams. I snorkeled for ninety minutes and again was the last person to leave the water. Red-and-blue starfish glowed on the coral, and I ran my hands over blue sea stars and nudibranchs thick as pipes and spotted with orange.

In Madang we rode in a green Toyota Commuter. From the ceiling of the van frangipani dangled in loops. Painted in white on the side of the van was "ARE YOU READY? JESUS IS COMING SOON." The van took us outside to Bilbil, a village known for its pottery. Planted beside the road to the village were cocoa, cassava, and papaw, the fruits of this last hanging down like giant udders. While Vicki examined jugs, deciding not to buy one because she thought it would be broken during the flight back to the United States, I wandered through the village. Walls of most huts were bamboo, and the roofs, sago palms. Tacked on a wall beside the door of a hut was a poster. The poster was a foot and a half square and depicted a soccer team, the NGIP Muruks from Rabaul, a member of the PNG Big League and winner of the Cambridge Cup in 1989.

From Bilbil the van took us to Riwo, where men and women danced in grass skirts and loincloths. They wore headdresses decorated with white feathers and necklaces strung with pig tusks curving like new moons. On the sand by the sea stood a table. On it dried pots and pans. Above and to the left of the table an outhouse jutted over the water. When the *Crown Monarch* left Madang, I noticed an outhouse with six stalls sticking out over the water behind a village. When the boat sailed, I always saw things. Above Milne Bay a long waterfall tumbled through the Owen Stanley Mountains like the will-o'-the-wisp. I wanted to notice more and venture into the great deep of thought. Cruises, though, run shallow, resembling life itself. The things one sees on a cruise or in life are just observations. Only by hammering and forcing can one create the illusion of a picture.

I declared our souvenirs when we disembarked in Cairns. "That suitcase," I said to the customs officer, pointing at a swollen red bag, "contains souvenirs: reed baskets, wooden carvings, and necklaces made from shells." "The whole bag?" he said, looking dismayed. "Wait," he said, awareness suddenly smoothing his brow, "aren't you American?" "Yes," I answered. "Aren't you going to take all this back to the United States?" he asked. "In five weeks," I said. "Well, then," he answered; "Customs in the United States can deal with this lot. Go on through." From the dock we returned to the Holiday Inn and, after leaving the suitcases in our suite, spent the rest of the day in souvenir shops. In them we met many passengers from the cruise. We greeted each other like old friends. We chatted with people with whom we had never talked while on board the *Crown Monarch*, asking questions about families and future plans. "There she goes, a little island of light sailing into the blue beyond," Vicki said that night as we stood on our balcony at the Holiday Inn and watched the *Crown Monarch* leave port on another cruise

Travel was addictive. The next morning at eight-thirty we were on a catamaran headed for Green Island. I spent three hours and forty minutes snorkeling, my skin wrinkling like a tired, leaky balloon. Because I recognized birds and trees, place was familiar, and I felt at home. A flock of gray-breasted white eyes swirled around picnic tables in a green dust. A green-winged pigeon scurried through leaf litter. Perched on the limb of a coral tree two Eastern reef herons resembled ornaments removed from tacky birdbaths. A rose-crowned fruit dove hunched on a branch, its pink breast glowing. Ghost crabs dug holes in the sand above the waterline. An ambrax butterfly wavered through a bushy thicket, the white patches on its wings shaking like semaphores. Above the beach nicker nut vine bristled, its seedpods resembling green pincushions. "The great deep didn't affect you," Vicki said, "you have started identifying birds and trees again. It doesn't take much to satisfy you."

The next day we flew back to Perth. That evening when I kissed Eliza good-night, I found a letter lying beside the bed of Clarabell, the doll Santa Claus brought Eliza for Christmas. "Dear Clarabell," the letter read; "Oh, how I adore you. Your voice rings like music. Your hair is like gold. Whenever I see you my heart dances. Alas, I cannot reveal my identity. But here are some clues: one, my hair is brown; two, I have been on a cruise. We went 3,552 miles. But I am still the same. Your secret admirer."

Some of the Best

We returned from Cairns on Friday, July 1. Sticking through the daisies in front of the house was a For Sale sign. On the kitchen table lay a note from a real estate agent saying that he had scheduled an open house for July 2, from eleven to twelve in the morning. "I hope you won't mind," he wrote. I slept late on Saturday. A light drizzle blew across the yard. A pair of ring-necked parrots waddled across the grass, water pearling yellow, blue, black, and green atop their feathers. A spotted turtle dove crouched beside a rock, the patch over his neck glistening in the rain like a saddle blanket. Suddenly the parrots tossed the water off in a spray and flew over the back fence. The dove rose in an arc. Flipping sideways it spun through the silky oak by the garage, its wings clattering. At the door stood the real estate agent, a couple beside him. "I'm sorry," he said; "I wrote the wrong time on my note. The open house starts at ten o'clock, not eleven. I hope you won't mind."

On July 8, we were going to leave the house for good. "Today is all right," Vicki said, "but during the week I have to pack, and I don't want to be disturbed." "You won't be," the man said. While we ate breakfast people trooped through the house. "Are the floors under the rugs hardwood?" a man asked me. "I hope you don't mind if my little girl uses the toilet," a woman said. "I like muesli, too," a man said, peering into my breakfast bowl. Tuesday morning another real estate agent telephoned. "My client wants to look at the house now," she said; "I hope you won't mind." "I mind," I said; "we are leaving on Friday. You can see the house then." "No," she said; "my client wants to see it now. Besides I am going on holiday on Friday." "He and you," I said, hanging the telephone up, "need to learn self-control."

Days unraveled into errands. On Thursday, I sold the Toyota back to Brooking Mazda. When I purchased the car in September, Rod Evans told me to return it in August. "We will buy it back," he said, "for about what you paid for it." "And they did," I told Vicki later that day; "can you imagine that happening in Connecticut?" Vicki and I usually own cars for a dozen years, long enough to become sentimental about them. Before I drove the Toyota to Brooking, Vicki patted its hood and said, "Good-bye 8NJ-O78. You've been a trooper. I hope Rod finds you a home with a warm garage."

Our round-trip ticket from Connecticut to Australia allowed us one stopover. Ten months earlier we flew directly to Perth. In February, I had scheduled the stop in Fiji on our return flight. On Wednesday, I booked a holiday at The Fijian, a resort, an agent said, "with plenty of coral near the beach." Worry is the consort of Holiday. "What will we do with our luggage on Fiji?" Vicki asked. "Let me worry about that," I said. And worry I did, not simply about the holiday, but as the end of the year approached about everything associated with leaving. In August we were taking the train from Perth to Sydney. Where, I worried, would we store the luggage on the train and how would we get the bags to the hotel? Throughout the week I nagged Vicki, urging her to throw away things. On Monday I went to the university bookstore and filled the car with cardboard boxes. That night I packed books, the children's pencils and drawings, and baskets of memorabilia from school, most of which I wanted to "recycle." "Do you want the children to throw everything away and just forget that they were ever in Australia?" Vicki said.

The next morning I mailed seven boxes at the university post office. Postage to the United States cost $248. Although we were leaving Melvista on the eighth, we would not leave Perth until August 1. From the eighth until the twenty-fourth we would be in the Kimberley. For the time we were away, I stored our possessions in a garage owned by the university. Before selling the car on Thursday, I carted a duffel bag, eight suitcases, and eleven cardboard boxes to the garage. From Martin Thompson, a wildlife artist, I bought three pictures: one of a red kangaroo, the others of ring-necked parrots and kookaburras, birds that frequented the yard. The pictures were twenty-one inches tall and twenty-five wide. "I love them," Vicki said, "but how will we get them home." "Let me worry about that," I said. During the last week on Melvista, I fretted so much about luggage that Vicki banished me from the house. I spent most of the week at the university.

Friends described plights of acquaintances who almost had to take out mortgages in order to cover the cost of excess baggage. "You'll be all right so long as you don't let a woman process your bags in Sydney," one person said. "No," a tall bachelor said, "women are wonderful. I always go to a woman, and I never have trouble." "Yes," another person said, "women are better than men, especially Chinese women. They don't want to offend customers, so they don't charge for excess weight." "Don't under any circumstances go to a Chinese," someone else told me later; "they stick to the rules. A couple of years ago in Singapore, a Chinese at the check-in counter made my friend David leave a suitcase behind. The bag contained souvenirs from David's vacation. He paid to have the bag sent air freight, but the bag disappeared, and he lost some wonderful things including pieces of old China and a wall hanging decorated with egrets."

We left 12 Melvista, and Perth, at 6:50 in the morning on the eighth. Despite leaving most of our luggage behind in the garage, worries accompanied me, resembling a heavy backpack. "Do you think the bags will be there when we return?" Vicki said; "somebody could break in and steal them." "Trust me," I said; "the garage is locked, and the bags are safe." "But how do you know they are safe?" Vicki asked. "I just know," I said, picking up *Panorama*, Ansett's travel magazine. I studied the map of Australia in the back of the magazine. I read the names of places aloud: Wagga Wagga, Coober Pedy, Mount Isa, Emerald, and Gove. In imagination I crossed Arnhem Land, sailed across the Gulf of Carpentaria, and wandered down Cape York Peninsula. I roamed the Great Sandy, Gibson, and Simpson deserts.

I turned the hourglass of my life upside down and examined the past as it sifted through memory. My parents were loving, and my childhood was happy. I lived in a house appointed with words like *responsibility, decency,* and *integrity.* If my childhood had not been happy, I wondered, would my life have been so conventional? Mother answered my question. "Fortune smiled on you. Never stop being thankful. Instead of fretting about what did not happen, forget yourself and help others." Suddenly the voice changed to that of Vicki. "Sam," she said, "Edward and Eliza won't eat breakfast. Do something." In front of me sat a gray tray sagging with sausage, bacon, scrambled eggs, tomatoes, a roll and butter, marmalade, orange juice, and macadamia cookies. "This is lunch," I said to Edward while putting on earphones for the radio; "eat something then give the rest to Francis." By eleven o'clock Eliza and Edward and even Francis, who grazed across three breakfasts, would be clamoring for lunch.

For a while I listened to Mozart in hopes of drifting past Arnhem Land out into the Arafura Sea toward Never-Never Land. Rarely can I sleep on airplanes, however. Instead I thought about the time ahead, four nights at the Cable Beach Club followed by twelve days traveling through the Kimberley. I arranged the trip, telling Vicki the details later. Vicki likes routine. Anything that disrupts routine upsets her, and she refuses to plan trips. "Can you name anything else you could have done to make our last weeks in Australia more complex?" Vicki said while packing. "No," I said, lying, wishing I had scheduled an excursion to Kakadu in the Northern Territory.

Four months had passed since I booked our stay at the Cable Beach Club. I did not confirm the reservation before leaving Perth. What will I do, I thought, if the reservation has gone astray? In Connecticut whenever I become fretful, I walk in the woods. Invariably something diverts me. I took the earphones off and forced my eyes to walk. Three rows ahead of me sat two young aboriginal men. Both wore baseball caps, the one-size-fits-all type, decorated with the logos of athletic teams. One cap was black. A red knob perched on top looking like a flattened cherry while a block of red letters ran across the front, the letters spelling BULLS, white outlining them like mortar around bricks.

The other cap was dark blue. Printed in silver letters across the back of the cap was SHAQ ATTACK. Stitched beneath the letters and hard to see from three rows away was Reebok, the name of the company that manufactured the cap. On the left side of the cap was 32, the number worn by Shaquille O'Neal, a center on the Magic, a professional basketball team in Florida. When I asked Edward the name of the team for which O'Neal played, he was astonished. "Edward," I said, "sports are not the sort of thing to which serious adults pay close attention." When we landed in Broome, I discovered that the driver sent by the Cable Beach Club to fetch guests at the airport did not have our names on his list. A drizzle was falling when we left Perth. In Broome the sun was as warm as an eiderdown. Vicki smiled when she stepped out of the plane. "This is going to be a good vacation," she said as we walked toward the club van, adding, correctly as it turned out, "the reception desk will have our reservation."

Seventeen stone lions, all with their hair carefully curled, squatted on their haunches atop blocks, forming a half-moon before the entrance to the Beach Club, waiting, it seemed, for the crack of a trainer's whip before roaring into life and performance. Stone horses stood beside paths that turned like circus rings. The horses were alert, their short tails raised, their mouths open sucking in air, and their legs tensed to the edge of prancing. In the lobby of the club a reef sprayed like a garden out of a black vase five feet tall. Tied to stalks, a bouquet of conches, clams, starfish, fans of coral, and chambered nautiluses bloomed like flowers. On the reception desk sat a wicker basket lumpy and pink with Lady Williams apples. I ate one after registering. An aviary of bird paintings hung from the walls. Beside the desk palm cockatoos groomed themselves across a canvas six feet tall and four feet wide, cheeks red and feathers rising sharp over their heads like tomahawks.

Later that day I dug a field guide out of my backpack and returning to the lobby went bird-watching. I slipped silently through the room and identified cockatiels, crimson rosellas, a bush stone-curlew, silver gulls, a nankeen night heron, black ducks, and a sulfur-crested cockatoo. While creeping up to a white-breasted sea eagle, I tripped on the corner of a rug. Luckily appetite dulled the bird's awareness. Having just pulled a fish from the water, the eagle did not hear me stumble. Except for blue-and-yellow macaws, all the birds in the room were native to Australia. Later in the Taronga Zoo in Sydney, I saw blue-and-yellow macaws. "Those birds in Broome probably escaped from a zoo," I said to Francis, explaining that I doubted the macaws would succeed in establishing themselves in Australia. For me a bird on the wall was almost as good as a bird on a limb. Sprinkle imagination on the paint, and a canvas flutters into life, song darting from it in bright streaks.

Modeled on the small homes in which pearl divers once lived, bungalows at the Beach Club also stirred my imagination. An airy veranda surrounded the bedroom of our bungalow. Tucked out of sight on one side of the bungalow were a bathroom and a small kitchen. Over the bungalow a tin roof rose to a point, cooling the building and resembling a silver tent. Painted green and red, lattice stitched like lace across the screens surrounding the veranda, turning hard sunlight into shadowy bars. On the veranda itself wicker chairs gapped, inviting travelers to rest and tumble into cool sleep. Above the bed a fan beat slow circles. For a while I lay on the bed and imagined myself a real storyteller, a man who had sailed dark, hot seas and sat in dusky corners, clutching bottles of black rum. I wore a soiled yellow Panama hat and a white shirt with a frayed collar. The fantasy did not last long. Fantasies of parents are usually short-lived. "Come on, Daddy," Eliza said, "we want to explore the beach, and Mommy said you have to go with us." I shed imagination and put on my "extra-large" blue bathing trunks, the lining of which had pulled loose from the seams. Whenever I swam, the lining twisted into a knot shaped like a loaf of French bread, kneading my doughy lower regions, forcing me to baste them afterward with zinc oxide. After casting a wistful glance at the veranda, I accompanied the children to the beach to search for golden doubloons.

In my family, vacations lend themselves to literary doings. Eliza won't travel without some of her gang of friendly stuffed animals. On this trip she took Kitty and Fuzzy, the latter a dumpy panda. Kitty kept a diary while she stayed at the Beach Club. I found the first page on the seat of a wicker chair. "We had macadamia cookies for breakfast," Kitty wrote. Later, Kitty continued, "We took a nap. Then Mommy gave us drawing lessons after which she took us for a walk." Kitty also wrote poetry. On Eliza's bed I found "When They Met" by "Kitty Pickering." "When they met, the birds sang. / When they married, the deer frolicked. / When they had a child, the fish leapt with joy. / When they died, God opened His Arms."

Except for being able to nap, Kitty's doings resembled my own. For breakfast I ate cornflakes bought in downtown Broome. I sprinkled raisins and crushed macadamia cookies over the cereal. I walked about the club and looked at the gardens. Streams curled between bungalows. While red and green bridges arched above the streams, palms draped over them: pandanus jagged with sharp leaves; fan and fishtail palms; then royal palm, the trunks of this last bulging in the middle, parallel green lines crossing the swellings at intervals, making trunks resemble stacks of gray crowns, each crown a different size. River red gums leaned over the streams then turned up in the sun, their trunks gleaming like white ladders. Weeping figs spread wide, their green canopies thick and low, resembling covers on vegetable dishes. Flowers burned at the top of African tulip trees.

Fruits dangled heavily from sausage trees, the leaves of the trees stiff and inflexible, "opinionated and stern," Francis said, "German like the sausages." Bougainvillea wound like needlepoint through lattices, while ixora bloomed in red and orange bushes. On yellow oleander, flowers resembled trumpets. When Eliza discovered a dead cat on the shoulder of a road half a mile from the club, she sprinkled oleander blossoms over the body. "Kitty thought we ought to do something," she explained. By the steps to our bungalow straw-necked ibis hunted through the lawn, and honeyeaters sputtered through a fig tree. A family of small green frogs lived behind the water tank above the toilet in the bathroom. Shy, they came out only at night.

When I was not roaming the grounds of the club, I was often on Cable Beach itself. Waves were small and rolling, just right for a father with children. We bodysurfed, and I was the champ. I resembled other fathers on the beach. Many were middle-aged with deep-dish stomachs but with slender, younger, forklike wives. Each morning the children and I clambered over rocks. We found green sea slugs resembling bits of indoor carpeting. The children filled bags with shells: periwinkles, limpets, and spidery gray conches. Unlike doubloons, which could be spent to pay for excess baggage, the shells became baggage and were carefully packed to take back to the United States.

North along Cable Beach nudity was fashionable. Twice I ambled north, not so much to gaze at invigorating sights as to reach the bush. Sweet bird of youth had long since ceased roosting on the shoulders of the swimmers I saw. Almost all the people who swam naked were middle-aged, and as they dove into the surf, their rumps rose and fell like brown stones bundled about in a heavy swell. Over the dunes behind the beach lay another natural world across which agile wallabies bounced and grasshoppers broader than my palm spluttered into noisy flight. I squatted beside a patch of purple mulla mulla and watched a brahminy kite slide between dunes. A gecko skittered into a clump of spinifex grass then looked out warily, holding himself so high off the sand that he appeared posed.

At sunset I swam. From the horizon, color streamed upward in wet lines, damp and vitality seeping out of the lines the higher they climbed, garish orange turning yellow then fading to silver and finally light blue. Along the ocean and beach color ran sideways, the ocean dark blue with black shadows collapsing into clumps under waves. At water's edge the beach glistened like satin. Damp spots resembled orange pools. Close to the dunes the sand was silver, becoming tarnished as night approached. Swimming made me hungry. Twice we ate on the patio beside the freshwater pool. We lingered over dinner. Above the patio coconut palms shook lightly like feathers. From tennis courts came the thump of balls, the noise not resembling belches as it did in the daylight but instead the suction of an old pump, one by a back door, a hydrangea white with blossoms beside it, a cedar bucket cool on the well cover. Other nights we took taxis into Broome and ate at Tongs, a Chinese restaurant.

At the club a guest could book a fishing trip, a ride on a hovercraft, or a scuba-diving excursion. Many tours were available, and a stack of pamphlets lay on a table in the lobby. I thumbed them, not searching for a tour but hoping that an odd pamphlet might spill out. Located at the club was, I discovered, a "Relaxation Centre," offering, among other things, "Beauty Therapies," "Guided Healing," "Rebirthing," "Flotation Therapy," and "Reiki." Rebirthing was, I read, "an inner process of self-learning that uses a conscious connected breathing technique to help re-experience and thereby re-evaluate life's events." "What does that mean?" Vicki said. "I don't know," I said, "but finding out costs fifty dollars. Reiki is cheaper at thirty-five dollars." "What is that?" Vicki said. "Haven't you heard of Reiki?" I said reading the pamphlet. "The word Reiki means Universal Life Energy," I explained. "By enhancing the life force with Reiki energy the body can mobilize its healing resources to reverse the disease process, physically, emotionally, and mentally." "Oh," Vicki exclaimed, "the bus is here, and we can go shopping."

During the day we explored shops in Chinatown, eating ice cream cones when we grew weary. We bought a wardrobe of shirts, some with *Broome* stitched across the chests, others pulsing with life, both animal and vegetable, palms blown into nests by wind or a school of silver fish gliding through a scarlet sea. Vicki bought me a T-shirt, the only souvenir shirt I took home from Australia. On the front of the shirt was a rectangle resembling the side of an aquarium. Two saltwater crocodiles thrashed through the aquarium, tossing foam about them in white clouds, their eyes red with anger. Several shops resembled attics, dusty with knickknacks, things made by great-aunts at adult education classes: hazy blue-and-pink paintings, mugs decorated with pudgy dancing puppies, and earrings pimply with colored beads. Shelves sagged, weighed down by zoos fashioned from seashells: owls, elephants, puffer fish, pigs, giraffes, lovebirds, mice, kittens, and Ninja Turtles, these last armed with swords and carrying shields.

Vicki spent much time looking at pearls. My wallet was shallow, and I could not dive into it overnight and fish out cash enough for a necklace. Even so, I also enjoyed looking at pearls, especially black ones, their luster shimmering between night and day. If the children had discovered a treasure chest on the beach I would have bought a black pearl. "Daddy, instead of a pearl," Eliza said, "why don't you get the ultimate Australian souvenir, a tattoo?" "What kind?" I said. "A kangaroo," Eliza said; "a kangaroo could hide in the hair on your back."

Edward read every book about crocodiles in the Nedlands Library. Consequently we spent an afternoon at Malcolm Douglas's Crocodile Farm. A wire fence surrounded the farm. Suspended on it were small signs warning, "Guard Dogs Patrol at Night." "Why would crocodiles need to be guarded by dogs?" Francis asked. I couldn't answer the question. Only someone who had never seen a crocodile burst out of a mud hole would consider breaking into a crocodile farm. A guide tossed chickens and red slabs of kangaroo to Gus, Aggro, Three Legs, Henry, Happy, and Santa Claus. The jaws of the crocodiles banged together with a loud metallic thunk when they snatched at the meat and missed. Still, the crocodiles ate less than we did in Broome. Most of the time they lay basking in mud, resembling horny duffel bags, not one of which had a maw large enough to swallow the laundry of shirts Vicki bought in Chinatown.

Children and wives insist upon regular meals. On Saturday we went to the market on the lawn surrounding the Broome Courthouse. We roamed stalls for two hours, keeping our energy stoked up with butterfly cakes, a heart surgeon's delight consisting of a vanilla cake sprinkled with confectioner's sugar and soggy with dollops of cream resembling liquid butter; pineapple and coconut drinks; green chicken curry; fried noodles; and "Judy's Fresh Fried Lumpia," this last an egg roll stuffed with seafood and vegetables. I listened to an aboriginal man singing country music. He sounded as if he were born in east Tennessee. Instead, though, of leaving Carthage and Red Boiling Springs behind him, he left Hall's Creek and made his way to Broome, not Nashville.

Beneath a fat gum tree aging hippies sat on the ground beating wooden drums and playing stone flutes. I wondered what sort of lives the musicians led. All were tall and skinny, not one carrying a tray of butterfly cakes around his middle or bending under a backpack swollen with excess baggage. The music was monotonous, though, and soon I wandered to a table, bottles of jam, chutney, and honey shining on top: strawberry and passion-fruit jam; walnut and green mango chutney; and honeys: wild wattle, bloodwood, and Great Sandy Desert. After leaving the market we walked up Hammersley Street to "Kimberley Kreations." While I looked at paintings in the gallery, the children sat on the porch and rubbed a gray marble cat.

Later that afternoon I swam in the ocean, and the children swam in the freshwater pool. "What a marvelous experience for the kids," acquaintances in the United States said when I mentioned spending a year in Australia. The experience was marvelous, not, however, for the children but for their parents. Often I had trouble believing that I was in Australia. The children never experienced disbelief. Instead of doing what I thought fabulous, riding waves in the Indian Ocean, the children preferred swimming in a pool.

After swimming I cooked steaks on the patio. A green frog hopped under the table. I caught him and to save him from being stepped upon turned him loose under a hedge of ixora. The evening was cool, and after dinner as I lay in bed, jasmine wafted through the screens, turning the bungalow vanilla. That night I dreamed I wrote a children's book entitled *The Smallest Ear*. The book described the unhappy childhood of the smallest ear of corn in a bushel basket. The ear was so little that even worms neglected him. The other ears in the basket teased him. Some bullied him, scratching him with their massive shucks. He had no friends, but he worked hard to ripen, and before he became a dry cob, he saw his kernels turn fields green. On paper the book is absurd. In dream it was a best-seller, enabling me to spend another year in Australia.

In Broome I looked at pearls in Linney's on Dampier Terrace. The building housing Linney's was new. Attached to the wall by the front door was an engraved brass plate declaring, "This building was officially opened 26-3-94 by Peter Murray, A Giant Kimberley Character." Early on July 12, Peter Murray picked us up at the club. Peter owned a company called "Kimberley Safaris," and three months earlier I booked a tour with him, an eleven-night, twelve-day trip called "The Best of the Kimberley." The trip covered twenty-seven hundred kilometers, taking us first to the best-known tourist spots in the region: Windjana and Geikie gorges, Tunnel Creek, and the Bungle Bungles, "suburbia," Peter labeled them. After four nights the tour drifted from suburbia into the central Kimberley: through Springvale Station, across the Ord River through Bedford Downs Station, slicing between the King Leopold Ranges and the Durack Range at Teronis Gorge. From the Upper Chamberlain River, the trip turned west, crossing Tableland Station, heading south across the Traine River through Glenroy and Mornington Stations to Sir John Gorge.

After two nights near the gorge we drove northwest through Mt. House Station to the Gibb River Road, where we turned south toward Derby and Broome. Eleven people made the trip including Peter and his helper, Tom. The four tourists on the trip, other than Vicki, the children, and me, were women: Faye, a businesswoman who had known Peter and his wife for years, then "the three ladies," Margaret, Leslie, and Barbara, friends from childhood, now in their fifties, who had traveled together before, both rough and soft, preferring, they noted, the rough, seeing it as more natural. All three were knowledgeable botanists and bird-watchers. Throughout the trip I dogged their footsteps, aiming my binoculars where they pointed. Amenable, hardy, and industrious, the ladies were ideal companions. Moreover, they were home folk. Margaret and Leslie attended Nedlands Primary when they were children, and although Barbara went to primary school in Cottesloe, she lived in Nedlands, a quarter of a mile away from the house on Melvista.

Although Peter and I were the same age, the mental worlds we inhabited were vastly different. Peter grew up around cattle. In the 1980s he and two partners leased 7 million acres of land. During the economic recession Peter went brisket, short plate, and flank up, losing everything, $25 million overnight, he said. From the financial carcass Peter must have sliced off a bit of round, for in addition to the tour company, he owned a gas station, a share in a pearl farm, and the franchise for Avis-Rent-a-Car in the Kimberley. I wondered what led Peter to build the cattle empire. All people eventually fail, letting themselves down whether directly through physical illness or intellectual blindness, or indirectly by choosing the wrong friends or advisers. Peter overreached, but not out of arrogance. He did so, I decided, because he was Australian. History is short in Australia, and school does not teach limitations. In the United States people are often educated beyond dream and initiative. The longer one's education, sometimes, the narrower his skills. School makes a person aware of his weakness and ignorance. Instead of shaping people willing to take risks, education produces thoughtful people, individuals who ponder and who talk and write more easily than they act. Rather than overreaching, the educated may underreach. Rarely do I celebrate the monumental. Instead I examine the small, shuffling trees and flowers through pages like porcelain figurines. I have been in schools so long that I cannot imagine managing anything other than a modest book.

The same soil that made Peter nurtured Tom. Raised on a farm, Tom was a master of machines. He left Albany and came to Broome, seeking relief for arthritis. In Broome he served as a justice of the peace and took on assorted jobs in order to gather money for Northern Outback Traders, a company he established to sell clothes in aboriginal communities. Tom was the only person I met in Australia who used the word *mate*, ending almost every sentence with it rather than a period. Occasionally Tom read poetry to the children, ballads describing fossickers and bushrangers.

Peter took two vehicles on the trip, the first a Ford Maverick truck with a dual cab and a flat bed, the second an OKA, a white cabin on big wheels, a land boat capable of swimming over stones in dry creekbeds. Beyond suburbia, in fact even within the Bungle Bungles, we traveled on "Purgatory Roads," tracks that kept hell and heaven vital in the imagination, the mind forever envisioning the hellish jolt ahead while dreaming of the asphalt left behind. Seats filled the first three-fifths of the OKA, two bucket seats in the front, behind them two padded bench seats, the first seating three people, the second four at a pinch. The remaining two-fifths of the OKA served as pantry, kitchen, and storeroom. Wooden panels boxed in this last part of the OKA. When we stopped, Peter raised the two side and the back panels. Stacked behind them were shelves, hooks, storage bins, coolers, and refrigerators, these last powered partly by a solar panel on the roof above the driver's head.

Foodstuffs, tools, and cooking utensils had specific shelves or boxes allotted to them. Peter expected participants on tours to learn the system quickly, so they could help in setting up camp and with the cooking. The ladies were immediately handy. In contrast I fumbled about, never quite learning whether something belonged in the red or the green box. For want of anything better, Peter made me wine steward. Although I was unable to master Peter's opener and frequently had to spear corks with a nail file, I found the task congenial. Peter packed fifty-four bottles of wine into the storeroom, all of which were moderately expensive, at least in comparison to the cooking wines Vicki and I drank in Perth. On the trip the group knocked down forty-four bottles, all twenty-four of the reds and twenty of the whites, this in addition to several cases of beer.

Four people rode in the Ford. The Ford was lower and did not plunge and toss like the OKA. Peter drove the OKA, and Tom, the Ford. Since Peter knew the tracks, he led. The land was dry, and the OKA stirred dust into tunnels and plumes, some red, others orange or white, all the colors dry as bone. Unlike the air-conditioner in the OKA, that in the Ford was broken, forcing people to open windows. After riding in the Ford, people looked red and feverish. Along with food and tools, some swags and duffel bags were packed in the bed of the Ford; others were lashed to the rack on top of the OKA. We traveled lightly, Vicki fitting our belongings into two duffel bags. Peter advised us to bring four "tops" and two or three pairs of shorts apiece, warning that clothes would quickly become soiled. Still, I did not wear most things Vicki packed for me. Dirt did not bother me. Only when my clothes resembled the color and texture of gorges in the Napier Range did I take them off. Instead of pulling clean clothes out of the duffel and disturbing Vicki's packing, I washed the old clothes in a blue plastic bucket. The clothes dried quickly, and I was able to put them back on almost within an hour. Getting dirt out was difficult, and my clothes weathered. "Although this shirt is not as old as a Devonian coral reef,"

I said one afternoon to Vicki, "it is almost as spectacular, particularly at sunset when the sediment glows."

All of us carried backpacks. In mine I crammed binoculars, a fly net, sunglasses, a pair of old jogging shoes, and two guidebooks, *Birds of Australia* and *Plants of the Kimberley Region of Western Australia*. In her backpack Eliza packed Fuzzy and Kitty, changes of clothes for both, Kitty's diary, then an omnibus volume by James Herriot describing his years as a veterinarian in Yorkshire and including the novels *All Creatures Great and Small*, *All Things Bright and Beautiful*, and *All Things Wise and Wonderful*. Bigger and heavier than the duffel bags were our swags, sleeping bags consisting of a groundsheet resembling a brown tarpaulin, a foam mattress two inches high, sheets, two blankets, a pillow, and a comforter. As soon as we started setting up camp, Edward climbed on the top of the OKA and tossed the swags down. Also on the roof of the OKA was a plastic tube containing iron stakes, each seven feet long with an arrowhead at one end, the other end flattened like the head of a railway spike. One by one Edward handed me the stakes, and after Vicki selected a campsite, I pounded the stakes into the ground above each swag, nailing them into the earth with a heavy hammer resembling a diminutive sledgehammer. I drove the stakes in the ground near our pillows at a sixty-degree angle, so that they would jut out over the swags. From the stakes Vicki hung mosquito nets. Moonlight turned the nets silver, and they shimmered like gouts of water splashing white over a big rock then spreading out in an icy skirt. Vicki and I and the children were the only people who slept under nets. In the *West Australian*, Vicki read articles describing the dangers of Ross River virus. Moreover at least one person in Hall's Creek had contracted Australian encephalitis.

Sleeping under the stars was more appealing in poetry than in fact. Nevertheless I slept well. Some nights I watched the moon roll across the sky like a pearl in a bowl, usually a silver pearl, lumpy and natural, but at full moon a golden, artificial pearl. Every morning I woke at sunrise. As bars of light streaked the sky, blue wafted up from the ground. When light diffused over the horizon, turning soft and downy, the blue changed to green and I got up and brushed out my swag. Later I brushed out the children's swags. I used a vegetable brush. I knelt on the ground, and by the time I finished my back was stiff. No matter how bare the ground on which we unrolled the swags, dunes of sand and prickly saltwort swept over the groundsheets during the night. Sometimes I brushed broods of lethargic ants out of the tarpaulin. No matter where we put the swags, ants were nearby, usually underneath the swags themselves. By dusk, however, most ants disappeared into nests. Those I found on the groundsheets in the morning were probably workers who, having been confused by the swags, were unable to find ways back to their nests. Although Vicki once found a small brown scorpion in grass under Edward's swag, insects did not bite us.

Once I brushed out the groundsheets and took down the mosquito nets, Vicki folded the sheets and covers. Afterward we rolled the swags, both of us on our knees trying to squeeze them into tight bundles. Never have I been able to tie any knot other than a Gordian knot. Once a swag resembled a hot dog bun, I pinned it to the ground so that it would not unravel and Vicki cinched ropes around it, fashioning knots with names smacking of the sea and the *Cub Scout Handbook*.

The children carried the swags to the OKA. Afterward we ate breakfast. My breakfast was always the same: a bowl of granola, "yuppie food," Peter called it, two pieces of lightly buttered toast, then several cups of tea. No matter how much milk I poured into the cup, the tea was always muddy brown. In contrast to my nibbling, the ladies were stalwart trenchermen, joining Peter, Tom, and Francis in a cattleman's breakfast of bubble and squeak and whole carcasses of meat: steaks, chops, and sausages proud with shank and chuck, rib and loin. After breakfast as well as after dinner and lunch, I helped wash dishes, specializing in drying and, as Vicki put it, "minute talk." Toward the end of the trip the children washed dishes. Only five or six children went on Peter's trips during the year. Not only were the trips comparatively expensive, but they were really for adults. Our children thrived, however, and never complained. "Don't they ever fight?" Tom asked.

In great part, days were organized around meals. Lunches were quick, eaten beside rivers or cattleyards and consisting of sandwiches made from leftovers, usually meat covered with condiments including a spread of bush flies. Every lunch I swallowed a fly or two, washing them down when they hung in my throat with a beaker of Coca-Cola.

When Peter ran out of Coca-Cola, I drank Mineral Springs, seltzer mixed with assorted fruit juices: lemon, orange, and mango. Peter liked to reach camping spots by four in the afternoon. Preparations for camping started about an hour earlier, Peter and Tom stopping and all of us piling firewood on the vehicles, usually snappy gum. Black cockroaches the size of thumbs nested in the wood, and at campsites Francis spent hours rescuing them from the fire, putting them on the trunks of rotten trees far from the flames.

We camped near water. Stored in the OKA were lengths of hose and a pump, and if one wanted a shower, he could take it. I usually showered not to clean myself but to scrub splinters out of my legs. I wasn't successful, and for a week after the trip ended, red welts covered my hands and ankles. For dinner we ate a slaughterhouse of steaks, chops, roasts, and sausages. Served with them were vegetables: pumpkins, onions, cabbages, potatoes, and carrots. We sat on folding chairs around two low green tables. The chairs were old and small, and during the meal they sank into the ground, pushing our knees toward our chins. The meat was heavy, but red wine buoyed it up, floating it down the gullet, and I ate great slabs. After washing dishes and putting utensils away, people sat around the tables, the fire flickering yellow on their faces. Peter told stories describing high jinks in the Kimberley and boyish days past. Rarely did I sit long. I could match neither Peter's tales nor the ladies' capacity for wine. Moreover, not even blind Homer could have enticed me to sit long after the moon rose. Practically every night I went to bed before anyone else, including the children.

In May, I drove from Broome to Derby. I drove so fast that the landscape rushed past in a wind. In the OKA I had the leisure to observe. Moreover, while Peter drove on asphalt I could write. Taking notes while we bumped along tracks crossing cattle stations was impossible, one letter an ellipse, still and sober atop a line like a swallow resting on a wire, the next tumbling off drunkenly, loops flapping like feathers, bold strokes turning like wrists. As we drove to Derby, I noticed wattle, caustic bush, needleleaf grevillea, beefwood, and bauhinia, its small green leaves resembling pudgy wings, fluttering and making trees quiver, almost as if they were mirages. Termite mounds splattered the land. At times they resembled galls stuck to the ground. Other times I thought them haycocks or tombstones, or herds of thick Herefords grazing across fields. In the central Kimberley the mounds were rounder, heavy lumps of earth rolling macromastic then hanging pendulous.

We talked about boabs throughout the trip. Even after the trees became commonplace, Vicki and I marveled at their appearance, the fleshly vaselike trunks, bare limbs twisting up and outward over the lip of the vase forming inverted bowls, the sky clear between the branches, resembling bits of blue pottery, the branches themselves cracks running crazed, darkening and making the bowls seem ancient. Vicki watched for big trees, and we measured several by walking around them, the largest taking twenty-one steps. One night we slept under a boab. Limbs wrinkled above us, seeming to cling to the sky like ivy to a stone wall. "You are sleeping," Faye told Eliza, "outside the prince's castle." We were not the only people attracted to boabs. Generations had carved their names into the soft bark, ranging from Bill and Coreen just outside Derby to Joe in 1916 and ZIY in 1914 on a boab in a mustering yard near the headwaters of the Upper Chamberlain River. In 1922 Walter Pidman carved his name on the prince's castle. Above creekbeds the trees grew in files. On slopes they resembled sconces attached to walls. Occasionally trees divided and trunks pressed against each other, belly to belly, the upper branches entwining in fleshly nonchalance.

Never before had a tree made me affectionate. Boabs did not affect Vicki the same way, and when I suggested a dalliance under a particularly large tree, she said, "Jesus, how mundane." No matter the landscape I cannot escape the ordinary. "Babe," I said to Vicki in the Bungle Bungles, "how about a little of the old Bungle Bungle." The suggestion fell upon dry soil, so I went bird-watching.

Brown quail switched through high grass hunting for insects. Five cockatiels sat still in a dead gum, and long-tailed finches sputtered around a dripping water faucet. A dingo padded silently across a creekbed, and donkeys stared across a yellow field, their ears straight and sharp, making them appear taller and more alert than their domesticated relatives. That night at dinner the children discussed eradicating feral, or nonnative, wild animals. "Why destroy so few animals?" Edward said. Like donkeys, cattle and sheep, he noted, had been brought to Australia. Why not end all feral activities, Francis said, mentioning building highways and dams, mining for gold and diamonds. Eradicating things feral, the children decided, was arbitrary and whimsical.

In Derby, Peter stopped at a grocery, and Vicki and I bought supplies, plastic bags full of bite-size candy bars: Mars, Bounty, and Nudge, this last produced by Cadbury and consisting of a hazelnut center wrapped in an eiderdown of caramel and milk chocolate. I ate my first Bounty standing by a bicycle rack in front of the grocery. Three days later I finished the bag. Sight-seeing drained energy. Just south of Derby we stopped at the Boab Prison Tree, a large hollow tree in the middle of which constables supposedly confined prisoners overnight. Resembling ants pouring through a nest, tourists swarmed around the tree, climbing in then struggling to clamber out, pushing against others trying to get inside before their buses departed. Once inside the tree tourists looked weary and woebegone, determined to enjoy themselves but shackled to schedule and needing candy bars.

The first night we camped at Windjana Gorge, still suburbia, Peter emphasized, but a suburbia far different from planned neighborhoods and houses with two-car garages. The air was fat with the cries of little corellas. Fish leaped out of a smooth green pool, falling back into the water with a silver clink. Leaves on twin-leaf bloodwood rattled when I brushed against a branch. A freshwater crocodile floated like a shadow through the water. Boabs grew up the sides of the gorge, resembling statues in rock gardens. Figs dug into crevices, and humps of limestone spinifex clung to ledges. At sunset color streamed down bluffs and, resembling light bleeding through stained-glass windows, shone between a nave of passion-fruit vines turning paths into aisles rich with color: amber, red, pink, and orange.

The next morning as I walked through the gorge, wagtails and double-barred finches bounced about me like musical notes. A striated paradalote jittered through a paperbark in a scramble of yellow, black, and white. A gray butcherbird darted ahead of me, landing on a stump then dropping to the ground, next flying low through the scrub, always watching me, probably thinking that I was following him. Returning from my stroll I met many walkers, almost all middle-aged and cheery with good wishes. Having outlived the small vanities of appearance, perhaps even of identity itself, the walkers looked keenly at the landscape and seemed pleased just to be alive.

Our second stop in suburbia was Tunnel Creek. Snow bush grew beside the road in white hummocks, and on kapok trees yellow flowers spiraled out of the ends of bare branches. The distance through the tunnel was seven hundred and fifty meters. "Daddy," Eliza said as we crossed to a sandbar, the water cold over our thighs and the end of the tunnel a tube of thin light, "this reminds me of Narnia." In C. S. Lewis's *The Lion, the Witch, and the Wardrobe,* children walked through a wardrobe into another world. Near the end of the tunnel, light thickened, and a portcullis of sharp rocks gleamed. River red gums leaned over a green pool. A freshwater mangrove gripped a wad of dirt, the tree's gray bark bound so tightly to the trunk that it seemed sewed on. A Leichardt pine grew in a green shadow. Behind the pine pandanus palms frayed into fans. On a slope above the creek blossoms on prickly grevillea unfurled into yellow and red shreds. Through rocky ledges the roots of figs fell in chords, strings that played to the imagination, not the ear.

Imagination works better when one is alone. Instead of deep cords I heard shallow hilarity. A skinny man with long hair chased a large woman in a skimpy bathing suit around the edge of the pool, splashing water on her bottom. "Don't you wish," Eliza said, holding my hand as we waded back through the tunnel, "that we had been alone in Narnia?" In the tunnel, we met a busload of Japanese tourists. They walked in single file and carried small flashlights. From a distance they appeared mysterious, seeming participants in an ancient rite, pilgrims wending their slow way underground to a ceremonial cavern. "Sometimes it is best to be alone," I said to Eliza, squeezing her hand, "but at other times having people around is nice."

That afternoon we drove to Fitzroy Crossing, dubbed Silver City because of the beer cans dumped in vacant lots and along the shoulders of the road, even in the bed of the Fitzroy River. When aborigines were nomadic, they made things out of natural materials. When the items were discarded, they decayed. Instead of lingering on top of the ground as garbage they became part of the earth. Old ways persisted. Although aborigines purchased food and drink packaged in plastic and tin like all people in Australia, they behaved in part like nomads, dropping trash as they ambled through days. Because aborigines lived in settled communities and because much present-day trash was not biodegradable, litter accumulated, tarnishing the landscape.

Near Fitzroy Crossing we rode a flat-bottomed boat through Geikie Gorge. Every tourist we had met during the day was on the boat, so many people that I longed to be elsewhere. A guide pointed out fresh-water crocodiles basking on sandbars. "I counted fifty-six crocodiles," Eliza said. Although the boat wallowed through the gorge weighed down by a landfill of tourists, the passengers made almost no noise, treating the excursion like a religious experience. The silence irritated me. The water was smooth, and amid the quiet, I imagined myself zooming through the gorge on water skis, the boat pulling me roaring like rapids, my skis yellow, huge saltwater crocodiles painted on them. On the upturned front tip of each ski, a crocodile's mouth gapped white. Down the gullet disappeared tourists, on the right ski a woman in red tights and with a bottom as big as a watermelon, on the left a man cradling a case of beer under his arm. The writing on the side of the case was blurred, and I couldn't tell if the beer was Emu Export or Victoria Bitter. Clearer was a tattoo on the man's right forearm, a blue cross. Encircling the upper part of the cross like a halo was the word *REPENT.*

Rarely am I misanthropic for long. A female black-necked stork tiptoed daintily through a shallow bay, her eye golden and her neck green and blue in the afternoon light. Never had I seen the stork before, and while watching it I drifted away from the boat. A pelican dozed on a spit of gray sand while a little pied cormorant perched on a low branch of a river gum. An osprey flew through the gorge, curving around a bluff bulging like an iron stove. A darter clutched a snag and spread its wings. On a flat, cane grass waved wide and green. Through hunks of limestone halfway up a slope a coolibah curved, its white trunk splotched by patches of weathered orange bark. A whistling kite soared high above the gorge.

"Are you a writer," a girl sitting next to me said, seeing me jot down observations. "Not much of one," I said, closing my notebook. "I want to be a writer," the girl said, pausing for a moment before she asked, "Where are you from?" The girl was a student in secondary school in Perth. "If I don't become a writer," she said; "I want to teach kindergarten. Small children are sweet." "Good luck," I said to her when the boat docked and I stood to leave; "I hope you write lots of happy books." "Thank you," she said smiling, "I hope so, too."

I slept well that night. The next morning blue-winged kookaburras woke me, their racketing exhilarating and making me laugh. In the morning birds often entertained us: long-tailed finches in the Bungle Bungles, and beside a creek on Bedford Downs Station, silver-helmeted friarbirds and red-tailed black cockatoos. At times the sky seemed a garden blooming with birds. A little eagle glided over our campsite on the Upper Chamberlain. Forty white-backed swallows roosted in a river red gum, twenty-four on an upper limb, sixteen on a lower. Flocks of budgies blew across the plains, wrinkling like sheets of translucent green paper. White-quilled rock pigeons bounded upward through gorges, seeming to leap rather than fly over boulders. Spinifex pigeons ran between hummocks of grass, feathers over their heads waving like red flags, their plump bodies rolling and lumpy.

Near Annie Springs sixteen fork-tailed kites brooded over a dusty paddock. In a cattleyard a brown falcon perched on a branch staring over the plain like a sentinel. Beside a creek a gray shrike thrush hunched into a limb, white leaves bristling about him like long feathers. While brolgas strolled silently across a low field, a flock of lemon-tinted honeyeaters stirred through a bauhinia in a commotion. From a bank above Mary Pool a pair of rainbow bee-eaters hunted insects, swooping out in lines from a river red gum then swirling through gold-and-blue scribbles in order to catch their prey. Two sulfur-crested cockatoos groomed themselves on a branch of the same tree. Higher in the tree a red-winged parrot twirled slowly through a bush of leaves. Six gray-crowned babblers bounced over a dark log, fussing and following each other almost like monkeys.

Trees also marked our passage through the Kimberley. Twice we spread swags under wild plums, the bark sweeping around the trees in currents of tight gray shakes, bushes of leaves at the ends of twigs resembling green dust mops. One night a limb from a bloodwood stuck out over my swag. The limb was broken and resembled an upper arm, thickening near the tree into a shoulder. A hive of English bees nested in the limb and swarmed about me like gnats. One morning we hiked along a stream to a swimming hole. Teatrees grew beside the path in clumps, and the seedpods of cockroach bush shined like varnish. Leaf beetles sunned themselves, color swirling through their shells like oil. A white-faced heron stood immobile on a bank. Nearby a water monitor lay on a rock, its body resembling a thick twist of leather. Boulders and slabs of bluff surrounded the pool. At one end of the pool stood a mangrove, its roots grasping rocks like fingers. The mangrove was old and gnarled, and knobs resembling black warts protruded from the trunk. I studied the tree. The trunk reminded me of the face of an aged poet, his nose swollen, his cheeks wrinkling into gullies, pulling the flesh into seams. While inclination remained quick, ability decayed, and the poet was sour, dreaming about sweet sailor boys but awakening to dry impotence. "Did you notice that tree by the pool?" Eliza said later; "I thought it looked like a teddy bear." "I thought it resembled an elephant," Edward said. "No, a dragon," Francis said, "a smiling dragon celebrating his birthday."

On the way to the Bungle Bungles we stopped for groceries in Hall's Creek, and the children ate chocolate Wedges. People shuffled beside the street and sat in circles drinking. A woman sitting on the ground threw clods of dirt at her companion. He turned his back to her and, bending over, resembled a nut. Yells suddenly flew upward like kites blown off the ground. The sounds wavered in the air for a moment then tumbled silently back to earth. A man lay in a stupor under a bush. A thin young mother drifted across the highway, leaving a small child to cross the road alone. Three days later Peter bought gas in Turkey Creek. Outside the station stood three video machines. The machines were broken, but local children played them anyway, pushing and banging them. A small metal sign stood beside the door to a grocery at the station. Painted on the sign was a Scotty, a red line drawn through the dog. Above the picture were the words "No Dogs Allowed on This Veranda." "This curb isn't a veranda, is it, Daddy?" Eliza said. "No," I said. "I wish we had a Scotty," Eliza said when I handed her a chocolate Wedge.

We spent two days in the Bungle Bungles, the first day following trails into Echidna Chasm then Mini-Palms Gorge. Sandstone melted across sight in layers, orange silica and black lichens protecting the white rock underneath from rapid erosion. Outside Echidna Chasm cassia bloomed in yellow racks. Palms grew up the sides of the chasm, rising straight like tall chimneys. Termite mounds clung to sheer walls.

The farther I walked the narrower the trail became, and I felt as if I were climbing through a bronchial passage in a lung. Walls pressed close then towered straight while a breeze blew down the path as swift as water.

The Mini-Palms trail followed a dry creekbed. In the bush silverleaf grevillea was yellow and red with flowers. On miniritchie bark peeled upward in small red curls. The trail ended in a cave, the walls of which rose in sheets then flowed together in pink seams. Small palms grew in rows across the floor of a canyon, resembling plants neat on the ledge of a window. The sides of the canyon were damp, and ferns spilled from cracks, reminding me of wallpaper pulling loose in an old house, first buckling then roiling out in heavy bows before drying and shredding. Although I climbed on a slab of limestone leaning against the wall of the canyon, I could not identify the ferns.

Rarely does a traveler see clearly. Sometimes he bumps his head against a silver box or tramples lemon grass into perfume. Most of the time, though, he does not know how to observe, much less interpret. On the floor of the canyon I found a piece of notepaper, five and a half inches long and three and three-quarters inches wide. The paper was lined, and around the margin flowers resembling honeysuckle blossomed in red and blue horns. Written in blue ink by a ballpoint pen with a fine tip was, "Joan at Plaza," followed by two unreadable words then the number "820000." "What does that mean?" Edward said. "The writing is in code," I said; "deciphering the message will take time." Of course I never figured out the message, but that's all right. Travelers learn to appreciate bits of things and to be satisfied by glimpses.

At the ruins of a homestead not far from Bedford Downs, Francis and I dug through a dump, turning up rusty cans and brown glass bottles. Stamped on a bottle was "This Bottle Always Remains the Property of the West Australian Glass Manufacturers Proprietary Limited." On the top of an oil drum was "B. A. RHEEMAUST." "Daddy," Francis said, "wouldn't it be fun to dig here all day. There is no telling what we would find." Schedule prevented our staying. Instead we hurried over tracks toward Tableland Station, along the way passing yellow hibiscus, red bundles of bunch speargrass, and scraggy cabbage gum, lemony with blossoms.

The second day in the Bungle Bungles we went to Cathedral Gorge. Holly grevillea blossomed along the roadside, the flowers red clumps at the ends of limbs looking snagged as if floodwaters had stranded them. From a distance the bungles rumpled out of the land, "rows of kilns," Francis said, "some red hot, others lukewarm, some cool." A nutwood grew deep within Cathedral Gorge, its bark corky and sticking out from the trunk like scales on the spine of a crocodile. Francis picked up a flat rock then dropped it to the sand. The rock fell with a thunk, and the sound echoed through the gorge. I wanted to sing "What a Friend We Have in Jesus," but a group of tourists appeared, and I stopped singing before I started. Later Vicki and I wandered up Piccaninny Gorge by ourselves. Rarely had we been alone on the trip, and once more the old bungle bungle came to mind. Suddenly a girl appeared. Her face was red, and she had been crying. "I'm lost," she said, "how do I get back to the carpark?"

After we left the grocery in Turkey Creek days folded into each other. Soon I lost track of time and almost place. Small moments glittered: tea beside the Traine River, in front of me blue water lilies rising on long stems out of a green pool, the flowers resembling cut-glass chalices. Crimson finches darted above the water, blinking in the sun like flames. Paperbarks leaned over the pool, their leaves dangling like skirts of linen. At Sir John Gorge we fished for barramundi. "The first stage," Peter explained, "is to catch a bream to use for bait." Eliza and I fished together. Neither of us reached the first stage. My socks and shoelaces, however, reeled in their limit of burrs from Mossman River grass. The burrs were sharp and hard, and when pulling them out I bloodied my fingers.

At the end of the day I stepped into a crevice, dropping in up to my hip. My right leg twisted, and I fell backward. For a moment I thought I had broken my leg. Blood streamed down my ankle from cuts along my calf and up my thigh. Beneath my knee appeared a purple dent two and a half inches long. Around the dent flesh rose in hot swollen red loaves. To keep the swelling down I soaked my leg in the Fitzroy River. "Good bloody bait," Vicki said, "maybe you will catch a barramundi now." For the rest of the trip my leg was swollen. "For the first time in your life," Vicki said, "you have a shapely calf, dent or no dent." Although the leg did not hurt when I walked, it ached when

I lay down. Embarrassed about stepping into a crack, I mentioned the mishap only to Vicki. Edward and Eliza, though, saw me fall. "Suppose you had broken your leg, Daddy," Edward said, "what would you have done?" "Maybe the Flying Doctor would have come," Eliza said; "that would have been exciting."

On the way back to Broome we camped beside the Lennard River. The next morning we went to Lennard Gorge. Blossoms were pink on kurrajong. Above a pool sides of the gorge towered red and orange. From a distance light seemed to fizz softly through the water. My leg aside, the days in the Kimberley made me coltish, and instead of stuffing myself into the blue bathing suit and feeling like a sausage, I jumped naked into the pool. "Daddy," Eliza said later, "you looked like Tarzan." "You need a new bathing suit," Vicki said; "that flesh-colored one with the small tassel on the front is a bit worse for the years."

We arrived back in Broome near sunset. The moon was full, and when it rose above Roebuck Bay, the mudflats reflected the moonlight, creating, a brochure said, an illusion of a golden staircase. Vicki, the children, and I stood on the terrace of the Mangrove Hotel and watched the light spool across the bay. "That was pretty, but so were the grasses in the Kimberley," I said, trying to remember them: buffel, rice, cane, bundle bundle, and tall spinifex, silver with seed and blowing like foam. Later that evening we walked down Carnarvon and ate at Tongs. "Where have you been?" the waitress asked; "we have missed you." The next morning we flew back to Perth. "Daddy," Eliza said as she placed macadamia cookies on a tray for Kitty and Fuzzy, "you don't want to leave Australia, do you?" "No," I said; "seeing friends in Connecticut again will be nice. But Australia is a wonderful country, and I've seen only a little of it." "But you've seen the Kimberley and that's some of the best," Eliza said, "and when you write about things, you will see them again."

Embers

The end of our year resembled the beginning. As we spent our first week in university housing at 17 Myers Street, so we returned for the last week. Trees and flowers that bloomed when we arrived bloomed again. Sour sobs poked yellow through the grass. Once more I crushed the blossoms of Geraldton wax and rubbed the paste into my palms. On coral trees blossoms stuck out like scarlet coatracks. Birdcalls that once seemed foreign were now familiar: the fluting of magpies, the caterwauling of ravens, and ring-necked parrots ringing like doorbells. I spent evenings wandering the university trying to impress place on my mind. I sat in the grass in Whitfield Court and watched Winthrop Hall seep through colors at sunset, the pale orange limestone ripening into gold. In the Tropical Grove, I listened to wattlebirds and kookaburras. Eliza accompanied me on walks, and one night we saw a brush-tailed possum.

Edward and Eliza attended Nedlands Primary. A new term began at John XXIII, but Francis stayed home, designing computer networks. Every morning I went to the English department. I was very fond of the people in the department, and when I said good-bye I was nervous my voice might crack, so I pasted good cheer across my words. On Eliza's last day at Nedlands Primary, Mrs. Odgers's class had a surprise party for her. When Vicki and I walked to school to meet Eliza, little girls stood outside the classroom crying. "Nuts," I said to Vicki, turning around, "I can't take this. You will have to bring Eliza home." Edward's friends gave him an Australian Rules football. The boys signed it, and that night as he tossed it up in the living room, he burst into tears. "Daddy, I don't want to go home," he said. The next day Edward gave Robbie his purple basketball, and both Sophie's and Hannah's mothers brought their daughters by to say good-bye to Eliza again.

Worry kept me from becoming morose. During the year our possessions multiplied. In the last week I mailed five more boxes back

303

to Connecticut in hopes of reducing our excess baggage. "You didn't mention baggage in the Kimberley," Vicki said; "now that's all you talk about." The day before leaving Perth, I spoke at the Local Government Week Conference held at the concert hall. "I am spending my last day in Perth working," I said to Vicki, "because you won't throw anything away, and the airlines are going to charge a fortune for our suitcases." I rode a bus downtown and arrived at the concert hall an hour and a half before my talk. Companies set up booths in the lobby of the hall. Seven new tires stood before Goodyear's booth, resembling an unwrapped tube of licorice Lifesavers. Parked by the Ausplay booth was a red-and-yellow plastic helicopter seven feet tall. A yellow slide unraveled from the cabin of the plane, and from the top a green propeller stuck up like a daisy that had lost most of its petals. Minter, Ellison, Northmore, and Hale labeled themselves "the local government lawyers." A man in a gray coat handed me a flyer. On the front was a red corral. Inside the corral a small herd of red letters stirred about angrily, bellowing: "UNEMPLOYMENT! ROAD TRAUMA! POLLUTION! COST OF LIVING!" Black letters ran like asphalt across the bottom of the flyer. "FIX AUSTRALIA, FIX THE ROADS," the letters said. Inside the auditorium flags hung in pleats. "These are governments of banners," a woman said. Sewed on the flags were the names of shires and towns: Koorda, Wickepin, City of Bayswater, Yilgarn, and Narembeen. On some flags crests were colorful with black swans, yellow sheaves of wheat, and Sturt's desert pea red as sunset.

"How did the talk go?" Vicki asked later that afternoon. "Fine, I bored the asses off five hundred people," I said, then asked; "what did you do?" "We walked along the foreshore and ate ice cream cones at Matilda Bay, just like we did after we arrived," she said; "the day was beautiful. Buildings in downtown Perth shimmered like ice cubes, and the Swan River seemed a pool, runoff from the cubes spreading wide and silver."

At eleven the next morning Dennis Haskell and George Seddon drove us to the East Perth Railway Station, Dennis stuffing his van with our luggage and George filling his sedan with Vicki and the children. George and Dennis helped me check our luggage onto the baggage car. Then they said good-bye. At one o'clock we boarded the *Indian Pacific*. Ahead lay sixty-nine hours on the train, two days and three nights during which we crossed Australia, traveling 2,704 miles from Perth to Sydney, by way of Adelaide. Neither Francis nor Edward had ever been on a train, and Eliza had only been from Perth to Bunbury on a school outing. I was excited. I had not taken a train trip in twenty years. Near the apartment in Nashville where I lived when I was young a railway trestle crossed West End Avenue. Father and I walked along the tracks together. While Father clutched my left hand, my eyes roamed the right-of-way, searching for loose spikes, flattened pennies, and treasures tossed from windows or flushed down toilets. We counted cars on passing trains and read the names of railways painted on the sides. Coupled in stanzas, the words *Norfolk and Western, Santa Fe,* and *Union Pacific* resembled poetry, the sounds singing in imagination like the rails themselves.

Years later when I stayed at my step-grandfather's house in Virginia, I walked through woods using railway tracks for a path. Often I found dead box turtles. The turtles burrowed through gravel under the rails, trying to reach the other side of the right-of-way. Drafts from passing trains bounced them across ties. Sometimes I found a live turtle and took it into the woods far from the tracks. At night trains rushed past my step-grandfather's house roaring through sleep, wheels and cars clattering like bones, the whistles thick streaks, at first black and silver in my imagination then rising and curving blue out of hearing, the headlamps yellow funnels, insects drifting into them where they swirled for a moment before being sucked into the engine.

The engine pulling the *Indian Pacific* was green and yellow. At Tarcoola I walked the length of the train. It consisted of twenty passenger cars, three car carriers, and two flatcars. Chained to the first flatcar were two vans. The other flatcar was empty. On the carriers a mesh of struts and supports wrapped around twelve automobiles. Our sleeper was car ARM 954X, or D, as a sign put it. Exteriors of the sleepers were rippled and silver. Across the side of the cars flew the emblem of the *Indian Pacific,* a wedge-tail eagle, its body brown, wings curved in flight, the tips of its feathers golden. While Edward and Eliza shared accommodations, Francis had a compartment to himself. Vicki and I shared a deluxe suite. The room was twice the size of a normal first-class room. In addition to a private lavatory we had a sitting area in front of a window. Soft chairs surrounded a round table. Our lower bunk was a double bed, not a twin. On the table perched a metal bucket, ice piled around a bottle of Yellowglen, a pinot noir chardonnay, a gift from the railway. The wine, the label declared, was "a stylish wine in the classic tradition," showing "fresh fruit aromas with a hint of cashew nut and fresh yeast." Next to the bucket was a box of candy, Cadbury's Black Cat Chocolates. After the train left the station, the conductor brought us drinks, the children cups of hot chocolate and Vicki and me a pot of tea.

"Nothing goes better with tea and hot chocolate than candy," Vicki said, stripping cellophane off the box. Eating is more important on a trip than it is at the kitchen table. Eating domesticates the unfamiliar and imposes routine upon the extraordinary. For tea Vicki ate a brandied apricot nougat followed by a hunk of Turkish delight. Francis bolted a strawberry cream and a fruity plum. Edward had a slab of peanut brittle then a vanilla caramel, while Eliza topped a piece of royal fudge off with a dark hazelnut whirl. Rarely do I eat candy. Instead of munching the nut caramel Vicki offered me, I drank tea and imagined sipping wine as the evening clicked through orange into blue. That night Vicki and I drank the wine, not around the table as I imagined, holding our glasses against the fading light, watching the evening star break into yellow splinters. Instead we sat on the lower bed, our backs against the wall of the compartment, legs thrust out akimbo, resembling logs jammed into a sawmill. The children confiscated the table, turning the top into a battlefield for an endless game of war, converting our comfortable chairs into command posts.

We ate at second sitting: breakfast at eight in the morning, lunch at one in the afternoon, and dinner at seven. Four people could sit at a table in the dining car. Since there were five of us, we sat at two tables across the aisle from each other. Vicki and I always joined one of the children, so that other people who sat at the tables would not eat only with children. For two nights Paul, an electrical contractor from Melbourne, sat at one of the tables. On a whim he had bought a round-trip ticket on the *Indian Pacific*, joining it at Adelaide. He stayed in Perth only four hours, taking the return trip back to Adelaide the same day. "I needed a break from things," he said; "I called my wife from Perth to tell her where I was. Boy, was she surprised." Vicki and I liked Paul. Later, when he left the *Indian Pacific* in Adelaide to catch another train back to Melbourne, he waved good-bye as we pulled out of the station.

On a trip one quickly grows fond of strangers. Standing alone on the platform, Paul looked forlorn, and we felt sad as he shrank into the distance behind us. Our other table mates were two Dutch women, longtime companions who raised a family together. "This trip is the new bathroom in our house," they said, explaining that after building the bathroom themselves they borrowed money from a bank, supposedly for construction of the room but really for the trip. The women were fun. "What a wonderful trip," Vicki said, "rolling through the night across Australia on the *Indian Pacific*, drinking red wine, and laughing with two Dutch dykes. Could life get any better?" "No," I said, "I don't think so."

The trip seemed short, the hours passing swiftly like the sleepers under the rails. Occasionally I read, but mostly I sat in front of the big windows in our room and watched the landscape peel across sight. Outside Perth, vineyards were bushy and green, and fruit hung in yellow bulbs from lemon trees. In the Avon Valley knobs of granite protruded from hills, resembling bowls resting on their sides in drying racks beside sinks. Beyond the Avon Valley farmland rolled gently. York and salmon gums ran along the edges of fields like picket fences. At the tips of branches leaves bunched together in patches. With no forest behind the trees to create dark and shadow, light shone through the limbs, making the trees resemble bristles left on an old broom, "one beaten ragged," Vicki said, "sweeping the land into wheat."

The *Indian Pacific* stopped in Kalgoorlie, long enough for passengers to take a quick tour of the city. I stayed up for the tour. Unfortunately we arrived in Kalgoorlie behind schedule, and the tour was canceled. Still, I walked the platform and looked down the main street. The night was cool, and the fragrance of marijuana hung thick in the air. "Did you smell that?" an American said to me; "this isn't California, is it?"

The next day the train crossed the Nullarbor, the great flat limestone plain, "four times," a brochure said, "the size of Belgium." Blue bushes grew in stubbles. White rocks lay scattered about almost as if they had spilled out of a huge saltshaker. "It makes me so sad," Vicki said, looking out the window; "this is such a pitiful place." The train stopped at Cook, the halfway point on the Trans-Australia line. Cook, a sign declared, "The Queen city of the Nullarbor." South of the rails ran a broad gravel track. Across the track was a line of prefabricated houses, the line two houses thick in places. "How would you like to spend a year here?" I said to Francis. "I wouldn't," he answered. There was something in me that wanted to explore and appreciate every place. "But think about the snakes and lizards we would see," I said. Francis did not answer.

I got off again when the train stopped in Tarcoola. In front of a building two men kicked a football back and forth. A fire burned in the parlor of the Wilgena Hotel. The hotel was painted red. Nailed outside were signs advertising "Eagle Blue Beer." Across each sign flew an eagle, a banner twisting in his bill like a snake. Printed on the banner was "Naturally Brewed Light Bitter Beer." The post office in Tarcoola served as agent for the Commonwealth Bank. A sign on the counter read, "*Three Days* notice required for withdrawal of $200 and over."

That evening I bought two halves of champagne from the bar on the train. Before dinner I sat at the window and watched the sunset wash by. Switches of myall swept past, their branches black against the orange light. From the ground, gray rose then turned blue. I drank the champagne and nibbled Arnott's NIK NAX, "baked wheat snack crackers," the box declared, "baked not fried." At dinner Paul treated the Dutch women and Vicki and me to wine. Paul thought the women sisters. "Men and women are made for each other," he said innocently; "what I don't understand is how men could like men and women could like women." "Oh, it just happens," I said, and four of us giggled.

I got up early the next morning. At Keswick Station in Adelaide eleven journalists boarded the train. They stayed on for ninety minutes, interviewing me and taking pictures in the dining car. People who walked through the car stared at me, all except the children, who strode past, eyes fixed on the wall ahead, their expressions frozen in embarrassment. At a crossroads outside Adelaide the train stopped. On the shoulder of the road a van waited for the journalists. A television crew set up cameras in the middle of the road, and as the train pulled slowly away, they filmed me standing in the doorway of car D waving good-bye to Australia. "Daddy," Eliza said when I returned to the room, "you are just like Madonna. Reporters follow you everywhere."

For a long time I looked out the window. The morning was overcast. Grass stuck to fields outside Adelaide like a green skin. Distant hills puffed up into blue mounds. Trees were so scarce that when I saw them, they reminded me of trademarks stamped on the backs of greeting cards. Cattle and sheep milled about the fields. Abandoned farmhouses slumped into red piles. Often I saw dead sheep, their bodies rumpled fleeces. After Peterborough the land dried. At Broken Hill, I wandered the platform. Dark heaps of mullock loomed over the tracks. Outside the town power lines sliced sight into blocks, reducing vision to slag, I thought, turning away from the landscape. Later near Menindee emus bounced like mops through fields. For a while Vicki and I counted kangaroos. She saw a dozen before dinner, and I saw seven. That night I began to worry about luggage again. "How," I said to Vicki, "are we going to get it all to the hotel?"

When I woke the next morning, the train was twisting through the Blue Mountains above Sydney. The sky was pink, and a purple breeze curved along the horizon. "Don't worry about the bags," Vicki said; "money solves such problems. We can use the bundle you were paid for the speech in Perth." While I piled bags up in the luggage room at Sydney Central, Vicki hailed a taxi, a station wagon. The driver helped me stuff half our luggage into the back of the car. Then he took Vicki, Edward, and Eliza to the Marriott on College Street. After dropping them off, he returned to the station for Francis, me, and the rest of the luggage. "So far so good," I said after our bags were stored at the Marriott, "but I dread going to the airport."

Vicki and the children had not been to Sydney, and I filled their hours with sight-seeing. I led them from the Cahill Expressway down through the Royal Botanic Gardens to Farm Cove. We climbed the steps of the Opera House then took one of Captain Cook's tours of the harbor. A group of Americans stood in front of us, waiting to board the boat. Their voices sounded harsh. "They are from California," Edward said, "not Connecticut. We don't sound like that." We took an elevator to the top of Sydney Tower, the trip down lasting seventy-five seconds from the door's closing at the top to its opening at the bottom. We roamed the Art Gallery of New South Wales, and I imagined hanging Eugene Von Guerard's painting of Milford Sound in New Zealand in our living room. A silver sky glowed above ragged mountains. Beneath the mountains a pool spread like a mirror. "That's a little old-fashioned, Sam," Vicki said. "I am old-fashioned," I said. When we left the gallery a disturbed man stood on the steps outside the building shouting, "Fuck." "This isn't Perth," Edward said.

In the Strand Arcade we watched hatters molding Akubras to the heads of customers. We rode the Monorail and looked down streets. Excavations for new buildings gaped like cavities. In the cavities dark pools of green water shone, yellow construction equipment clumped around them like plaque. We spent a day at the Taronga Zoo. Eliza and I got separated from Vicki and the boys on the Taronga Road. We found them at the "Coca-Cola Bottlers Chimpanzee Park." On seeing Eliza a young chimpanzee banged on the glass of an observation window. When Eliza pressed her hand flat on the glass, he put his hand against the glass on the other side of the window. Eliza looked at him for a moment then burst into tears. "I don't like this, Daddy," she said. Beside a garbage can stood a sign urging people to "Do the Right Thing." Thirty yards away an Andean condor sat on a dead limb. The cage was too small for the condor. He should have been soaring in the silence above white mountains, his wings curving like breaking waves. Inside the cage the condor folded into a lump, almost as if he were shrinking into himself to escape the noise littering the air about him.

We explored DFS, the duty-free shop on George Street. Tour buses parked outside the shop. Inside tourists coursed through the aisles like rushing water, eddying and buying. Apart from ourselves and two other people, "Germans," Francis said, the customers were all Japanese. Every afternoon I bought a cake at the Renaissance Patisserie on Argyle Street, and we sat in a back room and ate it while drinking tea. At night we walked along Campbell's Cove. A photographer took pictures of a newly married couple standing under a lamppost outside the Park Hyatt. Behind them the city flickered and jangled like a poker machine.

We did much eating and shopping. At the Australian Music Centre, Vicki bought a tape of didgeridoo music. The tape, the clerk said, was the best recording of didgeridoo music he knew, this despite the music's having been played by a white man, recorded in Arizona, and printed in Germany. At the Aussie Bear next door to the patisserie I bought a circus of stuffed animals: a koala for Edward, an emu for Francis, an echidna for Eliza, and for Vicki, Numby, the numbat.

"Don't you want a honey possum," Vicki said to me. "No," I said, "you are my little honey possum." The owner of the store heard my answer. "You are all right," she said; "I'd like to clone you for my friends."

Tourists, especially those who wander about on foot, wear dull clothes. In Sydney I wore baggy khaki trousers; an old striped shirt with a collar, a greenish imitation madras shirt that faded in the washing machine instead of bleeding in the sun; thick gray socks; and jogging shoes with heavy soles, a brand called Hi-Tec that I bought for $56.95 in Perth and that I wore in the Kimberley, the red soil so permeating the uppers of the shoes that they looked as if they had been dug out of a clay pit. Over my shirt I wore a blue sweatshirt bought at the bookstore at the University of Western Australia. Emblazoned in red and outlined in white across the chest of the shirt were the letters UWA. Underneath the letters appeared the university crest. In the center of the crest a black swan preened himself. Under his feet curved a banner reading "SEEK WISDOM." Wearing the sweatshirt, Vicki beside me, my head turning to watch the children, I appeared sappy and conventional, a middle-aged father who spent his time worrying about luggage, a man whose thoughts were duller than the blade on a battered lawn mower.

People could read me as easily as they read my sweatshirt. Often tourists travel not so much to discover the exotic as to escape platitudinous lives. They travel in hopes of breathing life into dream, in hopes of becoming a character in their fantasies, for a moment shaking loose from the trammels of mundane identity. Rarely does the tourist succeed. To replace a wardrobe or change a state of mind for a vacation is too difficult. No matter where people travel they wear their identities, much as I wore the sweatshirt. Of course one still dreams of scrambling the letters across his chest, for a blink of time becoming an intriguing mystery, the stranger at the inn in whose footprints rumors swirl like dust.

One night we ate in the Tandoori Palace, an Indian restaurant on Oxford Street. A few of the customers in the Tandoori Palace seemed to live comparatively unconventional lives. At least they dressed unconventionally. Some wore leather, decorated themselves with chains, and hammered rings and plugs into their faces. Others must have tossed men's and women's clothes into a big laundry basket and then reaching in put on whatever came to hand.

On an earlier trip to Sydney, I ate in the restaurant. I was alone, and I noticed people at other tables. As I waited for my meal, I shaped a colorful and imaginary me who was the focus of curiosity. On this trip, however, when I entered the Tandoori Palace herding Vicki and the children before me, I could not indulge imagination. I did not have the leisure to create fantasy or notice other people in the restaurant. Walking tired Eliza. Once we sat down, I struggled to keep her awake until the meal was served. Moreover, Eliza and Edward were hamburger and french-fried-potato children. To get them to taste then eat onion bahajees and samosas, lamb pasanda, chicken mumtaz, and Makhani gosht drained my energy and kept my attention glued to the dishes on the table. "That was a great meal," Vicki said as we walked to the hotel, "but did you see how the people behind us were dressed? They looked like Halloween." "No," I said. "You missed a sight," she said; "at times I felt like I was eating in a circus."

The next morning we flew to Fiji. At eight-thirty we boarded the Airporter, a shuttle bus that ran between the airport and hotels in Sydney. Attached to the rear of the shuttle was a luggage van big enough to hold our suitcases. At the airport I joined people waiting to check in for Qantas flight 291. I studied the ticket agents behind the counter. "Don't let the tall blond check you in," I heard a woman say to a friend; "I have had her before. If your bags are an ounce overweight, she'll charge you." I narrowed my choices to two women, the first a pudgy dark-haired clerk with a happy smile, the second a Chinese woman who processed bags and passengers rapidly. She prided herself on speed and efficiency, so much so I decided she would probably ignore excess baggage. When I reached the front of the line, the tall, blond clerk beckoned me. "Would you like to go ahead," I said turning to two women standing behind me; "I haven't got our tickets ready."

"Thank you," the women said and stepped forward. "Next," the Chinese woman said. "Gosh, do I love this country," I gushed as I approached the counter; "we have been here a year, and everything has been wonderful." "That is nice to hear," she said taking our tickets and adding, "just put your luggage on the scale." She didn't waste time looking at the weight or counting bags. After I left the counter, I looked back. The two people whom I let ahead of me stood in front of the tall blond. Their faces were red, and I saw the blond point to the scales and shake her head. "You are a piece of work," Vicki said as we walked toward Customs. "Damn straight," I said.

Euphoria never lasts long. When I booked the holiday in Fiji, I asked the agent in Perth if I could store bags at the airport on the island. The agent telephoned Nadi and learned that bags could be left at Airport Security. "But," the agent warned, "there is quite a bit of crime in Fiji, and I don't think your bags will be all that secure. I wouldn't leave anything at the airport." Our resort was an hour from the airport. Although I hired two cars to take us to the resort, the cars were small, not big enough for a year of possessions. At Nadi, Vicki and I filled two trolleys and rolled them to Airport Security. Busy chatting on the telephone, the clerk in charge did not waste time on us. "Put labels on your bags," he said, handing me a handful of tags. "Tear off the numbers and give them to me, then put your bags in there," he said, pointing to a room, the doors of which stood open, facing into the terminal. People milled about the building, some leaning against the wall beside the door. "We'll have to leave the bags," I said to Vicki; "I'm too tired to think of anything else. But our year is gone. We'll lose everything."

I booked us into The Fijian for four nights and five days. Located on a small island, Yanuca, The Fijian was a big resort, consisting of at least 413 rooms, some of them family rooms, others suites and bures. I thought the children would find more to do at a big rather than a small resort. I was right. "This holiday stuff," Edward said after two days on Yanuca, "is tiring." By the time Vicki and I stored the luggage at Airport Security, night had fallen. While Vicki and Eliza rode in one car, Francis, Edward, and I rode in the other. I was tired, and the drive seemed endless. Out of politeness the driver talked to me. The man's English wasn't good, and conversation was labored. Sitting in the backseat, the boys dozed. When silence gapped like a pothole, I paved it over with words. Not only was I weary, but I was hoarse when we reached The Fijian. "This was a good trip," the driver said; "we had a good talk. I hope to drive you back to the airport at the end of your vacation and have more good talk." "That would be fine," I said.

We stayed in room 482, a family room in the last building at the edge of the island. In Fiji, as in the Marriott and a score of other hotels, we bumped against each other, bed pressed to bed, suitcase leaning against suitcase. If a "with-it" person, to use contemporary slang, has to have his own "space," we were an old-fashioned family, sharing dressers, towels, toothpaste, and all habits and quirks. When five people share a room, privacy lodges elsewhere. Slipping away to the bathroom, or anywhere for that matter, without someone noticing and commenting is impossible. Likewise, ignoring someone traipsing into the bathroom is also difficult. As a result of living close, much of our conversation was earthy, particular and personal rather than distant and elevated, matter to be churned through bowels rather than mulled by brain.

"So what," Vicki said on my speculating about the effects of our travels upon the children. "Flowers grow in black dirt, not in air. Beside," she continued, "you are naive if you think this year will influence the children. Name something that happened when you were ten that shaped your life." "I can't remember anything," I said; "maybe I was never ten." "Maybe you still are ten," she said, pointing to a plastic box in my hand.

Inside the box was a small gecko. At one end of the room glass doors opened onto a lawn. At night geckos slid across the doors, their bellies white against the panes. Just before talking to Vicki, I caught a gecko to show the children. "It is green, not white," Francis said. "Silver-green like the light that shines through the palms in the middle of the day," Eliza said. Grass stretched like a rug from our door to a line of coconut palms and hog plums. Fruit draped from the trees, the coconuts resembling big green tears, the hog plums large white eyeballs, black pupils at their tips. Beyond the palms the land sloped down to the ocean. Not far offshore waves tumbled over a reef, the froth resembling a shaggy white eyebrow. In the shallows hunks of coral thrust up from the sand, freckling the surface of the water, splotching it brown and green.

We ate buffet breakfasts at the Takali Terrace, one of the restaurants at the resort. Included in the price of the room were Vicki's and my breakfasts. I paid for the children's breakfasts. Although the breakfasts never varied, I paid a different amount each morning. One day I paid $13.20 for three meals, the next $27.00, the next $21.80. "Prices in Fiji are arbitrary," a man sitting nearby said after hearing me discuss a bill with Vicki. "That's part of Fiji's charm," he continued; "I've come here for twenty years. Sometimes I pay too much, sometimes too little. In the end prices even out. Take things as they come and don't worry." Matters came oddly. Sometimes waiters gave us four glasses at dinner; other times they gave us six. Forks and spoons appeared in strange clutches, three of one, seven of the other. Although we ordered our meals at the same time, one meal usually appeared ten minutes before the rest, "the runaway engine," Francis called it. Invariably another meal showed up later than the others, "the caboose," Edward said.

One night Fijians entertained guests at the resort by walking on hot coals. The man who described the performance spoke English. Much as waiters got orders and numbers slightly wrong, so his English was a little off. We "would grow goose bumps" watching the performers, the man said. In sketching the history of Fiji, he noted that "scientists have done a lot of diggings and findings out." When a king died in the old days, he went to "the happy hunting ground." Before Christianity came to the islands, Fijians were cannibals. Now, he said, "fresh water eel rates very highly on the local menu," adding, "you don't want to see us chasing after each other for a free meal." "I wonder," Vicki whispered, "if Fijians find it odd waiting on people whom they would have eaten two hundred years ago?" Once missionaries taught Christianity, "the Ten Commandments was followed from one to ten to the very last syllable in all the tribes." Recently people's behavior had slipped, the man said, explaining that "meat pie and the beer may have changed them."

I followed the advice and relaxed. Once a day I walked around the island. Beside paths hibiscus and poinsettia bloomed red, and from ornamental ginger, flowers dangled, resembling strings of oval shells. A flock of red-headed parrot finches skipped through the grass under a frangipani. A spotted fantail sidled along a limb, a white stripe over his eye resembling a brow, another streaming back from the corner of his eye like a tear. A mongoose scurried across a road. The animal's body bounced forward, resembling furry bundles jerking on the coils of a tightly wound spring. The roots of mangrove trees dug into the shoreline like long fingers. A gray reef heron stood still beside a tidal pool. Across the causeway linking Yanuca to the mainland a man plowed a small field with a team of horses, one of the horses white, the other brown. Along the coast toward Nadi hills rose from the sea in crumbling layers. Bare and ocher-colored, they appeared cooked, baked in the sun so long they dried. As I looked at the mainland an African tulip tree bloomed behind me, the flowers whooshing upward in jets of red flame. From raintrees seedpods hung like black parentheses. In the breeze the light pods on Ben trees crinkled and shimmered out of substance, almost becoming erasures.

One morning Vicki and the children bought sun hats. While Vicki sat in a folding chair, a man wove palm fronds into shape, sizing the hat as carefully as salesmen selling Akubras in the Strand Arcade. When he finished the hat, the man twisted fronds into the shapes of birds and stuck them into the hat. One afternoon I played Ping-Pong with Edward, beating him three times, the scores being 21 to 12, 11 to 3, and 21 to 11. Another afternoon Eliza and I played bowls against Edward and Vicki. Eliza could not roll the balls far, and we lost 17 to 12, "charging back," as Eliza put it, from a 9 to 1 deficit. At night we usually ate a buffet dinner. The buffet cost $17.50 each. Never did Eliza and Edward eat my money's worth. "When I pay seventeen dollars for a pip-squeak's dinner," I told Edward one night, "I expect him to eat everything."

Twice a day I snorkeled, spending at least four hours in the water. The first day I got burned. Before I went into the water, Vicki covered me with sunscreen, not, however, for snorkeling, but for the beach, rubbing great white gouts into my face, neck, arms, chest, and back. A snorkeler floats on his stomach, and that night the backs of my ankles and the upper part of my behind were burned, my bathing suit having slipped down below propriety. In the water I saw damsel and angel, lizard, hawk and squirrel fish; coral trout; snappers; and assessors, some of these last yellow, others blue turning green when they shifted in the light. I followed butterfly and bannerfish like a member of a marching band trudging behind a drum-and-bugle corps bright with flags.

I floated through colors, fish spinning around me like neon ribbons: green, orange, purple, red, yellow, and violet. Flounder buried themselves in sand while butterfly scorpionfish twirled through coral, their fins rowing orange and black. Devil scorpionfish hunkered on the bottom resembling dusty stones. Banded sea kraits foraged through coral and pushed themselves down holes in the floor of the ocean, shaking like black-and-silver ropes. "We call them the friendly sea snake," a Fijian said. The snakes were common, and by the end of the vacation I could find them whenever I wished. Indeed, I knew where many creatures lived: moray eels, two-spot damselfish, rock cod, and smooth cornetfish. "I could stay here forever," Vicki said one evening as she sat on the Takali Terrace, sipping "A Taste of Honey," a yellow drink in a tall glass, a slice of pineapple clinging to the side of the glass in a half-moon, a cherry perched above like a red bonbon.

Every morning a porter slipped the *Fiji Times* under our door. I read the shipping news and dreamed of roaming the South Pacific. The *Clydebank* sailed from Rotterdam at the end of August. After stopping at Hamburg, Hull, Antwerp, Dunkirk, and Le Havre, it left Europe in its wake. On November 6, the boat reached Papeete. On the eleventh the boat docked at Apia, then in quick succession Suva, Lautoka, Nouméa, Santo, Honiara, Lae, Rabaul, Kimbe, and Madang. I read the names aloud. "Wouldn't it be fun to attend this," Vicki said, showing me an advertisement for the Bombay Dhamaka Show, a "block buster," sponsored by Indiana Showbiz, "Promoters of Magic King Junior Mangal." "See Humpty Dumpty dance on stage and make you laugh," the advertisement stated. Also appearing in the show was Shika Swarup, Miss India for 1992, doing "sizzling dances from the heroine of film CHEETAH."

When he landed in Fiji, our pilot banked sharply then slammed down on the runway. I gasped. During the year I flew so much that I traveled beyond nonchalance. One night in Perth a wind shear tipped our plane to the left. To compensate the pilot jerked the plane back to the right, so far that I thought we might roll over. "Wasn't the landing fun, just like a roller coaster," Edward said. "Yes," I lied. We left Fiji at one o'clock at night. In hopes of anesthetizing myself I drank three piña coladas, the only drinks I had during the stopover. The drink did not work. I could not fall asleep. Every time the plane throbbed through turbulence I grabbed the arms of my seat and squeezed tightly until the flight smoothed out.

In Los Angeles we waited seven hours at the terminal for our next flight. My nerves did not settle. Once our flight was airborne I kept thinking the plane too low. I was sure we would slam into a mountain, this despite the pilot's telling us that he was flying at 32,000 feet. Because I was nervous and couldn't sleep, I stared out the window.

Below the plane cities glowed like embers. Emblems of the year in Australia, I thought, for a moment forgetting fear and becoming mournful. "Vicki," I said, turning to tell her that I wanted to return to Australia. She was asleep, and I got no further than her name. At nine o'clock the next morning we landed in Hartford. A white limousine waited for us. "Daddy, it is almost as if we never went to Australia," Edward said before asking, "are you unhappy to be back?"

To have told Edward that I was sad would have been silly. I knew that he and I, all of us, would soon be content in Storrs. "No, Edward," I said; "I am so thankful to get off airplanes that I can't be unhappy." That afternoon I walked around our yard. George followed at my heels. Goldenrod and New England asters leaned over the driveway, their heads heavy with blue and yellow buds. In the woods behind the house spotted cort bloomed, the mushrooms purple above the leaves. The rhododendrons I planted a year ago had grown eight and a half inches. A nuthatch bustled down the side of a black birch, and a gray squirrel bundled across the grass. I crushed the leaves of mockernut hickory and ground the fragrance into my hands. I telephoned the Daffodil Mart in Gloucester, Virginia, and ordered bulbs for the dell. I was too tired to select varieties, so I said, "Just send me one hundred and fifty dollars worth. You choose them." The next morning I carried my bicycle out of the basement and pumped up the tires. Then I rode over to the Cup of Sun. Voula and Jerry were behind the counter. "Sam!" Voula exclaimed when I walked through the door, "you are back. Everybody has missed you!" "The first muffin and cup of coffee are on the house," Jerry said; "How was Australia?" "I loved Australia, and I miss it," I said; "but I am happy to be home."

About the Author

Samuel F. Pickering, Jr., teaches English at the University of Connecticut at Storrs. A much sought-after speaker, he is the author of six previous collections of essays, including *Let It Ride,* available from the University of Missouri Press.